DUE DATE	RETURN DATE	DUE DATE	RETURN DATE

ACTIVITIES 1922–1932

The Collected Writings of John Maynard Keynes

THE COLLECTED WRITINGS OF
JOHN MAYNARD KEYNES

VOLUME XVIII

ACTIVITIES 1922–1932

THE END OF
REPARATIONS

EDITED BY
ELIZABETH JOHNSON

MACMILLAN

CAMBRIDGE UNIVERSITY PRESS

FOR THE

ROYAL ECONOMIC SOCIETY

Published for the Royal Economic Society by

THE MACMILLAN PRESS LTD

London and Basingstoke
Associated companies in Delhi Dublin
Hong Kong Johannesburg Lagos Melbourne
Singapore Tokyo

The Syndics of the Cambridge University Press
32 East 57th Street, New York, NY 10022, U.S.A.

Macmillan ISBN 0 333 10730 0 excluding U.S.A. and Canada
C.U.P. ISBN 0 521 21875 6 U.S.A. and Canada only

Printed in Great Britain
at the University Press, Cambridge

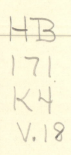

CONTENTS

GENERAL INTRODUCTION

This new standard edition of *The Collected Writings of John Maynard Keynes* forms the memorial to him of the Royal Economic Society. He devoted a very large share of his busy life to the Society. In 1911, at the age of twenty-eight, he became editor of the *Economic Journal* in succession to Edgeworth; two years later he was made secretary as well. He held these offices without intermittence until almost the end of his life. Edgeworth, it is true, returned to help him with the editorship from 1919 to 1925; MacGregor took Edgeworth's place until 1934, when Austin Robinson succeeded him and continued to assist Keynes down to 1945. But through all these years Keynes himself carried the major responsibility and made the principal decisions about the articles that were to appear in the *Economic Journal*, without any break save for one or two issues when he was seriously ill in 1937. It was only a few months before his death at Easter 1946 that he was elected president and handed over his editorship to Roy Harrod and the secretaryship to Austin Robinson.

In his dual capacity of editor and secretary Keynes played a major part in framing the policies of the Royal Economic Society. It was very largely due to him that some of the major publishing activities of the Society—Sraffa's edition of Ricardo, Stark's edition of the economic writings of Bentham, and Guillebaud's edition of Marshall, as well as a number of earlier publications in the 1930s—were initiated.

When Keynes died in 1946 it was natural that the Royal Economic Society should wish to commemorate him. It was perhaps equally natural that the Society chose to commemorate him by producing an edition of his collected works. Keynes himself had always taken a joy in fine printing, and the Society, with the help of Messrs Macmillan as publishers and the Cambridge University Press as printers, has been anxious to give Keynes's writings a permanent form that is wholly worthy of him.

The present edition will publish as much as is possible of his work in the field of economics. It will not include any private and personal correspondence or publish letters in the possession of his family. The edition is concerned, that is to say, with Keynes as an economist.

Keynes's writings fall into five broad categories. First there are the books which he wrote and published as books. Second there are collections of articles and pamphlets which he himself made during his lifetime (*Essays in Persuasion* and *Essays in Biography*). Third, there is a very considerable volume of published but uncollected writings—articles written for newspapers, letters to newspapers, articles in journals that have not been included in his two volumes of collections, and various pamphlets. Fourth, there are a few hitherto unpublished writings. Fifth, there is correspondence with economists and concerned with economics or public affairs.

This series will attempt to publish a complete record of Keynes's serious writing as an economist. It is the intention to publish almost completely the whole of the first four categories listed above. The only exceptions are a few syndicated articles where Keynes wrote almost the same material for publication in different newspapers or in different countries, with minor and unimportant variations. In these cases, this series will publish one only of the variations, choosing the most interesting.

The publication of Keynes's economic correspondence must inevitably be selective. In the day of the typewriter and the filing cabinet and particularly in the case of so active and busy a man, to publish every scrap of paper that he may have dictated about some unimportant or ephemeral matter is impossible. We are aiming to collect and publish as much as possible, however, of the correspondence in which Keynes developed his own ideas in argument with his fellow economists, as well as the more significant correspondence at times when Keynes was in the middle of public affairs.

Apart from his published books, the main sources available to those preparing this series have been two. First, Keynes in his will made Richard Kahn his executor and responsible for his economic papers. They have been placed in the Marshall Library of the University of Cambridge and have been available for this edition. Until 1914 Keynes did not have a secretary and his earliest papers are in the main limited to drafts of important letters that he made in his own handwriting and retained. At that stage most of the correspondence that we possess is represented by what he received rather than by what he wrote. During the war years of 1914–18 Keynes was serving in the Treasury. With the opening in 1968 of the records under the thirty-year rule, many of the papers that he wrote then and later have become available. From 1919 onwards, throughout the rest of his life, Keynes had the help of a secretary—for many years Mrs Stevens. Thus for the last twenty-five years of his working life we have in most cases the carbon copies of his own letters as well as the originals of the letters that he received.

There were, of course, occasions during this period on which Keynes wrote himself in his own handwriting. In some of these cases, with the help of his correspondents, we have been able to collect the whole of both sides of some important interchange and we have been anxious, in justice to both correspondents, to see that both sides of the correspondence are published in full.

The second main source of information has been a group of scrapbooks kept over a very long period of years by Keynes's mother, Florence Keynes, wife of Neville Keynes.

From 1919 onwards these scrapbooks contain almost the whole of Maynard Keynes's more ephemeral writing, his letters to newspapers and a great deal of material which enables one to see not only what he wrote, but the reaction of others to his writing. Without these very carefully kept scrapbooks the task of any editor or biographer of Keynes would have been immensely more difficult.

The plan of the edition, as at present intended, is this. It will total twenty-nine volumes. Of these the first seven are Keynes's published books from *Indian Currency and Finance*, in 1913, to the *General Theory* in 1936, with the addition of his *Treatise on Probability*. There next follow, as vols. IX and X, *Essays in Persuasion* and *Essays in Biography*, representing Keynes's own collections of articles. *Essays in Persuasion* differs from the original printing in two respects: it contains the full texts of the articles or pamphlets included in it and not (as in the original printing) abbreviated versions of these articles, and it also contains one or two later articles which are of exactly the same character as those included by Keynes in his original collection. In *Essays in Biography* there have been added a number of biographical studies that Keynes wrote later than 1933.

There will follow two volumes, XI–XII, of economic articles and correspondence and a further two volumes, already published, XIII–XIV, covering the development of his thinking as he moved towards the *General Theory*. There are included in these volumes such part of Keynes's economic correspondence as is closely associated with the articles that are printed in them.

The next thirteen volumes, as we estimate at present, deal with Keynes's *Activities* during the years from the beginning of his public life in 1905 until his death. In each of the periods into which we divided this material, the volume concerned publishes his more ephemeral writings, all of it hitherto uncollected, his correspondence relating to these activities, and such other material and correspondence as is necessary to the understanding of Keynes's activities. These volumes are edited by Elizabeth Johnson and Donald Moggridge, and it is their task to trace and interpret Keynes's activities sufficiently to make the material fully intelligible to a later generation. There will be a further volume printing his social, political and literary writings and a final volume of bibliography and index.

Those responsible for this edition have been: Lord Kahn, both as Lord Keynes's executor and as a long and intimate friend of Lord Keynes, able to help in the interpreting of much that would otherwise be misunderstood; Sir Roy Harrod as the author of his biography; Austin Robinson as Keynes's co-editor on the *Economic Journal* and successor as Secretary of the Royal Economic Society, who has acted throughout as Managing Editor.

Elizabeth Johnson has been responsible for the *Activities* volumes XV–XVIII covering Keynes's early life, the Versailles Conference and his early post-1918 concern with reparations and international finance. Donald Moggridge has been responsible for the two volumes covering the origins of the *General Theory* and for all the *Activities* volumes from 1924 to the end of his life in 1946.

The work of Elizabeth Johnson and Donald Moggridge has been assisted at different times by Jane Thistlethwaite, Mrs McDonald, who was originally responsible for the systematic ordering of the files of the Keynes papers and Judith Masterman, who for many years worked with Mrs Johnson on the papers. More recently Susan Wilsher, Margaret Butler and Leonora Woollam have continued the secretarial work. Barbara Lowe has been responsible for the indexing. Susan Howson undertook much of the important final editorial work on these volumes.

NOTE TO THE READER

In this and subsequent volumes, in general all of Keynes's own writings are printed in larger type. All introductory matter and all writings by others than Keynes are printed in smaller type. The only exception to this general rule is that occasional short quotations from a letter from Keynes to his parents or to a friend, used in introductory passages to clarify a situation, are treated as introductory matter and are printed in the smaller type.

Most of Keynes's letters included in this and other volumes are reprinted from the carbon copies that remain among his papers. In most cases he has added his initials to the carbon in the familiar form in which he signed to all his friends. We have no means of knowing whether the top copy, sent to the recipient of the letter, carried a more formal signature.

Crown copyright material appears by permission of the Comptroller of Her Majesty's Stationery Office.

The editor also wishes to thank Eric Warburg and Sir Sigmund Warburg for their courtesy in supplying copies of Keynes's correspondence with Carl Melchior and of Melchior's diary account of Keynes's visit to Berlin in June 1923, and Joachim Kratz for his kind interest in making an English translation of the diary extract.

Chapter 1

THE DECLINE OF THE MARK, 1921–1922

The editing of the 'Reconstruction in Europe' supplements, culminating in the publication in December 1923 of *A Tract on Monetary Reform*, expanded Keynes's writing interests beyond their previous focus on reparations and war debts to the broader field of the international monetary system. It was at this time, during 1922 and 1923, that he made his most concerted efforts for a rational treatment of Germany—officially, as an expert adviser on the state of the mark, and unofficially, as a speaker and writer; publicly, in the columns of the *Nation*, and privately, in attempts to influence both British and German acquaintances in high places.

Linked with the reparations problem was the question of the health of the German mark, which dropped disastrously in value with every Allied endeavour to enforce payment for war damages. Early in 1921 Keynes predicted that once actual reparation payments started, the mark would collapse. The prediction occurred at the end of an explanatory article on the foreign exchanges which cautioned speculative holders of marks who were gambling on the eventual prosperity of Germany.

Keynes produced the article in February in response to a request by *La Nación*, Buenos Aires, for him to write on any subject that he pleased. In sending the manuscript to his American publisher, Alfred Harcourt, for placing in the American press, he remarked (6 February 1921) that it was 'not an article to which I attach any particular importance—decidedly, indeed, a second-grade article...'. Harcourt replied (24 February) that he thought Keynes spoke 'rather too slightingly of it'; after trying the *Saturday Evening Post* and the *New Republic* he sold it to the financial section of the New York *Evening Post* for $50. Here it is given in the form in which it appeared in England in the *Manchester Guardian Commercial*.

From the Manchester Guardian Commercial, *24 March 1921*

WILL THE GERMAN MARK BE SUPERSEDED?

The object of this article is to deal with a popular mistake about the foreign exchanges which seems to be extremely common. It is popularly supposed that the future of the exchange value of a country's currency chiefly depends upon its intrinsic wealth in the form of natural resources and an industrious population, and that a far-sighted man is right to expect an ultimate recovery in the value of its money if the country looks likely to enjoy in the long run commercial or industrial or agricultural strength. The speculator in Rumanian lei keeps up his spirits by thinking of the vast resources of that country in corn and oil, and finds it hard to believe that Rumanian money can in the long run be worth less than the money of, say, Switzerland. The speculator in German marks bases his hopes on the immense industry and skill of the German people, which must, he feels, enable her to pull round in the long run.

Yet this way of thinking is fallacious. If the conclusion of the argument was that in the long run the Rumanian peasant and the Rumanian proprietor ought to be able to live comfortably, or that an industrial nation like Germany must be able to survive, the conclusion might be sensible. But the conclusion that certain pieces of paper called bank notes must for these reasons come to be more valuable than they are now is a different kind of conclusion altogether, and does not necessarily follow from the former. France was the richest country in the world, not excepting England, when, in the last decade of the eighteenth century, her paper money, the *assignats*, fell, after five years' violent fluctuations, to be worth nothing at all on the bourses of Lisbon and Hamburg.

Against recovery

War, revolution, or a failure of the sources of the national wealth generally begins the depreciation of a paper currency. But the recovery of this money to its former value need not result when the original calamity has passed away. A recovery can only come about by the deliberate policy of the govern-

2

ment, and there are generally weighty reasons against adopting such a policy. In the case of the money of the French Revolution, the depreciated notes were simply swept away, and their place taken by a new currency of gold. I do not remember any case in history in which a very greatly depreciated currency has subsequently recovered its former value. Perhaps the best instance to the contrary is that of the American greenbacks after the Civil War, which eventually recovered to their gold parity, but in their case the maximum degree of the depreciation was moderate in comparison with recent instances. The various sound currencies existing throughout the world in the years before the war had not always existed, and had been established, many of them, upon the débris of earlier irretrievable debasements.

For it may not be in a country's interest to restore its depreciated money, and a supersession of the old money may be better than its resuscitation. A return even of former prosperity may be quite compatible with a collapse in the value of the former currency to nothing at all.

Let me apply some of these considerations to the case of the German mark. As I write there are about 250 marks to the £1 sterling, but within the last twelve months the rate has been as high as 360 and as low as 120. As the par value of the mark is 20 to the £1 sterling, German bank notes are now worth less than a tenth of their nominal value. Even without a Bolshevik government matters can be much worse than this; for the bank notes of Poland or Austria are worth less than a hundredth of their nominal value. But for the purposes of our argument let us take the less extreme case of Germany.

Germany today

Now it is well known that at the present time there are many causes at work which are tending to make the value of the mark progressively worse even than it is at present. The

3

expenditure of the government is about three times its revenue, and the deficit is largely made up by printing additional notes, a process which everyone agrees must diminish the value of the notes; Germany's commercial exports (i.e., excluding deliveries under the Treaty), although showing some substantial recovery from the worst, are still short of her absolutely essential imports, and thus the balance of trade is against her; the economic condition of her neighbours, Russia and the fragments of the former Austro-Hungarian Empire, which used to be her best customers, make impossible any early revival of trade with them on the pre-war scale, and these very adverse conditions are present and operative, in spite of the fact that as yet Germany is not making current payments on account of reparation up to the standard, or anything like it, of even the most moderate proposals for a settlement of the Allies' demands. If and when these demands materialise in payments the difficulties of the budget and the difficulties of the trade balance are certain to be aggravated.

Who would benefit?

But let us put aside these considerations for the moment, and look a little further ahead. Most of those who look for a recovery of the mark are not thinking of this year, or even, probably, of next. They believe that ultimately Germany will pull round, and that when this occurs the mark will recover also.

Now though the process of the depreciation of money (i.e., the rise of prices) is easy, though painful, the reverse process of appreciation (i.e., the fall of prices), though difficult, is also painful. The upset to the economic organisation of a country caused by falling prices is quite as bad, as we have all been finding out lately, as the upset caused by rising prices. Both are bad, but once we have suffered the evils of rising prices, they are not obliterated by following them up with the evils

4

of falling prices. This applies everywhere, but in Germany there are two special considerations which it is my particular purpose to emphasise in this article.

Germany has a national debt which now amounts to 350 milliards of paper marks, and is likely to amount to a still higher figure before equilibrium has been obtained in her national finances. If the mark were to double in value—far more if it were to increase tenfold—the money burden of the service of this debt would remain the same, but its real burden would be proportional to the increase in the value of the mark. The portion of the German revenue (measured in goods) which would have to be paid over as interest to the holders of the German national debt would be increased in the same proportion. That is to say, German resources, which would otherwise be available, in part at least, for reparation, would be diverted to the German propertied classes. The Allies would hardly allow this. Yet the only alternative, a partial or complete repudiation of the German debt, is a precedent which they might hesitate to encourage.

Furthermore, the holders of the German public debt, who are mostly Germans, are not the only persons into whose pockets an improvement in the value of the mark would put a great deal of money. There are also the foreign speculative holders of German currency. It has been estimated by the experts of the German government that the amount of German money held abroad and of credits granted to Germany by foreigners, by far the greater part being in terms of paper marks, amounts to about 70 milliards of paper marks, of which something less than half is held in the form of actual German paper money. We can probably reckon therefore that the amount of German bank notes and bank balances held more or less speculatively outside Germany is not less than 50 milliards of paper marks. At the rate of exchange—250 marks equal £1—these holdings are worth £200 million. But at par they would be worth £2,500 million, and even at 100 marks equal £1 they would be worth £500 million. As a speculative holding of German notes yields the holder no interest, he presumably does not intend to keep them as a permanent investment and is only waiting for an opportunity of realising them at a profit. A permanent improvement in the value of the mark would entail, therefore, paying over to foreign speculators very large sums of money which would otherwise be available for reparation. There would be no great advantage to Germany in this, and the Allies would hardly allow the claims of the speculators to rank in front of reparation.

Against Allied interests

In addition, therefore, to all the usual difficulties of reinstating a fallen currency, there are strong reasons in the case of Germany for thinking that a reinstatement cannot be undertaken. Germany has two classes of foreign creditors to deal with—the Allies, who have reparation claims which are expressed in terms of gold marks, and the foreign speculative holders of German bank balances and of German currency, which are in terms of paper marks. To increase the value of the paper mark in relation to the gold mark benefits the latter at the expense of the former. It is not particularly in the interests of the German government to pay over huge sums to foreign speculators, and it is decidedly contrary to the interests of the Allied governments. Whatever temporary fluctuations there may be, it is therefore extremely unlikely to happen.

I do not expect, therefore, a permanent recovery in the value of the German paper mark. Possibly it might be stabilised at some very high figure to the £1 sterling. But if the Allies persevere with their reparation demands the mark is much more likely to continue its fall until the final stage is reached, when the simplest and most sensible course will seem to be to supersede it altogether by some new unit. And all this may happen even though in the end Germany may have recovered a considerable measure of her economic strength.

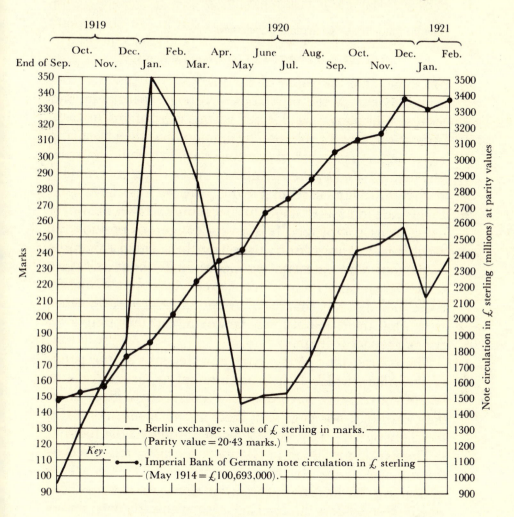

The Allies' London Ultimatum of 5 May 1921 demanded that Germany pay over the sum of 1 milliard marks during the course of the summer. The pressure of complying with this demand, combined with the unforeseen division of Upper Silesia between Germany and Poland, caused the steadily depreciating mark to reach a new low in November. From 247 marks to the pound in May, it dropped to 1,041 in November. Keynes, writing in the *Manchester Guardian*, continued to see the future value of the mark depending on the policy of the Allies.

From the Manchester Guardian, *9 November 1921*

RECORD DEPRECIATION OF THE MARK

For some time the value of the mark was maintained to a certain extent by the purchases of foreign speculators and because Germany was not yet paying reparations in cash. Early in the year I published the opinion that when Germany had to begin to pay cash to the Allies the mark would collapse. The fall, initiated by the attempts of the German government to obtain foreign currency for this purpose, may have been largely due in its later stages to speculators all over the world losing heart completely. It is a very dangerous position for the currency of any country to be held abroad in vast amounts by persons who entertain erroneous ideas about its future value. When once these preconceived ideas are thoroughly upset they discover that they have no rational idea whatever as to what their holding may be worth, and they fling it on the market accordingly.

The future value of the mark now depends on the policy of the Allies, which I shall not attempt to forecast. But as recent movements have loosened everybody's ideas from their previous moorings, and these are all at sea, it is useful to steady ourselves by looking again at some of the facts.

The existing inflation in Germany is usually measured by the volume of the Reichsbank's note issue. This is a little misleading. We have to pay attention also to the treasury bills, which their holders can turn into cash at an early date, if they want to. If the exchange value of the mark remains at its present level and German internal prices become adjusted to it, a far greater volume of notes than hitherto will be required to carry on the business of the country. Bankers and others hold as little as possible of their liquid resources in notes, which carry no interest, and the balance in treasury bills. If prices rise violently they will have to turn more of their treasury bills into notes. This will appear in a corresponding increase of the Reichsbank note issue on one side of the account, and of its holding of treasury bills on the other side. Thus the increased note issue may be far greater than the new inflation occasioned by the government's currency deficit, and may reflect the pre-existing potential inflation of past unfunded debt. The increased note issue will, therefore, be better described as a *result of the collapse* of the exchange than the other way round; and it will be quite outside the control of the government, which would have no remedy except a refusal to meet its treasury bills on maturity.

The complete inadequacy of the existing note issue to an exchange of 1,200 to the pound sterling, once internal prices begin to adjust themselves to the latter, is shown by the fact that the value at this exchange of the whole circulation is below £80 million, which is less than a fifth of the British note issue, although Germany uses notes much more and cheques much less than we do. There is the further paradoxical result that, since the gold reserve of the Reichsbank is worth nearly £60 million, their total circulation of notes valued at the present rate of exchange (and leaving out of account the unfunded debt) is covered by gold to the extent of 75 per cent, a figure only rivalled by the Federal Reserve Bank of the United States.

The aggregate treasury bills amount to about 215 milliard marks, of which more than 90 milliards are already held by the Reichsbank. If, therefore, the whole of the balance of these was cashed out by their holders into notes the circulation would rise to a figure worth no more than £180 million at an exchange of 1,200. This rate of exchange seems therefore to discount a good deal of future inflation due to the Allies pressing their demands and Germany trying to meet them.

9

One other figure is interesting. Earlier in the year the amount of German bank notes and bank balances held more or less speculatively outside Germany was estimated at 50 milliard paper marks. At the rate of exchange, then prevailing, of 250 marks to the pound these holdings came to the formidable figure of £200 million. Now they are worth little more than £40 million, a much more manageable figure. If the foreign holdings were bought at an average exchange of 200 (and a large part was bought at a lower rate than this), the speculators have at present prices lost something like £200 million.

So far, therefore, foreign speculators have not only paid the whole of the indemnity up to date, but much more besides. No wonder that the speculative market is upset. The position is very artificial—though I do not believe a word of the silly stories that the German government could be so bold or so mad as to engineer on purpose what will in the end be a great catastrophe for their own people, whether the mark reacts or falls farther.

In December 1921 the German government asked to postpone the reparation payment due the following May. Premier Briand meeting with Lloyd George at Cannes agreed to a partial moratorium, but his defeat by Poincaré in the Chamber of Deputies broke off the conference.

In England the slump of 1921 dragged on into 1922, unemployment increased, and while financial opinion in some quarters rallied round the cry for a protective tariff, there was a more general feeling that Britain must export to survive and for that she needed customers, including the Germans. Keynes was suddenly preaching to the converted. In France, however, with Poincaré in command, an uncompromising attitude towards Germany persisted. The Chamber of Deputies spent an entire session deploring, in the words of Keynes's old critic, André Tardieu, 'the Anglo-Saxon theory of economics and financial phenomena dominating the world', the chief practitioners of which were J. M. Keynes and the *Manchester Guardian*.

A combination of events in June 1922 helped to set off the final 'flight from the mark'. The first of these was the negative recommendation of the committee of bankers appointed by the Reparation Commission to examine the feasibility of an international loan to Germany. Large cash payments by Germany and increased foreign exchange speculation were followed by the assassination of Walther Rathenau, who as foreign minister was personally associated with the policy of fulfilling Germany's reparation obligations—the culmination of a series of disheartening occurrences. In July Germany asked for a moratorium of two and a half years, but Poincaré was willing to grant only a brief stay and demanded payment, whereupon the mark fell catastrophically.

A meeting of Lloyd George and Poincaré with the other Allied premiers was called to take place in London on 7 August. During July some articles appeared in *The Times* suggesting that the Allies should pay their debts to Britain in 'C' Bonds (bonds covering the amount of reparation as determined by the Reparation Commission still owing after the payments scheduled in the London Agreement were taken into account). These bonds, comprising the largest part of the German debt, were generally agreed to be worthless. The *Times* articles attracted attention and Poincaré let it be known that he favoured such a proposal, which would compensate France for reduction of Germany's debt by reduction of her own.

In what was interpreted as an attempt to cut the ground from under Poincaré's feet, the British government issued the Balfour Note on inter-allied debts on 1 August. In the first instance this communication was in response to a request by the United States for payment of the interest accrued since 1919 on her wartime loans to Britain and liquidation of the capital borrowed over the next 62 years. The Balfour Note stated that while hitherto Britain had made no demands for repayment from her Allies, she must now collect enough from them and from Germany to pay what she owed to the United States. The announcement contributed to the further decline of the mark.

It was at this time that the first 'summer school' of the Liberal Party was held at Oxford. These summer schools were study conferences for the purpose of examining the party's attitudes on current problems, and Keynes's presence as a speaker became as much of an institution during the twenties as the meetings themselves. On 4 August, the day after the Balfour Note was debated in the House of Commons, Keynes addressed the gathering on the Liberal policy on reparations and war debts. The circumstances aroused lively interest and Asquith himself presided at the meeting. (Keynes stayed with Asquith at his country house near Oxford for the occasion.) The speech was published in full in the Liberal *Westminster Gazette*.

From the Westminster Gazette, *5 August 1922*

A MORATORIUM FOR WAR DEBTS

I do not complain of Lord Balfour's Note, provided we assume, as I think we can, that it is our first move and not our last. Many people seem to regard it as being really addressed to the United States. I do not agree. Essentially it is addressed to France. It is a reply, and a very necessary reply, to the kites which M. Poincaré has been flying in *The Times* and elsewhere, suggesting that this country should sacrifice all its claims of every description in return for—practically nothing at all, certainly not a permanent solution of the general problem.

The Note brings us back to the facts and to the proper starting point for negotiations.

In this question of reparations the position changes so fast that it may be worth while for me to remind you just how the question stands at this moment. There are in existence two inconsistent settlements both of which still hold good in law. The first is the assessment of the Reparation Commission, namely 132 milliard gold marks. This is a capital sum. The second is the London Settlement which is not a capital sum at all, but a schedule of annual payments calculated according to a formula; but the capitalised value of these annual payments, worked out on any reasonable hypothesis, comes to much less than the Reparation Commission's total, probably not much more than half.

But that is not the end of the story. While both the above settlements remain in force, the temporary régime under which Germany has been paying is different from, and much less than, either of them. By a decision of last March Germany was to pay during 1922 £36 million (gold) in cash *plus* deliveries in kind. The value of the latter cannot be exactly calculated, but, apart from coal, they do not amount to much, with the result that the 1922 demands are probably between a third and a quarter of the London Settlement, and less than one-sixth of the Reparation Commission's original total.

It is under the weight of this reduced burden that Germany has now broken down; and the present crisis is due to her inability to continue these reduced instalments beyond the payment of last month.

In the long run the payments due during 1922 should be within Germany's capacity. But the insensate policy pursued by the Allies for the last four years has so completely ruined her finances, that for the time being she can pay nothing at all; and for a shorter or longer period it is certain that there is now no alternative to a moratorium.

What, in these circumstances, does M. Poincaré propose? To judge from the semi-official forecasts, he is prepared to cancel what are known as the 'C' Bonds, provided Great Britain lets France off the whole of her debt and foregoes her own claims to reparation.

What are these 'C' Bonds? They are a part of the London Settlement of May 1921, and, roughly speaking, they may be said to represent the excess of the Reparation Commission's assessment over the capitalised value of the London Schedule of Payments, and a bit more. That is to say, they are pure water. They mainly represent that part of the Reparation Commission's total assessment which will not be covered even though the London Schedule of Payments was paid in full.

In offering the cancellation of these Bonds, therefore, M. Poincaré is offering exactly nothing. If Great Britain gave up her own claims to reparation and the 'C' Bonds were cancelled to the extent of France's indebtedness to us. France's claims against Germany would be actually greater, even on paper, than they are now. For the demands under the London Settlement would be unabated and France would be entitled to a larger proportion of them. The offer is therefore derisory. And it seems to me to be little short of

13

criminal on the part of *The Times* to endeavour to trick the people of this country into such a settlement.

Personally I do not think that at this juncture there is anything whatever to be done except to grant a moratorium. It is out of the question that any figure low enough to do Germany's credit any good now could be acceptable to M. Poincaré, in however moderate a mood he may visit London next week. Apart from which it is really impossible at the present moment for anyone to say how much Germany will be able to pay in the long run.

Let us content ourselves, therefore, with a moratorium for the moment, and put off until next year the discussion of a final settlement, when, with proper preparation beforehand, there ought to be a grand conference on the whole connected problem of inter-governmental debt, with representatives of the United States present, and possibly at Washington.

The difficulties in the way of any immediate settlement now are so obvious that one might wonder why anyone should be in favour of the attempt. The explanation lies in the popular illusion, with which it now pleases the world to deceive itself—the international loan. It is thought that if Germany's liability can now be settled once and for all, the 'bankers' will then lend her a huge sum of money by which she can anticipate her liabilities and satisfy the requirements of France.

In my opinion the international loan on a great scale is just as big an illusion as reparations on a great scale. It will not happen. It cannot happen. And it would make a most disastrous disturbance if it did happen.

The idea that the rest of the world is going to lend to Germany, for her to hand over to France, about 100 per cent of their liquid savings—for that is what it amounts to—is utterly preposterous. And the sooner we get that into our heads the better.

I am not quite clear for what sort of an amount the public imagine that the loan would be; but I think the sums generally mentioned vary from £250 million up to £500 million. The idea that any government in the world, or all of the governments in the world in combination, let alone bankrupt Germany, could at the present time raise this amount of new money (that is to say, for other purposes than the funding or redemption of existing obligations) from investors in the world's stock exchanges is ridiculous.

The highest figure which I have heard mentioned by a reliable authority is £100 million. Personally I think even this much too high. It could only be realised if subscriptions from special quarters, as for example German hoards abroad and German-Americans, were to provide the greater part of it; which would only be the case if it were part of a settlement which was of great and obvious advantage to Germany. A loan to Germany, on Germany's own credit, yielding (say) 8–10 per cent, would not in my opinion be an investor's proposition in any part of the world, except on a most trifling scale.

I do not mean that a larger anticipatory loan of a different character, for example issued in Allied countries with the guarantee of the Allied government, the proceeds in each such country being handed over to the guaranteeing government so that no real money would pass, might not be possible. But a loan of this kind is not at present in question.

Yet a loan of from £50 million to £100 million—and I repeat that even this figure is very optimistic except as the result of a settlement of a kind which engaged the active goodwill of individual Germans with foreign resources and of foreigners of German origin and sympathies—would only cover Germany's liabilities under the London Schedule for four to six months, and the temporarily reduced payments of last March for little more than a year. And from such a loan, after meeting Belgian priorities and army of occupation costs, there would not be left any important sum for France.

I see no possibility therefore of any final settlement with M. Poincaré in the immediate future. He has now reached the point of saying that he is prepared to talk sense in return for an enormous bribe; and that is some progress. But as no one is in a position to offer him the bribe, it is not much progress; and as the force of events will compel him to talk sense sooner or later, even without a bribe, his bargaining position is not strong. In the meantime he may make trouble. If so, it can't be helped. But it will do him no good, and may even help to bring nearer the inevitable day of disillusion.

I may add that for France to agree to a short moratorium is not a great sacrifice, since on account of the Belgian priority and other items, the amount of cash to which France will be entitled in the near future, even if the payments fixed last March were to be paid in full, is quite trifling.

So much for the immediate situation and the politics of the case. If we look forward a little, I venture to think that there is a clear, simple and practical policy for the Liberal Party to adopt and to persist in.

But M. Poincaré and Mr Lloyd George have their hands tied by their past utterances. Mr Lloyd George's past in the matter of reparations is the most discreditable episode in his career. It is not easy for him, whose hands are not clean in this matter, to give us a clean settlement. I say this although his present intentions in this matter appear to be reasonable.

All the more reason why others should pronounce and persist in a clear and decided policy. I was disappointed, if I may say so, in what Lord Grey [Liberal leader in the House of Lords] had to say about this at Newcastle last week. He said many wise things but not a word of constructive policy which could get anyone an inch further forward. He seemed to think that all that was necessary was to talk to the French sympathetically and to put our trust in international bankers. He put a faith in an international loan as the means of solution which I am sure is not justified. We must be much more concrete than that, and we must be prepared to say unpleasant things as well as pleasant ones.

The right solution, the solution that we are bound to come to in the end, is not complicated. *We must abandon the claim for pensions and bring to an end the occupation of the Rhinelands.* The Reparation Commission must be asked to divide their assessment into two parts— the part that represents pensions and separation allowances, and the rest. And with the abandonment of the former the proportion due to France would be correspondingly raised. If France would agree to this, which is in her interest anyhow, and would terminate the occupation, it would be right for us to forgive her (and our other Allies) all they owe us and to accord a priority on all receipts in favour of the devastated areas. If we could secure a real settlement by these sacrifices, I think we should make them completely regardless of what the United States may say or do. In declaring for this policy in the House of Commons yesterday, Mr Asquith has given the Liberal Party a clear lead. I hope that they will make it a principal plank in their platform. This is a just and an honourable settlement, satisfactory to sentiment and to expediency. Those who adopt it unequivocally will find that they have with them the tide and a favouring wind.

But no one must suppose that, even with such a settlement, any important part of Germany's payments can be anticipated by a loan. Any small loan that can be raised will be required for Germany herself, to put her on her legs again, and enable her to make the necessary annual payments.

It will be recalled that at a meeting of neutral financiers at Amsterdam in November 1919 Keynes himself had been responsible for drafting a memorial to the League of Nations putting forward a proposal for an international loan (*JMK*, vol. XVII, pp. 128–50). It should be noted, however, that this proposal emphasised that the primary qualification for any country wishing to receive credit must be to have set its own financial house in order.

At the London Conference Poincaré would not hear of a moratorium without 'productive guarantees' from Germany—the appropriation of certain state resources, customs receipts, and 25 per cent of the value of her exports—measures which the British were unwilling to allow. They proposed a milder alternative scheme which Poincaré rejected, and the conference broke off.

Towards the end of August Keynes was invited to Hamburg to take part in a World Economic Congress meeting during Hamburg Overseas Week —'one of the innumerable German propaganda weeks', in the words of the *Daily Telegraph*—organised by the city's commercial community to encourage the restoration of normal trade relations. It was Keynes's first visit to Germany since the war. He left England Wednesday, 23 August; dined with his friend Carl Melchior, who lived in Hamburg, 25 August; made his speech on Saturday morning, 26 August, the closing day of the Congress, and dined with the committee that evening; lunched the next day with Wilhelm Cuno, the general manager of the Hamburg-Amerika shipping line, who was soon to become Chancellor—and was back in London within a week. (He knew Cuno as one of the German economic experts at the peace negotiations, and as a contributor to the *Reconstruction in Europe* supplements.) During the visit he sent two dispatches to the *Manchester Guardian* on conditions in Germany.

Keynes was given an enthusiastic reception in Hamburg. 'His remarks', observed the *Daily Telegraph*, not disingenuously, 'are reported in the German press at a length and with a prominence which is usually reserved for the heads of governments.' Keynes spoke in English and was introduced by Cuno as 'the man most responsible for the changed attitude of the English-speaking world towards Germany'. He was greeted with prolonged applause and cries of '*Hoch*'. The Hamburg correspondent of the partisan *Manchester Guardian*, describing the event, wrote:

> As Keynes delivered his address...enunciating the guiding principles with the clarity of the classical British economists, one had no longer the impression of one foreigner speaking to others and to Germans; the Congress revealed itself as a session of representatives of the 'Commercial Commonwealth' of Ricardo.

HAMBURG ADDRESS

Amidst the disheartening incidents of the moment, it is easy to underestimate the rate of progress of public opinion. It is necessary to look back a little way to appreciate the extraordinary change. Two and a half years ago, when I published a book, my opinions were those of a small and powerless minority. The general conclusions I then expressed are now accepted by the whole world, except that many people would now go further than I did then; and even France would, in fact, be well satisfied if she could now secure terms as good as those for proposing which I was charged, a very short while ago, with every kind of motive except a preference for the truth.

But whilst, hitherto, this movement of opinion has had great political significance, it has not had an equal practical importance. To substitute demands four times the possible for demands eight times the possible is progress of a kind; and then to come down to twice the possible is again progress. But it is still a politician's job. There is no room for the expert, the technician, the scientist, until the politicians have come down to something that can really happen.

So far this has not occurred. One of the greatest misfortunes for Germany has been the fact that there has been no incentive whatever for the exercise of sound financial ability in the conduct of her affairs. However skilful and persistent the German experts might have been in their efforts to stabilise the mark or to balance their budget, it is certain that the Allies would have raised their demands proportionately and so have rendered these efforts absolutely unavailing. In such a situation there was simply nothing to be done, and it was expecting the impossible of human nature to suppose otherwise.

I venture to predict, however, that the day of scientific, administrative and executive skill is at hand; not this year indeed, but next year. And when once this phase is reached, it is not impossible but that progress may be extremely rapid.

In the meantime there are two dangers ahead, the gravity of which I find it difficult to estimate. The first is that the Allies may delay too long and that the disintegration of German life may have proceeded too far for a recovery. You can judge better about this than I can. But I do not believe it. Such great and complex organisations as a nation can suffer a gradual degradation of their standards of life; but they cannot suffer any sudden catastrophe except by their own frenzy.

The other danger is that France may actually carry into effect her threat of renewing war. I do not believe this either. One or two years ago France might have acted thus with the necessary inner conviction. But not now. The confidence of Frenchmen in the official reparations policy is utterly undermined. They know in their hearts that it has no reality in it. For many reasons they are reluctant to admit the facts. But they are bluffing. They know perfectly well that illegal acts of violence on their part will isolate them morally and sentimentally, ruin their finances, and bring them no advantage whatever. The real risk only arises if France, from quite other than financial and economic motives, decides that chaotic conditions in Germany would be to her political advantage.

I should not be surprised if the immediate situation were solved by M. Poincaré allowing his representative to be outvoted in the Reparation Commission. He may make harsh speeches and inflict futile minor outrages, as in the expulsions from Alsace Lorraine. But he will not act on a big scale. Indeed his speeches are an alternative, not a prelude, to action. The bigger he talks, the less he will do. If he intended serious action, he would certainly speak smoothly, so as to reduce as much as possible the irritation amongst his allies. But if he means to do nothing, then he must talk loudly to satisfy his own public.

I may be wrong about this. For I, in common with nearly all Englishmen, regard the idea of violence in this connection as so futile as to be incredible; whereas the continent of Europe is inclined, I think, to regard the advantages, and consequently the likelihood, of military action more seriously than we do.

Nevertheless I think Germans will do well to keep cool and not be too much alarmed. At any rate I can assure you that the vast majority of Englishmen of all classes, and, I believe, of Italians and Americans also, would regard acts of violence at this juncture with anger and detestation.

Let me return to my main topic. I think the time is approaching when practical proposals will obtain a hearing. It is, therefore, worth while for German financiers to examine the possibilities, as experts not as politicians, and to have their proposals ready.

Now there are certain difficult questions connected with reparations which are the affair of the Allies rather than of Germany. The connection with inter-allied debts for example, the division of the proceeds between the Allies, and the question of a priority for the devastated areas. The question also of abandoning the demand for pensions, that most hateful and dishonourable breach of the Armistice conditions, is one that must be raised by the Allies and not by Germany, who has signed the Treaty containing it.

The business of Germany is to think out what kind of scheme of payments she is able and ready to carry out.

Now there are two methods of payment, on which the attention of the German experts has been much concentrated lately, but which I believe to be illusory and undependable. The first of these is the payment of the earlier instalments by means of a large international loan, and the other is payment by means of deliveries in kind.

Both of these ideas have had political value hitherto. It has been useful for Germany to be able to say—yes, we will pay at once, if we can be given a loan to pay with. This form of words has softened the underlying negative. And it has been useful for France to substitute the vast international loan illusion for the vast reparation payments illusion, in proportion as the latter illusion grew weaker. And imaginary schemes for payment by deliveries in kind (apart from deliveries of coal, which are, of course, very much of a reality) have played a very considerable part in the various ephemeral

21

settlements which have been concocted to satisfy public opinion during the past three years. It has assisted Germany in obtaining a reduction of cash payments to be able to offer vast deliveries of goods, provided the French consumer asked for them, on a scale which clearly could not occur in reality. About this French and German politicians have been in a friendly tacit collusion.

But when we abandon political illusions and try to approach the facts on their merits, then we shall be wise, I suggest, to depend on neither of these methods.

An international loan of not less than 4 milliard gold marks, which is the lowest figure generally contemplated, cannot be raised on any possible terms—that is to say in the form of new money for remittance out of the country in which it is raised. To believe in the possibility of a transaction on this scale is to make a fundamental mistake about the character of international finance. Moreover, the notion that a large part of this could be subscribed out of German balances abroad can only be based on a mistaken estimate as to the amount of these balances. I have heard many high estimates of these, often from German sources, which I feel confident are erroneous. I am sure that such German balances do not exceed 2 milliard gold marks and may well be less and that this sum includes a substantial amount required for the purposes of current trade. A subscription of even 1 milliard from German sources to an international gold loan would be a remarkable and improbable achievement.

When a really satisfactory settlement has been concluded, a foreign gold loan up to as much as 1 milliard altogether may be possible for the purpose of stabilising the mark and putting Germany on her feet again. But the vast loan for the purpose of making reparation payments for the first two or three years at the rate of (say) 2 milliards a year is a chimera.

There is only one kind of international loan which can play a part in the reparation settlement on a large scale—namely a German loan floated in the countries of her creditors, in substitution for those countries' own internal debt. A German loan, floated in France, with or without the guarantee of the French government, of which the whole of the proceeds would accrue to France, would be a sensible and practical arrangement, decidedly helpful to French finances. I hope that an issue of this kind may form a part of the final settlement.

Apart, however, from a loan of this description, it is, I am sure, most inadvisable to make any settlement of the problem dependent on raising an international loan on a large scale.

But not only is it impracticable to obtain the cash elsewhere than from Germany herself. It is also, in my judgment, unpractical and uneconomical to attempt to substitute for cash payments deliveries in kind. I include under this criticism deliveries of coal as well as of other articles. I believe that Germany would be in a much better position to make payments if she is left absolutely free as to the method of making them. By compelling Germany to deliver specific quantities of coal we tend to diminish and not to increase the total contribution she will be able to make towards reparation. Attempts to prescribe payment in a particular way, whether by deliveries of coal and other materials or by what Monsieur Poincaré calls 'productive guarantees' will diminish Germany's capacity to make other payments by more than they will benefit the Allies who receive them.

Assuming, then, that the final settlement should take the form of a series of cash payments effected by Germany in whatever method she judges best, with complete liberty on her part to trade freely, what sort of sum is practicable?

It is obvious to everyone that for the moment a moratorium is necessary and unavoidable. It is, however, very difficult to say how long such a moratorium should last, or at what rate Germany should commence payments when it comes to an end. I think, therefore, that there must be considerable elasticity in the earlier period. I throw out the following as a suggestion of the lines on which a solution might be sought.

Let the total liability of Germany, apart from payments already made, be fixed at 40 milliard gold marks, and let this sum be due in 1930 or thereabouts. Any sums paid *before* that date would then be deducted from the sum due as at that date, together with 6 per cent compound interest calculated from the date when each payment was made up to the due date in 1930. Beginning with 1924 these should be a minimum payment of a milliard a year. The sum still outstanding in 1930 should then be paid off by a series of gradually diminishing payments spread over 15 years.

In this case it would be in Germany's interest to pay as quickly as possible. But at the same time her Treasury would be given an adequate period during which no demands could be imposed from outside in excess of its current capacities.

I give these figures as a starting point for a discussion. I am not certain that Germany could pay this sum. It may not be possible to name any figures with confidence until the results of the moratorium are visible. But if we are to have any definitive solution in the near future, we must endeavour to bring the discussion to concrete details.

Provided a settlement on these lines were combined with, firstly, the abolition of deliveries in kind; secondly, the dissolution of the Reparation Commission; and thirdly, chief of all, the termination of the occupation of the Rhinelands, I believe that Germany would have been set a financial problem which it would be possible for her technicians to solve, and expedient for her politicians to promote.

I do not mean to suggest to you that a settlement on these lines is practical politics at present. I do not think it is. But there is no harm in being a little ahead of the development of opinion. I do suggest that the time has now come when practical men in Germany can usefully give their minds to the construction of schemes from the point of view of what can

24

in fact be carried out, rather than with a view to placating ill-informed and transitory public opinion in France or anywhere else. Germany must have her ideas ready and endeavour to think out the details of a policy which is not merely a paper policy or a diplomatic policy, but one which she can carry out and means to carry out. It is perfectly possible that some time in the course of next year a grand general conference may be held. And it is better to have one's ideas thought out in advance rather than improvised at the last moment under the pressure of the momentary political situation.

For the moment there is, as I have said, and as everyone admits, no alternative to a moratorium. This is required to give Germany time to recover from the reaction which must result from the inflationary boom of the last two years. Time is also necessary to devise schemes for steadying the mark and for balancing the budget. I do not take an optimistic view of Germany's immediate prospects. A disastrous reaction from the boom seems unavoidable. But on the other hand the budgetary problem during the period of the moratorium does not strike me as very difficult. And once a settlement has been come to with the Allies I see no great obstacles to a stabilisation of the mark, though I think it will be imprudent to attempt any material improvement in its value above the level which is established at the date when the settlement is effected. Surely the position of Germany is to be sharply distinguished from that of Austria or Poland or Russia. The underlying conditions are of a totally different kind. In such a situation as exists at this moment it is difficult to be hopeful. But when once a settlement has been effected what are now impossible problems will be rapidly soluble.

One must not lose sight of the other side of the balance sheet in an orgy of inflation such as Germany is suffering from. The burden of the internal debt is wiped off. The whole of Germany's payments to the Allies so far, whether for armies of occupation, pre-war debts, or reparation, have been entirely discharged by the losses of foreign speculators. I do not believe that Germany has paid a penny for these items out of her own resources. The foreign speculators have paid the whole of these liabilities and more too. Thus Germany is free from many of the budgetary problems which oppress other countries. Unless the whole of the Continent is thrown into disorder by military acts, some measure of recovery ought not to be difficult to achieve.

Whilst, therefore, Germany has still much to go through, I see no reason for despair. If we are to take a long view the most serious aspect of the situation arises from the population problem. Germany, in common with most other European countries, will suffer a degradation of the standards of life if she allows her population to expand further.

I wish I knew what young Germany is thinking and feeling; in what directions it seeks satisfaction for its emotions and outlet for its energies and talents. The strength of the young republic and the apparent determination of the German people to avoid the foolishness and the violence both of monarchist reaction and of communist revolution have excited the quiet admiration of peaceful people everywhere. Most of the valuable things in life have very little to do with international affairs. But there is one necessary condition for everything good: peace. I can imagine dominant sentiment taking such a turn amongst Germans as to render restored Germany a bulwark of the peace of Europe.

On 18 August, following a large cash payment by Germany, the mark fell 875 points in 24 hours, reaching a new low of 5,575 to the pound sterling. This was the crisis situation described in Keynes's first dispatch to the *Manchester Guardian* which he wrote within the second day of his arrival in Hamburg.

THE DECLINE OF THE MARK

From the Manchester Guardian, *26 August 1922*

FLUCTUATIONS OF THE MARK

The latest crisis in the exchange value of the mark has completely disorganised business. The violence of the fall is due to the complete absence of support, the Reichsbank, which lacks resources as a result of its last payments to the Allies, standing aside altogether and not helping the market as it did on some previous occasions of collapse. The amount of business done is not large, and even a transaction of £10,000 either way would have a significant effect on the rate. Thus a continuance of violent fluctuations either up or down is to be expected.

The demand for foreign valuta for forward delivery has been so acute that lately a holder of bank balances could sell them in exchange for sterling and buy them back again for delivery a month later at a rate of profit of 60 per cent per annum. In effect, the forward market in Hamburg has broken down completely, and transactions can only be carried out for cash.

This is one symptom of what is becoming the leading phenomenon of the German financial situation—namely, the extreme shortage of cash. The fall in the exchange value of the mark has so far outstripped the rate of inflation that the amount of Reichsmark bank notes and bank balances is at the present depreciated value quite insufficient to carry on the business of the country. Thus an unprecedented stringency of money is developing which, unless it is soon relieved, will bring much business to a standstill.

Another aspect of the same phenomenon is the fact that businesses which use imported raw materials are becoming unable to buy enough material to keep their factories fully employed, simply because the amount of paper marks involved is so huge in relation to their capital that their credit facilities are unequal to financing it. Thus a continuance of the present situation must lead to unemployment for this reason alone.

Meanwhile internal prices do their best to keep pace with the exchange, but are quite unable to keep up with it. Official fixed charges are falling to a ridiculous real cost, with further adverse consequences to the budget. For example, it is possible today to send a telegram of 20 words inside Germany at a cost of a halfpenny in English money. To take a different sort of example, eggs in Hamburg have risen in price 50 per cent since last week, but even so they are obtainable at four a penny in English money. It costs as much today to have a pair of boots soled as it cost last week to buy them new.

How far the fall in the exchange has outstripped the actualities of the situation as measured by the existing inflation is illustrated by the fact that the gold value of the Reichsbank's note issue has now fallen to £25 million, with the result that it is covered by the Reichsbank's gold reserve more than twice over!

Clearly the situation is unstable in the extreme and the result of panic. If France commits acts of violence and illegality there is no saying what may not happen in the present social and economic situation of central Europe. But if a moratorium is conceded, which the whole world knows to be necessary and unavoidable, a very sharp reaction may be experienced. Today's value of the mark discounts events which have not yet occurred.

Keynes's second despatch to the *Manchester Guardian*, written the same day as he addressed the Hamburg congress, belied the optimistic tone of his speech.

From the Manchester Guardian, *28 August 1922*

GERMAN PEOPLE TERRIFIED BY UNCERTAINTY

The situation in Germany is very anxious. I did not appreciate until I came here how near Germany is to a nervous breakdown. The effect of the crashing fall of the mark on the sentiment of the general public is terrifying and disintegrating.

The prices in the shops change every hour. No one knows what his week's wages will buy at the end of the week. The mark is at the same time valueless and scarce. On the one hand the shops do not want to receive marks, and some of them are unwilling to sell at any price at all. On the other hand, in Hamburg yesterday the banks were so short of ready cash that the Reichsbank advised them to cash no cheques for more than 10,000 marks (about one pound sterling), and some of the biggest institutions were unable to cash their customers' cheques for payment of weekly wages. The public is pessimistic and depressed and has lost all confidence.

In these circumstances everyone's thoughts are involuntarily directed to all the dangerous elements which lie under the surface of German life. It is remembered that the effective weapon of the young republic against the reactionary organisations was the general strike, and that hitherto the working classes have rallied to the government because employment has been good and the means of livelihood sufficient. But what sort of a winter can Germany expect? If the exchange continues as it is now unemployment is inevitable, because businesses have insufficient cash credit to purchase raw materials and to keep their factories in operation. Wages will not be able much longer to keep pace with the cost of living.

Rationing proposals again

At the same time the weather of the past month has injured the harvest. Proposals are already on foot to restore food kitchens and rationing and all the apparatus of the war period. An industrial country like Germany cannot support without a breakdown of its economic machinery these terrific fluctuations in its standard of value.

I find, therefore, widespread apprehension that general

unemployment and difficulties about food will be regarded by the masses as indicating the failure of the present regime, with the result that they will be lukewarm in its defence. In such circumstances a new *Putsch* from the Right or from the Left might overwhelm the Government in Berlin. It is not uncommon to hear it said in Germany today, 'We are on the edge of civil war.'

This pessimism may be justified. But I fancy that the extreme nervousness caused by the crash in the exchange leads Germans, like other people in a nervous breakdown, to exaggerate a little, by dwelling on them too much, every cause for anxiety. If the present crisis could be satisfactorily solved there might be a chance of recovery.

Immediate action needed

But if this result is to be achieved immediate action by the Allies is urgently required. Germany must be given a breathing space during which she can be free from demands for money and from threats of invasion. An unconditional moratorium must be declared without further delay.

If Great Britain wants to save the situation the time has come when she must have a positive policy of her own and must insist on it. So far we have been content to moderate the disastrous policies of France. I do not know what M. Poincaré really intends at this juncture. But if it is his intention to precipitate a crisis, then he must be told in the clearest manner that Great Britain will throw the whole of her authority against him. Everyone knows that M. Poincaré's proposals are imbecilities. It is intolerable that for such things the health of Europe should be put to hazard.

On 31 August the Reparation Commission meeting in Paris voted against a motion by the British delegate, Sir John Bradbury, to grant Germany an unconditional moratorium until the end of the year and adopted instead a Belgian proposal that she should pay the instalments due, not in cash but in six months' treasury bills, to be guaranteed. (The manner of the guarantee was to be a matter of disagreement; finally, on Belgian insistence, the Reichsbank reluctantly acquiesced to the use of its gold as security.)

Writing to *The Times* the same day as the Reparation Commission was meeting and before its decision was known, Keynes discussed the difficulty of getting the Germans to agree to a guarantee pledging the Reichsbank's gold and characteristically suggested an ingenious solution. He withdrew the letter (the typed carbon remained in his files marked 'withdrawn'), presumably when the news of the adoption of the Belgian proposal reached London.

To the Editor of The Times (*dated 31 August 1922—withdrawn*)

Sir,

If the reports from Paris are to be believed, France will not vote for an unconditional moratorium and Great Britain will not vote for a conditional moratorium. In this case, the way to escape a crisis is to avoid a vote on this issue.

Under the schedule of reduced payments for this year the net sum still due from Germany in cash up to the end of 1922 does not exceed some £13 million. The whole of this is due to Belgium in virtue of her priority.

Belgium's present attitude is dictated rather by loyalty to France than by a belief in the wisdom of French policy. It is said that Belgium is prepared to help a solution by accepting from Germany six-month bills for the above sum.

If such bills were simply drawn in gold on the German Treasury, Germany would probably agree. But Belgium requires that they should be guaranteed by the Reichsbank's gold, or, which comes indirectly to the same thing, by the German joint stock banks. This condition is unacceptable, because, once Germany gives up the quasi-independence of the Reichsbank's gold, she will be open to continual pressure until nothing is left of her final reserve.

Is there no third course? It is foolish to disorder the whole affairs of Europe for £13 million. At this junction there is nothing to be done but to gain time. I suggest that it would

31

be in Great Britain's interest for her to guarantee the necessary bills herself. I appreciate the Treasury objection to such a course. But I believe that Germany would honour these bills. By this means Germany would have met her liabilities up to the end of the year, and the question of a moratorium would not arise.

Of course this is no solution. But whilst public opinion has been enormously enlightened during the last three years—in France as well as elsewhere—*more time* is still needed before a real settlement is possible; more time for European opinion to crystallise in concrete proposals, and for America to re-enter with her counsels the European arena.

I am, etc.,

[copy unsigned]

Keynes devoted his eighth *Reconstruction in Europe* supplement to a discussion of the problems of reparation and the devastated areas. As the leading article he put forward an expansion and elaboration of his Hamburg speech. In it he recorded an extreme disillusion—such as he rarely allowed himself to show in public—born of watching four years of fruitless conferences.

During this period Keynes was well supplied with the successive proposals for the readjustment and scaling down of reparation payments being concocted by Basil Blackett at the Treasury. Some of these memoranda explored the possibilities of reparation in kind. Finding them unread by anyone in the Cabinet, Blackett sent them to Keynes, intimating that 'if an unfortunate accident should lead to their publication...in the *Manchester Guardian*', he should not be unduly distressed. Keynes, however, persisted in regarding payments in kind as an illusion, as his Hamburg speech and this article strongly indicate.

From the Manchester Guardian Commercial, *28 September 1922*

IS A SETTLEMENT OF THE REPARATION
QUESTION POSSIBLE NOW?

Nothing is settled; yet a way out is required before time can allow a significant change in surrounding circumstances.

There are no material obstacles to a wise solution. Nor are there any longer psychological obstacles on the part of the great public; for general opinion longs for a solution, and hardly cares any more what it is, if only it will work. If we were not governed by individuals who are fettered by the foolishness or the insincerity of their past words the elements necessary for a settlement would exist now.

The problem has two sides: the magnitude of the burden to be imposed on Germany; and the concessions to be offered France, to reconcile her to the disappointment of her larger expectations. Politically the two questions are bound up together. But logically they are distinct. If the Allies intend to get from Germany all they can, the total to be fixed can have nothing to do with a subsequent adjustment of obligations amongst the Allies themselves. Otherwise we fall into the fallacy, which deceives many Frenchmen, that the extremity of France's need enlarges Germany's capacity.

The following pages deal with the first problem, and I have not space here to deal with the second fully. But I may repeat briefly, what I have often said before, that if we can promote thereby a general settlement, Great Britain should forgive France (and her other allies) the whole of their war debts to her and should forgo the whole of her own claims to reparation; and should act thus irrespective of what America may do or say.

When I wrote on this subject in 1919 I was of the opinion that, apart from her immediately transferable assets, Germany could not pay more than 2 milliard gold marks (£100 million) as a continuing annual payment, and that it would be wise to ask of her somewhat less. At the time of the peace conference the so-called moderate men used to seek a compromise on the basis of some figure between 5 and 8 milliards. The latest proposal put forward by M. Poincaré (see the draft scheme reprinted from *Le Temps* in the first appendix to this article) [omitted here] amounts in effect to 3½

33

milliards; and I expect that he would really be content with the figure of 3 milliards which has often been on the lips of the 'experts' during the last eighteen months. Recent signs indicate that the British government would now favour a figure in the neighbourhood of 2 milliards.

If, therefore, Germany could pay something between 2 and 3 milliard gold marks a year, it might not be difficult to devise an acceptable settlement. But, whilst the *maximum* limit of reasonable estimate remains, in my judgment, at 2 milliards, this does not mean that Germany could promise so much with a firm intention of fulfilment. Beyond 2 milliards one is in the realm of fantasy: but not before the neighbourhood of 1 milliard is reached are we in the field of high probability. I think it probable that Germany could, after a short breathing space, pay 1 milliard gold marks annually for a period of years, and it would not be unreasonable to exact a pledge from her to do so. Although it may not be demonstrably *impossible* that she could pay 2 milliards, yet this is so unlikely that we should get no settlement of the question by compelling her to promise it.

Yet if the most reasonable expectation is that Germany can only pay something between 1 and 2 milliards, then—even though public opinion would really accept *any* solution—it is doubtful whether the politicians now in authority have enough courage and good sense to propose a scheme which Germany can honestly accept. It may need new men, of whatever political colour, who are fairly free from past commitments, to make the speedier progress which Europe's state imperatively now demands. Since, however, we require a settlement soon, we must hope, nevertheless, that the obvious trend of opinion will help our existing authorities to move quickly. In this hope I propound below the outline of a scheme which contains in it the seeds of peace and is not incompatible with the mentality and sentiment of the day.

There are certain preliminary conditions which are necessary to any lasting settlement.

(1) At the first opportunity Germany must be assured of a moratorium at least up to the end of 1923. The present method of giving her a respite for a few weeks at a time is childish and useless. I do not agree with the view, expressed by so many authorities outside Germany, that the present state of Germany's finances and of the mark exchange is entirely her own fault. Although her actual reparation payments have been small and paid for by foreign speculators, the uncertainty, the continual crises, and the expectation that, on the least sign of improvement, the Allies would increase their demands and go on increasing them until a collapse ensued have made sound finance impossible. The utmost efforts which Germany could have made would not have yielded a tenth part of the Allied demands of the past three years, and could only have served to postpone each successive collapse by a few weeks at most. In these conditions a continuing fall of the mark was inevitable, and with a rapidly depreciating currency the problem of the budget must be, for the time being, insoluble. Under a moratorium of reasonable length financial reform will be technically practicable. But unless the financial and industrial reaction from the recent boom runs its course rapidly the moratorium period should probably cover 1924 as well as 1923.

(2) Reparation deliveries in kind should be abolished, with the exception of manufactured or semi-manufactured goods directly required for the repair of the devastated areas. These latter, which are useful in principle, are not likely, however, if we judge from recent experience, to amount to much in practice, partly on account of the opposition of the French industrialists. The coal deliveries, on the other hand, are injurious to the whole economic system of Europe, and greatly reduce Germany's aggregate capacity to pay. Let anyone who doubts the viciousness of the present system read the

35

striking articles of M. Delaisi and Herr Lübsen in the seventh of these special numbers. The coal deliveries are indefensible, and I urge most strongly that they must disappear from any settlement which is to be lasting. The only argument in their favour hitherto has been the fact that a certain quantity of coal has always been forthcoming even when cash payments have broken down. I admit that, as long as we follow the unfruitful policy of grabbing whatever is tangible regardless of its effect on what we shall get in the long run, there is something in favour of the coal deliveries. But compulsory deliveries, which pay no attention to the natural geography of coal or to the relative urgency of demands for it, can form no part of a productive scheme of reparations.

(3) As soon as a definite resettlement of reparations has been achieved, the Reparation Commission should be dissolved and such limited duties of supervision as may still be necessary should be handed over to the League of Nations.

(4) The occupation of the Rhinelands must be terminated. This sword in Germany's side wounds Europe and does France no good.

With these preliminaries settled the best chance of a settlement is to be found in a plan which does not necessarily require from Germany more than 1 milliard (£50 million) a year, but provides for certain defined supplementary payments in the event of certain contingencies. Plans on these lines have often been considered. But they are worth considering again. For they seem to offer an escape from the dilemma that we must either repeat the mistake of compelling Germany to subscribe to promises which she does not see her way to fulfil (which will merely lead to a repetition of the present state of affairs), or fix a figure which opinion in France will certainly consider too low and which may in fact turn out to be less than could have been obtained.

I print in the appendix to this article [omitted here] two suggestions along these lines which have reached me from Germany. They are from authoritative sources, and I invite particular attention to them. I combine them in the following plan with some further suggestions of my own.

First, as regards the fixing of the amount. The real burden depends on whether the sum fixed is reckoned as due immediately, with an annual payment for interest and sinking fund pending discharge of the capital, or whether interest is postponed for a few years and discount allowed on earlier payments. The Treaty of Versailles contemplated the former arrangement by which if, as is the case, Germany takes some years to recover her productivity, the sum due mounts up to a fantastic total by the operation of compound interest. The alternative arrangement of not charging interest for a time may be criticised as being a mere camouflage for a reduction of the sum due. But from another point of view there is a justification for it. It is not clear that reparation is a proper case for the application of the commercial principle of compound interest. To demand that Germany should repair all the damage done instantaneously is obviously to demand the impossible. It should be sufficient if she can repair it over a period of time; and it is straining a point against her to charge compound interest in respect of the inevitable interval of time which must elapse before her reparation can be complete. It is reasonable, therefore, to fix a date by which she must make good the original damage and only to charge her interest in so far as her task is not completed by that date; and it is expedient, in order to give her an incentive to pay promptly, to allow a discount in respect of payments before that date.

I suggest, then, that the date of payment for the sum due be fixed at 1935, that Germany be allowed discount at the rate of 6 per cent per annum for payments made before that date and be charged 6 per cent per annum (of which 5 per cent shall reckon as interest and 1 per cent as sinking fund) on sums still outstanding after that date.

This being the scheme, at what figure should the capital charge be fixed? I suggest, tentatively, 40 milliard gold marks: partly because, after deducting the dishonourable claim for pensions, I do not believe that a higher claim than this can be justified in accordance with the terms of Armistice; and partly because a liability of this amount due in 1935 will work out, in terms of annual payments, in the neighbourhood of the maximum burden which it is reasonable to lay on Germany.

The way this would operate may be illustrated as follows. If Germany could begin by paying forthwith at the rate of 2 milliard gold marks (£100 million) per annum, she would have approximately completed payment by the due date of 1935; which hypothesis is unlikely to be realised, since, even if Germany rises to a maximum capacity of 2 milliards annually, she certainly could not begin such payments immediately. If she could only pay 1 milliard a year, she would just keep level with the interest but would never succeed in paying off the capital. If she could pay 1½ milliard a year, commencing in 1925, she would have completed her task in about 1950. These illustrations indicate that my suggested figure errs in the direction of being too large. I am sure that it is useless to discuss a higher figure. The most expedient result might be reached by making certain deductions, in respect of payments already made, from the aggregate of 40 milliards.

What minimum rate of payment should be required during the period before 1935? In order to satisfy everyone that as much as possible is being obtained, it may be well to combine several criteria of payment.

(1) Beginning with 1925, the aggregate annual payments not to fall below 1 milliard.

(2) Germany to make available for public issue a series of gold bonds up to as large an amount (within the limits of her

total liability) as the public would absorb year by year on the lines explained in appendix II below; half the proceeds of any such issues prior to 1925, up to a maximum of 1 milliard altogether, to be retained by Germany; the balance of the proceeds up to 1925 and the whole of the proceeds thereafter to be paid over to the Allies as an addition to the annual minimum of 1 milliard; but the service of such loans to be deducted from the 1 milliard.

(3) France to be entitled to requisition from Germany the supply of any labour and materials that are directly required for the repair of the devastated areas.

(4) An index of annual payment, based on the volume of Germany's foreign trade, to be compiled on the lines explained in appendix III below, and the figure thus arrived at to be substituted for the minimum of 1 milliard whenever it exceeds this amount.

For my own part, I do not believe in the likelihood of a large-scale international loan to Germany in the near future. But the above plan leaves open the possibility of additional receipts from this source in the earlier years, to the full extent that the collective judgment of the world considers German credit to deserve them.

Just as the second provision covers the possibility of a great recovery in German credit, so the fourth provision allows for the contingency of a great recovery in German trade. In either of these events the Allies will be paid off earlier and the reparation question got out of the way the sooner.

The above is a sincere attempt, based on technical considerations, to propose a settlement of reparations which may be workable and productive.

The most fundamental criticism which could be directed against it is this—that, whilst it may be moderate and ingenious and not obviously foolish, it is based nevertheless on the same wrong economic philosophy of the modern world as the Treaty of Versailles itself—that is to say, on false analogies due to misunderstanding the driving forces, of the nineteenth and twentieth centuries. I do not perceive the underlying forces of the modern world clearly enough either to frame the criticism explicitly or to know how it should be answered. But moving for a short time to a different plane of thought from that of the preceding paragraphs, let us try to elucidate a little what this criticism means.

All these plans, moderate and immoderate, clever and crazy alike, assume that we shall undoubtedly return shortly to arrangements not very different from those of 1914—an accelerating world of peace, foreign trade, foreign investment, expanding industrialism, capitalistic individualism, and, above all, of increasing economic well-being. Out of the surplus which will accrue to everyone in these conditions Germany can very well transfer year by year to France, and Great Britain to the United States (for it is not now expected that any parties except France from Germany and the United States from Great Britain will exact the financial obligations arising out of the war), sums comparable to those by which in pre-war days they were wont to augment the aggregate of their foreign investments. Justice requires it and economic fact allows it.

These liabilities between nations are likened, in these plans, to liabilities between well-established business houses; and it is assumed that the method of payment will be much the same as in the case of a loan to Brazil floated by Rothschilds. Indeed, the analogy is carried so far that 'moderate men' expect to find the solution in the bankers and big issue houses anticipating by a 'financial operation' the actual payments which are to be provided hereafter out of the sweat of German brows. Yet perhaps, this critic hints, the respectable and honoured bankers who sat on the Bankers' Committee in Paris this spring, on whose wisdom and capacity the peaceful, moderate, commonsense business world placed so much trust and hope, were nearly as crazy as the representatives of the City of London who, in 1918, advised the Prime Minister what Germany could pay.

The critic who would raise these sour and sceptical questions would accuse the world of two deep misunderstandings —one of the past and one of the future.

He would point out, first, that when a government defaults there is no legal process for dealing with it, as there is between individuals, and that no profitable method exists of bringing pressure to bear; that, generally speaking, nothing but motives of self-interest deter a government from defaulting whenever the burden is heavy in relation to its resources; and that these motives usually consist in an expectation of borrowing more new capital than the burden of interest on previous loans. It is foolish, therefore, to suppose that any means exist by which one modern nation can exact from another an annual tribute continuing over many years. He would point out, further, that the great pre-war trade of industrial nations was developed on a basis of credit, long or short, and that no nation can win new markets in any other way; yet exports which are to be the means of paying an indemnity must be on a cash basis. And as for foreign investments, it is a decision to suppose that these were mainly built up by means of an export surplus. In the beginning the snowball may be started by a small export surplus, or more probably by the profits of merchants in foreign trade, but thereafter it piles up by the operation of compound interest and the re-investment of the interest on previous loans. In 1914 the principal capitalist nations, which were investing largely abroad, actually had an export deficit, and their new investments were wholly provided for out of the interest on those they already had. It is, therefore, a mistake to argue from the pre-war foreign trade and foreign investments of Great Britain or of Germany that an industrial nation can

41

provide year by year a large export surplus. There is probably no recorded case of an industrial nation, without new resources to exploit, providing an export surplus of as much as £20 million a year. Thus even a figure of 1 to 2 milliard gold marks is a serious exaggeration—half a milliard would be nearer the truth.

Our critic, thinking along these lines, would add that the reparationists make another, final, mistake about the nature of the modern economic world, in supposing that national wealth can be built up by a foreign tribute, even if it is paid. Knowledge, skill, organisation, and a proper balance between the factors of production are infinitely more important than a tribute of goods or cash. France has, in fact, found no great difficulty in rebuilding in a short space of time the bulk of her destroyed property without external assistance, and Germany, if she had been allowed to do so, could probably have almost finished the job by now. One has only to compare the number of houses destroyed in France with the new houses built in Europe each year in normal times to perceive that the reconstruction of the devastated areas is, in relation to the productive resources of Europe, a very small affair. To have compelled Germany to rebuild northern France and Belgium with her own hands would have imposed on her a task within her capacity of which the carrying out would have had no harmful reactions. But to compel her by political and military pressure to find a supply of foreign resources by the roundabout processes of foreign trade may, by upsetting the equilibrium of industrial production and by rendering existing organisation useless, cause far more loss than gain. In short, as soon as we have reduced the payment to what is possible we soon perceive that its collection may be more trouble than it is worth, and that the path of true wisdom surely lies in cancelling the whole thing.

Perhaps this critic goes too far—though it is not easy to answer him. But when he passes to the misunderstanding of the future he alarms and impresses me more. So far he has been pointing out that, even if we get back to pre-war conditions, the reparation game is not worth the candle.

But suppose that we cannot reckon any longer on the ever-increasing economic well-being, under cover of which so much could be ignored, then the Europe established by the now crumbling treaties of the Paris Conference runs extraordinary dangers. If Bolshevist Russia and Turkey ruled by victorious reactionaries have added to them the economic ruin of central Europe and industrial unrest which declining standards will provoke elsewhere, we are faced with possible combinations of events which may make the most careless afraid. European civilisation requires support from every quarter, to escape decline. The young republic of Germany may still prove one of its good friends. Western Europe has need of the German republic, of reconciliation with her, and of joint defence against the dark forces.

The reparation conferences of the past three years between the prime ministers of France and England may seem to the future student amongst the most frivolous and misguided episodes of history, and those who attended them the blindest of statesmen. We waste our time with nonsense while bigger events are shaping.

Our affairs have been conducted since the Armistice with insincerity and incompetence. For four years no question has been settled on its real merits. In spite of his great gifts, master of conciliation and persuasion, yet because he appeals to all that is shortest in view, backwards in memory and forwards in prevision, Lloyd George has proved himself the least capable of enduring and constructive statesmanship of any man who has held long power in England. Perhaps we lose our time in devising paper schemes, and ought to concentrate energy on the political strife which alone can free us from the methods and the persons who have led us where we are.

43

Keynes put his opinion as to the likelihood of the repayment of war debts more bluntly in a letter to the American lawyer Paul Cravath who had sent him a report of a speech by Herbert Hoover (17 October 1922) which had received considerable comment in the Press. Hoover, who at this time was a member of the American Debt Funding Commission, had stated his conviction that the Allied debts to the United States could be paid within a reasonable time and without undue strain.

From a letter to PAUL CRAVATH, *23 November 1922*

I read the full text of Hoover's speech with a good deal of interest. From the academic point of view there is indeed a good deal in what he said. It is from the practical and political point of view that I feel it to be open to damaging criticism.

In particular he seemed to assume all through that there was no question that the debts would be paid if the United States demanded them, so that it was merely a question for Americans to make up their minds whether self-interest would be better served by asking and receiving or by forgiving. But the real fact of the matter as regards the European debts is that there is not one chance in a million that a penny will be paid in any case. The debts are merely a diplomatic weapon which can, for sentimental reasons, be used with effect if it is applied at the right moment. But there is a serious danger that the United States will refrain from making any constructive proposal to Europe until the value of this particular inducement has become obviously nil.

On the economic side I do not think it can be disputed that, assuming Europe was willing to pay, the United States could somehow or other receive the money in course of time, provided they were willing to re-arrange their industries accordingly, ruining some and making the fortunes of others, and in general scrapping the major part of manufacturing industries for export.

I also thought he blundered rather in suggesting that cancellation would ruin the basis of credit. What may be

44

injurious to international credit would be, not cancellation, but repudiation; and one of the great arguments, in my mind, in favour of timely cancellation, will be that it will prevent the awkward precedent of repudiation, which precedent might tend to get extended to other cases quite different in their nature and origins from the inter-governmental debts arising out of the war.

Keynes's other contribution to the eighth *Reconstruction* supplement was an article on 'Speculation in the Mark and German Balances Abroad' to which he had devoted considerable investigation. Towards the end of July he had sent off letters asking for specific information on the subject to banking acquaintances in Germany and the neutral countries.

On 29 August 1922 the francophile *Times* editorially criticised Sir John Bradbury's advocacy of an unconditional moratorium for Germany as an attitude not 'helpful' to France. Depicting Germany as financially intact and merely unwilling to pay, this leading article referred to 'above all...a huge sum, estimated at eight or nine hundred millions sterling, safely invested in foreign securities or lodged in foreign banks'. This was not what Keynes had discovered in his researches and immediately on his return from Hamburg, which was the same day as the editorial appeared, he wrote to *The Times* in protest.

To the Editor of The Times, *30 August 1922*

Sir,

In your leading article of today you quote an estimate of eight hundred or nine hundred millions sterling for the sum 'safely invested in foreign securities or lodged in foreign banks' on German account. I do not know who is responsible for this estimate. But as the result of an investigation, which I hope to publish shortly, I am satisfied that it is a misapprehension of the facts, being about six times too high.

The figure of one hundred millions sterling for the sum held abroad by German investors, above the capital required for trade purposes, given by the Chancellor of the Exchequer in the House of Commons on 3 August, is probably about as good an estimate as can be made. At any rate, one hundred

45

and fifty millions sterling would be an outside valuation of the free resources of Germany held abroad.

I am, etc.

J. M. KEYNES

To this *The Times* appended a sarcastic footnote:

Perhaps Mr Keynes, when he publishes the result of his investigation, will give us the total of German balances held abroad as 'the capital required for trade purposes'. Our leading article yesterday made it quite clear that the estimate of eight hundred or nine hundred millions sterling embraced both the amounts invested in foreign securities and the amounts lodged in foreign banks on German account.

The same letter moved the *Insurance Record* to remark testily:

Mr J. M. Keynes has entered the lists once more on behalf of his German friends. It is an essential weakness of our country that, at critical moments, some Englishman or other can always be found to give our case away...

Keynes referred to *The Times*'s estimate in his article giving the results of his investigation. Among the distinguished bankers he had consulted in preparing it were Carl Melchior; Dr G. Vissering, head of the Dutch central bank; C. E. ter Meulen of Hope and Co., Amsterdam, and Marc Wallenberg of the Stockholms Enskilda Bank. Keynes asked them for three items of information:

1. The amount of German foreign balances deposited abroad or in the country in question (*a*) in the form of bank balances, and (*b*) in the form of foreign securities.

2. The amount of bank notes of the country in question held on German account.

3. The amount of German balances that were necessary for foreign trade and the amount representing the 'flight from the mark'.

He received careful, lengthy replies. Early in September he sent copies of his draft of the article to his informants asking for their criticism, in particular concerning his estimates for bank balances held in Germany on foreign account. To Rudolf Lob of Mendelssohn and Co., Berlin, he wrote (7 September):

Your estimates of Germany's foreign balances are, I think, lower than those which I have obtained from any other source. But the more I enquire into the statistics of this question the more convinced do I become that most of the estimates are grossly exaggerated and that something about on the scale you suggest is very much nearer the truth.

46

From the Manchester Guardian Commercial, *28 September 1922*

SPECULATION IN THE MARK AND GERMANY'S BALANCES ABROAD

Ever since the Armistice there have been strong incentives to individual German citizens to withdraw their assets outside Germany—the desire to hold some portion at least of their capital beyond the vagaries of the fluctuating and depreciating mark, the fear of Allied demands for the confiscation by the German government of any assets within its jurisdiction, and the hope of evading the crushing burdens of prospective taxation.

This 'flight from the mark' has powerfully impressed the imagination of the outside world. The vast sale of marks by Germany, which has been the counterpart of the purchase of marks by the foreign speculator, has been thus explained, in forgetfulness of the facts that these sales were made not only for 'flight' but also by German industrialists for the purchase of raw materials, and by the German government for the purchase of grain and to pay the clearing house for pre-war debts and the Reparation Commission for its cash demands.

The sums thus accumulated in foreign centres, held in secret and hard to calculate, have grown in the minds of the credulous and the ignorant to legendary dimensions, suitably put into words by *The Times* which, in its leading article of 29 August 1922, estimated at eight or nine hundred millions sterling the sum 'safely invested in foreign securities or lodged in foreign banks' on German account. These huge figures have become, for those who deal in emotional statistics, at the same time the symbol of German obliquity and the measure of her ability to disgorge resources under pressure.

The exact figures of these foreign-held hoards are undiscoverable. But there are two methods, neither of them better than approximate, of estimating their general magnitude.

Foreign assets can only have been accumulated by Germany out of sales of marks in excess of those required to discharge other liabilities. If we can estimate the probable maximum sum obtained by such sales and the probable minimum part required for other purposes, we are left with a figure for the maximum amount of surplus resources still held abroad. The other method is the direct one of selecting those countries in which the bulk of the assets is believed to be, and of enquiring from the bankers of those countries how much they suspect they hold on German account.

I will begin with the indirect method. Since the Armistice Germany has had to sell mark notes, mark balances, and mark securities to meet three main demands for foreign currency—(1) cash payments to the Allies, (2) her adverse balance of trade, and (3) the 'flight from the mark'.

The figures for (1) are known precisely. Germany has paid in cash to the Reparation Commission £77 million, and to the clearing house, for the settlement of pre-war debts, £38 million, making a total of £115 million.

Official figures for (2) are also available, but are, at the best, not more than approximately accurate. Imports and exports, calculated in milliards of gold marks, have been recorded as follows.

	1919	1920	1921	1922 (6 months)
Imports	6·6	7·0	4·5	2·2
Exports	1·76	5·1	3·4	2·1
Excess of imports	4·84	1·9	1·1	0·1

Thus for the whole period the excess of imports has amounted to about 8 milliard gold marks. [The McKenna Report (April 1924) put the figure at between 9 and 10 milliards.] These figures are subject to two principal errors, operating, however, in opposite directions. On the one hand, there were large irregular importations, especially during the earlier years, through the occupied area—'the hole in the west'—which escaped computation. On the other hand, there has been an under-valuation, partly as an unavoidable result of the falling value of the mark and partly to evade customs duties, which under-valuation is said to have affected exports more than imports. In some cases exports have been valued at the internal price (*Inlandpreise*) instead of at the higher price actually charged to foreigners (*Auslandspreise*).

The earnings of the mercantile marine contributed nothing worth mentioning towards discharging this net adverse balance. Indeed, if the purchase of ships abroad is allowed for, the balance would be the other way. Interest earnings on foreign investments were also negligible, and were much more than offset by repayments on account of debts incurred during the war in the adjoining neutral countries.[1]

Exports of gold, however, amounted to about 1·25 milliard gold marks. Payments by tourists and travellers, in excess of similar disbursements by Germans, must not be left out of account. But into Germany there has been no large-scale incursion by American tourists.

Altogether the adverse balance, on account of what are generally called the visible and invisible items of trade, seems, on the basis of these figures, to have reached 6 milliard gold marks, or £300 million. Adding this to the cash payments under (1) we have a total exceeding 8 milliard gold marks, or £400 million. Most authorities give a somewhat higher figure.

We are left, then, with this result. German assets abroad accumulated since the Armistice cannot be more than the amount by which the purchases of foreign speculators in the mark exceed £400 million (gold).

How much have these speculators thrown away? No one knows accurately. But certainly enormous sums. Nothing like

[1] For example, Germany in 1919 owed Sweden in round figures 500 million kronor, practically the whole of which was repaid in the course of 1920–21. Considerable sums were also repaid to Holland; and lesser amounts to Switzerland, Denmark and Norway.

it has been known in the history of speculation—so large and so widespread. Bankers and servant girls have been equally involved. Everyone in Europe and America has bought mark notes. They have been hawked by itinerant Jews in the streets of the capitals, and handled by barbers' assistants in the remotest townships of Spain and South America. The argument on which bankers bought was the same as the argument on which servant girls bought: Germany is a great and strong country; some day she will recover; when that happens, the mark will recover also, which will bring a very large profit. So little do bankers and servant girls understand of history and economics.

By this means Germany has already had her much-discussed international loan, and on the easiest terms imaginable—as for interest, most of it bears none; and as for capital, only such proportion is repayable as Germany may herself decide when she comes to fix the value of the paper mark (at marks 5,000 = £1 the speculators have lost on the average 96 per cent of their capital). How dramatically fate has rewarded the foolishness of Versailles! Germany was to pay the rest of the world many milliards between then and now; but the same economic ignorance that made the world clamour for the Treaty has caused the bankers and the servant girls to pay to Germany many milliards which they will never see again.

Yet it must not be supposed that Germany, too, has not paid a penalty. In the modern world organisation is worth more in the long run than material resources. By the sale of paper marks Germany has somewhat replenished the stocks of materials of which the war and the blockade had denuded her; but she has done it at the cost of a ruinous disorganisation, present and still to come. She has confiscated most of the means of livelihood of her educated middle class, the source of her intellectual strength; and the industrial chaos and unemployment, which the end of the present inflationary boom seems likely to bring, may disorder the minds of her working class, the source of her political stability. The money of the bankers and the servant girls, which would have been nearly enough to restore Europe if applied with prudence and wisdom, has been wasted and thrown away.

But though the sums thus provided have been very large, we must put some check upon our estimates and keep them within the limits of reason. Speculators in marks can take their security in any of three ways—(1) in Reichsbank notes, (2) in balances held for their account in a German bank, or (3) in German mark bonds. (In addition, a relatively small amount has been expended by foreigners in the purchase of actual German properties, and the shares of industrial undertakings. But this is either a speculation on Germany's recovery or an attempt to take advantage of a temporary divergence between the internal and external values of the mark. It is not a speculation in the recovery of the mark itself.)

As regards (1), most authorities have placed the amount held abroad at the end of 1921 at between 25 and 30 milliard paper marks. The gold cost of these depends, of course, upon when they were bought. At the end of 1919 the total note issue of the Reichsbank was 36 milliards, against 22 milliards at the end of 1918. Since German prices doubled during 1918, some additional amount must have been required at home, and it seems difficult to suppose that more than (say) 5–7 milliards were exported in this year. By the end of 1920 the Reichsbank issue had risen to 69 milliards, but prices had more than trebled (the average for 1920 being seven times the average for 1918), so that, again, more must have been required at home, and 7–10 milliards seems a maximum allowance for export. By the end of 1921 the Reichsbank issue was 114 milliards; but prices were nine times the 1918 level, so that even if the internal circulation was able to get along with as little as four times the volume of notes of 1918,[2] there would

___

[2] If Reichs- and Darlehens-Kassenscheine be taken into account, the presumed proportionate increase for internal circulation is a little less. These supplementary

only be room for a further export of 14 milliards at the most, making a total export of 26 milliards over the three years.

Now we may estimate that in 1919 the average price paid by speculators for paper marks may have been about 20–25 per cent of the nominal gold value, in 1920 7 per cent, and in 1921 5 per cent. Combining these estimates with those given above, we have a minimum of 2 milliard gold marks and a maximum of 3 milliard gold marks for the amount expended by foreigners in the three years 1919–21 on the purchase of actual Reichsbank notes. The additional notes exported during 1922 may be large in volume, but cannot, in view of the very low value of the mark, have added very much to the gold value. Thus 3·5 milliard gold marks seems to be the outside estimate of the total proceeds of the sales of paper marks up to date.

This estimate is less than some estimates generally current. Even so, I believe that it is still too high. Certainly it would be difficult to justify a higher one. I have heard estimates of 7 or 8 milliard gold marks. But if foreigners had bought every single bank note issued by the Reichsbank since the Armistice, at its value on the day it was issued, the total would not amount to so large a figure as this.

The total of balances held by foreigners in German banks must be known approximately to German bankers. But I have not heard any close estimate of it. Some of these balances may be for large amounts; but the number of individual holdings must be far less than in the case of bank notes. The foreign holders of German bank notes probably number millions of individuals; but those who have taken the trouble to open special banking accounts in Germany can hardly exceed

notes rose from 10·5 milliards at the end of 1913 to 14·1 milliards at the end of 1919, but fell to 12·3 milliards at the end of 1920 and to 8·5 milliards at the end of 1921. Thus, assuming an export of 26 milliards, the total remaining circulation would have risen from 22·8 at the end of 1918 to 96 at the end of 1921.

in number 100,000–200,000 persons.[3] If we suppose that, directly or indirectly, 300,000 foreigners have opened bank accounts in Germany and have remitted £500 each on the average, we reach a total of 3 milliard gold marks. It seems an extravagant hypothesis, but as our object is to arrive at a maximum estimate we will let it pass.

We come next to investments in German bonds, mainly government and municipal. The issues of such bonds in which, to judge from stock exchange transactions, foreigners are interested on an important scale are strictly limited in amount. For example, the German 3 per cent and Prussian 3 per cent and 3½ per cent, which are the chief securities dealt with in London, amount *altogether* to about 9 milliard *paper* marks. I have no basis for an estimate of these investments, except the consensus of opinion that they are decidedly less important than (1) and (2). In view of this, perhaps 1·5 milliard gold marks is adequate as a maximum estimate.

So far we have 3·5+3+1·5 = 8 milliard gold marks as the sum expended by speculators in the paper mark. If we put down purchases by foreigners of shares and properties in Germany at 1 milliard gold marks, this would bring the credits to 9 milliard gold marks against debts for excess of imports and reparation and clearing house payments of 8 milliards (see above). [The McKenna Report set the figure up to 31 December 1923 at between 9·1 and 10·2 milliards.] On this basis Germany could only have accumulated surplus foreign assets to an amount of 1 milliard (i.e. £50 million). [The McKenna Report figure was 1·2 milliards.] In calculating her gross assets, however, it is necessary to add to this the amount of short business credits which she has raised in

[3] Many banking accounts in terms of paper marks are kept, however, especially in Holland, in non-German banks outside Germany, or in foreign branches of German banks. Corresponding balances must be kept, of course, by such banks in Germany itself; but the effect is to concentrate the balances and to diminish the apparent number of separate holdings. A single Dutch bank, for example, may hold in the hands of its German correspondent as much as a milliard paper marks on behalf of its clients as a whole.

foreign currency in the international money markets. If this sum is roughly estimated at ½–1 milliard, we are left with gross foreign resources of 1½–2 milliards, i.e. £75–100 million (gold).

There are many doubtful items in the above calculation; but I feel confident that the error is in the direction of putting the figures too high all round, rather than the opposite. It would not be easy to frame any reasonable hypothesis which would result in the surplus of 5 milliard gold marks often alleged by respectable authorities;[4] whilst the surplus of 16 to 18 milliards lately estimated by the *Times* leader-writer is about on a par with reparation expectations of £20,000 million.

The longer that I study these statistics the stronger does my own personal impression grow that all the figures given above, on both sides of the balance sheet, are exaggerated. I do not believe that Germany has really had an adverse trade balance of 8 milliard gold marks since the beginning of 1919;[5] and I do not believe that speculators in the mark have furnished as much as 8 milliard gold marks during the same period. A reduction of each of these estimates from 8 to 5 milliards would be more consistent with the whole available corpus of known facts and relevant probabilities.

In order to obtain the grand total of Germany's foreign assets, it is necessary to add to the above the remnant of her pre-war foreign investments. This cannot be much. Her investments in Russia, Austria-Hungary and the Balkans have been lost, those in the Allied countries and the United States have been liquidated or sequestrated, those in the neighbouring neutral countries of Europe were sold or offset by borrowings during the war. There remain very few countries of importance, of which only the Argentine is significant,

[4] I have heard this figure mentioned both by a high German official and also by one of the best informed of neutral bankers.
[5] More than half of this alleged total is attributed to the year 1919, when the collection of statistics was very faulty.

together with such investments in the United States and Allied countries as have escaped the vigilance of the liquidators through registration in other names. The total cannot exceed ½–1 milliard gold marks.

The upshot, then, of an enquiry on these lines is that Germany's total foreign resources may be worth between 2 and 3 milliard gold marks, from which must be subtracted the short-term credits she owes. Thus I make her free foreign assets below £100 million.

Now for the alternative method of approaching the problem—the direct method of enquiring how much Germany holds in each foreign country. Here we are outside the field of published statistics. The only way is to consult the judgment of prominent bankers in the countries chiefly concerned. The following estimates are based on replies which I have obtained from such quarters. I find that, generally speaking, my informants put at a much more moderate figure the amounts in their own countries, where they are speaking from their own knowledge, than those in other countries, where they are relying on hearsay.

So far as bank balances are concerned, it is generally agreed that the greatest amount is held in Holland. The most authoritative guess I have had given me is 270 million florins (450 million gold marks), but guesses of competent authorities have also ranged up to as high a figure as 600–700 million florins (say, 1 milliard gold marks). In Scandinavia the amounts are not important: perhaps 65 million kronor in Sweden, 31 million kroner in Denmark, and 10 million kroner in Norway—say 110 million gold marks altogether. In Switzerland, where securities are largely held on German account, bank balances are not believed to be equally important. Balances in other neutral countries, such as Spain and the Argentine, are not considered significant, apart from the requirements of current trade. The two remaining centres of importance are England and the United States. But here the problem is confused by the likelihood of the balances being often held in the names of nominees. I am told that whereas at first balances were mainly held in Holland, those in London and New York have been materially increased of late. So far as New York is concerned, I have heard the figure of $50–100 million mentioned, with the lower figure much more probable than the higher. Judging from the general magnitude of the most reliable estimate for Holland, it looks as if German foreign bank balances might run to as much as 1 milliard gold marks altogether. But it will be seen that the evidence is very incomplete.

One other way of looking at the problem is also useful. The number of individuals in Germany who are at the present time sufficiently well off to keep substantial foreign balances is strictly limited. Taking first of all balances of a small amount individually, a well-informed banker, who has approached the question from this point of view, thinks that we should be putting the figures very high if we estimated the number of individuals at 30,000, and the average balance kept by each of these persons in foreign countries at 10,000 gold marks, which would yield a total of 300 million gold marks. Taking next the big balances, which in some cases might reach from 5 to 10 million gold marks, and for a few individuals even more, he believes that 1,000 such balances, averaging 300,000 gold marks each, would be a fully adequate estimate, yielding a further 300 million gold marks, which makes 600 million gold marks altogether, or not much more than half the maximum of 1 milliard tentatively suggested above.

As regards foreign bank notes held by Germans, it seems that only Dutch and United States notes are held in large amounts, though British bank notes may also reach a significant figure. The estimate I have obtained for Dutch bank notes is 250–300 million florins (400–500 million gold marks); the total circulation of the Bank of the Netherlands is not sufficient to permit of much more being held in this way. The estimate for Swedish bank notes is 10 million kronor and for Danish bank notes 20 million kroner.[6]

I know of no reliable estimates for American or British notes. But, again proceeding on the general magnitude of the Dutch and Scandinavian estimates, a total of something like 1 milliard gold marks is indicated as a maximum for foreign bank notes of all kinds.

The number of individual Germans owning foreign bank notes is, of course, very much greater than the number owning foreign bank balances; but, on the other hand, the average holding is much smaller. If we were to suppose that 100,000 individuals in Germany hold foreign bank notes and that the average holding is 2,000 gold marks (= £100, which seems extremely high as an average), we should reach a total of 200 million gold marks, which is only one-fifth of the maximum of 1 milliard suggested above. This surely indicates that the figure of 1 milliard is too big—it would require that half a million individuals should hold foreign bank notes to an average value of £100 each.

For new purchases of foreign investments by Germans I have seen no estimates having any sound statistical basis. Until lately German investors have not thought it safe to buy important quantities of securities on the London, New York, or Paris stock exchanges, whilst the volume of suitable stocks obtainable elsewhere is limited. No doubt Germans have purchased some important interests in Holland, and participate in some businesses in Sweden and the Argentine. Their holdings of Dutch treasury paper are put at 10 million or 15 million florins. No authority I have consulted puts German purchases of negotiable stock exchange securities so high as half a milliard gold marks.

This method of inquiry confirms, therefore, for what it is worth, our previous conclusion that the total of Germany's

---

[6] Professor L. V. Birch, however, has estimated the holdings of Danish notes in central Europe as a whole at 100 million kr. (*Nationalokonomist Tidskrift*).

foreign resources probably falls short of 2 milliard gold marks and certainly cannot exceed 3 milliards.[7] For my own part, I believe that her net resources in the form of foreign bank balances, foreign bank notes, and negotiable foreign investments are not likely to exceed £75 million. I put the extreme range of reasonable estimate between 1 and 3 milliards, with the most probable figure much nearer to the lower than to the upper limit.

A letter from the head of the German Reichsbank, Rudolf Havenstein, arrived too late for Keynes to take it into account in writing his article. 'To my great regret,' Havenstein wrote (13 September), 'I am not in a position to give exhaustive or adequate answers to the three questions asked, as every attempt so far to obtain any tolerably exact figures has failed.' This statement, however, prefaced a letter on ten foolscap-sized pages that went into each of Keynes's questions in detail. Keynes wrote in reply:

To RUDOLF HAVENSTEIN, *4 October 1922*

Dear Dr Havenstein,

I beg to thank you most sincerely for the very full and illuminating letter, no. 17819, which you were kind enough to send me on the 13th September in answer to my enquiries.

Unfortunately this letter reached me just too late for me to be able to make use of it in my article, which had to go to press a day or or two before your letter reached me. I have sent you a copy of this article under separate cover.

Fortunately, however, what you say mainly went to confirm the conclusions of my article; except that your arguments make me even more confident than before that most current estimates of German balances are grossly exaggerated. I begin

---

[7] This conclusion is also in general conformity with that reached by the Chancellor of the Exchequer, who said in the House of Commons on 3 August last: 'There has been a certain amount of exaggeration in regard to Germans exporting capital. An estimate on my part can be only a wild guess, but I do not think that, above the capital required for trade purposes, the sum held abroad by German investors is more than £100 million sterling.'

to feel that, even in mentioning the figures I have mentioned, I have compromised a little with the prevailing opinions, and that a strictly scientific view would have led to a lower figure. Indeed, I am not sure that I cannot accuse you of falling a little under the same influences!

Whilst at the conclusion of your letter you state your opinion that you think the total sum involved is unlikely to exceed a sum of £100 million sterling, I cannot but feel that the general trend of the letter up to the last sentence prepares the mind for a materially lower figure.

Your observations as to the comparative value of the alleged foreign holdings with the market price of the ordinary shares of German companies is particularly striking.

Yours sincerely,
[copy initialled] J.M.K.

Keynes had sent a draft of his article to Reginald McKenna, chairman of the London Joint City and Midland Bank, who was about to depart for the United States to address the American Bankers' Association on the reparations problem. McKenna wrote (20 September 1922) that the article was not only 'extremely interesting' but

...so convincing that I have reduced the estimate that I gave in my American address of Germany's external assets to something not less than two hundred millions sterling. Unreasoning faith tells me that this is really below the mark, but I don't wish to state a figure materially different from yours. I include of course in my estimate investments as well as balances.

McKenna's speech was given within a week of the publication of the eighth *Reconstruction* supplement and the two were linked editorially by more than one journal as cool, enlightened views of the situation. Keynes took the opportunity to address a letter to *The Times*, but the copy is marked in pencil 'not published'.

To the Editor of The Times (*dated 5 October 1922—unpublished*)

Sir,

Mr McKenna's great speech before the American bankers brings the reparation question on to a new plane of discussion.

His estimate of the present value of Germany's capacity to pay is enormously below the lowest estimate published by anyone hitherto, and his arguments go some way towards showing that my own estimates, which were avowedly given as outside estimates, have probably erred in the direction of being too high.

His main propositions, on which any rational policy must be founded, deserve general acceptance; namely that a long moratorium is advisable, that Germany's present capacity to pay is limited to that proportion of their existing foreign assets which her nationals will voluntarily surrender, that her future capacity depends on her future export surplus, and that in past experience no industrial nation has ever had in normal circumstances a large surplus of exports.

But I am confident, after much enquiry, that Mr McKenna's estimate of the amount of Germany's existing foreign assets is excessive. A week ago, in the eighth special supplement of the *Manchester Guardian Commercial*, I gave the results of my enquiry in detail. The outside maximum is £150 million, and, in my own belief, the figure is not likely to exceed £75 million. Mr McKenna's figure of £200 million is, indeed, not so very far from my maximum; but then my maximum is already an outside figure.

In the time at his disposal Mr McKenna obviously could not give the details on which he based his estimate; so that I cannot compare his data with my own, which are already available to the public. But I may mention one illustration which shows up vividly how unlikely it is that Germans in their present impoverished condition could afford to hold abroad so great a proportion of their total resources in a form which for them is necessarily very speculative. Mr McKenna's figure of £200 million would buy up all the ordinary shares of every company in Germany, *plus* every German bank note whether circulating at home or held by foreign speculators, *plus* the whole of the deposits of every bank in Germany, and still leave enough over to buy up the whole of the bank notes and the whole of the bank deposits all over again.

I am, etc.,

[copy unsigned]

The decline of the mark accelerated rapidly towards the end of 1922, the rate dropping from 5,074 to the pound sterling in August, to 14,145 in October and 32,146 in November. The German government invited a group of independent financial experts to come to Berlin to discuss the feasibility of stabilisation. It was announced that Keynes accepted this invitation 25 October; the other members of the group, which arrived in Berlin 2 November, were Gustav Cassel, R. H. Brand, Jeremiah W. Jenks of Columbia University, Dr G. Vissering of the Dutch central bank, the Swiss banker Leopold Dubois, and B. Kamenka.

According to Lord D'Abernon, the British ambassador in Berlin, writing in his diary (*An Ambassador of Peace:* Volume 3, *The Years of Recovery*), the scheme to invite foreign experts to explore the possibility of stabilisation was the result of conversations in which he participated with some of the more progressive German banking authorities. He had suggested 'the name of Cassel—an old friend of mine—and of Keynes, of whose ability I have the highest opinion'. Chancellor Wirth was told by the opponents of reform that 'Cassel and Keynes were both men of extreme theoretical views and quite indifferent to what anybody else thought on their own subject. He therefore watered them down by adding to their number...'

Keynes sought help from Sir John Bradbury, the British representative on the Reparation Commission, who had recently made a public statement on the situation created by the fall of the mark. Speaking in his own behalf and not as a representative of his government, he had put forward a plan for a general settlement, but warned that unless Germany acted decisively and demanded a moratorium for two years, no serious progress could be achieved.

To SIR JOHN BRADBURY, *20 October 1922*

Dear Bradbury,

Your latest proposals as summarised by the journalists are barely intelligible. Is any more authentic version available? I enquire particularly because I have just received a request from the German govt. to go to Berlin for a few days to discuss what ought to be done about stabilising the mark, and I want to be as well informed as I can about the whole position up to date.

Keynes's handwritten note was kept in Bradbury's papers (T 194/9) together with a copy of Bradbury's reply.

From SIR JOHN BRADBURY, *23 October 1922*

My dear Keynes,

Here is a copy of my memo. It is in no sense confidential having been sent out to the press for publication by the Reparation Commission. The British Press has however been too full of internal politics to insert it and the French Press has boycotted it!

I also enclose a note showing why I thought 1000 marks to the dollar a practicable rate for stabilization on the 4th October. I should not be so sanguine today!

The main idea of my plan is to relieve the German budget of all peace treaty charges except the service of a bond issue which would be made at the rate of about 3 milliard gold marks a year until either (*a*) a situation is reached in which a general settlement can be negotiated or (*b*) saturation point is reached (subject however to asking for something additional on current account if the state of the budget permits).

If a general settlement does not intervene a point will be reached at which it will become obvious that the service of the outstanding bonds is as much as Germany can stand and the rest of the liability will have to be written off.

I could of course have made this underlying idea much clearer in the drafting but if I had I am afraid the welcome of the proposal in France would have been even warmer than it has been!

Yours sincerely,
JOHN BRADBURY

The experts were asked three specific questions:
(1) Was stabilisation possible now?
(2) If not, what conditions were necessary?
(3) What actual measures should be taken to achieve stabilisation?

Keynes, Brand, Cassel and Jenks signed a majority report dated 7 November. They stated that immediate stabilisation was necessary to save Germany from complete financial collapse and to safeguard her creditors.

It would be possible only under three conditions: a moratorium of at least two years in respect of Germany's Versailles obligations; some modest support from an international consortium to engage public confidence and supplement Germany's own efforts, and finally, a balanced budget.

The signers of the majority report believed that it would be imprudent to attempt stabilisation except at a low value of the mark. At the time that they were writing the rate was 7,000 marks to the dollar; they visualised some improvement with the restoration of confidence and regarded a rate between 3,000 and 3,500 marks to the dollar as appropriate. The situation was 'unprecedented', in the words of the majority report, in that, at a rate of 3,500 marks to the dollar (17,500 to the pound), the gold reserves of the Reichsbank amounted to about twice the value of the note issue. 'No currency has fallen into decay with so great a potential support still unused.'

In outlining a plan to bring about stabilisation, the majority report set out a number of measures making use of these gold reserves to buy paper marks at a fixed rate to the dollar and to buy and borrow foreign exchange. This was its main difference from the minority report, signed by Vissering, Dubois and Kamenka, which made everything depend on a large loan, to be organised by an international committee of bankers.

While Keynes was in Berlin Bradbury had sent him a scheme for restoring the German currency while risking only a small part of the gold reserve. Other than this, no working papers or drafts concerning the report remain among Keynes's papers and there is no indication as to whether any particular part of it was due to Keynes's influence or was drafted by him.

New events quickly followed the publication of the two reports. On 14 November the Wirth government fell—not because of disagreement over the stabilisation proposals but because the Socialists, the strongest party in the Reichstag and the strongest supporters of stabilisation, refused to work with the industrialists whose motives were believed to be suspect in this matter. Before this government departed, however, they sent a note to the Reparation Commission stating that an external loan of 500 million gold marks was a preliminary condition of stabilisation; to this sum they proposed to add an equal sum and by buying marks abroad would endeavour to push the value of the mark upwards—*not* the advice given in the majority report.

Keynes wrote to thank Melchior for the arrangements made for his stay in Berlin and for the help of Herr E. Kocherthaler, a colleague of Melchior at M. M. Warburg and Company.

Dear Melchior,

I owe you a very great debt of thanks for the arrangements which you made possible during my stay in Berlin. Indeed, I do not know what I should have done without Kocherthaler. He was quite invaluable. With a somewhat long experience of assistants, I do not think that I have ever been so well served. I am very grateful to him and to you.

It is rather difficult to make out from the public press just what has been happening since I left Berlin. But so far as I can understand from the latest communication of the German government to the Reparation Commission, their scheme contains one element which, in my judgment, is hopelessly unsound. That is to say, if I understand them aright, they propose, not to attempt to stabilise the mark at a fixed figure, but to use their resources to intervene for its support on foreign exchange markets at rates which will be varied from time to time.

It is my firm belief that so long as any element of uncertainty is allowed to remain, nothing can possibly be done, and it is probable that resources so employed will be dribbled away without effecting their purpose. But perhaps I misjudge what is suggested. If it is possible to send me a copy of the exact text of their communication, I shall be very grateful for it.

My impressions on returning to London confirm very strongly the view which I expressed in Berlin, that the prospect of raising a loan here in advance of stabilisation is practically non-existent. No doubt in the event of a long moratorium of four or five years the position will be changed, but I should think that there is no real prospect of such a long relief being granted at the present time.

I think, therefore, that the German government are psychologically mistaken in putting foreign assistance in the forefront of their plan; and are technically mistaken as to the manner in which they would employ any resources they can obtain. But I fear that this is not very unexpected to me after what I saw of them in Berlin. Their lack of psychological flair seemed to me to be only equalled by their lack of technical competence.

Let us hope that the new government is going to be better. I wonder from what elements it will be composed. Rashly predicting from a distance, it looks to me as though there would be, in the first instance, a government a little more to the right than was Wirth's, and a little more under industrialistic influences; but that such a government cannot survive for long, and will be succeeded by something looking primarily to Socialist support. From what I saw in Berlin, I was disposed to put more hopes on the Socialists than on the Industrialists in any matter concerning stabilisation. It is a terribly demoralising thing for a country to have everyone, whether he wants to or not, speculating against his own currency.

The report on stabilisation signed by the four of us has had a very good publicity in England, and has, I think, had in the aggregate a better press than anything with which I have been connected in recent times. Whether we are right or wrong, I think that what we there put down does truly represent the instructed opinion of England. I enclose a leader from the *Financial Times* and also one from *The Times*, as I have these handy. But they are only two amongst many of very similar tenor.

Will you kindly show this letter to Kocherthaler, and thank him again from me for all his work.

Yours sincerely,
[copy initialled] J.M.K.

The leader from *The Times* that Keynes sent to Melchior, although complimentary about the advice given to Germany in the majority report to pull herself up by her own bootstraps, could not resist a remark about the doctrine of self-help not being popular in that country among those who had been led astray 'by some professors of economy, notably by a gentleman who signs the present report'.

Keynes's impression that he had passed on to Melchior—that the German government proposed to intervene in support of the mark on the foreign exchange market at varying rates, instead of stabilising it at a fixed rate—was evidently conveyed to the head of the Reichsbank, Herr Havenstein, who wrote to Keynes (4 January 1923) at considerable length to correct what seemed to him a misunderstanding. Havenstein maintained that the rate could be fixed only after a preliminary experimental phase in which the mark was allowed to respond automatically to the international trade situation, subject to such intervention as might be needed to eliminate the effects of speculation.

To RUDOLF HAVENSTEIN, *17 January 1923*

Dear Herr Havenstein,

I am very much obliged to you for your important and interesting letter of the 4th January. The question is too big a one for it to be easy to discuss it in correspondence. But I owe it to your letter to attempt, in reply, to make out as clearly as I can where it is we agree and where we differ.

The prior question of all is whether a stabilisation plan for the mark is possible at all at present. I hold the view that in the absence of a moratorium it is not possible; but that with a moratorium, of which unfortunately there seems no prospect at present, it is possible.

After answering this first question in the affirmative, there comes next the question of the method of stabilisation to be adopted.

You express your letter as though the chief difference between us related to the answer to the second question. But from what you say subsequently I am not at all sure that our main difference is not really about the first question. The greater part of your letter is directed, it seems to me, to the argument that the conditions in Germany are at present such that even with a moratorium any project of stabilisation would be extremely rash. I admit great force in your arguments. But nevertheless, I do not agree with them, mainly I think because I do not attach the importance that you do to statistics of an adverse balance of trade. If I felt confident that I could control the budgetary position, I should not doubt my capacity, in Germany's present situation, to control the exchange. As soon as the supply of new currency is limited, I do not see how it is possible that the balance of trade should be adverse. I believe that the point of view which looks first to the balance of trade, and seeks for an improvement in that first of all, or alternatively to the support of a foreign loan, is deeply erroneous and has not penetrated to the true process of causation lying behind current events.

I am not impressed, therefore, by arguments about the balance of trade. I am only impressed by arguments about the budgetary position. It is for this reason that, in the absence of a moratorium, the position seems to be hopeless. But once a moratorium is granted I see no insuperable obstacle to budgetary equilibrium. Indeed, when I was in Berlin, the Treasury officials whom I heard agreed with this view.

When we come to the second question, I cannot help thinking that your views are dominated by your deep pessimism about the first question. If the time is not ripe for stabilisation at all, then it might be prudent, even though the scheme was called a stabilisation scheme, to make it in effect something very much less. If, on the other hand, stabilisation is feasible, then the very meaning of the word necessitates, it seems to me, that the exchange should be fixed, and I can see no object in any prolonged preliminary oscillations. I do not think that it matters very much what rate is selected, provided it is reasonably in accordance with the existing facts; that is to say, I should take some figure between the external and the internal value of the mark at the date of stabilisation. But within those limits I should regard the determination of the exact amount as rather a secondary point. On the other hand, I should be very much opposed to a rate which attempted to raise the value of the mark, as I believe this would bring about all sorts of untoward consequences. But equally I should, for obvious reasons, be much against a rate which meant any further depreciation in the external value of the mark.

If the time is not ripe for definitely fixing the mark, I see no object in intervening on the market at all. The plan of intervening from time to time, in order to punish bear speculators, or for any other purpose, would, it seems to me, fritter away resources without attaining any solid object.

In fact, the root of my dislike for what I understand to be your proposal is that it seems to me to be really not a technical method at all, but a compromise between those who are in favour of stabilisation and those who are against stabilisation. I should far prefer, to this compromise, the definite victory of one or other of the two parties. I recognise that your own pessimistic view has great support behind it, both from facts and from opinion. It may very well be that the whole thing is premature at present. I do not accept this view, but I appreciate the arguments. But I see no purpose in any middle course between letting this view prevail and pursuing the opposite view with vigour.

In any case, however, I fear that this discussion is no better than academic for the time being. I need not say that I regard the present operations of the French government [they occupied the Ruhr on 11 January] with violent disapproval. I think that their action is wrong on law, and on morals, and on expediency. But things have got to work themselves out, and it is useless in the meantime to attack the technical problem either from one point of view or from the other.

I have put my opinions frankly, in the interests of clearing up the question. I know that you will understand and appreciate. I have much valued your letter.

Yours very truly,
[copy initialled] J.M.K.

The eleventh issue of the *Reconstruction in Europe* supplements was devoted to the foreign exchanges and European banking. Keynes's introductory article, 'The Stabilisation of the European Exchanges—II', was a reconsideration of the subject with which he began the series in the light of eight months' experience. In the same issue he printed several comments on his earlier article, including a letter from Joseph Caillaux, the former French premier and finance minister.

Caillaux contended that since people 'prefer bankruptcy to the acknowledgment of their insolvency', it was necessary to envisage

a limited inflation by means of an increase in the precious metals, which would have the double result of reducing the weight of the enormous State debts and of restoring very gradually the monetary systems which have not been too hopelessly demoralised.

Asking permission to publish what had been originally written as a personal letter, Keynes replied:

From a letter to JOSEPH CAILLAUX, *18 July 1922*

I have read with very lively interest your letter of the 21st June on the question of devaluation.

I recognise the political obstacles arising out of prejudice and popular ignorance, and I agree that for this reason the adoption of the remedy is likely to be long delayed.

The existence of popular hostility to the scheme is a good reason why politicians should be afraid of advocating it. But this does not make it any less the duty of economists to seek to alter public opinion. The experience of the last three or four years teaches, I think, how quickly public opinion is capable of moving in the face of events, even in directions which were thought impossible a very short time ago. Moreover, you agree with me in seeing no other solution, and put your faith, therefore, in something suitable dropping from heaven. So until that something drops, I shall persevere.

My next move in the debate will be to take up the issue again in a forthcoming supplement of the *Manchester Guardian*...

From the Manchester Guardian Commercial, 7 December 1922

THE STABILISATION OF THE EUROPEAN
EXCHANGES—II

Eight months ago, in the first number of these supplements, I put forward certain general principles for stabilising the exchanges of Europe.[8] In this short interval much has happened. I return to the same topic with my opinion changed on some points by further reflection and by the course of events, but unchanged on others.

Devaluation

In my former article I argued that no attempt should be made to restore to their old parity those currencies which were depreciated by more than 20 per cent below their former value. This doctrine has since been supported by the authority of the Genoa Conference, whose resolution in its favour has proved to be in accordance with an overwhelming weight of instructed opinion.

Nevertheless, while the Genoa resolutions affirmed the doctrine in general, representatives of the countries chiefly affected took the opportunity of explaining that it must not be applied to them in particular. Signor Peano, M. Picard, and M. Theunis, speaking on behalf of Italy, France, and Belgium, joined in declaring that, so far as each of these countries was concerned, they would have nothing to do with devaluating, and were determined to pursue the policy of restoring their respective currencies to their pre-war value. This was probably dictated by political rather than intellectual considerations; but that enlightened self-interest should have

---

[8] In this article I suggested as a basis of discussion certain rates at which the leading exchanges might be stabilised, providing a margin of 5 per cent between the fixed rates at which notes would be redeemed and those at which they would be issued. By an unfortunate misprint, for which I deeply apologise to many perplexed readers, the columns of the table were transposed, so that the redemption and issue rates respectively appeared reversed.

led these three individuals to deny the consequences of what their intellects had just affirmed is a measure of the immense difficulty of carrying into practice any scientific attempt at stabilisation. No European government has yet declared itself in favour of *stabilising* the value of its money, as distinguished from *improving* it, which renders monetary conferences futile for the present.[9] The end must be willed before it is useful to discuss the means. Thus, it is more necessary to reassert in plain language the simple, governing facts than to work out the technical details of an actual plan.

The burden of internal debts

If the quantity of a currency can be controlled, then sooner or later its value can be stabilised. This simple truth still holds good. The quantity of a currency can be controlled unless the government is in financial difficulties. This also holds good, although when the sickness is far advanced a tentative stabili-sation may have to precede budgetary equilibrium.

What are the sources of a government's financial difficul-ties? It may be living in current expenditure beyond its means in current income. This extravagance is never beyond cure by firmness and economy, though the State may be forced to confine its functions, beneficent or grandiose, more nar-rowly than its ambitions demand. But financial difficulties may also beset a State because its contractual liabilities, fixed in terms of money, have reached an intolerable proportion of the national income. This is a question of the distribution of the national burdens between different classes rather than of aggregate State expenditure in relation to aggregate national wealth; but, nevertheless, if the fixed charges of the national debt bear too high a proportion to the national

---

[9] The solution is not likely to come by joint, simultaneous action. The experts of Genoa recognised this when they 'ventured to suggest' that 'a considerable service will be rendered by that country which first decides boldly to set the example of securing immediate stability in terms of gold' by devaluation.

income, it may offer a problem insoluble by orthodox methods. The active and working elements in no community, ancient or modern, will consent to hand over to the *rentier* or bond-holding class more than a certain proportion of the fruits of their work. When the piled-up debt demands more than a tolerable proportion three solutions are possible. First, repudiation, which as regards internal debt may be ruled out at present in Western Europe; second, a capital levy, which is the best solution on merits but is difficult to explain or understand, as the ignorance of the solid arguments on either side in the columns of the Press has lately exhibited; third, the depreciation of the monetary standard in which the debts are expressed, whereby the real burden of the debts is diminished in exactly the same proportion in which the monetary standard is depreciated. This expedient cannot be defended on its merits. Its indirect evils are many. Instead of dividing the burden between all classes of wealth-owners according to a graduated scale, it throws the whole burden on to the owners of fixed-interest–bearing stocks, lets off the *entrepreneur* capitalist and even enriches him, and hits small savings equally with great fortunes. But it is the line of least resistance; the responsibility for it cannot be brought home to individuals; it is, so to speak, nature's remedy, which comes into silent operation when the body politic has shrunk from curing itself.

Now in the countries of Europe lately belligerent the third expedient has already functioned on a scale which reduces the real burden of the debt by from 50 to 100 per cent. In Germany the national debt has been by these means practically obliterated, and the owners of small savings have lost everything, whilst the same conjuncture has enabled some capitalist *entrepreneurs* to multiply their fortunes. In France the real burden of the debt is less than half of what it would be if the franc stood at par; and in Italy only a quarter. The owners of small savings suffer quietly, as experience shows, these enormous depredations, when they would have thrown down a government which had taken from them a tenth of the amount by more deliberate but juster instruments.

In these circumstances advocates of devaluation take a middle course. They accept the *fait accompli*. So far from repairing the evils of depreciation, a reversal of the process superimposes new evils. But a restoration to parity of the heavily depressed currencies, were it desirable, would be impossible, if only because it would raise the real burden of the internal debts (that is to say, the proportion of the earnings of the active class transferred from them to the *rentier* class), in an intolerable degree. On the other hand, when once this impossibility is understood and faced, devaluation may bring stabilisation and the avoidance of a further depreciation within practical politics.

My point may be well illustrated by some particulars relating to France.

Excluding altogether the external debt of France, her internal debt now exceeds 250 milliard francs. Further borrowing definitely anticipated for the near future, together with loans on reconstruction account guaranteed by the government, will bring this total to the neighbourhood of 300 milliards by the end of 1923. The service of this debt will absorb about 18 milliards per annum. The total normal receipts under the budget of 1923 are estimated at this same figure of 18 milliards. That is to say, the service of the debt will shortly absorb, at the present value of the franc, the entire yield of taxation. Since other government expenditure in the ordinary budget (i.e., excluding war pensions and future expenditure on reconstruction) cannot be put below 11 milliards a year, it follows that, even on the unlikely hypothesis that further expenditure in the extraordinary budget after 1923 will be paid for by Germany, the yield of taxation must be increased permanently by 60 per cent to make both ends meet. If, however, the franc were to depreciate to (say) 100

73

to the pound sterling, the ordinary budget could be balanced by taking little more than at present of the real income of the country.

In these circumstances it will be difficult, though not impossible, to avoid the subtle assistance of a further depreciation. In the light of the figures now available, I was probably too optimistic in my previous article when I suggested that the franc might be stabilised at 52½ to the pound sterling. But what is to be said of those who still discuss seriously the project of restoring the franc to its former parity?

In such an event the already intolerable burden of the *rentier's* claims would be more than doubled. It is unthinkable that the French taxpayer would submit. Even if the franc was put back to par by a miracle, it could not stay there. New inflation due to the inadequacy of tax receipts must drive it anew on its downward course. Yet I have assumed the cancellation of the whole of France's external debt, and the assumption by Germany of the burdens of the extraordinary budget after 1923, an assumption which is not justified by present expectations. This fact by itself renders it certain that the franc cannot be restored to its former value. Yet no Frenchman of influence, so far as I am aware, with the sole exception of Professor [Charles] Gide,[10] has admitted this truth. At the Genoa Conference M. Picard [of the Bank of France] was able to deny it without being considered ridiculous. France dwells in a deep pit of ignorance.

If we look ahead, averting our eyes from the ups and downs which can make and unmake fortunes in the meantime, this question of what amount of dead-weight internal debt is tolerable to the active earners of the community is fundamental. The level of the franc is going to be settled in the long run not by speculation or the balance of trade, or by any such fleeting influences or secondary symptoms, but by the

[10] Perhaps M. Loucheur must also be mentioned as an exception. [Louis Loucheur had been Ministre des Régions libérées in the Briand government.]

proportion of his earned income which the Frenchman will permit to be taken from him by taxation to pay the claims of the *rentier*. The level of the franc exchange will continue to fall until the commodity value of the francs due to the *rentier* has fallen to a reasonable proportion of the national income, having regard to the habits and mentality of the country.

In a private letter addressed to me by M. Caillaux, which he allows me to print at the conclusion of this article, there is set forth a philosophical defence of those who are unwilling to face the problem of devaluation. M. Caillaux writes with grace and knowledge. But what is it he says? He invokes a philosopher's stone which shall save the face of the franc by making gold worth as little as itself. Certainly, we must direct to this the genius of our laboratories! What a fine way out of the reparation question, with cartloads of newly manufactured gold crossing the frontier, and M. Poincaré right after all!

But, above everything, M. Caillaux tells me that in these matters the world is not governed by reason, echoing as it were the voice of M. Hanotaux in one of our earlier supplements [*JMK*, vol. XVII, p. 426]. Is France such a madhouse that her elder statesmen end with no conclusion but this?

Perhaps. I, too, do not find the world particularly rational. Nevertheless, those may do best who listen in time to the voice of reason and the cries of Cassandra.

The evils of deflation

The magnitude of the internal debt in most European countries is, therefore, the fundamental reason why it is impossible to restore the value of their currencies to their former value, and why even the project of stabilising them at their present level may be too optimistic.

But even if it were possible, it would not be desirable to raise the value of the currencies, or, in other words, to lower the levels of prices to their former standards, once they have become adjusted to other standards. I have little to add to what Professor Irving Fisher has written with overwhelming force and lucidity in his article printed below ['Devaluation versus Deflation']. I should like to compel every banker and politician in Europe to learn it by heart. He deals, however, primarily with what justice demands and only secondarily with what prosperity requires.

The policy of gradually raising the value of a country's money to (say) 100 per cent above its present value in terms of goods means giving notice to every merchant and every manufacturer that for some time to come his stock and his raw materials will be constantly depreciating on his hands, and that everyone who finances his business with borrowed money (whether in the form of debentures, bank overdrafts, or bills) will in the end lose 100 per cent on his liabilities (since he will have to pay back twice as much in terms of commodities as he has borrowed). Modern business, being carried on by *entrepreneurs* largely on borrowed money, must necessarily be brought to a standstill by such a process. If the business world really believed that the Government and the State Bank were capable of carrying out such a policy as the above, they would have no choice but to retire from enterprise for the time being. The only sensible course in such circumstances is to realise one's assets, pay off all money liabilities, and sit tight on one's bank balance until the *funeste* process is over. Probably the business world would be a little more sceptical than that. But even the possibility that such a process of deflation might set in would compel them to curtail their enterprise; and if the government were to score an initial success and a certain improvement was effected, the fear of its continuance must necessarily depress trade. The mechanism of the modern business world is even less adapted for violent fluctuations in the value of money upwards than it is for fluctuations downwards. And for what good purpose or desirable end would all this upset be engineered? None at all that I have ever heard of.

Yet let not the reader suppose that Professor Fisher and I are flogging a dead horse. These things need to be said and to be repeated. When I visited Berlin lately to discuss the stabilisation of the mark, I found an influential authority arguing that it would be a wise policy to raise the value of the mark to thirty times the value ruling at that time. A restoration of their currencies to the pre-war par is still the declared official policy of the French and Belgian governments. I hear that Signor Mussolini has threatened to double the present value of the Italian lira—a fearful threat indeed if it could be carried out, and one to avoid which the Italian people would be ready, I should think, to submit to almost anything! But would so good a politician as Signor Mussolini have propounded, even in bravado and exuberance, such a policy as this if he had understood that, expressed in other but equivalent words, it was as follows: 'My policy is to halve wages, double the burden of the National Debt, and to reduce by 50 per cent the prices which Sicily can get for her exports of oranges and lemons'?

Finally, one country—Czechoslovakia—has, on a modest but sufficient scale, been making the experiment. Comparatively free from the burden of internal debt, and free also from any appreciable budgetary deficit, Czechoslovakia has been able, in pursuance of the policy of her finance minister, Dr Alois Rasin, to employ the proceeds of certain loans, which her credit enabled her to raise in London and New York, to improve the exchange value of the Czech crown to about double the level which seemed to me eight months ago, with reference to the circumstances existing at that time, a rate at which she could hope to stabilise the crown with advantage to herself. Owing to the rapidity with which under the above favourable conditions it has been possible to effect the improvement, the country has not suffered as severely as she would if the change had been slower and more prolonged. But it has cost her an industrial crisis and serious unemployment. To what purpose? I do not know. Even now the Czech crown is only worth a sixth of its pre-war parity; and it remains unstabilised, fluttering before the breath of the seasons and the wind of politics. Is, therefore, the process of appreciation to continue indefinitely? If not, when and at what point is stabilisation to be effected? Meanwhile the foreign resources, which might have been employed during the past six months to secure a definite stabilisation, are no longer intact, and it will not prove easy to replenish them. Czechoslovakia was better placed than any country in Europe to establish her economic life on the basis of a sound and fixed currency. Her finances were in equilibrium, her credit good, her foreign resources adequate, and no one could have blamed her for devaluating the crown, ruined by no fault of hers and inherited from the Habsburg Empire. Pursuing a misguided policy in a spirit of stern virtue, she has preferred the stagnation of her industries and a still fluctuating standard.

Seasonal movements

It is often supposed that if a country's budget, currency, foreign trade, and its internal and external price levels are properly adjusted, then, automatically, its foreign exchange will be steady. On the other hand, so long as the above elements are not properly adjusted, then no scheme to fix the exchange can succeed. So long, therefore, as the exchanges fluctuate—thus the argument runs—this in itself is a symptom that an attempt to stabilise would be premature. When, on the other hand, the basic conditions necessary for stabilisation are present, the exchange will steady itself. In short, any deliberate or artificial scheme of stabilisation is attacking the problem at the wrong end. It is the regulation of the currency, by means of sound budgetary and bank-rate policies, that needs attention. The proclamation of convertibility will be the last and crowning stage of the proceedings, and will amount to little more than the announcement of a *fait accompli*.

There is a certain force in this mode of reasoning. But in one important respect it is fallacious.

Even though foreign trade is properly adjusted and the country's claims and liabilities on foreign account are in equilibrium over the year as a whole, it does not follow that they are in equilibrium every day. Indeed, it is well known that countries which import large quantities of agricultural produce do not find it convenient, if they are to secure just the quality and the amount which they require, to buy at an equal rate throughout the year, but prefer to concentrate their purchases on the autumn period. Thus, quite consistently with equilibrium over the year as a whole, industrial countries tend to owe money to agricultural countries in the autumn and winter, and to repay in the spring and summer. The satisfaction of these seasonal requirements for credit with the least possible disturbance to trade was recognised before the war as one of the most important functions of international banking. A most admirable organisation had been devised for the purpose, and the seasonal transference of short-term credits from one centre to another was carried out for a moderate banker's commission.

It was possible for this service to be rendered cheaply because, with the certainty provided by convertibility, the price paid for it did not need to include any appreciable provision against risk. A somewhat higher rate of discount in the temporarily debtor country, together with a small exchange profit provided by the slight shift of the exchanges within the gold points, was quite sufficient.

But what is the position now? As always, the balance of payments must balance every day. As before, the balance of trade is spread unevenly through the year. Formerly the daily balance was adjusted by the movement of bankers' funds, as described above. But now it is no longer a purely bankers' business, suitably and sufficiently rewarded by an arbitrage profit. If a banker moves resources temporarily from one country to another, he cannot be certain at what rate of exchange he will be able to bring them back again later on. His profit is no longer definitely calculable beforehand, as it used to be; unforeseen movements of the exchange may involve him in heavy loss; and his prospective profit must be commensurate with the risk he runs. In fact, the seasonal adjustment or credit requirements has ceased to be arbitrage banking business, and demands the services of speculative finance.

Under present conditions, therefore, a large fluctuation of the exchange may be necessary before the daily account can be balanced, even though the annual account is level. The exchange must fall (or rise, as the case may be) until either the speculative financier feels sufficiently confident of a profit to step in or the merchant, appalled by the rate of exchange quoted to him for the transaction, decides to forgo the conveniences of purchasing at that particular season of the year and postpones a part of his purchases.

The services of the professional exchange speculator, being discouraged by official and State banking influence, are generally in short supply, so that a heavy price has to be paid for them, and trade is handicapped by a corresponding expense, in so far as it continues to purchase its supplies at the most convenient season of the year.

The extent to which many of the exchange fluctuations which have troubled trade during the past three years have been of the nature of seasonal fluctuations, and therefore due not to a continuing disequilibrium but *merely* to the absence of convertibility or 'pegging', is not, I think, fully understood.

During 1919 there was a heavy fall of the chief European

exchanges, due not to seasonal influences but to the removal of the inter-Allied arrangements which had existed during the war. During 1922 there has been a rise of the sterling exchange, which is independent of seasonal influences. During 1923, or at some later date, there *may* be a further non-seasonal collapse of some of the Continental exchanges due to certain persisting features of their internal finances. But during the three years since the autumn of 1919 the fluctuations have been *mainly* seasonal, as the following table shows:

	Percentage of dollar parity					
	Sterling		Francs		Lire	
	Lowest	Highest	Lowest	Highest	Lowest	Highest
1919–20	69	82	31	44	22	32
1920–1	69	82	30	45	18	29
1921–2	73	92	37	47	20	27
1922–3	90	—	34	—	20	—

The comparative stability of the highest and lowest quotations respectively in each year is very striking, and indicates that a policy of stabilisation at some mean figure would probably have been practicable; whereas, on the other hand, the wide divergences between the highest and lowest are a measure of the expense and interference that trade has suffered.

Even in the absence of any decided long-period tendency of an exchange to rise or fall, a big seasonal fluctuation is inevitable so long as each country, influenced both by the hope of its currency rising and by the fear of its falling, shrinks from taking the plunge of an attempt to avoid both.

Exchange demoralisation

If seasonal pressure is a reason why even a fairly healthy currency requires a policy of definite stabilisation, there is an equally strong reason for endeavouring to fix, at however low a level, a very sick currency.

It is convenient for the citizens of a country to keep in the form of money (in the widest sense) a certain proportion of their total real resources—a proportion determined by the habits and business practices of the community. If R represents their total resources measured in terms of commodities, and K is the proportion of them kept in the form of money, and if N is the number of units of money in circulation, then P, the value of each of these units in terms of commodities, is given by the equation $NP = KR$.

Now, apart from periodic changes in the value of R, that is, in the community's aggregate real wealth, P, the value of its money, may tend to depreciate either because N, its quantity, is increasing or because K is diminishing.

Depreciation generally begins with an increase of N. But if the depreciation is severe enough or continues long enough, it becomes greatly accentuated and proceeds more than in proportion to the increase of N, because of a diminution in K through a loss of confidence in the money. Depreciation involves every individual in loss to the extent that he holds his resources in the form of money or of claims to money when it takes place. Sooner or later he begins to protect himself against such losses by changing his habits, so as to hold in this form, even at the cost of great inconvenience, a smaller proportion of his resources than before.

When this process sets in seriously a currency system is in great danger, and depreciation may proceed at a tremendous rate, quite independently of the increase in the volume of the circulation. Every kind of shift is attempted by a population which has lost faith in its own currency. Everyone tries to put himself in a position in which he will not lose, even though legal tender money continues to depreciate. And before long this comes to mean that many persons will have put themselves in a position in which (from the limited standpoint of

82

their immediate cash interests) they actually stand to gain by a further fall. When, taught by past losses and excusably struggling for self-preservation, a whole population becomes a 'bear' of its own currency, the psychological obstacles to a remedy are almost insuperable. This has been the situation in Austria; it is becoming the situation in Germany; and other countries should take notice in time.

Connected with this phenomenon I seem to observe a significant change of atmosphere. Ever since the Armistice it has been the view of the great public that a return of the leading currencies to their pre-war status was to be anticipated sooner or later. The prevalence of this opinion, and the 'bull' speculation it encouraged, have helped the leading currencies to maintain their values all through the ups and downs of the last three years. But disappointment has at last produced its natural consequence. The public has seen the rouble go and the krone go and the mark go; and its mood has suffered change. The instinctive bias of general sentiment is now, I think, becoming 'bearish' of European currencies, possibly with as little reason capable of being explained as when previously it was 'bullish'. But the new atmosphere is dangerous, and is one more reason against drifting too long without a policy.

Conclusion

I draw the conclusion, on the whole, that the European exchanges will fluctuate briskly for some time yet. Instability is likely to continue until, on the one hand, the stronger currencies have reached par again (though perhaps at the cost of prolonging industrial depression and requiring some painful adjustments); and until, on the other hand, some of the weaker have fallen much further than at present, even though they may be saved, just in time, from joining in the abyss the rouble, the krone, and the mark.

Nevertheless, I marvel at the lethargy and apparent impotence of what may be called, for short, the forces of capitalism. They are running the most enormous risks in all Europe. Nothing but peace and moderation can serve their cause. Yet who has heard of the great bankers of Paris publicly representing to their government the risks of its present policy?[11] The system upon which they live depends, as we are often reminded, on the validity of money contracts. So long as the value of money is chaotic, the basis of contract is undermined. Yet the bankers of Europe think it more 'cautious' to point out the difficulties of any scheme of prompt action (and there are plenty ready to the hand of a critic) than to urge that at all costs and at all risks something of the kind must be attempted, lest there come at last the final stage of *sauve qui peut*, when everyone thinks more of saving something from the wreck for his individual self than of the interests of the system to which he belongs.

It might have been supposed that the conservative elements of Europe would have been those to feel most concerned at the present course of events. But, in fact, it is left to the Socialist parties to raise a decided voice for reason and moderation.

If the events which are unrolling before our eyes result in profound modifications of the structure of European society it will not be the work of the doctrines of Marx, nor of the disciplined force of international labour, but of the timid and short-sighted ways and stupid heads of its own conservative leaders.

[11] Some of our own bankers, however, are now speaking out boldly.

Chapter 2

NEW GOVERNMENTS, NEW ATTEMPTS AT SETTLEMENT, 1922–1923

The new German government headed by Wilhelm Cuno was an uneasy coalition with a predominantly industrial interest. Its prospects for success were not favourable. Melchior wrote to Keynes (2 December 1922):

I have returned today from Berlin where I spoke with several members of the new Cabinet. I hope that in Germany we shall now proceed to ...a more active policy of our own as far as the reparation questions are concerned. In view of the actual French designs it is, however, doubtful whether such attitude may still have any practical results...

The French were rumoured to be planning to take over authority in the already-occupied Rhinelands and to expel unfriendly German officials, confiscate German property and seize the Ruhr coalfields.

Melchior's letter of 2 December crossed the following letter from Keynes written a day earlier. Melchior's letter of 21 November defending the German Note, to which Keynes refers, was not kept in his papers. The Note in question was the German Note to the Reparation Commission of 14 November, the day that the Wirth Cabinet resigned, which stated that Germany could not stabilise the mark without the support of a foreign loan, and asked for a moratorium on all payments except those to devastated areas.

To CARL MELCHIOR, *1 December 1922*

Dear Melchior,

Thanks for your letter of November 21st. I quite see that the German Note can be defended on the basis of its being ambiguous and not really deciding clearly in favour either of the four experts [signers of the majority report on the stabilisation of the mark] or of the three experts [signers of the minority report].

But I cannot feel sure that it is good policy for Germany at this date to continue putting forward ambiguous proposals which do not bring matters to a clear head. It all depends on how much time there is still left for parleyings. The view that there is a great hurry to get things settled may very likely be erroneous; there is generally more time than one thinks. But certainly the present policy of the German government seems to be based on the theory that a delay of three or six months will be of no great consequence, since a Note of this kind certainly hinders matters rather than pushes them forward.

The only chance, in my opinion, would be for Germany to put forward a very good and clear-cut offer, which could then be supported by some of the Allies, who could demand at the same time that those who did not accept such a proposal should put forward a workable alternative.

Nevertheless, I am ready to agree that such a course would very probably be useless now. I take rather a pessimistic view, as I think you know. The reparation question seems to me to be rapidly passing out of the economic sphere. The more thoroughly we convince France that she cannot hope for much money in the near future, either from reparation or from an international loan, the more decidedly does she turn her thoughts towards securing other supposed advantages.

I do not think it at all likely that any settlement of economic questions will emerge from the forthcoming conference [of Allied premiers]. On the other hand, I think there is a considerable chance that France will decide, in effect, to annex Germany up to the Rhine frontier. Though she may threaten to occupy the Ruhr also I am very much more doubtful whether she really intends to do this. That part is probably a bluff. But the annexation of the Rhinelands is practical politics.

Attempted action by France of this kind lifts the whole matter, of course, quite outside the economic sphere. What its immediate and ultimate reactions will be on the situation of France and Germany respectively, who can predict?

There are just two other points on which I would like to say a word: (1) Everything I hear from the best-informed quarters convinces me that I by no means exaggerated, when I was in Berlin, the utter impossibility of a loan either here or in New York. The thing, even on a small scale, is quite outside discussion. (2) I think you will hardly find a prominent politician in England who is not astonished and dismayed at the extraordinary weakness of the German government in its personnel; in its absence of any decided policy; its perpetual attempts, not to do things on their merits, but to try and find out some useless formula which will not offend; and in the terror, no doubt natural, of France under which it seems continually to labour. Cannot anything be done to remedy this? Is there no one in Germany capable of calling out in a clear voice, both to Germany and to the rest of the world? I had hoped that Cuno might be going to form a government of all the best elements in Germany. But, from the small knowledge I possess, the Cabinet he has collected together looks a wretched affair. Am I right, or not?

Yours sincerely,
[copy initialled] J.M.K.

Melchior replied (5 December) that he had again been in Berlin where he had tried to bring about 'a clearer, more detailed and more concrete declaration' by Germany in the Note that was to be published before the conference of Allied premiers in London that same month. At the conclusion of this letter, which analysed the possible outcome of events from the German point of view, he told Keynes that he had brought the contents of Keynes's letters of 17 November (p. 64) and 1 December to the notice of Dr Cuno and of the foreign minister and the minister of finance, and could 'only hope that your words may contribute to clear the exceedingly menacing and possibly tragic situation'.

In England Lloyd George's Coalition government had come to an end with the Carlton Club meeting of 19 October. The general election that followed brought Andrew Bonar Law to power at the head of a Conservative government. Stanley Baldwin was the new Chancellor of the Exchequer. Keynes had known both men since his days in the Treasury;

Keynes, Baldwin, and Bonar Law's influential private secretary, J.C.C. Davidson, were all members of the United University Club.

Two immediate problems facing the new government were the approaching Paris conference on reparations in January and negotiations with the Americans over the funding of the British war debt. Keynes lost no time in seeking to extend his influence behind the scenes; he corresponded with Sir John Bradbury, the British delegate to the Reparation Commission, over Bradbury's plan (below, p. 93) and in December he had appointments with both the Prime Minister and the Chancellor.

Bonar Law invited the premiers of France, Belgium and Italy to meet him in London 9 December for a preliminary discussion before the Paris meeting with the Germans in January when a large payment was due. They had before them a 'Preliminary Note of the German government for a provisional regulation of the situation' which proposed to balance the budget and meet payments in kind by stabilising the mark and replacing reparations with a gold loan. In the tense and foreboding atmosphere of French military threats and German financial disaster, journalists feared that nothing would materialise but 'the policy of the china dogs'—Bonar Law and Poincaré sitting ornamentally across from each other.

There were rumours at this time that the United States was beginning once more to take an interest in intervening in Europe. Keynes put his qualified hopes in the new situation into an article that he wrote at the request of the New York *World*. The *World* distributed this article in North and South America; in the Chicago *Daily News* it appeared beneath the headline 'WANTS U.S. TO WARN FRANCE AGAINST GRAB'. It was published in England in a more dignified format by the *Manchester Guardian* on the opening day of the conference.

From the Manchester Guardian, *9 December 1922*

THE NEED FOR A CONSTRUCTIVE BRITISH POLICY

We are approaching a critical stage of a question which has now dragged on so long that the world may, through *ennui*, underestimate its gravity. So far each conference, dealing with unrealities, has ended with a paper solution, which has served the double purpose of saving faces and of making a gradual progress away from fantasy to truth. Meanwhile Germany's economic life has decayed by stages perceptible, but not so sudden as to provoke extreme crisis.

Because approach to the edge is slow, it does not follow that there is no edge. Now it is no longer easy to avoid a decision which involves sudden consequences one way or the other. We should therefore view the prospect with clear eyes, and consider its possibilities beforehand. The following are its bare outlines.

I

No competent person disputes that Germany cannot pay reparation in the near future, and that a postponement of her liabilities, certainly for two years and perhaps for five years, cannot be avoided. Any proposal to the contrary is, therefore, not bona fide; that is, it is intended, not to secure payment, but either to crush Germany's economic life or to extort from her some non-pecuniary concession.

II

There is not quite so complete a unanimity about the possibility of Germany's satisfying her creditors out of the proceeds of an international loan. In my judgment, the Great Loan is as big a hoax as the Great Indemnity. I believe that the leading bankers of London and New York agree with this. Certainly a loan on Germany's credit to pay France is impossible in London; investors would not subscribe and, if they would, the authorities of the City, believing that we have no surplus of resources beyond our commitments, would not allow them. American bankers say that it is equally impossible in New York. No international loan, which involves real investment and is not merely a substitute of one document for another, is within practical politics; except perhaps a moderate sum for the purpose of stabilising the mark *after* the reparation problem has been wisely settled.

III

Public men in France are now nearly convinced of the truth of my first proposition. There is more illusion about the loan. But France is beginning to understand that there is no money in that either. It is in this disillusionment that the biggest danger lies. The more completely we convince France that there is no chance of her obtaining immediate assistance towards the aid of her financial difficulties, either out of Germany herself or out of an Engish and American loan, the more inclined she is to seek compensations of a different kind and the less incentive does she feel to limit her actions within the bounds which public opinion in England and America would approve. Hitherto France has pursued both policies of keeping Germany weak and trying to draw wealth from her. Since the second policy is no longer fruitful, one reason for not pushing the first too far is greatly weakened.

IV

It is possible therefore that it may now be the deliberate aim of the French government to promote what was avowedly her policy during the Peace Conference—namely, to extend her frontiers to the Rhine by transforming the present occupation into what would be, though not perhaps in name, a virtual annexation. She may also threaten an advance into the Ruhr. But although such an act might open out interesting possibilities for her industrialists, the suggestion is probably a bluff. Unlike measures in the Rhinelands, it is a serious military operation. Unlike the Rhine frontier, the occupation of the Ruhr is no part of permanent French policy; it would be a mere demonstration. Moreover, the Ruhr occupation would throw the whole of Europe into chaos and rapidly lead up to an impossible situation; whereas some political changes in the present occupation of the Rhinelands might be carried through in such a way as to avoid, for the moment and on the surface, any catastrophic change from existing conditions. Thus the cooler heads in France are likely to hang back from the Ruhr, whilst at the same time perceiving in the Rhine policy an intellectual coherence which the other lacks.

V

Nevertheless, if France seizes the Rhine provinces, this act will be one so disastrous to herself, to Europe, and to the prospects of future peace that the whole world, including even America, should do whatever lies in their power, by protest and by inducement, to dissuade France from creating in Europe a situation at least as evil as in any former days. The Rhinelands have a population of 8,500,000 Germans. No part of Germany is more traditionally German. What madness to suppose that France will increase her security by incorporating these alien lands within her administrative system!

VI

These surmises are not certain; but we ought to be prepared for the contingencies they contemplate. What ought we to do? It would have been a great help if Germany could have tabled an offer so clear and honourable that general opinion could have accepted it as a basis of discussion not to be pushed aside. But there is nothing to be hoped from Germany in her present condition of demoralisation and inner weakness. Left to herself she will continue to make ambiguous offers, to sign anything under threats, and to do little to save herself from a steady descent into chaos. No plan will come from her. It must come from us.

91

VII

Has not the time arrived for the British government to frame a constructive policy on lines which they themselves recommend on its merits and think right and reasonable? It must provide for an interim period of relief for Germany; it must impose conditions on her as to the steps she must take to put her affairs in order during this period; and it must settle what she is to pay at the end of this period. But it must include proposals of the utmost generosity towards France, as regards her priority and her effective share of reparation and her war debt to ourselves. We must sacrifice nothing of our rights except in return for a solution. But there is almost no sacrifice we should not make to get a good settlement. Our offer should involve real concessions, and should not be contingent on the action of the United States.

VIII

By such an offer we shall have made our position and our policy clear. To its support we must summon all wise and moderate influences. In putting it forward we must make it plain that we will not tolerate the alternative of violence. If there is to be a departure from the pathway of peace, we must leave no doubt that we shall not be content with a passive protest, but will invite to joint consultation the leading governments of the world. The alternative of violence must not be permitted by default of courage and unity amongst the friends of peace.

As this article is written for the American public as well as for the English and the European, I should like to ask the question—whether in this case we could rely on effective support from the United States. In our financial and economic proposal to France we should do well to lay down no condition which does not depend on ourselves alone. But if the question is lifted out of the economic into the political sphere, can we reckon on the American people intervening with their whole authority on the side of peace?

The conference was marked by some signs of good will. Even *The Times* considered editorially that the German Note was the first reasonable German offer, although too vague and too hurriedly put together. Poincaré found it not worth discussing; he attributed the improvement in tone to his own threats in the Ruhr and concluded that this was the only way to influence Germany. The conference adjourned 11 December until 2 January when the premiers were to meet in Paris, and asked the Germans to revise their proposals over Christmas.

In preparation for the approaching conference Sir John Bradbury presented a plan for fixing the German liability and writing down and settling the European inter-allied debts. This plan, which evolved from the earlier Bradbury proposals of 6 October and 2 November 1922, was first submitted to the Chancellor of the Exchequer on 1 December; Bradbury revised it, on 15 December, by considerably altering the form and machinery in order to make it easier to grasp.

Bradbury sent copies of all four different phases of the plan to Keynes (who saw the first two versions at the time of the report on the mark). He commented on the version of 1 December in the memorandum that follows. It is undated and does not indicate for whom it was written, but both Baldwin and, more especially, Bonar Law would have appreciated the remark about Monsieur de Lasteyrie, Poincaré's finance minister, from past Treasury dealings with the French.

In Bradbury's version of 15 December he adopted a variation of Keynes's suggestion of an international clearing house for the collection and sharing of both reparations and inter-allied debts.

SIR J. BRADBURY'S PROPOSALS

Sir John Bradbury's new scheme seems to me most brilliant. It is very ingenious, and I think that the ideas underlying it are fundamentally sound nearly all through.

The great objection to it is its intricacy and obscurity. On the other hand it covers the whole ground. Though fairly familiar with these matters, I had to read it through three or four times before I grasped it, and I should doubt whether Monsieur Poincaré or Monsieur de Lasteyrie would ever do so.

My general comments are the following:

(1) It is very advantageous to ourselves, much more so than various alternative schemes which have crossed my mind from time to time. I think that this advantage is secured without being unfair to anyone else. But the scheme is, in my judgment, a fair and just one all round, rather than one which represents any particular sacrifice on our part. We should have to recommend it as fair and reasonable rather than as generous and disinterested. I do not know that this is an objection. But if the French ever understand the scheme they will notice that we come out of it pretty well, which may not increase their willingness to accept.

(2) The scheme appears to be materially more severe on Germany than it actually is. Even so, I think that the total effect is too severe. If the additional annuities under 1(*b*) were left out I should like the scheme. Alternatively the annuity under 1(*a*) might well be reduced to 2 milliards and the rate of interest under (6) reduced correspondingly to 5%. The precise figures, however, are a matter of opinion, and it is more important to consider, at this stage, the general principles.

(3) Under the heading of general principles, there is one addition to Sir John Bradbury's scheme which would, I think, enormously improve it. I suggest that there should be substituted for the Reparation Commission a commission of inter-governmental debt which should be responsible for the administration of inter-allied debt as well as of reparation, and should act as a clearing house. This commission should be instructed to pay to any creditor the net balance due to him under the settlement as a whole. In that case any net creditor would be entitled to notify the commission at any

time that they would accept for their share payment at Germany's option in certain forms other than those prescribed. The effect of this would be that so long as France was getting the net sum to which she was entitled it would be entirely the affair of the other net creditors as to how Germany paid the balance or whether she paid it at all.

The idea underlying (3) above leads up to an alternative general line of approach which I think is worth considering. It would not be so advantageous to ourselves as Sir John Bradbury's scheme, but it would be immensely simpler and is one to which it would be rather difficult for France to object before the bar of public opinion. It depends on the principle mentioned above that if France obtains the whole of what she is entitled to on balance in settlement of inter-governmental debt it is no longer her affair what happens about the rest of Germany's liability.

France has already agreed to the London Settlement. That, as the permanent scheme which is law at the present time, must form our starting point. Under this scheme Germany's annual liability partly depends on the volume of her exports. (a) On the hypothesis of 6 milliard exports her annual liability is 3·56 milliards. (b) With 10 milliard exports her liability is 4·60 milliards. On hypothesis (a) France's share is 1·85 milliards; on hypothesis (b) 2·39 milliards. Roughly speaking, France's liability to the United States and to the United Kingdom for her governmental debts, including accumulated interest, amount, at 5% interest and 1% sinking fund, to 1½ milliards per annum as a round figure. Since 10 milliards is a very optimistic hypothesis for Germany's exports, France's net expectations under the existing settlement, quite apart from any further concessions to Germany, are at the outside 1 milliard. At any rate, as a diplomatic point it is very much worth while, I think, to emphasise this. The schemes which are attributed to Monsieur Poincaré in the newspapers, so far from representing any concession, would put

France, even on paper, in a better position than she is in now.

My suggestion is, then, that the London Settlement be left for the present unchanged, but that its operation be postponed for five years. France's liabilities to her creditors shall be postponed for the same period. If at the end of that period the sum due from Germany to France under the London Settlement is x milliards per annum and the sum due from France to her creditors is y milliards per annum, then France shall be granted the two following concessions.

1. There shall be a priority in her favour on Germany's payments to the extent of her net credit of $x-y$ milliards.

2. The priority in her favour shall be not less than 1 milliard, even though $x-y$ is less than 1 milliard.

3. France's creditors will only require payment from her to the extent that Germany's payments in excess of France's priority render this possible.

On the other hand:

4. France shall agree that any excess due from and paid by Germany beyond her priority shall be paid to France's creditors in discharge of France's liabilities, and as regards this sum in excess of France's priority Germany shall be allowed to pay in any form that may be acceptable to those to whom she is paying it, or not to pay at all in so far as those to whom the money is due choose to let her off.

In the above I have considered France only. A complete scheme would have to take account of the other claimants to reparation also.

Under this scheme France is asked to make no concession whatever on the London Settlement, except as regards a moratorium for a certain period. On the other hand, when the moratorium comes to an end she has a definite priority of at least 1 milliard a year and does not have to pay her own creditors except in so far as money is available for the purpose from Germany.

The scheme is not contingent on the United States coming into it, although it would work much better if the United States did come in. It would be quite sufficient for the real purpose of the scheme if the United States was formally given the option of coming into it.

The effect of the whole thing would be that with the minimum disturbance of the existing situation the question of how much Germany will be required to pay in future beyond the figure of 1 milliard would virtually lie in the hands of the British and American governments.

Keynes had an appointment with Bonar Law on the evening of 19 December, presumably to discuss the coming conference. He produced his own plan for a settlement, signed and dated 23 December 1922. A copy of this was kept in his papers with an official envelope marked PRIME MINISTER—in which it must have been returned—posted the 23rd and addressed to himself, c/o Lytton Strachey Esq., The Mill House, Tidmarsh, Pangbourne.

KEYNES'S PLAN FOR SETTLEMENT

I. *The settlement with Germany*

A. The moratorium

No cash payments prior to 1 January 1927, and no deliveries, except France to be entitled to demand 500,000 tons coke monthly, Belgium 250,000 tons coal monthly, and Italy 250,000 tons coal monthly, the value of these deliveries to be credited to Germany under *B* (iii) below.

The moratorium to be subject to the following conditions:

(i) The gold reserves of the Reichsbank, together with the proceeds of an internal loan, to be applied to the stabilisation of the mark forthwith.

(ii) No increase in the floating debt beyond a figure to be approved; and no deficit in the budget after 1923.

(iii) The above measures to be carried out to the satisfaction of an Allied commission of three sitting in Berlin with full

97

powers to demand information on all financial and economic matters.

(iv) This commission to be empowered, in the event of its instructions being disregarded, to demand additional coal deliveries up to a further 750,000 tons a month, Germany to receive, in this case, no credit or payment for any part of the 1,750,000 tons monthly; and, in the event of the failure of these coal deliveries, to demand that the State coal mines be handed over to it.

B. The permanent settlement

Beginning with 1 January 1927, Germany to pay:

(i) A fixed prior-charge annuity of 1½ milliard gold marks for 25 years, secured by a first charge on (1) the customs, and failing their sufficiency on (2) the coal mines.

(ii) A fixed second-charge annuity of ½ milliard gold marks for twenty-five years, secured by a second charge on the same assets as in (i).

(iii) In any year, either before or after 1927, Germany, after meeting her fixed obligations as above, to make such additional payments as she is able; the occupation of the Rhinelands to terminate when such additional payments (including the value of deliveries during the moratorium period), together with 6 per cent compound interest from the date of their payment, amount to 5 milliard gold marks.

Sanctions

In the event of default in respect of the annuity *B* (ii), the securities to be administered on behalf of the owners of the second-charge annuity.

In the event of default in respect of the annuities under both *B* (i) and (ii), the Rhinelands to be reoccupied, if previously evacuated under (iii), and the securities to be administered on behalf of the owners of the annuities in default to the extent necessary to make good the default.

II. *The settlement between the Allies*

1. The prior-charge annuity of 1½ milliard gold marks to be divided between the Allies, other than Great Britain, in the Spa proportions.

2. The second-charge annuity to be accepted by Great Britain in satisfaction of all her claims both for reparation and for inter-allied debt.

3. The additional payments under *B* (iii) to be divided between all the Allies in the Spa proportions.

J. M. KEYNES
23. 12. 1922

Keynes also had an appointment 18 December with Baldwin. The Chancellor of the Exchequer was preparing to depart on his mission to Washington to accomplish the other settlement that was due, the arranging of the terms of Britain's war debt to the United States.

To STANLEY BALDWIN, *16 December 1922*

Dear Chancellor of the Exchequer,

I enclose an extract from a lecture I gave last week before the Institute of Bankers, which deals with a matter which may perhaps interest you with reference to our debt to America. (The rest of the lecture dealt with the question of where and whether sterling could be stabilised in terms of the dollar.)

When I see you on Monday there are two points of detail which I should like to mention in particular—(1) make sure that [E.] Rowe-Dutton [of the Treasury] has copies with him of one or two of the most important dispatches which we sent to America when we were originally borrowing money, and (2) the exact argument as to the effect which the tariff has on this whole problem.

Both of these are a little in the nature of debating points, but might nevertheless be useful.

Yours sincerely,

[copy initialled] J.M.K.

In addition to giving a series of four weekly lectures on current monetary problems to the Institute of Bankers in November and December (*JMK*, vol. XIX), and to making sure that the new government received the correct advice, Keynes was also looking after the last two issues of the *Reconstruction in Europe* supplements—and attending to his other ordinary duties in London and Cambridge. On the same day as he saw Baldwin—18 December—he was moved to write a 'letter to the editor' in some exasperation. It was written from his four-storey house at 46 Gordon Square, and was headed:

THE NUISANCE OF A TELEPHONE

To the Editor of the New Statesman, *23 December 1922*

Sir,

I venture to lay my plaint before you because I expect that many of your readers may be in the same situation. For the convenience of my intimate friends, to call up taxis, and to speak with tradesmen and business houses, I find a telephone indispensable. But I have no private secretary and my study is on the third floor.

The result is that at no time during the day can I rely on a quarter of an hour's uninterrupted work. Any unconcentrated person who finds it easier to ring up than to write a postcard, any hostess making up her party, any American tourist to these shores who thinks he would like a few words with me, is entitled by the existing conventions, *and is able*, suddenly and at any hour to interrupt my business and make me attend to theirs.

I write, therefore, to invoke your powerful aid to initiate a new and improved code of manners. I suggest that to ring up a private house, in any case in which a postcard or a letter would do equally well, should be thought inconsiderate; that a stranger should have no more right to use the telephone of a private house than to open the front door; and, above all, that it should be bad manners, except amongst intimate friends, to issue an invitation on the telephone, which gives the guest no time, without apparent rudeness on his part, to consider whether he is really free and whether he wants to accept.

It might be reasonable to except from these rules, if desired, cases where the rung-up is an American or a female, since I understand that their more (or is it less?) highly strung natures are exhilarated by the perpetual possibilities of a call. But should not those, who dislike being rung up, be permitted to place a warning symbol against their telephone number in the book?

Yours, etc.
J. M. KEYNES

The extract that Keynes sent to Baldwin was from his fourth Institute of Bankers lecture, on 'Devaluation Applied to Sterling', given 5 December 1922. Speaking of repayment of the American loan, he said he was

a little alarmed at the light-hearted way in which some authorities talk about the supposed ease with which we can discharge that liability.

I quite agree that if we are called upon to pay it we must pay; but I think it is a great mistake to pretend that it would be an easy thing to pay, or that it will not create very great disturbance to all parties concerned. We have to think out a great deal more carefully than we have what the exact course of events is likely to be.

He agreed with McKenna that it would be within Britain's capacity to meet the necessary sum of $300 million annually from the funds now lent to foreign borrowers. These borrowers would have to be accommodated in the United States. He explained that this would not be a simple transfer but that the transition period during which these funds would be diverted from the London market to the New York market would be uncertain and difficult and might necessarily result in 'all kinds of interference with the freedom of finance which is the essence of the success of London'.

Unless the diversion could be arranged,

there will be enormous difficulties in our paying the interest on this loan.

101

We could not do it merely by an alteration of exports and imports without undergoing a significant change in our level of life...it is not likely that we shall discover quite the right way to do it possibly for a few years to come.

During the transitional period, Keynes pointed out, it would be very difficult to stabilise sterling—the government's aim—at the old par or at any level whatever.

Both the Americans and the British professed to regard the war debts as purely business obligations; however, certain remarks of the American ambassador, George Harvey, had given the British reason to hope that they could obtain substantially better terms than they subsequently got. Keynes was moved to start an article on the subject—handwritten in pencil, two pages of manuscript remain, headed as follows:

GREAT BRITAIN'S DEBTS TO AMERICA

It is easy just now to gain considerable credit on both sides of the Atlantic by asserting that Great Britain seeks no abatement of her war debt to the government of the United States, will pay in full, and will pay at once. The state of mind behind such statements is a little complex. Partly pride; Great Britain does not dishonour her bond; if required to pay, she pays up to the limit of sacrifice—which sentiment is so capable of passion that the greater the irritation, if such were to spring up, the more impatiently would pride urge discharging gold westwards. Partly a discretion of taste, that concessions must be offered not asked. Partly a desire not to complicate the urgency of a European settlement with this other problem, a hope that America may help us to be wise, and an instinct that a claim for ourselves would hold her back. But partly also a half-calculated diplomacy—an impulse that this is the tactful and judicious way to talk at the present stage of the proceedings, mixed with a readiness to change the tactics on signs that the talk is being taken a little too seriously.

This last element is detected by many Americans, and poisons the brew a little; yet Americans also are largely responsible. It is common for them to tell us: the time is not yet ripe, public opinion is not ready, would not stand for it; if you agree to pay readily, you will find it to your advantage afterwards. By such conversations and with these mixed origins the well-intentioned half-sincerity flourishes.

But in fact we want important concessions in the funding of our debt. No Englishman thinks it right or just or expedient that we alone of those who have subscribed to literal bonds should be required to fulfil them without abatement; and airy allegations to the contrary bear no true relation to the real facts of the national sentiment.

Baldwin returned from the United States with terms far less favourable than he and others had hoped for—the settlement amounted to annual payments of $161 million for ten years and of $184 million for 52 years thereafter. These terms were hotly discussed in the Cabinet, Bonar Law being much opposed to their acceptance.

On the day that the Cabinet was meeting, 30 January, Davidson passed on to Baldwin an extract from a letter that he had received from Keynes. The extract, as it is preserved with Baldwin's papers, is typewritten, marked 'Received 4.15 p.m. 30. 1. 1923'.

From a letter to J. C. C. DAVIDSON

I hope, on the whole, that we refuse the American offer, in order to give them time to discover that they are just as completely at our mercy, as we at France's and France at Germany's; it is the debtor who has the last word in these cases. We could reply quite politely that we have made the best offer we can in the present circumstances of uncertainty, and that if they want more they must wait until the general position clears up and we know what we are going to get from France and Germany. We'll therefore re-open the matter in two years time and meanwhile have no objection to the interest mounting up on paper at five per cent, although of course we can't pay this.

103

Below the typed quotation the following remark is written in pencil, in an unidentified hand:

These pure finance people are interesting.

Hawtrey says 'jump at it'.

Baldwin succeeded in convincing the Cabinet that he had done all that he could, and the next day Bonar Law had to give way. He was persuaded to relent by Reginald McKenna, who was originally opposed to these terms; the City was also in favour of acceptance. According to Lord Beaverbrook, Bonar Law, McKenna and Keynes were the only opponents of the settlement in public life.

Andrew Boyle in his biography *Montagu Norman* dates the animosity between the governor of the Bank of England and Keynes from this time. Norman, who accompanied Baldwin on the mission to the United States, asked Keynes to call on him (9 November, following Keynes's return from Berlin) for advice before the Washington visit. The two were in agreement regarding the economic situation in Germany. But Keynes's 'passionate objections' to the terms of the American settlement—according to Boyle— were reported to Norman by others and he never asked Keynes's advice again, thinking of him, Boyle said, as 'a clever dilettante with a great potential for public mischief'.

When two months later Ambassador Harvey (in a speech at a dinner honouring Baldwin) reaffirmed his conviction of the business character of the American loans, the New York *World* cabled Keynes, asking him for 'any comment you would care to make'. He replied by cable (1 March 1923) diplomatically, and clearly influenced by changing events:

> I am asked to comment on Mr Harvey's speech. I have said nothing about the debt settlement hitherto because I have been somewhat divided between two feelings. On the one hand, as the Treasury official who knew most closely at the time the exact circumstances in which the debt was incurred, I cannot pretend to feel satisfied about the justice of the way in which the financial burden of the war is working out. On the other hand it is an immense thing that there should be a settlement if it helps England and America to feel and act together about the new war with which France is distracting Europe. If some joint policy results, that will be worth everything.

'The new war' was the French invasion of the Ruhr, 11 January 1923. Before this happened, the Allied premiers met in Paris as scheduled 2 January. While Keynes professed to cling to some hope, the general atmosphere was not promising.

NEW ATTEMPTS, 1922–1923

From the Westminster Gazette, *1 January 1923*

SUPPOSE THE CONFERENCE BREAKS DOWN?

I see no good reason why this week's reparation conference should fail. It may be assumed that any proposal from Great Britain will be generous to France and will aim at getting from Germany as much as can be got (for that is not less in the interests of Great Britain than of France). The present British Cabinet is not likely to be soft towards Germany or hard towards France; their record points in the opposite direction. If, therefore, France is chiefly thinking of the restoration of the damage done, a difference of principle between the two governments can hardly arise.

Nevertheless recent reports from Paris indicate a distinct possibility that France may prefer political and military objectives to the economic compensations with which alone the reparation question is properly concerned; and that Monsieur Poincaré is determined to seize this opportunity to take forcible measures against Germany of a kind which no British government could approve. We ought, therefore, to consider beforehand the possible results of a breakdown of the conference and of separate action by France.

I anticipate that, as usual, the immediate economic results will not be as sensational as might be supposed. The worst situations are those which develop slowly over long periods and are never announced in the stop-press column of the newspapers. There exist already over a large part of Europe situations worse than the gloomiest prophets foresaw; but they did not come into existence at a stated moment. So it may be again. A sensational denouement can only come about through a political event—a strike in the Ruhr, a fall of government in France or a reactionary *Putsch* in Germany. The final consequences of an act which will destroy the credit of France and Germany at the same time will not be seen all in a moment.

105

What forms can the action of France take? She can extend either her military occupation or her civil administration. She will doubtless commence with the latter, either by ousting the German administration from the area west of the Rhine which French troops already occupy, or by attempting to enforce French administration in the district of the Ruhr.

If she limits her measures to the Rhinelands, which she already occupies, and proceeds from step to step delicately, the immediate effects may not be very striking. If she includes in them a new customs frontier at the Rhine, she may add to the impoverishment of Germany without enriching herself. There is no way in which Germany could put up an effective resistance to any of these proceedings.

The administration of the Ruhr on the other hand is a different affair altogether. Here passive resistance to the French officials would be an obvious retort, and the officials would soon be calling for military support. Yet as a *permanent* military proposition, as distinct from a temporary demonstration, the Ruhr occupation is a desperate expedient. What military commander could feel comfortable with his forces sprawling through that entangled area in the midst of a dense hostile population?

For these reasons one would assume—if it were not that Monsieur Poincaré is capable of any stupidity—that the Ruhr occupation is a bluff, but that French administration of the Rhinelands is really intended.

What arguments against these proceedings could one address to a Frenchman who was thinking only of immediate French interests and who could not be reached by an appeal based on the obvious dangers to the future peace of Europe?

I should, first of all, remind him of the dangerous position of the franc, and how, more than in any other country, the financial system of France depends on the maintenance of her credit. So far she has avoided the worst results of inflation because of the implicit faith of her people in the value of

French *rentes* as an investment and their willingness to save and lend prodigious sums to their government. But this confidence will collapse if the franc, in terms of which the loans are expressed, becomes of doubtful value. Many conditions already exist conducive to a deterioration of the franc exchange. It is believed that the Paris financial world is beginning to be a 'bear' of it on a fairly large scale, just as Berlin has been of the mark. Any action which impairs the international credit of France may have startling repercussions on her economic situation. France's financial position is not such as to give her any margin at all for playing tricks, or even for disregarding worldwide opinion.

But I should emphasise even more strongly that separate action by France at the present stage probably means an absolute end of reparations. By acting in accordance with the best opinion as to how much Germany can really pay, France can still hope to obtain eventually a very substantial sum. But if she takes forcible measures, she will probably get nothing at all. She will get nothing for several reasons. In the first place she will, by the effects of her action on Germany's credit and industry, have rendered it impossible for Germany to pay her. In the second place she will, by breaking the Treaty herself, have given Germany justification for declaring that, the Treaty being rendered void by France's own act, Germany's acceptance of liability falls to the ground. But above all, *she will have shot her bolt*. When France has occupied the Ruhr and is administering the Rhinelands, Germany will have nothing more to fear. France will have done her worst. For if she tried to push her occupation further and further into Germany, she would only make herself more and more vulnerable and exposed to the ultimate *revanche*. If Germany were refusing at this moment to make payments within her capacity, threats and sanctions might be useful. But that is not the actual situation. Germany's only motive in paying reparations is for the sake of a quiet life. For a quiet life she would in her present mood pay up to the limit of her capacity. But if France makes it clear that she is not to have a quiet life anyhow, Germany's motive for paying entirely disappears.

If these arguments do not weigh with Frenchmen, what will happen? The immediate consequences will depend upon how France's measures impress world opinion and how Germany reacts to them. That is to say, the *initial* factors are psychological rather than economic. It is therefore rash to predict them. I will limit myself, therefore, to a statement, not of probabilities, but of possibilities.

If France occupies the Ruhr, her action may impair the external credit both of France and of Germany, as measured by the foreign exchanges; with obvious results.

Partly because of the interference with her coal, and partly because of the exchange impossibilities in the way of importing necessary supplies of food and raw material, acute unemployment might be precipitated in Germany, which would quickly destroy the present compromise government and the balance of political power.

The combination of economic distress with patriotic rage might at last drive Germany desperate. A movement of violence from reactionary Bavaria, aided perhaps by the Communist left, would face us with a German government of an entirely different complexion and ideas of policy from those we have dealt with hitherto. The extreme docility towards the Allies, and even weakness, of recent German governments has been remarkable. It will not help France or Europe to replace them by more savage material, such material as we know with only too much reason to lie below the surface in Germany.

The final remedy might come through a revulsion of feeling in France, bred of disappointment and disillusion, not unaided by the fall of the franc. Perhaps this is the route by which Europe is destined to find the way out at last.

These are only possibilities. But what advantage is there to set against them? Will France by this train of events render herself safer? or richer?

Bonar Law presented the conference with a plan, attributed to Bradbury, that attempted to solve the reparations and European debt problems as a whole. Germany was to be given a four-year moratorium, apart from deliveries in kind to be credited. After that she must meet a schedule of fixed payments, some of which were to be determined by an independent tribunal at a later date, and these were to be covered by bonds on easy terms providing the incentive to find the money quickly. In addition Germany must stabilise the mark along the lines recommended by the experts' majority report, accept financial supervision and submit to seizure of her revenues and military occupation if she failed to meet these obligations. As far as the European debts were concerned, Britain was to apply the French and Italian gold deposits she was holding in part payment against them, bonds received by France in respect of the Belgian debt and by Italy were to be transferred to Britain, and the remaining debts were to be written off.

The conference lasted only two days. France refused to consider the British plan, as Britain did not intend to give up her own share of reparations while reducing the total sum. Nor would Poincaré accept a moratorium without more stringent guarantees; he called for an immediate seizure of 'productive pledges' amounting to French control of timber and coal production, customs revenue and coal and export taxes. As Poincaré put it, Britain and France were on opposite sides of a ditch without a bridge between them. This conference left off diplomatic manoeuvres and pretence; the positions were defined. Amid a certain amount of relief that they had agreed to disagree like gentlemen, the prime ministers parted in what some French wit termed the 'rupture cordiale'.

With the beginning of the new year the editorship of *The Times*, which had been hostile to Keynes since *The Economic Consequences of the Peace*, passed from Wickham Steed to Geoffrey Dawson. On 2 January 1923 Keynes received a letter from Dawson:

Dear Keynes,

Will it amuse you to write a letter—not necessarily a long one—commenting on the British scheme of settlement? I dare say you are engaged in doing it elsewhere, but I should be very glad to publish your opinion of the scheme if you cared to send it to me by tomorrow evening.

Yours sincerely,
GEOFFREY DAWSON

Keynes responded with a long personal letter instead.

To GEOFFREY DAWSON, *3 January 1923*

Dear Dawson,

I am much tempted by your invitation to me to write a letter to tomorrow's *Times*. But on account of the nature of my views, as indicated below, I am not sure that it would be helpful for me to express them over my own signature just at this juncture.

For your own information, my feeling about the British proposals as published in today's papers is as follows.

I think the British scheme a very fine performance intellectually. It covers the whole ground comprehensively and would work out in detail, which, considering the complexity of the case, is a considerable achievement.

I also think it strictly just; that is to say, the sort of scheme an impartial authority might put forward who had no eye on political considerations.

As regards Germany, it goes, in my judgement, to the extreme limit of severity. But it is the first proposal officially tabled which has made an attempt to be governed by reason, which in itself is great progress. When one is endeavouring to fix Germany's capacity one can attack the problem on one or other of two assumptions. If we suppose that the world in general and Germany in particular will go back in the course of the next three or four years to more or less pre-war conditions as regards international financial credit and scale of production, but with prices settled down at not below twice their pre-war level, then it seems to me quite conceivable that Germany might be able to carry out what the British proposal lays on her. If, on the other hand, there is no going back, and the future is going to be materially different from the past, with central Europe at a decidedly lower level for many years to come than that which she had attained to in 1914—all of which, having regard to what has happened, is exceedingly likely—then the present proposals go very far indeed beyond what would prove practicable.

The defence of the British proposals, and I think it is a valid defence, must be that at the present stage of proceedings one must necessarily draw up one's scheme on the first assumption, however sceptical one may be about its realisation. Personally, I do not believe Germany will ever pay anything like the sums mentioned in Bonar Law's scheme. But I see nothing outrageous or contrary to good sense, as I have done on every previous occasion, in tabling this as a paper scheme at the present stage.

My real criticism of the whole thing relates to its treatment of France. The details are so complicated that it is not easy to work out in terms of annual payments exactly what it all amounts to as between ourselves and France. But at a rough shot, I should say that when Germany begins to pay, the annual sum accruing to us will be not less than two-thirds of the annual sum accruing to France. Strictly speaking, there will be nothing unjust in this. But surely it is altogether outside practical politics that France could possibly agree to any such thing in combination, as is proposed, with a large scaling down of Germany's total liability. As soon as the French have worked out the arithmetic I should anticipate a howl. We have got to be far more generous than this to France if there is to be the remotest possibility of a settlement now.

Nevertheless, while personally I should go an enormous way further to meet France as to her share of the plunder before the conference was over, I think it quite likely that Bonar may be right in beginning with a perfectly just scheme of this sort; provided it is his intention, before the conference comes to an end, or at any rate before he breaks off conversations with Poincaré, to make a proposal of far more striking generosity. I think his policy should be to refuse any material modifications in the plan as it affects Germany, but to indicate at the last moment that he would go much further in meeting France if only they would accept the German part of the scheme.

I am so sceptical about any settlement resulting now that I feel the most important thing of all is to put ourselves in an impregnable position before the public opinion of the whole world, particularly the United States. If we were really going to get out of reparations the amount which we are claiming in the present scheme, the reasons for the United States to be generous towards us would be much modified. If, on the other hand, rather than precipitate a crisis, we offer France at the last moment a really substantial sacrifice, then our position is unassailable.

I do not know what Bonar Law's intentions may be. But I think he deserves everyone's support at the present stage; and I am not clear that it will help him if the French newspapers can say that even the notorious Francophobe Mr Keynes thinks the present proposals not nearly favourable enough to France.

Yours sincerely,
[copy initialled] J.M.K.

Dawson replied (4 January):

My dear Keynes,

I am most grateful to you for the very interesting letter which reached me last night. It was good of you to write, and I shall look forward one of these days to something for publication. Pray observe with favour my refusal to have you rung up on the telephone.

Yours sincerely,
GEOFFREY DAWSON

In a postscript Dawson asked if it would 'amuse' Keynes to write a review of a new book by Francesco Nitti, the former premier of Italy, *The Decadence of Europe: the Paths of Reconstruction.* The book was published and Keynes's review appeared in *The Times* on the same day that the Reparation Commission, with the sole opposition of Bradbury, declared Germany to be in voluntary default on coal deliveries and France gathered her troops for going into the Ruhr.

From The Times, *8 January 1923*

EUROPE IN DECAY

Signor Nitti lives in a country where the freedom of the Press is disappearing and those who utter unpopular opinions are forcibly purged of them. But he has not lost his courage. This new book of his is chiefly striking for its outspokenness. It is a new thing for one of the Allied premiers, who himself took a prominent part in the long series of reparation conferences just concluded, to burst out: 'If the public knew with what levity, with what fatuity, with what scepticism the greatest problems in the life of nations are so often discussed, they would not tolerate for long many of the very great blunders which now jeopardise the life of the world.'

Signor Nitti covers, a little discursively perhaps, but with a wealth of material, the whole of the European area—the Treaty, the subsequent conferences, the occupation, the economic problem of Europe, armaments, Turkey, Russia, the succession states of Austria-Hungary. In part he is traversing well-known ground, but there is no recent book of an equally comprehensive scope, and his frank treatment of such topics as the grave abuses attendant on the occupation, and the present position of armaments, will probably be new matter to many readers. In particular, France has a larger army than any country has ever had in modern times, much larger than the pre-war German army. Against France's 728,000 men (including the colonies) and 3,000 aeroplanes, of which no less than 800 are suitable for bombardment, Germany has an army of 100,000 with no aeroplanes, and a police force of 150,000. Rumania's army is double Germany's. Poland has nearly as many men under arms as Austria-Hungary had before the war. Jugoslavia and Czechoslovakia together have more soldiers than the United States. It is not easy, in face of these figures, to take seriously the alleged threat to France's security except as a remote contingency—unless indeed

France exposes herself, far extended in hostile territory, to the patriotic fury of a nation goaded to desperation.

Historic parallels

Two historical parallels adorn the narrative and are given an important place—Europe after 1815, and Rome after the victorious campaigns of Julius Caesar; the first to illustrate the wisdom of moderation after victory, the second to exhibit the unchanging character of the political diseases to which the victors in an exhausting war are liable.

The author's main purpose, however, is to denounce in unmeasured terms the present policy of France, as summed up in a passage quoted from Clemenceau:

'"I conceive of life after the war", said Clemenceau in the French Chamber, "as a continual conflict, whether there be war or peace. I believe it was Bernhardi who said that politics are war conducted with other weapons. We can invert this aphorism and say that peace is war conducted with other weapons."'

Signor Nitti considers that no compromise is possible between this policy and the policy, for example, of Great Britain. There can be no hope except in the complete reversal of the former. 'The resettlement of Europe will never take place', he argues, 'except by abandoning armies of occupation, re-establishing the sovereignty of every state, and abandoning absurd indemnities, which do harm not only to the morality, but also to the intelligence, of the victors.' Failing this, 'Europe sinks rapidly into decay. There is economic decadence, there is intellectual decadence, and, what is more grievous, there is moral decadence'; whence the title of his book.

A piece of savagery

Signor Nitti does not attempt to propound one more of those ingenious half-solutions which try to build up on the existing foundations. He regards the Treaty of Versailles as a piece of savagery incompatible with civilisation. He demands that we make a new beginning, without which we cannot stay 'this progressive decay of ours which all the peoples outside Europe look on at with mixed feelings of stupor and agitation'.

At a moment when European policy is at the parting of the ways, this book comes opportunely. On the other hand I do not altogether share the author's pessimism. The battle of opinion is already much more nearly won than he seems to think. Even France is not really so remote, I fancy, from a revulsion against the unrealities of her present régime. If the Poincaré policy fails, as it is bound to do, the way may be clear for a far better settlement than would have been possible before. Great risks are certainly present. If France actually proceeds to the full lengths against Germany which her present armed force permits, lasting and catastrophic consequences to Europe will ensue. Nor can we rely on an indefinite continuance of the extraordinary weakness which Germany has exhibited hitherto. But is it not also possible that France will shrink from the full consequences of her own acts? Two things may combine to prevent the worst from happening. The finances of France are too rotten for her to be able to proceed far without being pulled up by practical considerations. Coolly considered, M. Poincaré's policy is too much lacking in intelligence to be capable of inspiring in the mind of France that intensity of conviction which is necessary to carry out a big and dangerous game. Nevertheless, whatever may befall, Signor Nitti, having cast on the world this work of sincerity and passion, is entitled to the concluding words of his preface: 'Perhaps it will be one day a title of honour to have broken with the conventional language of falsehood, which weighs on us more heavily than our economic decadence, or our financial ruin.'

In the midst of the ominous events mentioned earlier Melchior wrote Chancellor Cuno, 8 January, the letter that follows, given here in the translation which he furnished to Keynes. (In the German version the extract from Keynes's letter was quoted in English.)

Dear Mr Cuno,

Since Keynes, although not a member of the government, is nevertheless a frequently consulted expert and attentive reporter, it may interest you to read an extract from one of his letters to me, which I quote below:

From a letter to CARL MELCHIOR, *5[?] January 1923*

At any rate, the British proposal marks, I think, an important definite stage of forward progress. You may think the burden on Germany too heavy. But the draft proposals are a fine intellectual performance, making an honest attempt to settle the whole question on more or less rational lines. But whether elaborate schemes like this are really going to be part of the operative machinery of the next ten or twenty years, I have my doubts.

I am, naturally, rather pleased that my government has adopted the report of which I was one of the signatories at Berlin, and have indeed gone so far as to include action on the lines of this report amongst their imposed conditions.

I wrote the above before the breakdown of the conference. We have now got, all of us, to be very cool and careful. I'm not sure that I don't envy Cuno his job!

Melchior added:

So you see that there are even people in the secure position of Cambridge professors who envy you. May this be a good omen!

Yours sincerely,
C. MELCHIOR

Keynes had not kept a copy of this letter to Melchior, evidently sent after 'the breakdown of the conference', but as Melchior, writing on 9 January, thanked him for his 'kind letter of the 5th inst.', presumably that was its date.

Melchior's letter of 9 January gave an account of his impressions of the Paris conference, which he had visited unofficially. After thanking Keynes for the last number of the *Reconstruction in Europe* supplements which he had just received, he continued:

From a letter from C. MELCHIOR, *9 January 1923*

I returned from Paris on Saturday. I did not intend to take an active part, but only wanted to get into contact with certain French circles. Neither has [Carl] Bergmann found occasion to enter into negotiations; for it would have served no purpose—after the French-English difference had proved to be so wide that it could not be bridged over—to submit the German plan which, by the way, I consider very reasonable, but which shows lower figures than the English scheme. [Keynes's estimation of Bergmann appears on pp. 290–2.]

As regards the latter, it is certainly an excellent work, but, in my conception, gives rise to the consideration of the following two points. The figures are too high and should therefore be divided into a fixed sum and another one contingent on some elastic factor, if one does not want to reduce it altogether. I also consider the proposed control inappropriate. No provision has certainly been made for the eventuality that the German minister of finances should not succeed in pushing through Cabinet and Reichstag the measures prescribed by the controlling authority; or in other words: the English plan—unlike the French one—contains no prescriptions for the event that the Cabinet and Reichstag reject such measures. If this omission was intended and if indeed only an obligation on the part of the minister of finances to make propositions should be established, the whole prescription would materially not have the importance which prima facie it appears to have, and we would more probably have to do only with a *coulisse*. I do not believe, however, that once such controlling authority is officiating things will work quite as smoothly, but think that, should Cabinet and Parliament refuse to accept the propositions made by the minister of finances upon decisions taken by the controlling authority, this might lead to very unpleasant and inner-politically unbearable conflicts. Also the regulations regarding the mode of voting do not in this connection offer sufficient guarantee. According to my opinion it would therefore be much better to waive such severe controlling provisions. If Germany is subjected to a tolerable scheme, she will herself have the very greatest interest to put her finances in order and to fulfil her obligations under such scheme. The accomplishment of such task will always be rendered easier, if undertaken voluntarily and not under force, for with a great nation the imponderabilia must after all be taken to a great extent into consideration. The absolute necessity to have due regard to this question of sentiment also speaks against the sanctions, in spite of the stipulation that they can only be inflicted upon unanimous decision. It is most important that the English scheme has adopted as one of the conditions the expert's report which also bears your signature. As you will have seen from the annex of Cuno's letter to Bonar Law, the German government had meanwhile already passed from the Dubois–Vissering report to yours.

How things may develop in France I cannot foretell. I am under the impression that for the present nearly the whole nation is backing Poincaré, though for two different reasons: whilst one party wants the continuation of Louis the Fourteenth's policy, that is to say the destruction of the German Reich and the annexation of all German land left of the Rhine, i.e. the greatest possible obstruction of German economic life and with it of the German State through the occupation of the Ruhr district, the other party—consisting of people who look upon the matter from an economic point of view and who stand in fear of France's political isolation—wants to give Poincaré this last chance to solve the reparation problem. Should his measures fail, his Cabinet will most probably be defeated and the crisis will then lead comparatively quickly to a solution and improvement. Should on the other hand the first mentioned, purely political-annexationist tendency gain the victory, we will in Germany probably have to face harder times than we have ever experienced since 1914. Cuno's Cabinet will then have to consider it its duty to muster all moral forces of the nation.

What position Great Britain and the United States will take, is, of course, the most important question. However weighty the English delegation's attitude in Paris may have been, we could not quite help thinking that it was as if upon his exit Bonar Law had said to Germany with the noble Prince Tamino in the *Zauberflöte*, viz:

> Ich kann nichts tun als dich beklagen,
> weil ich zu schwach zu helfen bin.
> ['I can do nothing but sympathise with you,
> because I am too weak to help you.']

Let us hope that the conflict in the European concert—which has, however, become so horribly disharmonious—will after all end as well as that in Mozart's opera. At the present moment, however, it does not look as if it would.

Yours sincerely,

C. MELCHIOR

On 11 January French and Belgian troops marched into the Ruhr.

Keynes replied to Melchior on 17 January. There is no copy of the letter in the papers but Melchior again forwarded an extract from it to Cuno (20 January), remarking, 'I continue to send you extracts from my correspondence with Keynes, the more so as I am quite convinced that his letters, even though addressed to me, are not intended exclusively for me.' The extract, which Melchior also provided for Keynes, follows:

From a letter to CARL MELCHIOR, *17 January 1923*

I quite agree, on merits, with your main criticisms of the English scheme. But I think they were put in on political grounds rather than for their merits. I think that the omission of any prescription as to what would happen if the Reichstag rejected the advice of the German minister of finance acting under the instructions of the control was intentional. It leads to the kind of anomalous situation which is commoner in the English constitution than in yours. But doubtless you are right that the control proposed would either have to be non-existent in practice, or would turn out to be unworkable.

All these discussions, however, have been rendered academic by events which have taken place since you wrote your letter. Things have now got to work themselves out by another route. I wish that I could gauge the depth of German feeling in the matter. The extent of the sacrifices which the average citizen is prepared to make rather than give way is going to dominate the eventual result, as against any possible political or economic considerations.

The proceedings of France are viewed by almost everyone in England with anger and disgust. You would be surprised at the number of people who say that their chief anxiety is lest Germany give way. The view is widely held that this time it is essential for Germany to hold out to the limit of her endurance. Our sympathies are profoundly with you.

There is good authority for the report that there has been lately official support for the franc exchange, which would, otherwise, have fallen much further. The turnout of business in the franc exchange has been quite considerable.

With this letter of 17 January Keynes had sent Melchior a copy of his letter to Havenstein written the same day (pp. 66–8). 'Those questions [concerning the stabilisation of the mark]', Melchior remarked in his reply of 2 February, 'as you state yourself appear already rather antiquated now that we are practically at open war and facing events, the consequences of which we are unable to weigh.'

He continued:

The resolutions which in view of the Franco-Belgian invasion our government has to take are clear and simple, although it will become increasingly sacrificial to carry them into effect. As to the decisions Germany has no choice whatsoever: for France in the first place does not want reparations but direct or indirect annexation and we must defend the fortress until the last day. The situation is somewhat similar to that in which Germany found herself a hundred years ago, when Napoleon succeeded in keeping her divided for seven years: only the general situation today is more dangerous for us. At that time the coalition was against France, but now—anyhow for the time being—it is with her, either through active support or through benevolent neutrality. We must therefore reckon with longer and harder times than those our country had to face at the beginning of the nineteenth century; however the possibility of more favourable developments originating out of the actual general confusion need not be contested.

I enclose for your own personal information [an] abstract from a letter which I received from a friend of mine, a high state official in Austria, and whose contents might interest you. The beginning of 1923 smells extremely badly.

Chapter 3

CORRESPONDENCE WITH A MUTUAL FRIEND, JANUARY–JUNE 1923

Making his annual report to the National Mutual Life Assurance Society, 31 January 1923, Keynes spoke what was uppermost in his mind:

So far as Europe is concerned, our chief concern must obviously be the critical situation in the Ruhr. A few weeks ago a settlement would have been possible by which, in the long run, substantial payments might have been secured from Germany. Now that France has chosen herself to tear up the Treaty and to break the peace of Europe, I much doubt whether any substantial reparation will ever be paid at all. The European system created by the peace treaties is rapidly breaking up, and France has embarked on a course, the final results of which on the continuance of high civilisation in Europe are not yet calculable. From our own selfish point of view, fortunately the world is large; and we must hope that those are right—and within certain limitations they may be —who believe that this country can, by prudence, maintain a decent life, in spite of violence and disorder across the Channel. We in England are, I think, a united people at the present time on the main issue, that we stand for peace, to a degree that only exists at important crises of our history.

On the day that France and Belgium entered the Ruhr Germany adopted a policy of passive resistance. All payments and all coal deliveries stopped; workers and miners struck; the German government drained money from the rest of the country for relief and financial support of the occupied territory. The French took control of the factories and mines, banks and customs; demonstrations were forbidden; mine owners were fined and high officials were expelled from the Ruhr. Food became scarce. The mark, which averaged 34,858 to the pound in December, dropped abruptly to

110,000 to the pound within the invasion's first week. British opinion was shocked by the French action but was not united enough as yet, in spite of Keynes's hopes, to take up a decisive stand against France.

In Melchior's words, the beginning of 1923 smelled extremely badly, but Keynes characteristically seized upon a dark hour to mount a new assault. The year had advanced into April when *Punch* printed some verses entitled 'Spring's Mixed Grill' (11 April 1923): after mention of rising prices, leaner purses and the income tax dodger (rhymed with 'the Oliver Lodger'), the poet found encouragement in his final stanza—

> And hope of salvation
> Revives and remains,
> For the rule of *The Nation*
> Is passing to KEYNES.

Publicly Keynes had spoken for the Liberal party in the October 1922 election; privately he had tried to influence Conservative policy through his acquaintance with Bonar Law and Baldwin. Privately he continued to keep his hand on the Liberal pulse; for example, he showed some concern over the public stance of Lord Grey, inviting him to a discussion on relations with France (which Grey could not attend). What *Punch* referred to was a further public attempt: with a group of Liberal friends he acquired a controlling interest of the Liberal weekly, *The Nation and Athenaeum*, with the intention of making it a forum for the livelier views in the party on current issues. Hubert Henderson was the new editor and Keynes the new chairman of the editorial board, on which Walter Layton made the third member.

The first issue under Keynes's aegis appeared 5 May 1923. In a typical Keynesian ploy the former price of 9*d* was reduced to 6*d*. The *Manchester Guardian* quoted a statement of policy by the new chairman in an interview published 4 May.

We shall be very much Liberal and not Labour. We are absolutely convinced that, whatever conclusions calculations of early office may lead to, there must in the long run be a place for Liberalism which has no commerce whatever with Conservative opinion, however moderate. Although we believe that the doctrinaire part of the Labour party is completely inadequate for the solution of our present troubles, we do sympathise with Labour in their desire to improve and modify the existing economic organisations so as to minimise what ought to be avoidable distress due to recurring trade depression and unemployment. We also attach enormous importance to international peace, which is, indeed, an absolutely necessary condition for all forward progress. We hope to offer a platform where a definite Liberal programme will be developed—a foreign policy which puts peace absolutely in the first place, and a domestic policy just as ready for change as Labour's, but offering remedies really relevant to the crying economic evils of the day.

Keynes kept a scrapbook of the unsigned pieces in the *Nation* that he wrote himself; he was responsible for much of the first issue, including the editorial foreword.

From The Nation and Athenaeum, *5 May 1923*

EDITORIAL FOREWORD

The present issue marks a change in the Editorship and control of *The Nation and Athenaeum*. Mr [H. W.] Massingham has edited *The Nation* since its foundation in 1907. It is he who has made the paper and has won for it its reputation for distinction and integrity. Few men have done more to keep the true spirit of Liberalism alive and its essential principles clear, in days of adversity and amid the temptations of electoral success. He never forgot that Liberalism was, in his own phrase, 'a larger and more fruitful thing' than the formularies of a political party; and no concession to mere expediency or to personalities has ever been countenanced by *The Nation*. We deeply regret the termination of his long connection with the paper. We shall do our best to continue his honourable traditions and to maintain and extend the influence of the paper in the political and intellectual life of the country.

We write our first leading article at a moment of extraordinary confusion of ideas and aims in the political world. Many of the old party programmes are either obsolete or accomplished. The new banners are not yet unfurled, or the lines of demarcation clearly drawn.

The problem of 'reunion', or, as it would be better described, of 'segregation', is not at all peculiar to the Liberal party. It is, in many respects, more acute in the Conservative party. And in the Labour party the question as to exactly who, in a tight place, really and truly at the bottom of his heart belongs to it, is just as difficult to answer. Nor is it quite so much a matter of personalities as many people make out— though personalities come in, too. It is mainly a question of where the party lines of the future are going to be drawn.

Now, as always, the political opinions of individuals stretch in a continuous series, each man separated from his neighbour in the row by a scarcely distinguishable difference, all the way from right to left—from Lord Carson to Lord Salisbury, to Lord Derby, to Lord Curzon, to Mr Bonar Law, to Mr Baldwin, to Mr Austen Chamberlain, to Sir Robert Horne, to Lord Birkenhead, to Mr Churchill, to Mr Lloyd George, to Sir Alfred Mond, to Lord Grey, to Sir John Simon, to Mr Asquith, to Lord Buckmaster, to Lord Haldane, to Mr Clynes, to Mr Webb, to Mr Ramsay MacDonald, to Mr Snowden, to Mr Lansbury, to Mr Newbold; graded on a scale of belief in the existing structure and objects of society, like Gibbon's theological barometer, 'of which the Cardinal Baronius and Dr Middleton should constitute the opposite and remote extremities, as the former sunk to the lowest degree of credulity, which was compatible with learning, and the latter rose to the highest pitch of scepticism in any wise consistent with religion'.

The present confusion of politics exists because no one yet knows where the new party fissures are going to break through. It shows, for example, no special lack of principle in Mr Lloyd George that he should flirt with the 'Centre party' on one day and with the Liberals on the next. He is unluckily placed—somewhere very near the spot where, when the world divides into continents, the waters will break through. He cannot yet tell on which side of him, when the Day comes, he will find dry land and a friend.

Our own sympathies are for a Liberal party which has its centre well to the left, a party definitely of change and progress, discontented with the world, striving after many things; but with bolder, freer, more disinterested minds than Labour has, and quit of their out-of-date dogmas. We should like to play a part in forming and expressing the new thoughts of the world which grows up since the war, and in building something to which enthusiasm is appropriate, and which is based on firm foundations of reason and good sense.

All through the nineteenth century questions of government and of religious opinion played a very big part in politics—the suffrage, Home Rule, the powers of the House of Lords, Catholic emancipation, church establishment, religious education, licensing. Of these great questions only the House of Lords—and that in a form which interests the country very little—lingers on alive. What sort of issues are going to take their place? Proportional representation, divorce reform, prohibition, eugenics, freedom of opinion and of propaganda on sex and birth-control problems? Perhaps. Some of these may be burning questions within ten years. But these are not the controversies at present which are tending to divide the country into solid groups of opinion. They cut across party divisions, and have not reached the crucial point at which people are prepared to sink their differences on other things to promote their agreement on these.

The great dividing questions of the near future seem to us to belong to other categories. They fall into two great groups: peace and disarmament; and the economic structure. The political aspect of both these problems is utterly different from what it was ten years ago. Before the war, the range of controversy upon British foreign policy was narrow. Groupings of great powers, with expanding ambitions and expanding armaments, faced one another; and the only basis of accommodation was an anomalous but long-established *status quo.* In such an atmosphere a British minister, intent on peace, must needs walk in the pathways of tradition. But today the old European order is dissolved, and the new forms are not yet shaped. The hopes of peace are staked upon the attainment of that ideal of a new international polity which has given birth to the League of Nations. In this work Britain may have a decisive part to play, for which a new type of foreign policy will be required, certain to lead to profound differences of opinion.

With the other problem the change is hardly less marked. From 1906 to 1914, a common economic policy united, for most practical purposes, the parties of the left—the development of social services involving public expenditure, and the raising of the money by stiffer taxes upon wealth. As an instrument of radical social change, this policy has been shattered by the weight of the war debt; and economic discontent is now focused on the vague issues of industrial control. Here the ideas of all of us are so confused and incomplete that the real points of controversy have scarcely begun to emerge. It is a mistake to suppose that 'socialism', whatever that may mean, is going to be the issue. It is merely a word, only useful so long as it cloaks decently the nakedness of Labour policy. The thing it once stood for is fifty years antiquated, the product of a different atmosphere, and is largely irrelevant to the real problems of today.

We have no programme to offer ready made. But we have our views of the lines along which sound policy must proceed. And we aspire to offer a lively spot where, out of controversy and conversation, a comprehensive policy may gradually take shape.

The new *Nation* drew strongly on Keynes's Bloomsbury and Cambridge friends. The first issue featured articles by Lytton Strachey and Virginia Woolf on the cover and Leonard Woolf was the literary editor. Among later contributors were Clive Bell, E. M. Forster, G. Lowes Dickinson, W. T. Layton, R. C. Trevelyan, Osbert Sitwell, George Rylands, Bertrand Russell, T. S. Eliot, Francis Birrell and his father Augustine Birrell and David Garnett and his father Edward Garnett. Simon Bussy, a Strachey brother-in-law, reviewed a show of paintings by Duncan Grant. Professor A. V. Hill, Keynes's physiologist brother-in-law, wrote 'An Apology for the Study of Frog's Muscle'. Pigou made an appearance as an essayist on 'Games'.

Keynes himself contributed a weekly page on finance and investment, the first being a commentary on 'The Rise in Gilt-Edged Securities' which attracted considerable notice in the financial press. And he figured in another guise in the 'Gossip of the Week' column of the same issue, which pointed out that all the 150 pictures being offered for sale by the London Group could be bought for one-quarter of what Augustus John was asking for one picture. 'Our City Editor recommends the former purchase as the better lock-up of the two' for a public gallery wanting, in Keynesian language, 'to instruct the young and enrich the future and render itself a repository of what is strongest and most promising in English art'.

The first issue also contained 'the first of a short series of articles by Mr Keynes' and promised that 'The second article to be published next week will deal with "The German Offer"'. This series was published in the United States in the *New Republic*.

When Keynes wrote the first article the ailing Bonar Law was still Prime Minister. Following the invasion of the Ruhr British opinion was gradually becoming convinced that the real interest of France was in military security and not in reparations. Most members of the government held the view that the occupation was illegal, but strong elements were still pro-French and no positive action was taken.

From C. MELCHIOR, *8 March 1923*

> Just these last days I had news from some gentlemen who had been in London and got into very close contact with circles connected with the government now in office. Those gentlemen, at any rate, were under the impression that in the entourage of the Prime Minister and at the Foreign Office the situation in England is not yet considered psychologically ripe, because just among the officials of the Foreign Office, in leading society circles, etc. the predominant feeling is still decidedly francophile, and that in those circles they do not exactly know how

England, if she makes up her mind to raise more positive demands, could carry them.

The situation of the forward market here has meanwhile entirely changed. Today f.i. [for instance] the price of spot London and the price of London for delivery end of March are even. The enormous differences these last months may be explained by the fact that the holders of foreign exchange fought a desperate fight for their holdings and borrowed money at exorbitant interest rates (up to 30 and 40 per cent) in order to provide for their requirements of paper marks (wages, costs, etc.), rather than departing with their foreign exchange.

The intervention by the Reichsbank in support of the mark, combined with a temporarily too strongly restricting discount policy, has altered this situation, and many holders of foreign exchange decided to sell their holdings, so that the Reichsbank's transactions in foreign exchange in support of the mark so far have caused no loss in its holdings of foreign exchange. In this respect I may refer to the details given in the letter which Dr Kocherthaler wrote you on the 28th of February.

The government will therefore still be able for a pretty long time to continue this intervention policy on approximately the same lines as hitherto, provided that no entirely new political moments turn up (f.i. a formal war between France and Belgium, and in the case probably also Poland, on the one side, and Germany on the other). Our government, in view of the actual finance-technical situation of the market, would even be in a position now to lower the foreign exchange rates still more; though I personally am in doubts whether it would be wise to go much further beyond what has already been done.

All these measures, as Kocherthaler wrote you already, are in the first place the result of political and not of financial considerations. The situation here could not have been held, if prices had leaped up still higher, which without an energetic intervention could not have been avoided. Moreover, it was, according to my opinion, also right from a finance-political point of view to bring about for the present a certain tranquillisation on the foreign exchange market. If—though it is surely not probable, but still not entirely impossible—the Ruhr action should end somehow, without any new and worse European catastrophe than [like] that of 1914–18 occurring, the present state of stability might to a certain extent be useful for the negotiations.

Yours sincerely
C. MELCHIOR

On 20 April, the British Foreign Minister, Lord Curzon, invited Germany to submit her own proposals for a settlement. The German Note in reply was presented on 2 May. This was the background to Keynes's first article for *The Nation*, which follows.

From The Nation and Athenaeum, *5 May 1923*

BRITISH POLICY IN EUROPE

Ever since 1919 it has been easy to show that our European policy has broken pledges, has treated with duplicity friends and enemies alike, and has been expressed in terms of fudge and make-believe. But one question still remained open: do such tactics pay?

At last we have the answer. Our tactics have got us nothing —neither reparations, nor European peace, nor trustworthy friends, nor prestige, nor security, nor the realisation of any national interest or any national ideal. It is a long time since the foreign policy of England has come so completely to grief as under Mr Lloyd George's second administration from 1919 to 1922. Mr Bonar Law, without the strength to construct a new policy, can only brood, sceptical and helpless, amidst the ruins. All the more reason why those party leaders who are free from personal responsibility for the events of the last three years should acquire clear utterance, and breathe new life and strength into their declarations of policy. Is not the time ripe, through the fulfilment of events and the progress of opinion, for a new and sharp statement of the aims and methods of British policy in Europe? It is not sufficient to mention the League of Nations. We want to know, for example, from Lord Grey, not merely that he would refer the Ruhr question to the League, but what steps he would wish the League to take, were this done.

I submit that, as a preliminary, the following simple principles are worth attention.

First, we must be extremely cautious and realistic in our estimates of what is possible or likely. Apart from other faults, the outstanding weakness of the peace treaties of 1919 was the assumption underlying them that the distribution of power and the harmony of arm existing on the day of the Armistice were *permanent*; whereas it should have been obvious to any sensible person that, when the war establishments had been demobilised, the balance of effective power would be totally disarranged, and that, to judge from all previous experience, the national policies of England, France, and Italy would soon diverge. The Turkish Treaty of Sèvres may have been the most extreme instance of the miscalculation of military forces; and the Austrian Treaty of St Germain of the disregard of economic possibilities. But it was scarcely less wide of the mark to assume in the Treaty of Versailles that we could attain our objects without, in some degree, the voluntary co-operation of Germany herself; or that it would be in the general interest to disarm Germany, yet to leave France with the largest army ever known in Europe in a time of peace.

The same type of error, however, is being made now by friends of my own way of thinking, the tone of whose complaints against British inaction seems to imply that we have much more power to put pressure on France than is actually the case. That a series of mistakes has, for the time being, reduced our European influence to vanishing point, is the only, but in a sense the unanswerable, defence of Mr Bonar Law and Lord Curzon. 'Benevolent impotence', says Mr Asquith. 'Just so,' replies Mr Bonar Law, 'I *am* impotent' —a complete, a triumphant retort! For Mr Bonar Law is never more at his ease than when he can say, without fear of contradiction, that the position is perfectly hopeless.

But whilst we are nearly, we are not quite, helpless. Our diplomatic problem consists in discovering what effective weapons we have and in calculating their exact strength. These certainly do not lie in the direction of using, or even mentioning, measures of force. It follows that they are limited to offering, or withholding, economic and financial inducements, and above all to leading and mobilising the public opinion of the world.

The suggestion of economic and financial inducements leads to my second point. We must seldom allow our practical policy to stray too far from the solid national interests. This is the hardest doctrine of all for high-spirited idealists. There are occasions when a nation can be quixotic; but only when its emotions are unusually stirred and unusually united. It is useless to frame a foreign policy on the assumption that it is our mission to set the whole world right. Intervention without a united force of public opinion behind it will be half-hearted; and that is the one thing which an effective foreign policy must never be. But the idealists need not be discouraged. There is plenty to occupy them in stripping away the false ornament from bogus national interests and discovering the real ones. More harm comes because national foreign policies are shoddy than because they are selfish. Moreover, in this particular case it is possible to prove, I think, that to offer certain economic and financial inducements to France *is* in the national interest.

The importance of influencing the opinion of the world enforces my third and fourth points. Our speech must be frank and in cool relation to the facts. This is not only agreeable in itself, but pays outrageously. In the huge arena of foreign politics, where *everything* sooner or later is found to be somewhere on the vast carpet, it is prudent to dismiss altogether the hope of universal deception. Even though opinion at home can be deceived by propaganda, which plays on popular sentiment and encourages what it pleases people to believe, it is quite impossible to do the same thing abroad —to make Germans believe that they could pay untold reparation, and Americans that it would be sound finance to lend large sums to Germany, and Russians that it would enrich them to pay the debts of the old régime. A country which hopes to influence the opinion of the world must take great pains to ensure that its public declarations are accurate and conform exactly to the facts.

Recent legends, anyhow, have done nothing but harm. The injury inflicted on Europe by the grand reparation legend is incalculable. Looking back, we can see that the policy pursued from 1919 to 1922, of steadily reducing the dimensions of the legend, but of never abandoning it in favour of the plain truth, has not worked well. With another legend—the grand international loan—which still possesses great powers of deception, I will deal in a later article. But there are also other legends, derived from the sentiments, natural during the war, as to the wholly virtuous intentions of all our Allies and the wholly depraved characters of all our enemies.

Speaking the other day in the House of Lords about the French invasion of the Ruhr. Lord Grey said: 'All of us sympathise with the aims and the justice of the objects which France has in view.' I suspect ingredients here from at least two legends—a legend that there is amongst Englishmen the same nearly unanimous sympathy with France as there was five years ago, and a legend as to the character of French aims. Doubtless Lord Grey was partly influenced in his choice of words by diplomatic manners and a desire to avoid the appearance of criticising a friendly country. But in so far as his words were not conventional, is Lord Grey confident that he knows what the aims of France really are, and that these aims include nothing with which he does not sympathise? Must we not penetrate beyond these phrases if we are to think out a foreign policy truly expressive of our national purpose? Lord Grey's opinions are very important to Liberals, and we are bound to scan his words closely if we are to know where the party stands.

Fourthly, we must return to the path of legality (i.e., it must not be sufficient, where the other party is helpless, to concoct a just plausible case for departing from the probable meaning of an engagement). This is an indispensable preliminary to regaining the confidence of impartial world opinion. As an earnest of our good intentions, we must, therefore, do what we can to repair the two most signal instances of doubtful faith towards Germany—the claim of reparation for war pensions, and the invasion of the Ruhr. We should formally renounce our claims to war pensions, and state plainly that, in our judgment, the Franco-Belgian invasion of the Ruhr is not countenanced by the most probable interpretation of the meaning and intention of the Treaty of Versailles. In a sense, such declarations would not make much difference. But in another sense they would, made with the whole authority of the British Commonwealth, have an extraordinary importance. At the least, they would do a little to restore respect for the due observance of legal form between nations—a respect which must be preserved and magnified, if projects of disarmament and the settlement of international disputes by peaceable procedure are ever to be practicable ideals. At present, eminent statesmen, even when they suspect that Germany may have been treated with bad faith, think it injudicious to say so emphatically. Is not this attitude inconsistent with advocacy of a League of Nations régime, in which the nations of Europe are to allow their security and just interests mainly to depend upon written engagements instead of their own armed strength! The supine attitude of other countries towards the question whether or not the Franco-Belgian invasion of the Ruhr is a just and lawful procedure seems to me more damaging to the objective of disarmament and arbitration than the fact of the invasion itself.

The German Note of 2 May proved disappointing. It was a compromise document, based on the same proposals that had been intended for presentation at the January conference of allied ministers. A new element, however, was an assertion of Germany's willingness to submit the terms of settlement to judgment by an international body of experts, as suggested by the United States Secretary of State, Charles Evans Hughes, in his speech of 29 December 1922. Leading off *The Nation*'s first issue of 5 May under the heading 'Events of the Week' was an unsigned account and commentary which was Keynes's immediate reaction to the German offer.

From The Nation and Athenaeum, *5 May 1923*

Stript of embroidery, the German offer is as follows—

1. A moratorium until 1927.

2. A payment of £60 million (gold) annually thereafter.

3. Additional payments of £15 million annually from 1929 to 1931, and of £30 million annually after 1931 (making in all £90 million annually), the decision whether and how these additional payments are to be made being left to 'an impartial international commission'.

4. If these annual payments can be anticipated by means of an international loan, all the better. But there is an important ambiguity here. The above annual payments represent 5 per cent interest and 1 per cent sinking fund of the suggested capital of the loan. Does this mean that, if these terms are not good enough (which would certainly be the case), the loan is to be issued below par?

5. Deliveries in kind to proceed on the same lines as before the occupation of the Ruhr, but to be reckoned as part of the above payments.

6. The offer is conditional on the evacuation of the Ruhr and the withdrawal of various other restrictions on German trade and menaces to her credit. This is clearly reasonable, since it would be impossible for Germany to make such payments unless her trade and industry were prosperous and secure from interference.

Mr Bonar Law's proposal of last January was for an annual payment of £100 million, instead of £90 million. But this full amount was to be paid from 1927, instead of 1931, and might in certain (very improbable) contingencies be raised to £125 million by the decision of an impartial body. Thus the German offer is not very far off our own government's terms, which naturally did not err on the side of leniency. It is, therefore, impossible for us not to regard them as a sincere statement of the utmost which Germany, under overwhelming pressure to do her best to reach a settlement, thinks she can really pay. But this is not all. Germany throws herself without reserve on the wisdom and justice of impartial world opinion. If her own scheme of payment is not acceptable, then let the whole reparations problem be referred to an international commission 'free from every political influence', whose decision she binds herself to accept. She binds herself, further, to accept *any* bilateral proposal for the avoidance of future war, and the guarantee of the frontier between herself and France. What further could she do?

A great responsibility rests on Lord Curzon. He invited this offer, and he is, therefore, bound to follow up any opening it discloses. He did not ask Germany to capitulate. He cannot have expected her to offer, out of hand, a sum of money which France would accept in her present mood. He cannot, therefore, have hoped for more than that she would make an offer not too far short of Mr Bonar Law's own figure, and would declare her readiness to accept alternatively the judgment of the world. His diplomatic task is one of enormous difficulty. But it is surely his duty to declare that Great Britain, as one of the signatories of the Treaty of Versailles, accepts the German appeal to impartial decision; and to call on France, if she does not accept it, to disclose in detail her own alternative proposals. At least this might clear the air and disclose, for good or evil, the real purposes of France. Failing a definite move by Great Britain, we have nothing now to look for but an intensification of the barren misery of the Ruhr.

France and Belgium replied jointly on 6 May. In their reply they announced that they would consider no German offer until resistance in the

Ruhr was relinquished and that they would not leave the occupied territories until Germany's reparation payments were discharged. The text was communicated to the British government only 24 hours before it was handed to Germany, thereby causing Curzon in the House of Lords and Baldwin in the Commons to protest this 'unnecessary precipitancy' in answering. Britain, it was announced, would present her own views to Germany; the British Note was duly delivered 13 May.

As promised Keynes gave his more considered reaction to the German offer, and in addition to the French reply, in the second issue of the new *Nation*.

From The Nation and Athenaeum, *12 May 1923*

THE GERMAN OFFER AND THE FRENCH REPLY

From time to time a trumpet is lifted to the lips of Germany. One expects a lofty and passionate strain of rebellious patriotism, or an unqualified simplicity cutting through the tangles, or the menacing note of desperation. One hears the gramophone record of a muddled drafting committee. From the days of Versailles until now the Notes of the German government have lacked both passion and persuasiveness. At each crisis of her affairs a timid and contorted document serves to re-arouse a baneful 'superiority complex' in the hearts of her oppressors. One might suppose that her statesmen, as well as her students, were nourished exclusively upon potatoes.

Heaven knows that propaganda is a sinful thing! But there is nothing wrong in writing a short sentence.[1] Throughout the world's Press the reaction of distaste to the German Note has been predominantly aesthetic—directed against the form and ignoring the substance. The peace of Europe, almost, is menaced by a prose style. Who, smiling at his German

---

[1] As a trifling but typical example, all the words in the German opening paragraph, except those which I have placed in italics, are redundant or objectionable—

It has always been the point of view of the German government, which they are induced to restate in the present international discussion, that questions, upon the settlement of which depend *the reconstruction of the devastated area*, equally desired by Germany, *and,* beyond that, *the economic restoration* and peace *of Europe, can find their solution only through mutual agreement.*

governess, could have foreseen that this national peculiarity would have turned out so important!

The faults of form are not only literary. It is a great error to have stated the offer in terms of an international loan instead of an annual tribute. All that Germany can do of herself is to provide annual payments, beginning as soon as possible and rising as high as possible. If, in order to help France, the rest of the world is prepared to capitalise and anticipate any part of these annual sums, that is their contribution, not hers. In fact, Germany is offering a huge annual tribute, up to whatever limit impartial opinion may think possible. But by making her proposal appear to depend on an international loan, impracticable in size and to be contributed by others, she has contrived to make it look a deception and an evasion at the same time. It is easy for her enemies to point out with truth that the loan cannot be raised, and that, if it could be, we and not Germany would be finding the money.

If, therefore, we want a plausible excuse for ignoring the German offer, we find it ready made. But if the real position is just the contrary, it is obvious that, so far from exploiting Germany's fatigue and perplexity, we must seek out the genuine heart of these impermeable paragraphs.

The substance of the German offer reaches, in my opinion, and perhaps exceeds, the limit of her capacity. Ignoring details capable of alteration, I find the following solid elements—

(1) After a moratorium of four years, Germany offers an annual payment commencing at £60 million (gold) and rising in certain circumstances to £90 million. This is very near the figure of £100 million which many authorities have given as the probable maximum. After all that has happened, it will be a surprising thing if more than this is ever paid. If we could get this, it would be madness to break the peace of Europe in the remote expectation of getting more.

(2) For the first time, Germany makes her offer uncondi-

tional on other alterations in the Treaty. Her proposal of two years ago, for example, was contingent on her retention of Upper Silesia, and that of four years ago on many other concessions. (It is instructive to note that the nominal figure of each successive German offer is less than that of its predecessor—100 milliards in 1919, 50 milliards in 1921, 30 milliards in 1923; which does not indicate that the application of force does much good. It is quite likely that the offer of 1925 will be 15 milliards, and that those of 1927 and thereafter will be *nil*.)

(3) In the event of this offer being deemed unsatisfactory, Germany declares her readiness to accept the decision of an international commission on the lines proposed by Mr Hughes on behalf of the United States.

In (1) Germany nearly reaches the figures of the British scheme of last January. In (2) she accepts the existing territorial settlement. In (3) she accepts the latest suggestion of the United States. It is impossible for England or America not to regard this as a sincere advance deserving serious consideration.

The French reply, sent without consultation with her Allies, offends against more important things than tact or style. The small, malignant figure of Poincaré lacks even the grim, ingratiating quality of the old grey owl, Clemenceau. One feels oneself in a black cavern, narrowing to a point through which nothing human can creep, nightmare narrowness.

France demands her bond and her forfeit too—to cut out Germany's heart and to exact the utmost ducat at the same time; greed and fear and revenge, overreaching one another, until they end in a sort of nihilism. It is not well to invoke the majesty of law in the act of outraging it, or to raise the plea of justice untempered by truth or mercy. The sneering reply of France closes the door on everything. It does not even grasp at a tangible object.

We are told that the effect of the Note on America 'is to

be found in a perceptible growth of public indifference to the whole business'. If England could detach herself from the European scene, the effect would be the same here. Not 'benevolent impotence' any longer; disgusted impotence. But we are not thus detached; and if, in face of the French attitude, Lord Curzon merely collapses, we shall have suffered a real reverse.

We must, at all events, hold open a door, keep a ray of light visible, and speak a few comfortable words. The statements of Lord Curzon and Mr Baldwin on Tuesday were satisfactory so far as they went. France having replied separately, we propose to avail ourselves of our right to do the same: what can we reply? One longs for a statesman who could speak with fire and strength, the spring of whose inspiration was not parched. One might think from their utterance hitherto that our ministers also are potato-fed. Nevertheless, Lord Curzon still has a stock of prestige and good intentions on which to draw, and an opportunity is now offered him if he will show some slight boldness.

More will depend on the tone of our communication than on its substance. We must build on the strong parts of the German Note, and lay particular stress on their willingness to accept impartial judgment. Even if, at the present stage, our reply is necessarily limited to banalities, let them be quiet and sensible banalities, small-talk if you like, but inviting the way to human intercourse. We can recognise German difficulties, admit the sincerity of her offer, anticipate a happier future, and ask some questions which might lead to a continuation of the correspondence. We ought, in truth, to go much further than this. But even a word of futile amiability might break the thickening atmosphere of set savagery.

The British Note of 13 May expressed disappointment with the inadequacy of the sum offered in payment of reparation by Germany and her failure to state precisely the guarantees she proposed to offer. However, the British government, said Lord Curzon, was persuaded that Germany in her own interests would 'reconsider and expand' her proposals so that they might become a basis for discussion. The Italian Note, delivered the same day, was similar in content to the British. Keynes made his comment under 'Events of the Week'.

From The Nation and Athenaeum, *19 May 1923*

Lord Curzon's reply to the German Note indicates that the British government drifts, and is still without a European policy. The degree to which Mr Bonar Law's Cabinet lacks both nerve and intelligence becomes painfully apparent in the face of big issues. The best that can be said of the reply is that in moderately polite language Germany is invited to try again, and that its pompous and condescending phrases are quite free from menace. The remarkable thing about it is the omission of any reference to the most important and promising feature of the German offer, namely, the proposal to submit to impartial arbitration the question of her capacity to pay—a proposal which Lord Curzon is scarcely entitled to overlook.

Suppose Germany were to submit an offer which the British government considered reasonable—has Lord Curzon made up his mind what he would do then? We know beforehand that the French government would not agree with us in considering it reasonable. Ought Lord Curzon, in such circumstances, to encourage the Germans to make their maximum offer, unless he is prepared to back them up in the event of this offer being a fair one? Is he prepared to do this? The contingency is a real one, because the existing German offer, when expressed in terms of annuities, is, in fact, not much short of Mr Bonar Law's own proposal of January last. Germany's wisest course would be to build her next offer on the Bonar Law scheme, pointing out clearly what parts of it, if any, need to be modified, and what parts she can accept.

British opinion could then judge whether the desired modifications were reasonable.

We may be reaching a decisive point in the tide of public opinion. So long as the British public believe that France is genuinely seeking reparations and that Germany is trying to evade payment, France will retain their sympathy, and will get the benefit of the doubt when she employs doubtful methods of pressure. Their confidence in France's object has been shaken in various ways, but not, so far, destroyed. A move which clearly exhibited the true purposes of France and of Germany to the ordinary, sensible Englishman would have an extraordinary importance. If France turned out to deserve our confidence, well and good. If, on the other hand, the average Englishman were to become convinced that France is menacing the peace of Europe, is ruining our trade prosperity, is depriving us of our share of a genuine reparation offer, and is spending money which she owes us on building aeroplanes not required against Germany—there would be a change of opinion in this country which would surprise M. Poincaré, and perhaps Lord Curzon, too.

Melchior, writing to Keynes 14 May, gave his personal view of the situation inside Germany and offered an explanation for the aesthetic shortcomings of the German Note that Keynes complained of. No copy of Keynes's letter of 10 May exists among his papers, so that it is not possible to say what information, mentioned by Melchior, Keynes sought, or what kind of 'suitable man' to supply it.

From C. MELCHIOR, *14 May 1923*

Dear Keynes,

Many thanks for your kind letter of the 10th instant. I shall try to find a suitable man who could supply you with the information you want, and I hope I shall be able to revert to this matter soon. Before Whitsuntide, however, I can probably not undertake any steps, because I am leaving for Holland tonight and shall not be back until the end of the week.

Meanwhile I may perhaps be permitted to give you below my personal views on the inner situation in Germany.

The Ruhr invasion and particularly the ever-growing hardships imposed on the population have created with us in Germany a considerably stronger feeling of unity than we have seen since 1918. Only the radicals of the left (Communists) and the radicals of the right (National-Socialists) resist, and these two elements oppose the 'Einheitsfront'. The National-Socialist movement in Bavaria has been shaken through the dominant party in Bavaria, the Bavarian Centre (the Catholic party) which is monarchistic and much more conservative than the 'Zentrums-Partei' in the Reich—which hitherto had favoured the National-Socialists in secret —having now turned against them. This was partly due to the National-Socialists having quite openly armed bands in Munich and in the country and thus endangered the State authority in the highest degree, and partly to the National-Socialists—a main point on whose program is the anti-Semitism—having on more than one occasion severely attacked Christianity as a Judaisation of Germany, whereby they have, of course, at once aroused antagonism on the part of the Catholic clergy. I do not believe that for the present any commotion from right or left, except perhaps some local disturbances, need be expected. Things would, however, get a different aspect, if the Ruhr action or the international political treatment of this question should lead to a far-reaching breakdown in Germany, in which case, however, I do not consider it impossible that riots will occur from both sides, which may eventually turn out rather sanguinary.

The English and Italian Notes have been published here this morning and, notwithstanding their most unpleasant tone, my personal impression is that they offer a chance for further negotiations. If there be such possibility, it should not be neglected.

I have read in the papers what you said about the German Note. I do not think it quite unjustified that it has been criticised abroad, as far as its form is concerned. It was not harmonious in style, too sober and therefore psychologically ineffectual. That was partly due to the unfinished state of affairs over here, which has developed since the revolution, namely that too many authorities have to be consulted, when such Notes are composed; the consistency and vigour of those documents must, of course, thereby suffer. It is for ourselves to find a remedy in this respect.

I cannot express any opinion, as to what attitude the German government is going to take vis-à-vis the English and Italian Notes. Regarding the guarantees, I think, more concrete information should be given. I personally considered it advisable that in the first German Note the guarantees were mentioned in rather general terms only, for I deemed it more expedient to reply to counter-enquiries in this respect, rather than submitting offers which perhaps would have been rejected at once. As to the height of the reparation payments, the German government will have to make up its mind, whether it will maintain the figures already named, in combination, of course, with the elastic factor of the impartial instance [arbitration], and point out that those figures, to its conception, are already the result of the most optimistic estimates, and that, if the question was to be dealt with from an economic and financial point of view, they represent a maximum; but that, if the German government should be mistaken in this respect, an increase through an impartial instance had been provided for. Should it, however, only be a question of naming some high figure, not for the purpose of finding a definite economic basis, but for the purpose of removing momentary political difficulties, the matter would have to be considered from a different point of view.

I must mention that what I have said is only an expression of my personal views, for I have no information regarding the attitude which will be taken in Berlin, nor shall I probably get such information still, owing to my departure tonight.

I should heartily welcome it, if you would carry out your intention to come over to Germany and lift the veil. I shall remain here until the end of June; in July I should like to take my holidays.

Yours sincerely
C. MELCHIOR

Keynes made his attempt to 'lift the veil'. On 16 May 1923 he addressed the following letter, marked 'Private', from King's College, Cambridge, to Chancellor Cuno.

To REICHSCHANCELLOR WILHELM CUNO, *16 May 1923*

Dear Dr Cuno,

I have of course been following recent events with deep pessimism and profound sympathy for the efforts you have been taking. Nothing, in my opinion, is of any utility at present, except something which makes clear to the average Englishman and the average American the true purposes of France and Germany respectively. It is hopeless to attempt to satisfy France. Any further reply you may make to Lord Curzon can have no object except to affect favourable British and American opinion. It may be useless to say anything. But I venture, very humbly, to enclose a suggestion of the line which a further reply might take. I have shown this suggestion to no one. The reply must be short and simple and dignified. What I suggest does not amount to anything novel. Please excuse my presumption in sending it. A foreigner naturally feels much delicacy in making a suggestion.

Yours sincerely,

J. M. KEYNES

Keynes's papers contain a copy of this letter and its enclosure made at Melchior's office at M. M. Warburg and Company, Hamburg. A draft of the enclosed 'Suggested German Reply to Lord Curzon' also exists in Keynes's own handwriting, marked 'Sent to Cuno / 16. 5. 23 / JMK'.

SUGGESTED GERMAN REPLY TO LORD CURZON

1. Germany made her recent offer in terms of a loan of which she would meet the service, because she had understood that an arrangement of this kind was contemplated by the Allies. She is equally ready to make it in terms of an annuity.

2. Germany is prepared to accept the general scheme of Mr Bonar Law's proposal of January last, provided that the amount of the annuity commencing in 1927 (i.e. the rate of interest on the first series of new bonds) is determined in due time by an independent tribunal as proposed in her previous communication. Germany is not prepared to undertake a defined payment unless she believes that she can fulfil her undertaking; and in present circumstances it is impossible for her to know that the amounts specified in Mr Bonar Law's proposal are within her capacity.

3. Germany has already agreed to discuss in detail the question of securities. The obstacle to the solution of this

question lies, not in any unwillingness on Germany's part to give securities, but in the difficulty of finding suitable securities. Germany is prepared, however, to accept Mr Bonar Law's proposal, namely to agree in advance in the event of a failure to pay any due instalment to hand over to the Reparation Commission or to any Allied power authorised to act on its behalf whatever revenues or assets of the German Empire or German States the commission or such power may select.

4. If only in the interest of the reparation payments themselves, Germany cannot agree to any occupation of her territory beyond the limits laid down in the Treaty of Versailles; and she regrets that reparation payments must remain materially impossible so long as such occupation continues.

Cuno's answer came through Melchior who wrote to Keynes on 22 May. In this letter Melchior discreetly intimated the lines along which the German government was thinking.

Again, there is no copy of Keynes's letter of 18 May which Melchior mentions. 'The change in the British Cabinet' was the expected change brought about by the retirement of Bonar Law. Baldwin became prime minister on 23 May.

From C. MELCHIOR, *22 May 1923*

Dear Keynes,

Many thanks for your kind letter of the 18th instant. I am delighted that we may look forward to your visit towards the end of June.

I wish to bring the following to your notice:

I had occasion to see our mutual friend—who spent the Whitsuntide holidays in the country near Hamburg—and to discuss matters fully with him. He showed me your letter of the 16th inst., to which he felt sure you would have no objection, being aware, as you are, of the friendly relations existing between him and me, and that you would not misapprehend that he has asked me to answer your letter. I would mention that besides him and myself nobody else knows of this correspondence, and that he is most grateful to you for your letter and your exceedingly important suggestions.

You are certainly right in pointing out that the reply must be short and dignified. In this connection we have to bear in mind that, though we must still consider the political situation in France—as far as her relations to Germany are concerned—as nearly hopeless, a solution can after all be arrived at only through negotiations in which also France will have to take part. The first aim we must have in view is to see how we can influence public opinion in England, perhaps also in Italy and even in Belgium—the feeling in Belgium, as you know, is not much in favour of the continuance of the Ruhr occupation. America, where at present they are making heaps of money and where, in accordance with the sympathetic human mentality, they therefore do not bother themselves about others' sufferings, appears to me most passive at this moment and can hardly be influenced. Besides, however, the French psychology must also be taken into account, and in our opinion it would not be advisable to revert too clearly to Bonar Law's scheme which in January last was quite formally rejected by the French and led to the breaking-off of the Paris Conference. I could therefore imagine that the German government in its reply should give expression to the following considerations:

(1) Amount. After having honestly investigated all possibilities, Germany had come to the conclusion that 30 milliards (20 plus 5 plus 5) represented a maximum, and that this figure was probably the result of too optimistic estimates and would exceed Germany's real capacity. In order to provide France with funds as soon as possible, Germany desired to raise this amount by issuing a loan with the least possible delay. As far as loans could not be placed, an annuity would have to be paid. In so far as a conscientious self-assessment is concerned, the German government, all the more because the economic situation in Germany was under prevailing circumstances getting worse and worse, could arrive at no better result. Germany would, however—and that is the main point—submit to any impartial instance [arbitration] in which the German interests would be duly represented, be it that this instance would decide for other figures, be it that another scheme, eventually even one that had already been proposed by one or the other of the Allies, would be adopted by it.

(2) Securities. As regards the securities, these would have to be offered in a more concrete form. State property and State revenues, railways, customs etc. have already been pledged by the Treaty of Versailles. It should further be stated, in which way German economic life is to contribute. I personally am an advocate of the gold mortgage which practically is nothing but a ground-tax payable in gold.

(3) Occupation. What you say in this respect, is absolutely correct.

146

I think that, with regard to the Belgian démarche in Paris, to the change in the British Cabinet and to the still necessary deliberations on this side, the German reply will no more be forthcoming in the course of this week.

I thank you again in the name of our mutual friend for your very valuable observations and should be much obliged, if, on receipt of these lines, you would telegraph me the word 'received', so that I may know that this letter has reached you safely.

Yours sincerely
C. MELCHIOR

Melchior wrote Cuno 25 May:

Re correspondence with Keynes

I assume that you have received my letter of 22 May, together with the enclosed letter from Keynes [which would be Keynes's letter to Melchior of 18 May] and the gist of my reply...

This morning I got a telegram from Keynes: 'Received replying'. Immediately I receive Keynes's reply I shall forward it to you. I am of course unable to judge from this short telegram if he has got in touch with the responsible people about the contents of the letter...

Keynes did not keep a copy of the reply for which Melchior was waiting —Keynes's reaction to the proposal being considered by the Germans. The text of his letter was supplied years later by Melchior's colleague, Max M. Warburg, when in 1942 he asked Keynes's permission to make use of the material in this and other of Keynes's letters to Melchior in writing his memoirs, *Aus Meinen Aufzeichungen* (privately published).

From a letter to CARL MELCHIOR, *24 May 1923*

I appreciate the point about not irritating France by referring too pointedly to the Bonar Law proposal. I think you are right. But

(1) a mention of the 30 milliard capital sum will mean that the new Note will lead to nothing.

(2) if the new Note is too like the old one, yet pretends to meet us, it will have no effect on opinion anywhere except irritation.

(3) I feel most strongly that it is important to get away from the capital sum (which is bound to fall short of what people here expect) and from the loan (which is absurd), and to speak in terms of annuities.

147

(4) In England I am almost alone in thinking 30 milliards about the limit of German capacity. The present Cabinet and its advisers strongly believe that Germany can pay more.

(5) The securities are of no real value and must be designed solely to influence opinion.

If any lump sum is mentioned, which I deprecate, it would be much better to make it 50 milliards at a lower rate of interest. But, in view of what you say, there is much to be said in favour of a very short answer to the effect that:

(1) Germany cannot increase her offer but reiterates her willingness to accept arbitration.

(2) She clears up any ambiguity as to what annuities she offered.

(3) She reiterates her willingness to discuss securities in detail.

(4) If the Allies are not prepared for conversations on this basis, there is no alternative to an indefinite continuance of the present situation, which Germany is prepared to face rather than enter into impossible undertakings which cannot be carried out and which merely perpetuate friction and uncertainty.

I consider the following two points important:

(1) If in fact the new Note is no advance on the old Note let this be proved plainly and even be boasted about.

(2) Let Germany instead of making moan about how badly she is being treated, insist rather on her capacity of indefinite resistance and even introduce a slight note of menace. Her present propaganda about how cruelly she is oppressed produces the impression that she will break down before long. *In the long run* firmness and a proud bearing will produce more effect on opinion than conciliations and moans.

Melchior replied on 26 May. His reference to Keynes's 'kind letter of the 20th' appears to be an error; Keynes's letter, which Warburg dated 24 May, discusses Melchior's letter of the 22nd.

From C. MELCHIOR, *26 May 1923*

Dear Keynes,

I thank you sincerely for your kind letter of the 20th [24th?] instant, which I have immediately transmitted to our mutual friend. I agree with you that, in view of the impossibility to place a loan of any importance at the present moment, it would be advisable to revert to the annuities scheme, which I have accordingly recommended.

In my opinion it would be impracticable for the present Cabinet to increase the capital amount. At the end of last December through Bergmann and again four weeks ago through the German Note 30 milliards, as far as the German self-assessment is concerned, has been declared to be the maximum. This same Cabinet can therefore not declare now, without falling into discredit at home and abroad, that it has meanwhile reconsidered the matter and come to the conclusion that now 40 to 50 milliards may be offered. The idea expressed by you that the interest might perhaps be reduced, would also be difficult to follow, as far as I can see. The German offer has been based on the, according to present circumstances, already low interest rate of the Treaty of Versailles (5% plus 1% amortisation). It would not be an easy matter to arrive at a still lower type. The only way left open, and also recommended by you in the first place, is therefore that of annuities.

I am writing you in a great hurry, so that this letter may still reach the mail in time; I may perhaps write you more on Monday, also about your article, which I shall read with the greatest interest.

I am studying with pleasure the newest numbers of *The Nation and the Athenaeum*. Unfortunately the number of the 12th of May, in which you wrote about the German offer, has—presumably owing to some delay in transmission—not yet come to hand; I hope, however, that it will arrive within the next few days. [When Melchior wrote (14 May) that he had 'read in the papers what you said about the German Note', he would have been referring to accounts by other journals of Keynes's *Nation* article.]

I thank you most cordially for the great trouble you have taken by your lucid and detailed observations, which are of the greatest value to us.

Yours sincerely

C. MELCHIOR

The article that Melchior looked forward to reading and promised to write about appears to be 'The International Loan'. Melchior referred to it in his letter of 28 May 1923 (p. 157); Keynes presumably sent him an advance proof. In it Keynes reiterated his conviction of the folly of all hopes based on this hypothesis.

From The Nation and Athenaeum, *26 May 1923*

THE INTERNATIONAL LOAN

The war accustomed us to vast credit operations between governments. Since the war, reconstruction loans, 'to stabilise the exchanges', have been a favourite panacea of philanthropists. In particular, many hopes of solving the reparation question and of satisfying France at the same time have been built up on the idea that, when once Germany's annual payments for reparation have been fixed at a reasonable figure, these prospective payments can be capitalised and anticipated by means of a vast international loan.

These hopes reached their highest point when a committee of bankers, which included Mr Pierpont Morgan, met at Paris in May 1922 and indicated that, on terms, great sums could be raised. Since that time sceptical doubts have increased about both the necessity and the possibility of such a transaction. Lord Curzon's recent complaint to Germany, that her proposal was made to depend on the feasibility of a loan, was a sign of this. Nevertheless, Germany made her offer in this form because she thought that this was the fashionable way in which to dress it; and the loan still figures in most paper schemes for settling Europe.

It is, therefore, worth while to repeat that the great international loan is an absurdity—an impossible and injurious chimæra. Germany, in any case, can only pay by annual instalments. It confuses the issue to introduce complicated provisions about a loan. But it also adds unreality to a discussion which, without this addition, has difficulty enough to keep in touch with facts.

The loan is chimerical because its suggested magnitude is out of relation to the capacity of the investment market for securities of this kind. The recent German Note mentioned a first loan of £1,000 million, and subsequent loans of a further £500 million. These figures correspond to those frequently mentioned in discussion, which range from £500 million up to £2,000 million. It is fair to the Germans to admit that amongst writers on this subject £500 million is often reckoned a low figure and £1,000 million not absurd. The idea is that the loan would be raised mainly in London and New York with some contributions from the neutral countries of Europe, and that the receipts would mainly accrue to France and Belgium. To the general public these figures convey no particular impression. To fix our ideas of magnitude let me quote some approximate totals of the volume of existing foreign investment.

The whole of the outstanding loans made by the British investor to the government of India, built up over a long period of years and largely taken in the form of British exports of railway material and the like, stand at less than £200 million. The loans, made by the British investor and now quoted by the London stock exchange, to the whole of the rest of the British Empire, dominion and colonial and provincial governments together, the accumulation of long years of investment in quarters specially favoured and specially trusted, stand at round about £500 million. The whole of the corporation and county stocks of the United Kingdom, quoted on the London stock exchange, are worth about £200 million. Thus the aggregate of the loans outstanding from the British investor to the governments of the whole British Empire and to the counties and corporations of the United Kingdom does not reach £1,000 million.

Most of the above loans are trustee securities by law—a privilege not likely to be granted to a German loan. Let us consider, therefore, a class of investment made without this privilege. The present value of all the loans made by the British investor to foreign governments throughout the world is approximately £400 million.

One more example will illustrate to the reader what an amount of capital £1,000 million represents. This figure is the total face value of all the stocks—debenture, preference, and ordinary—of the entire railway system of the United Kingdom (the present market value being about 10 per cent less).

The statistics of the present volume of savings in this country are not very reliable; but no one would place the total available each year for new foreign investment of all kinds above £150 million. Last year it barely reached £100 million. The total amount of foreign government loans floated on the London market in the two years 1921 and 1922 came to about £20 million altogether, and these borrowers had to pay on the average nearly 8 per cent.

Have I quoted enough figures to bring back proportion to the discussion? If Great Britain were to subscribe half of the suggested £1,000 million loan to Germany, it would mean that the whole of the British Empire and all other foreign borrowers could have nothing at all for four or five years. That is the borrowers' side. As for the lender, it means that the British investor would have to go on year after year lending all he had to Germany. We are obviously in the region of the wildest fantasy.

I conclude that, if Germany could borrow on her own credit in the London market £25 million at 10 per cent, it would be a remarkable achievement.

What about New York? Recently it has been far more difficult and expensive to float foreign loans in New York than in London. At the present time existing French government dollar loans stand in New York on about an 8 per cent basis; and Czechoslovak government dollar loans on a 9 per cent basis. It is not likely that either of these governments could get much new money in New York even at 10 per cent. Yet their credit stands, presumably, higher than Germany's would. The volume of foreign loans made by New York has sunk during the past year to a very low figure, and we have to go back to 1921 and the first half of 1922, when there was a short-lived boom in such securities, to find substantial amounts. But even in 1921 the loans to Europe did not really come to much. France secured on balance $70 million of new money, Denmark $40 million, Belgium $25 million. But then Great Britain paid off $150 million; so that even in 1921 the American investor lent nothing on balance to European governments. The only investments which attracted him on a large scale were pure speculations, such as mark banknotes where he hoped for 100 per cent profit and has suffered 100 per cent loss. The United States lends Canada a good deal, and a certain amount to Mexico and South America. But probably she has less surplus available for Europe than Great Britain has, and her investors are showing an even greater distaste for this type of investment.

In short, the £1,000 million loan is as nonsensical as general election reparation forecasts and as the alleged total of Germany's present balances abroad (also estimated by some at the good round figure of £500 million to £1,000 million). Why does such elephantiasis afflict this pitiful subject, that popular estimates are not just two or three times wrong, but generally ten times the truth? Has the peace of Europe ever been threatened before by arithmetical frenzy? It is, truly, an extraordinary state of affairs.

I have been speaking so far of proposals to borrow *new* money on Germany's *own* credit. If the loan were to be guaranteed by other powers, including Great Britain, some of the above arguments would not apply. The limit to the sums available for investment abroad would remain the same; but the degree of the investors' willingness to take a hand would, of course, be quite different. I hope, however, that any suggestion of a British guarantee may be ruled out. We must be prepared to make sacrifices in the interests of a settlement.

But the idea that, if Germany fails to pay the indemnity, we should pay it in her place, is intolerable.

There still remains, however, a type of loan to which none of my criticisms apply, namely, where no new money is required, but one form of bond is merely substituted for another. The possibility of a transaction of this kind is only limited by the willingness of the holder of an existing bond to accept another in its place. If, for example, the German government was to issue its bonds to the French government, which in its turn passed them on to the French investor, with or without its own guarantee, in exchange for French government bonds previously held, no technical or financial difficulty arises. The *Temps* has recently aired a proposal by which Germany would undertake to meet the service of the French loans which have been issued to provide for the expenditure on the devastated areas. This is sensible and practicable. There might be political advantages on both sides in getting German bonds well spread amongst the investors of France. But, financially speaking, it is a mere paper transaction; there is no essential difference between the payment by German of an annual sum to France for France to use in paying interest to her bondholders, and the payment by Germany to the bondholders direct. It would also be quite simple to substitute German bonds for the existing bonds of interallied debt. I do not include transactions of this kind under the designation of international loan.

The type of international loan which would be raised in London, New York, and the neutral capitals of Europe and credited mainly to France and Belgium is not only impossible but useless. France and Belgium have no need or employment for a huge lump sum of money. If it were to be credited to them in London and New York, they could do nothing with it except pay off what they owe to the British and American governments (which is not at all what they intend), or lend it out again, thus converting it back from a lump sum into an annual flow. Before the restoration of the war areas had commenced it might have been plausible to argue that a large lump sum of foreign money was required for this purpose. But, in fact, the restoration has proceeded very fast by means of loans raised at home. The financial difficulty of the French and Belgian governments is not in raising the money to pay for restoration, but in meeting the future interest on the loans which they have raised. The financial problem of France—so long, at any rate, as she does not pay what she owes to the governments of England and America—is one of internal, not of external, finance. The insufficiency of the annual revenue of the State to meet the service of her debt involves a constant threat of inflation, and thereby a depreciation of the franc. The remedy for this is not a lump sum of £1,000 million in London and New York, but annual receipts which can be employed to pay her bondholders without resort to inflation. The advocates of an international loan misconceive the character of French needs as well as the possibilities of the international investment market.

There is only one qualification to this; namely, in the event of the receipts from an international loan being employed to make annual payments to France and Belgium during a preliminary period whilst Germany was enjoying a moratorium. Such anticipatory payments would be useful to France and Belgium. But a proposal to raise the loan, whilst Germany is still in her present condition and prior to her recovering her credit and giving some tangible proofs of her willingness and capacity to pay, would be faced by even greater difficulties of persuading the foolish investor to risk his money than those already indicated. There can be few investors who would lend a penny to Germany on her own credit, whilst she is in her present plight, and before she can point to definite signs of recovery. The various political risks are far greater than can be compensated by any practicable rate of interest. A very small, half-charitable loan, on the lines

155

projected for Austria, designed to help Germany herself on to her legs again, is surely the utmost to be expected in the near future.

Let us, therefore, dismiss from the discussion the grand international loan, and concentrate on the essential question how soon and how much Germany can pay year by year.

The text of Keynes's next letter to Melchior has been supplied by Warburg. Keynes wrote to Melchior the same day as Melchior had written to him, 26 May, which was also the day that Baldwin's new Cabinet was announced. Lord Robert Cecil was made Lord Privy Seal, with special responsibility regarding the League of Nations. Baldwin intended to appoint Reginald McKenna as his Chancellor of the Exchequer, pending the finding of a parliamentary seat for him in the City; when this plan did not work out, he appointed Neville Chamberlain.

From a letter to CARL MELCHIOR, *26 May 1923*

The inclusion of Lord R. Cecil in the new Cabinet and the impending inclusion of McKenna makes a big difference. The balance of the government towards reparations is profoundly modified. There are now two very influential figures who do *not* believe in huge figures.

I am sure that in view of this the German reply ought to be delayed until Cuno has had time to take careful stock of the new situation. Also in view of the Belgian attitude to which you referred in your last letter and which is having important reactions in Paris. I am informed that there is a distinct possibility of a new orientation; perhaps even in a couple of months' time Loucheur taking the place of our dear old friend de Lasteyrie.

All this means that time is important. I think now that Germany should neither make a new offer nor reiterate her old one. But should simply write a very conciliatory reply asking for a conference at once or, if preferred, in three months' time. I can see very well what lines such a reply can take.

I have half a mind to pay you a flying visit in Hamburg next week-end, leaving London on Thursday or Friday evening.

With Keynes's papers relating to this time is a draft in his own hand addressed 'Dear Mr Prime Minister', but undated and unsigned. It embodies Keynes's idea of the personal appeal that Cuno might address to the British Prime Minister and takes into account his reading of both their characters. Unlike the suggested reply to Curzon it bears no notation to indicate that it ever was sent, and it does not appear (as does the letter to Cuno and its enclosure) among the correspondence between Keynes and Melchior that Max Warburg asked permission to use in his memoirs. It is as follows:

Dear Mr Prime Minister

Perhaps it is permitted in the unusual conditions of today for one holding my office to write a few words to one holding yours, as a private man, yet expressing feelings of public consequence.

I have held my office six months. It lies outside the scope of my career and my ambition. I would gladly lay it down. I accepted it with the thought that I might contribute something, because as a business man I have been trained to discuss frankly in international negotiations. I hoped to meet face to face those who speak for the Allied countries. But time passes by. Great misfortunes accumulate. I am imprisoned in Berlin, powerless to escape from the sterile interchange of diplomatic notes. I still think that we can only get out of this impasse by establishing a direct contact.

Melchior wrote again on 28 May.

From C. MELCHIOR, *28 May 1923*

Dear Keynes,
    Many thanks for your kind letter of the 26th instant. I wired you that my sister and I shall be quite delighted to see you here at the end of this

week. From all points of view I consider it quite excellent, if you would come over.

We on this side are under the impression that certain hopes may for the first time be entertained that the questions which have hitherto prevented the realisation of peace may be solved with the co-operation of the new English Cabinet. The great question, however, is whether we shall be able to bear long enough the strain at home and from abroad.

I think that Germany in her reply should say something definite, at any rate about the guarantees. That is necessary already, in order to compel our economic circles to take a decision on principle, and also in order to prepare legislatorial measures. Besides I quite agree with you that the new Note should, as much as possible, be kept in general terms and be as short as possible.

I have read your article regarding the international loan with the greatest interest; you are quite right. In this respect we are in close contact with our American friends, and the sum, which can be placed within the next few years, in our opinion ranges between 500 million and 1 milliard dollars, provided above all that it will be possible to excite the interest of the German-American community. The balance will have to be procured by annuities or, as you have already correctly pointed out on previous occasions, serve for the conversion of the inner [internal]- French debt.

Yours sincerely
C. MELCHIOR

(Melchior's reference to 'our American friends' would include Paul M. Warburg, brother of Max Warburg and a former member of the Federal Reserve Board. Cuno also had close connections in the United States and looked there for support.)

Keynes apparently saw Baldwin on 30 May. According to Baldwin's biographers Keynes asked for an interview with the new prime minister, saying:

I have something I want badly to ask you. I have had certain communications with Germany in the last few days. They may be going to do something not very helpful, yet might be influenced into more fruitful paths.[2]

The day Keynes saw Baldwin was the Wednesday before the Thursday or Friday that he planned to visit Hamburg. Neither Keynes nor Baldwin kept notes of this interview; indeed Keynes's meeting with the prime minister on the 30th is not recorded in his engagements book, although an appointment with McKenna for the same day is noted.

[2] Middlemas and Barnes, *Baldwin: A Biography* (London, 1969), pp. 180–1.

Keynes's engagements book notes only appointments in Cambridge for the weekend of 2 June—but in fact he was in Berlin from Friday evening to Monday morning, 1–4 June. On the morning of 4 June Melchior dictated an account for his diary which tells the full story.

In this account Melchior told how at Cuno's request he had travelled to Berlin the morning of 31 May and breakfasted with the Chancellor and Foreign Minister von Rosenberg. He was asked by them to review the German Foreign Office draft for the new reply and to prepare a counter-proposal of his own, which he did.

Keynes arrived in Berlin the evening of 1 June (Friday). He told Melchior that he had been sent by nobody and had travelled to Berlin rather than to Hamburg on his own initiative. However, before his departure from London he had talked with Baldwin for an hour and had dined with McKenna, the designated Chancellor of the Exchequer (who was convalescing from paratyphoid), and had discussed the matter of the German reply thoroughly.

According to Keynes, Baldwin and McKenna had a realistic picture of the possible size of German reparations. McKenna was even more sceptical than Keynes and had arrived at lower figures. On the other hand British Foreign Office officials had advised Lord Curzon that 50 billion gold marks was the appropriate amount. Keynes explained that reparations, originally the domain of the Treasury, had been transferred to the Foreign Office under Bonar Law. The responsibility was to be shifted back to the Treasury, but this would be gradual on account of Baldwin's personal consideration for Curzon, who had hoped to succeed Bonar Law as prime minister. It must be expected that there would be resistance from Curzon and the Foreign Office to a reasonable settlement.

Baldwin and McKenna thought that Germany should not put too much emphasis on an international court of arbitration because France would never agree to it. Stress on this might cause the French to ask that the matter be brought before the League of Nations (a move which Cecil would enthusiastically support) and, as one knew from the League's ineffectual handling of the Saar and Upper Silesia issues, such an outcome would probably be utterly disastrous for Germany. Many Englishmen believed that the French had bribed members of the League of Nations Council; England was not in a position to do the same in the German interest.

In Melchior's version of the German Foreign Office proposal he had departed from the original by beginning and ending with a request for oral negotiations. Feeling that he and Keynes were broadly agreed in their approach, he telephoned Cuno and asked whether he had any reservations if Melchior were to show his draft to Keynes. Cuno agreed to his doing so. Melchior and Keynes discussed the draft that same night (1 June) and Keynes suggested some changes.

On the morning of 2 June (Saturday) Cuno and Rosenberg had a detailed private discussion with Keynes; Melchior joined them towards the latter part of it when they took up the question of how to deal with the memorandum. After reading Melchior's draft Rosenberg had prepared a further one of his own in which he gave particular figures on annuities. Keynes and Melchior opposed the citation of figures on the grounds that they would be rejected out of hand by the French. It was decided to prepare a new draft taking into account Keynes's suggestions. This was done that afternoon.

On Saturday evening Keynes, Melchior and Rosenberg were the dinner guests of Cuno. The new draft of the afternoon was discussed and approved and Keynes made an English translation of it. On Sunday (3 June) Cuno, Keynes and Melchior had tea at Rosenberg's residence and made further small changes in the approved draft and its translation.

The German Cabinet was in a very difficult position regarding internal politics, Melchior related; both the Social Democrats and the majority of the Centre party, on whose support they depended, were demanding an offer with concrete figures—a point of view that Rosenberg shared. The view advanced by Melchior in his counter-proposal, reinforced by Keynes, that no detailed figures should be given, received support from an unexpected quarter. During Cuno's dinner party Saturday evening a secretary from the German embassy in London arrived with a draft proposal, put forward by some English businessmen associated with McKenna, which had been submitted to the ambassador, Herr Sthamer. Sthamer, as his courier reported, thought the English draft to be completely wrong and felt those responsible for it were without influence; he believed that only the Foreign Office, which stood for the Bonar Law plan, was important.

Although, as Melchior related, even Rosenberg became convinced that the memorandum in its present form was right, they were all aware that success was improbable. Keynes returned to London the morning of 4 June—'without doubt to prepare public opinion, especially at *The Times*'. The Germans emphasised to Keynes that if the English reaction was unfriendly the parties that had demanded a concrete offer would sweep the Cuno Cabinet away. If this happened they feared more radical elements would take over, with an outbreak of Communist disturbances and eventual civil war.

'I believe that Keynes convinced himself of the seriousness of the situation,' Melchior said, and I can only hope that he will exercise a good influence with the Press as well as with Bonar Law and McKenna.

He stressed...the result feared by us...was the very aim of the French. The big question was whether England would now find sufficient strength to counter these consequences and this would ultimately depend on the fibre of Baldwin's character and on his decision to act quickly. He [Keynes] could only say that he was hopeful, but that it was also possible that Baldwin would still remain passive for some time partly for the personal reasons vis à vis Curzon...The best that could be attained at present would be that Baldwin and McKenna would make some favourable remarks about the German Note and that the British Cabinet would then contact the other powers entitled to reparations with a view to obtaining the convening of an inter-allied conference at which England could propose a second conference which would include the participation of Germany. This would be the utmost that could be attained at present.

Tuesday, 5 June, was Keynes's fortieth birthday. Back in London, he received a telegram from Melchior: Heartiest congratulations hope next forty years will be splendid.

Typically, Keynes's trip to Germany provided extra grist to his mill; the financial information he had gathered furnished the material for his next 'Finance and Investment' column in the *Nation*.

From The Nation and Athenaeum, *9 June 1923*

THE SITUATION IN GERMANY

The German mark is worth less than the Polish mark, less than the Austrian crown. Nothing but the rouble now remains to be overtaken. The fresh collapse of the mark is a symptom of the progressive deterioration of Germany's economic position. Nevertheless, the adjustment between internal prices and external exchanges is now so rapid that the practical importance of the movement may be over-estimated. The exchange value of the mark is a phenomenon so much more definite, so much more intelligible than the vague and complicated shapes of the German problem as a whole, that we are tempted to substitute for the latter this shorthand symbol, so obligingly offered us in one word every morning. In truth the depreciation of the mark, resulting from actual and prospective inflation, is best looked on as a tax on the use of money levied by the government each day from a public still willing to pay it for the sake of the convenience of employing money in daily life instead of barter. Debts expressed in terms of money have long ceased to be of any importance; wages and prices are adjusted rapidly; and people in Germany now hold such small quantities of cash in the form of marks that the injury inflicted on individuals, even by a big collapse, is not so considerable as might be supposed. Even a well-to-do person will not hold more than a few pounds worth of marks. This turnover tax on money is inevitably unjust, because money is used for contracts and as a store of value, as well as a medium of exchange. But by now German economic life has so adjusted itself as to reduce to a minimum the injustice and inconvenience of the system. At the same time, this tax is the only one in present circumstances which the government can levy and collect fast enough to meet its needs.

Index numbers of prices are now calculated in Germany not every month, but every week. The result is remarkable. The general index number of prices (including 115 articles, of which only 14 are purely articles of import) has been as follows:

1923	Prices	Dollar exchange
January	2,997	4,279
February	7,040	6,647
March	6,378	5,070
April	6,554	5,823
May 1	7,790	7,548
8	8,424	8,653
15	9,153	10,000
22	10,771	13,274
29	12,195	14,285

The extraordinary rapidity of adjustment during May can only be explained by the fact that almost everyone in Germany now thinks and calculates in terms of the dollar exchange.

At the beginning of this week the note circulation of the Reichsbank was about 7,587 thousand million marks, and the exchange was 350,000 to the £ sterling. Thus the gold value of the entire circulation was only a little more than £20 million, which illustrates from another angle the small quantities of cash with which Germany can now get along. The government can probably pay its way with weekly receipts from inflation not exceeding £1 million a week or a tax of (say) 5 per cent on the present circulation, on the average of one week with another. Nearly 1 per cent a day! It is a strong inducement to economise the conveniences of cash. But it is not prohibitive. Suppose one carries, on the average, notes to the value of £1 in one's pocket-book (the average German carries much less); it is well worth while to pay twopence a day (this being the amount by which the £1 depreciates while it is in one's pocket) for the convenience of not having to barter with cabdrivers and shopkeepers.

Like the government, the other banks are constantly increasing the volume of their loans from the Reichsbank, being not at all deterred by the bank rate of 18 per cent, which is far below the rate at which they are able to lend the money out again to their customers. Obviously, the position is very unstable. No one will be content to pay the rates of interest now current unless he feels the utmost confidence that he will be able to repay the loan in a currency worth much less than that in which he is borrowing it. The present discounting of future possibilities may prove justified by events, as it has done hitherto. Nevertheless, the actual situation does indicate a heavy discounting of things which have not happened yet, and the present technical conditions would favour a quick rebound in the event of any favourable development.

By far the worst feature of the situation is the tendency

towards unemployment, which, after sinking almost to zero in the middle of last year, has now risen to a high figure, 5·7 per cent of trade union members being unemployed in March, and probably about the same now. The financial risks and difficulties of importing raw materials are leading to Germany's using up her small accumulations of commodities such as copper, cotton, jute, and the like, without sufficiently replacing them, which may mean yet further unemployment at a later date.

The extent to which production and employment are maintained in the Ruhr area itself in face of the blockade of exports and imports is noteworthy. Industrially, however, the Ruhr is an unusually self-contained area. One way and another it can use and work up a large proportion of its own output of raw products. But the fact that the plant has been overstrained and starved of normal repairs and renewals ever since 1914 is also an important feature of the situation. Much labour is now being employed in the repair and improvement of the Ruhr's own manufacturing plant.

In spite of increasing unemployment, the collapse of the exchanges, and the blockade of the most important industrial area, the experience of the war demonstrates the mistake which France makes in thinking that she can bring about Germany's capitulation by economic pressure of this kind. Great economic distress can be caused. But so long as most of Germany remains open to foreign markets Germany's economic situation will remain, at the worst, a good deal better than what she was able to endure for a long period during the war. As we pointed out recently, her harvest prospects are better than last year; she can buy essential requirements from abroad; and her reserves of foreign resources, whilst far smaller than is sometimes alleged, are appreciable, and have not yet been seriously drawn upon. Germany cannot be starved out. Provided, therefore, that Germany remains courageous and united in the exercise of this unprecedented weapon of passive resistance, a long time may elapse before this resistance can be broken down by purely economic causes.

Germany's Note of 7 June was conciliatory, reiterating her willingness to submit the questions of her capacity to pay and the amount and method of payment to an impartial international body. If large-scale loans should prove impracticable, she was ready to substitute a scheme of annuities, offering as guarantees the railways, a mortgage on the entire industry of the country and certain customs duties. 'In a matter so vast and complicated', the Note concluded, 'real progress cannot be made by the exchange of written documents, but can only be achieved by word of mouth at the conference table.'

Keynes remarked anonymously in 'Events of the Week':

From The Nation and Athenaeum, *16 June 1923*

The new German Note has been received by the British Press with a remarkable unanimity of quiet approval. A year ago it would have seemed incredible that *The Times*, the *Manchester Guardian*, the *Spectator* and the *New Statesman* should strike the same note on the European situation. Everyone agrees that, if our interest is in the economic problem of reparations, the Note offers as fair a basis of negotiation as we can expect. The method of ultimatums has been pursued for four years, mainly because the Allies' terms have been such that no one, least of all their authors, thought them fit for rational discussion. The general feeling that the time is now approaching for a conference at which Germany will be present is a natural accompaniment of the desire to return to reason. Future progress depends, not on anything that Germany can do, but on Mr Baldwin's success in handling France. It is a moment when 'diplomacy' has vast powers for good or for evil.

The Note is important for its tone and method of approach, rather than for what it adds to its predecessor. Lord Curzon's good advice to avoid irrelevant and controversial issues has

165

been followed, with the result that it is no longer possible to ignore the substance of the German offer by dwelling on side-issues and faults of manner and expression. The principal novelty is the development of the so-called 'guarantees' —the railways, the real estate, and the customs and excise of Germany. These having taken the place of the international loan as the fashionable trimmings of settlement, Germany has, quite properly, fallen in with Lord Curzon's hint to develop them. But, in truth, they are not, and cannot be, of much value. No one doubts that Germany can secure gross receipts in paper marks, which is all that these 'guarantees' can ensure. They do not touch the real difficulty as to how such receipts are to be converted into the equivalent of gold marks outside Germany.

A third paragraph which followed—on the attitudes of Italy, Belgium, and in particular France—was contributed by another writer.

Keynes reserved the space of the unsigned leading article of this issue for his considered thoughts on what the British attitude should be. He urged Baldwin to make a firm statement in favour of a settlement along the lines of the German offer and to put forward a scheme that would be acceptably generous to France. This was also the theme of an address that he made to the Royal Institute of International Affairs on 12 June.

From The Nation and Athenaeum, *16 June 1923*

THE DIPLOMACY OF REPARATIONS

The new German Note affords as fair a basis for the settlement of the *economic* problem of reparations as it is within the power of any German government to give. This is universally admitted by British public opinion. For the first time a stage has been reached at which the choice between alternative policies is *clear*. We cannot dissociate ourselves from the affairs of the Continent and the working out of the Treaty of Versailles, as the Americans have done. We must either seek a conference with Germany and throw in our influence on the side of a business settlement; or take our stand with France.

What does France want? M. Poincaré's declared policy is to bring about the capitulation of Germany and the signature by the German government of a blank cheque which has no relation (to quote a semi-official French statement) to 'Germany's so-called capacity of payment'—a repetition, that is to say, of the Treaty of Versailles. Since Germany has already signed such a document, a second signature would not advance matters. Indeed, as a method of getting paid, M. Poincaré's policy is so unreasonable, that he can only be supposed to aim at its political results.

We must examine, therefore, the fruits of the French plan. Neither the government of Dr Cuno, nor any other responsible government representing a majority *bloc* of the Reichstag, can concede the French terms. But the prestige of Dr Cuno's administration is not impregnable; the economic situation of Germany is bad; and the psychological situation very bad. If the French persevere with their pressure, and if Germany receives no encouragement from other quarters, the collapse of the present régime can be brought about in time. In this event the French terms would be subscribed by a government of Communists and Social Democrats of the extreme left—though not, of course, with the intention of paying. The Allies have the choice of payment from Dr Cuno or a signature from the Communists *à la Russe*. The advent to the Wilhelmstrasse of a government of the extreme left would yield a paper victory for France and a paper promise from Germany. It would probably be accompanied by disorder in many parts of Germany. But the consequences would not end there. The most lasting effect would be found in a weakening of the authority of the central government, and perhaps its complete disintegration. Berlin might sign; but, if so, the rest of the country would repudiate Berlin's authority. Berlin is weak already, and the tendency towards local independence is strong. We should see, therefore—in what precise form one cannot predict—a weakening of the federal structure and a practical autonomy amongst the States; one government in Bavaria, another in Saxony, a third in East Prussia; with the Rhinelands, and even the Ruhr, a province of the French Empire—until a new Bismarck arose and a new war. Reparations would be at an end, except in so far as France could exploit her new territory, or levy a tribute from the more accessible of the other States by recurrent threats of rapine, as the Goths did in the fifth century from the provinces of Rome. This, however, would be a secondary and disappearing feature of the new settlement. The main fact would be the devertebration of the German Reich, and the establishment by France of a military empire in Europe beyond challenge by any visible forces. France would have achieved what Germany was broken in attempting.

Such a project is capable of achievement. M. Poincaré may be deliberately pursuing it. In the light of history it is not improbable. Indeed, it is the old story. We are too much inclined in England to discredit the reality of aims which are not ours. We could not believe before the war that Germany was as stupidly bad as she told us she was; and now, ten years later, we cannot believe that France is as stupidly bad as M. Poincaré tells us she is.

Probably France as a whole is not what M. Poincaré makes her out. In a sense no country ever has a fixed policy. People's heads are not clear; some want one thing and some another; and everybody is susceptible to atmosphere and to the progress of events. But a point has been reached when we must be prepared to face the possibility of a European policy on the part of the French government directly opposed to ours, and must consider what action we can take in such an event.

The break-up of the Reich is no part of the policy of Great Britain. Politically, socially, and economically such a *dénouement* is dangerous to our interests. But we object for deeper reasons. Englishmen are very sincere in certain idealisms which they have cherished since the awfulness of war broke on them. We are not cynical enough to give them up without an upheaval of emotions which have more depth and disinterestedness than other countries may suspect.

Mr Baldwin's government will have, therefore, the support of the great majority of Englishmen if they re-enter the European arena with the determination to promote a settlement along the lines offered by Germany. If they have not the courage or the resource to do so, the opposition parties in this country must fight a great political battle to bring into office a government which has. In the meantime, we have reason to credit Mr Baldwin with good intentions. This being assumed, what can he do?

The first step is not difficult. He can state England's policy in plain language. He can say that, so far as we are concerned, Germany's Note offers an acceptable basis of negotiation, and that we concur with her in thinking that the time has come for oral discussion. We must not act without first endeavouring to secure joint action with our former Allies. But we do not need to wait for this before stating our policy. M. Poincaré has no delicacy in such matters; nor should we have. Open speech is required, both to stabilise the precarious position in Germany pending developments, and to indicate to France that the period of our quiescence is at an end. France will endeavour to prevent Mr Baldwin from speaking out by hinting that this will only make subsequent conversations more difficult. Let him not be taken in by this old diplomatic trick. A bold word now will make his future negotiations easier.

The next step is to secure the support of those who fundamentally agree with us, namely, Belgium and Italy. Neither of these countries has the slightest motive for wishing to sacrifice the actual receipt of reparation money to French political aims. To gain this support should, therefore, be within the compass of prudent diplomacy. Once this support is secured, France finds herself in a minority on the Reparation Commission. We shall do well, in this case, to follow M. Poincaré's example of acting on our juridical rights. Earlier conferences were rendered sterile by a polite convention that all decisions must be unanimous. M. Poincaré broke this convention and voted us down. We must be prepared, if we can, to do the same to him.

Whilst we take measures to augment our diplomatic strength, we must simultaneously woo France and be prepared to act by her with generosity in return for concessions to our point of view. But it is useless to speak her fair, unless at the same time we indicate what our course will be if she does not receive us fair. We have abundant evidence by now that to make free concessions to France does not mollify her in the least and only stiffens her presumption.

The means of pressure and inducement at our command are not very great. Nevertheless, there is scope for diplomacy. France's aims are not one and immovable, but many and subject to change. And whilst there is no visible force in Europe able to stand up to her, her strength will be steadily sapped by those invisible forces which ultimately destroy all seekers after the excessive.

Keynes seems habitually to have kept the envelopes of letters that he received from important people. He kept a plain envelope with only the name 'J. M. Keynes' in handwriting on it, presumably delivered by a personal messenger. It is marked 'from Cuno' in blue pencil in Keynes's own writing. The letter contained is handwritten.

No copy of Keynes's 'kind message 16 of June' remains, unless it was an advance proof of the foregoing article. Cuno's 'poor' English for which he apologised has not been altered; it has its own eloquence.

From W. CUNO, *16 June 1923*

My dear Mr Keynes,

I thank you so much for your kind message 16 of June and all the support you gave our memorandum. You were very successful indeed. I do whatever I can to keep the German people quiet in those very important days. That was one of the reasons that I made the trip to the western part of our country. The second reason was to get informations about the real situation. I was astonished how strong—in spite of all troubles they have—the people in the occupied countries is in the attitude to continue the passive resistance.

Especially the workmen declared, they are sticking to the passive resistance even if the German government were to ask for stopping it, before a solution of reparation and occupation has been found. You only can understand this attitude if you will realise the pressure laid upon the people by French troops, growing from day to day. I don't consider it as a clever move by Mr P. to strengthen the ag[g]ressive and hostile acts exactly during a time when the German government made the second step to clarify the complicated situation. The only reason may be to make the people breaking down before your government succeeded in opening the way for negotiations. I don't think he will succeed in trying it, but on the other hand you know our very difficult situation and therefore it is of the utmost importance that your government will not permit the French government to ask us for conditions which we are not able to accept. You know I am ready to do whatever I can to bring the problem to a *fair* solution but I never can accept conditions which I cannot fulfil, even if I would have to resign and to leave my place to anybody else, who may be willing to promise but never would be able to meet those conditions.

Excuse my poor English and the hurry I am writing.

With best regards
yours sincerely
W. CUNO

Chapter 4

THE RUHR IMPASSE,
JUNE–OCTOBER 1923

The new German Note was welcomed by *The Times* in a leading article (11 June 1923) as the first time that the German government had made proposals for payment which could be regarded as a real basis for further negotiations. Readers were reminded incidentally that there had been a time when the French government was not alone in expecting large reparations: 'It was Mr Lloyd George who first demanded these huge amounts.' Lloyd George protested against this remark in a letter to the editor published 13 June 1923. Keynes's comment on Lloyd George's reaction was printed the day following.

To the Editor of The Times, *14 June 1923*

Sir,

Mr Lloyd George's letter, published by you today, is probably concerned with the future rather than the past. It tells us more about what Mr Lloyd George is going to say than about what he has said. From this point of view one can only welcome it and applaud. But as a contribution to history it is subject to correction.

Mr Lloyd George writes that £2,500 million (present value) is the only figure he has ever been responsible for demanding from Germany. He forgets the following (let alone the general election of 1918)—

(1) In January 1921 he presented a Note to Germany demanding a series of annuities, the present value of which at 6 per cent was about £3,500 million *plus* 12 per cent of the value of Germany's exports for forty-two years. The present value of the last item cannot be exactly calculated, but it certainly brought up the total to £4,000 million. On 7 March 1921 Mr Lloyd George delivered an ultimatum to Germany

with his own voice demanding this sum, and threatening, failing acceptance, the invasion of her territory, which actually took place a few days later.

Mr Lloyd George reconciles this transaction with his present view by—

(a) using as his basis a German calculation which he described at the time as 'an offence and an exasperation';

(b) making a mistake in arithmetic; and

(c) forgetting the export proportion.

(2) In April 1921 Germany, through the United States government, offered the Allies £2,500 million (present value), the exact figure which, according to Mr Lloyd George's present view, the Allies had just demanded and were just going to demand. Nevertheless, this offer was treated as derisory and rejected without discussion.

(3) In May 1921 Mr Lloyd George presented an ultimatum to Germany demanding a fixed annuity of £100 million *plus* 26 per cent of Germany's exports, these payments to continue until the Reparation Commission's assessment of £6,600 million had been discharged. The present value depended on the volume of Germany's exports and came to some figure between (say) £3,300 million and £4,500 million, according to the assumption made. Failing acceptance of this by Germany, Mr Lloyd George threatened the occupation of the Ruhr. Mr Lloyd George now writes that this demand was exactly equal in present value to the German offer of the previous month —namely, £2,500 million. This is not what he said at the time. I have no idea how he reaches it.

I am, etc.,

J. M. KEYNES

The Times printed a second letter from Lloyd George on 15 June, in which he quoted from a speech that he made in 1918 as proof of his moderate attitude towards Germany then. The Times remarked editorially that there was 'indeed, no conceivable view of the reparations settlement which could not at one time or another be justified by his enthusiastic support'. This provoked a third letter from Lloyd George, published on 18 June, justifying himself by reference to Keynes's letter. He estimated the capital value of the German annuities proposed in January 1921 'at about £3,000 million.

> Mr Keynes says that if you calculate them on a 6 per cent basis for interest and sinking fund (a rather low percentage for such a security), even then they only come to £4,000 million. No 'incalculable sums' here.

Keynes protested in a letter written the same day:

To the Editor of The Times, *19 June 1923*

Sir,

I did not say that the present value of what Mr Lloyd George demanded from Germany in 1921 'only came to £4,000 million'. I said that it *certainly* reached that figure, making a minimum allowance for the 'incalculable' item. *Probably* it much overpassed this sum. Nor did I take '6 per cent for interest and sinking fund'; I took 6 per cent for interest alone.

But it is no good to complain about Mr Lloyd George's inadvertently twisting one's figures a little to make the best of a bad job. His main point—namely, that he never at any time really believed in vast reparations, does not surprise some of us and need not be disputed. Whether it is a suitable subject for him to boast about is another matter.

Yours faithfully,

J. M. KEYNES

A correspondent 'B' quoted M. Loucheur on Lloyd George's figures; the exchange tailed off with Lloyd George denying, 'whether M. Loucheur said so or not', that he had ever said any such thing.

This exchange between Lloyd George and *The Times* in June 1923 is an indication of how the British public attitude towards Germany had changed. Each party to the dispute took it for granted that he ranged himself on the side of moderation, in a position neither would have taken a few years earlier. Keynes celebrated *The Times's* new stand in 'Life and Politics', a column of editorial comment, following it with an anonymous dig at Lloyd George.

THE RUHR IMPASSE, 1923

From The Nation and Athenaeum, *16 June 1923*

The Times has published a series of leading articles on the German Note and on British relations to France which have been models of what a *Times* leader should be, now that the great paper has returned to its role of expressing with dignity and moderation the prevailing opinion of the governing circles of the country. How wonderful a relief to read the truth again in daily print!

The French public have, to our mind, an almost fantastic notion of what Germany can pay now and in the next few years. They seem to hold the view that they, a victorious nation, cannot pay a pound of their debts to us or a dollar to the United States; yet they are convinced that Germany, who is utterly defeated, can pay almost incalculable sums. There was a time when they were not alone in their error. It was Mr Lloyd George who first demanded these huge amounts; who insisted, against the terms of the Armistice, on the inclusion of pensions in the bill; who left to the French government, with their vast devastated areas before their eyes and with priority refused to them, no option but to make claims even more extravagant than at one time were our own—*The Times*, 11 June 1923.

Magna est Veritas et praevalebit!

The response which this leader in the 'Times' drew from Mr Lloyd George well illustrates the reasons which so many people feel for hesitating to co-operate with him. If Mr Lloyd George had admitted that he had changed his mind about reparations, everyone would have respected the admission. But the preposterous statement that he had *never* been responsible for demanding from Germany more than £2,500 million can only lower him in the public view. Apart from the ultimatums of 1921, which demanded much larger sums, the American representatives at the Peace Conference have narrated that the lowest figure he would then contemplate was double the above sum.

As the subject of his 'Finance and Investment' column in the same issue of the *Nation* Keynes took the happy outcome of the Austrian settlement.

From The Nation and Athenaeum, *16 June 1923*

THE AUSTRIAN LOAN AND REPARATIONS IN SOUTH-EASTERN EUROPE

The new Austrian loan has been an interesting experiment in international reconstruction. At last, after prolonged and complicated negotiations, Austria's liability to pay reparation has been suspended, her exchange has been stabilised, the leading powers of Europe have joined in guaranteeing a considerable loan under the auspices of the League of Nations, and she is now put on her legs again with financial resources, subject to the control of a commissioner-general appointed by the League, which will last long enough to give a real opportunity of reconstructing her economic life. The story of her emergence from a state of complete ruin is unique, and shows what can be done by goodwill when political and racial animosities do not interfere. The credit for this happy result must be shared amongst many, particularly the past and present financial controllers of the British Treasury (Sir Basil Blackett and Mr [Otto] Niemeyer), Mr Montagu Norman (the Governor of the Bank of England), Sir Henry Strakosch (lately chairman of the financial committee of the League of Nations), and Sir Arthur Salter, also of the League of Nations. But no one has better reason to feel proud and to rejoice than Sir William Goode, who, although he has been in Hungary during the last phase engaged on similar duties, has been Austria's bravest friend through everything and saved Vienna from disaster in her darkest days.

The restoration of Austria is by far the biggest piece of constructive work accomplished hitherto by the League of Nations. Perhaps it indicates that, for the present, the best scope for the League is likely to be found in fields which are not the subject of acute controversy between the major powers, but where, in the absence of the League, the necessary organisation and enthusiasm for constructive work would have been lacking.

The actual terms of the loan are interesting—6 per cent bonds issued at 80 (thus giving a flat interest yield of 7½ per cent), redeemable by 1943 by means of drawings or purchase. The average life of the bonds will be thirteen years, so that the total yield, including profit on redemption, is £8 12s 3d per cent. The service of the loan is to be charged on the customs duties and tobacco monopoly of the Austrian State, and is further guaranteed by the following powers in the proportions stated: Great Britain, 24½ per cent; France, 24½ per cent; Italy, 20½ per cent; Czechoslovakia, 24½ per cent; Belgium, 2 per cent; Sweden, 2 per cent; Denmark, 1 per cent; Holland, 1 per cent. Bonds for $25 million have been floated simultaneously in New York by Messrs Pierpont Morgan; and bonds for Kr. 11 million (issued at 98, carrying 6½ per cent interest) in Sweden. Spain and Switzerland are also to give assistance in some other form.

Bonds may be issued altogether up to about £29 million. The English investor has been asked to subscribe an amount of them which will cost about £9 million in cash. Thus the amounts involved are substantial. Yet the public have eagerly come forward with a heavy over-subscription. If we average the credit of the guarantors, the terms of issue seem about right. In effect, Austria has been enabled by the guarantee to borrow on about the same terms as those which Czechoslovakia was able to get on her own credit.

The satisfactory issue of the Austrian business emphasises the extreme harshness with which Hungary is being treated. A few weeks ago it seemed as if a suspension of reparation liabilities might be allowed to Hungary also, as a prelude to the reconstruction of her finances and the flotation of a loan.

The committee of the Reparation Commission for Hungary consists of representatives of Great Britain, France, Italy, and Jugoslavia. Great Britain and Italy proposed and supported a constructive scheme; France and Jugoslavia opposed it. And the committee being thus divided, the French chairman proceeded to use his casting vote in favour of pushing back Hungary into misery and confusion. This is in some ways the least excusable, because the most wanton, instance of the French policy of promoting ruin in the interests of political combinations.

Turkey having taken matters into her own hands, there only remains Bulgaria (apart from Germany) with a reparation problem to settle. Bulgarian reparations were fixed originally at £90 million. This has now been reduced to the comparatively moderate figure of £22 million, with payments secured on the customs spread over sixty years, the instalment for 1923 being £200,000. On 6 June the Sobranye ratified the settlement in the face of opposition based on the ground that Bulgaria was signing away her independence. On 9 June came a revolution, and within three days the Cabinet which ratified was in prison. The attitude of the new government to the settlement remains to be seen.

Was ever a greater curse than this invented in the name of justice?—this doctrine that it is positively our moral duty to ruin ourselves and our vanquished neighbours together, in an attempt to extract from them an enslaving tribute for a period of generations. One wonders sometimes why Socialists have not seized on the whole conception as the crowning crime of capitalism! Never before in history have the greediest conquerors or the most austere crusaders conceived such penalties and such shackles as we modern industrial nations have sought to fix, by a ghastly perversion of the notion of foreign investment, on whole peoples and unborn innocents.

Yet even a little time works miracles. It is just four years since we were bravely drafting clauses to take away her cows from starving Austria. Today we hand to her millions of money. The mild Viennese have conquered.

For a brief interlude in the summer of 1923 Keynes turned his attention to the composition of *A Tract on Monetary Reform*, the crystallisation of his major *Reconstruction in Europe* articles, which was to be published in December of the same year.

From a letter to FLORENCE A. KEYNES, *24 June 1923*

For the last week or two and for the next week or two I am doing very little for the *Nation* so as to be able to get on with my book, the scope of which, as usual, tends to grow a little under my hands. Then, after that, I sit in the Editor's chair for a fortnight while Henderson takes a holiday. I have at last got the business management side straight, by which I expect to save £1500 a year...

On 20 July he wrote, 'This week and next I am acting as Editor of the *Nation*, in addition to other occupations'—and returned to the problem of the Ruhr.

During June and the early part of July Germany's Note to the Allies remained unanswered. Communications passed between France and Britain, Poincaré insisting on the cessation of German passive resistance and adherence to the terms of Versailles, Curzon stating reservations as to the legality of the French invasion. Passive resistance was Germany's only weapon and the unoccupied part of the country was being financially drained to support the occupied area. Her economic collapse was imminent and threatened the well-being of Europe. Even the pro-French members of Baldwin's Cabinet began to feel that some decisive British action was necessary.

Editorially Keynes voiced his concern in 'Events of the Week'.

From The Nation and Athenaeum, *7 July 1923*

The situation between ourselves and France is, as we go to press, obscure but almost hopeless. Mr Baldwin, partly under the influence of certain elements in his Cabinet which do not entirely share his own sensible outlook, is straining every point in France's favour and craning his neck to detect a foothold of accommodation. If France wanted a compromise, she would certainly get it. The danger is that the present British government, terrified of a rupture, might go much too far to meet her. But reports from Paris indicate that M. Poincaré, convinced that the real divergences between French and British policy are fundamental, does not see any object in pretending that a compromise can be arranged between incompatibles. As regards his internal political situation, M. Poincaré never felt himself stronger than now. Believing that he can remain in the Ruhr until Germany sends new proposals, he has not the smallest intention of evacuating. Indeed, he considers France's situation as highly satisfactory all round. 'England', he says to his friends, 'will never follow French policy, and we will never follow hers. Therefore, we must act alone.'

Superficially, this line of thought is rational, however much madness underlies it. Indeed, M. Poincaré's frank admission of the utter unreality of the alleged *entente* between France and England is far closer to the facts than our vain clinging to the shadow of a ghost. Mr Baldwin will have to recognise that, at the present juncture, the project of winning France over to reasonable courses is vain. But what then? Europe has had no more anxious moment than now since 1918.

Writing to Keynes on 15 July, E. T. Scott of the *Manchester Guardian* feared that any salvation by the kind of international commission for which Germany asked would come too late to stay serious political and social upheaval. 'If and when the English Government is committed definitely to independent action may it not be necessary actually to assist Germany, if we can, to hold out against French pressure?' he asked. Weighing the alternative evils of widening the breach between England and France and 'the risk of having a corpse on our hands', he wrote:

The only thing that occurs to me as conceivably possible would be to help unoccupied Germany to stabilise the mark and equilibrate the budget on, I suppose, the lines of the Austrian scheme. But the conditions are obviously dissimilar and the difficulties so great that I am doubtful whether, even if the money could be raised, there would be a reasonable chance of success. On the other hand I can see nothing else that we can do if a social collapse in Germany is as imminent as is alleged. The government, I imagine, would not look at such a scheme unless it had strong expert backing, nor would it be worth while to propound it unless it were likely to be seriously considered. That is really my excuse for writing to you. I should be very grateful if you would let me know whether you think the idea merely hair-brained.

To E. T. SCOTT, *20 July 1923*

Dear Scott,

I am very much in agreement with what you say in your letter. Possibly there may be more favourable developments than you or I expect. But we certainly ought to be ready for a situation in which we have to give unoccupied Germany some definite assistance. In their present mood I do not think that the government would look at such a scheme as you suggest. But once things come to a head, if they ever do, and we have taken a decided stand, I dare say there may be some remarkable consequential changes of opinion both inside the Cabinet and outside.

As regards the technical possibility of stabilising the mark I think a great deal depends upon what under the imaginary régime the relations would be between occupied and unoccupied Germany. The principal cause of the vast inflation which is going on at this moment is to be found in the subsidies which unoccupied Germany is making to occupied Germany for the purpose of maintaining the resistance of the latter. So long as this expenditure goes on I should think that stabilisation is hopeless. If, however, it was merely a question of unoccupied Germany supporting itself without being drained by the needs of the occupied area I am personally of the opinion that a stabilisation scheme could be put into operation, particularly if there was British assistance behind it, within a remarkably short space of time.

But of course both your letter and mine are a good deal ahead of events, and heaven knows how long, at their present rate of movement, events may not take to catch up.

Yours sincerely,

[copy initialled] J.M.K.

Baldwin made a statement on 12 July summing up the British position. Both France and Britain, he said, wanted the payment of reparations and the recovered security of Europe; the difference between them was of means, not ends. The occupation of the Ruhr had not produced reparations and had endangered world economic recovery. The German Note of 7 June proposing an impartial investigation of her ability to pay could not be ignored and Britain would prepare a draft reply to it for the consideration of the Allies.

Keynes did his best to influence events. Commenting on the Prime Minister's statement in his *Nation* article of the following week, he welcomed it warily, at the same time conjuring up a dark warning.

From The Nation and Athenaeum, *21 July 1923*

MR BALDWIN'S PRELUDE

Mr Baldwin's statement may be the beginning of everything or of nothing. Is it the first bar of a completed tune? Or is he just humming to himself as he goes along, improvising note by note? Does he speak so softly at the outset for softness' sake or by reason of formidable things to come? Is it the feelings of France he seeks to spare or the feelings of his own colleagues in his own Cabinet?

It may be some time yet before we have the answer, quite for certain. Meanwhile, Mr Baldwin has, at least, surrendered nothing, and time, though it works dangerously in Germany, brings an ever-increasing weight of public opinion in Great Britain, in the United States, in Belgium, even in France underneath the concealing crust of the subsidised Paris Press, to support the voices of moderation.

Words in this case are important in a rare degree. Our task is to create psychological, not material, combinations. We have no intention in any circumstances of applying force to France. France, if she chooses, *can* ruin Europe, and *we* cannot prevent her. The inducements of friendship and generosity being, for the moment, useless, Mr Baldwin can make no progress unless he *alarms* France. His task is to alarm her without irritating her; and without bluff. He treads a delicate path, armed with the prayers of his countrymen and of prudent men everywhere, and with that simplicity which is not simplicity, granted to Englishmen from of old for the confusion of Continental logicians.

His strength lies in the facts. If France could see them clearly, she *would* be alarmed, alarmed not by us but by them. Our task is to foreshadow to her the real consequences of what she deems success. As Paris sleeps by night, we must raise forebodings to assail her mind, and spectres from the future she is creating. Her soldiers must see their forces dissipated, their exposed surface increasing, their scattered outposts victims of the guerilla; her diplomatists must anticipate an isolation gradually complete; her economists, the financial exhaustion of the government and the destruction of the *rentier* by the instrument of inflation; and her bourgeois, the annihilation beyond the Rhine of the old forms of society and the advance of new forms from the East. It is not the policy or the resources of Great Britain, but these matters, which threaten France. Our instrument for making her see them must be the force and sincerity with which we state and act upon our own prevision. This may bring us into open opposition to the government of France. But we cannot succeed in our objects unless the atmosphere we thus create serves to awaken the alarm of France, not about us, who in the last resort will remain passive, but about what is really alarming.

Whilst we alarm France, we must reassure Germany. M. Poincaré is calculating upon the early collapse of German resistance; and he may be right. He is delighted that Mr Baldwin should exhaust time in the exercises of politeness, because he hopes that meanwhile events will settle themselves in his favour. British opinion does not reckon enough with this possibility, or face with sufficient frankness the need to encourage Germany. We do not want German resistance to break down. Lord Curzon would regard the fall of Cuno's government and capitulation in the Ruhr as the worst news he could receive. The more slowly we move with France, the more necessary it is to give some slight comfort to Germany and to render a little support to the prestige of her existing régime. It is difficult to do this in a manner which is not distasteful to important sections of British opinion, and Germany must be content therefore with a few hints, gathering her comfort more from what Mr Baldwin did not say than from what he did.

It is impossible for Great Britain to be strictly neutral in the matter of the Ruhr, unless she remains passive and gives up the idea of having a policy of her own. If we oppose France in the Ruhr, we must admit that this means giving an, at least indirect, encouragement to Germany. British opinion moves from its old moorings very slowly and very reluctantly, and not at all unless the progress of events compels it. This is the tactical strength of M. Poincaré's position—he can still trade on the capital of the past, can still be outrageous with impunity by drawing on the accumulated stock of old loyalties. But if the British public become convinced beyond a doubt that he does not deserve their confidence, the balance of European politics will suffer an extraordinary change. Great Britain has never yet, since the Armistice, exercised her authority, because she has never felt sufficiently certain where her true course lay. This passivity, based on doubt rather than on weakness, has bred an illusion in France as to the weight of such authority if it is used.

The immediate danger, whilst diplomacy follows its slow

and winding course, springs from the weakness of Germany, from the deterioration of her economic life and the present mentality of her people. The economic effect of the Ruhr occupation is cumulative, and gets worse by lasting longer, mainly because of the enormous expenditure in which the support of the Ruhr industrialists and workers involves the Berlin government. Taxing by means of inflation is now almost the only serious source of revenue. They used to raise in this way the equivalent of about £1 million a week; they are now trying to raise by it nearly £3 million a week. The result is a complete breakdown of the currency, and a point may soon arrive when enough real resources cannot be raised to carry on the government and to support the Ruhr resistance, however many notes may be printed. That is to say, the Berlin government may become literally bankrupt. The inevitable difficulties of the situation are rendered worse by the facts that the financial direction at headquarters is weak and that the old-fashioned management of the Reichsbank is not equal to its new problems. The only favourable factor is the time of year—with the new harvest at hand and the season of cold still some months away.

Meanwhile, half the population is torn and divided against itself by fierce political dissensions, and the other half is apathetic. Neither the nationalists, nor the industrialists, nor the Communists, nor the makeshift compromise which governs, command the enthusiasm of generous and independent minds. The national spirit flickers, and burns nowhere with a pure flame. Disgust, disillusion, and despair have joined to weaken the sense of public spirit. The most significant feature of modern Germany is to be found in the inclination of the youth to avert their minds altogether from the political and economic problems of their country, to abandon 'Realpolitik' *in toto*, to become indifferentists to national questions, and to find elsewhere the springs of activity and enthusiasm.

M. Poincaré's confidence that German resistance can be

broken down is, therefore, not without some grounds. Naturally he is content that the diplomatic situation should develop as slowly as possible. So long as he can maintain the *status quo* without conceding anything substantial, he will doubtless do what he can to avoid an abrupt breach. He reckons that divided opinions in the Cabinet and the Tory party may cause Mr Baldwin to move so slowly that he will be too late.

A week later Keynes followed this Cassandra-like prophesying with a down-to-earth facts and figures article, its title echoing 'Is a Settlement of the Reparation Question Possible Now?' (p. 32) in the *Reconstruction* supplements. (Ten months' passage of time resigned him to the loss of the immediate adverb.)

From The Nation and Athenaeum, *28 July 1923*

IS A SETTLEMENT OF REPARATIONS POSSIBLE?

The negotiations between the governments of France and Great Britain, serious though they are in their possible consequences, are in the nature of preliminary sparrings. They are concerned, not with the settlement itself, but with the conditions prior to its discussion.

Whilst we are awaiting the issue of these preliminaries, it may be worth while to consider whether the elements for a settlement exist, provided the parties can be brought together to discuss it.

Germany's most recent offers mention a figure of 30 milliard gold marks (£1,500 million). Mr Bonar Law's proposal of last January was for 50 milliards *plus* a further problematical 17 milliards in the event of an arbitral tribunal deciding ten years hence that Germany can stand it. If an expert commission is summoned to reassess Germany's capacity, it will not be able to collect any material amount of relevant evidence which is not already available. It will probably aim, therefore, at hitting the mean of the best-informed 'moderate' opinions already current, which in fact range from

Germany's own figure of 30 milliards up to Mr Bonar Law's of 50 milliards. If the experts decide to fix a final, definitive figure, it will probably be 50 milliards at either 5 or 6 per cent. Possibly they may think it better to follow Mr Bonar Law's plan of two, or rather of three, stages—first a moratorium, lasting from two to four years; then the interest on 40 milliards (splitting, as arbitrators always do, the difference between 30 and 50); then, ten years hence, the interest on a further 10–20 milliards if an arbitral tribunal thinks it can be done when the time comes. From the point of view of the immediate burden on Germany, it makes a good deal of difference whether the annual payments are at 5 per cent without a sinking fund or at 6 per cent including a sinking fund. The extreme limits of the burden of such a decision would be, therefore, a minimum of £100 million per annum (40 milliards at 5 per cent) and a maximum of £180 million (60 milliards at 6 per cent).

Whether Germany could in fact pay such sums, is doubtful. I believe myself that even the smaller of the above figures will prove to exceed her capacity, unless she is allowed a longer period of recuperation than is likely. But the answer to this question, which only time can give for certain, is not of the same immediate importance as the question whether the elements exist for an agreed settlement now.

Subject to certain conditions to be mentioned below, I feel confident that Germany, whilst she will not pledge herself of her own motion to pay more than the 30 milliards she has already offered, would submit to judgment on the above lines at the hands of a body which, in the eyes of the world, could fairly claim to be independent and expert.

Would it satisfy the Allies? At the present time the minimum demand of France is 26 milliards *and* the cancellation of her inter-allied debts. Belgium demands 4 to 5 milliards in addition to the substantial sum she has already received in priority to the other Allies. Great Britain is assumed to demand the equivalent in annual value of what she owes to America, say 12 milliards. Probably 5 milliards would satisfy Italy, if her Allied debts were forgiven. 4–5 milliards would meet the claims of the minor Allies.

It appears, therefore, that 50 milliards *plus* cancellation of Allied debts would satisfy everyone. The above demands are so near to the Spa percentages (France's is avowedly based on them), that it would save quarrelling to stick to them exactly, which would lead to the following division:

British Empire	11	milliards	(£550 million)
France	26		(£1,300 million)
Italy	5		(£250 million)
Belgium	4		(£200 million)
Other Allies	4		(£200 million)

Thus

(1) a reduction of the German liability to 50 milliard gold marks,

(2) the division of this sum according to the Spa percentages, and

(3) a cancellation of inter-allied debt,

provide the outlines of a settlement which ought to satisfy all the Allies.

Probably the most business-like procedure would be to agree to this general scheme right off, and to refer to an arbitral tribunal, not the assessment of the capital total of the German liability, which for political reasons it may be convenient to fix at 50 milliards, even though this exceeds her probable capacity to pay—but the date at which Germany must begin to pay interest on this sum, and the question of allowing her temporary abatements in accordance with her developing capacity.

Germany can accept such a settlement provided there is a tribunal, in the fairness of which she can feel confidence, charged with the duty of determining the length of the moratorium and the rate at which payments are to commence thereafter. A complete moratorium for so long a period as four years, followed by a régime of payments at a very high level, is not the best possible arrangement. A complete moratorium for two years, or even less, should be sufficient, provided the annual payments thereafter commence at a low figure and are allowed to increase gradually. These matters cannot be settled now by any tribunal, however expert. The only immediate step likely to command general approval is the fixing of 50 milliards as the figure of Germany's nominal liability. The real usefulness of an arbitral tribunal must lie in the future.

The acceptance by Germany of any scheme, however, is likely to be contingent on certain general conditions. If the Allies wish to set up in Berlin some measure of control over her finances, Germany will probably go a long way to meet such demands. But if they wish to prolong in any shape the existing extensions beyond their Treaty rights of their hold over the Ruhr and the Rhinelands, the position is changed. This is probably a matter on which no responsible government in Germany can afford to make material concessions.

In undertaking a scheme of payment which is intended on both sides to be a reality, Germany submits her people and her economic life to a crushing burden. No nation, however helpless, will undertake such a thing unless in some shape it is made worth their while. A man may agree to surrender his possessions to avoid being beaten about the head. But no man will do so if he is to be beaten about the head in any case. If the occupation is to continue, the Allies will be already doing their worst, and Germany will have no incentive towards making a great sacrifice. If her political integrity and freedom are not to be restored to her, what does she gain by undertaking to pay a sum far in excess of what resistance in the Ruhr is now costing her? When Germany begins to pay, the suffering and distress which it will cause her people will be unbearable if they are to submit, as well, to indignity, dependence, and oppression of other kinds. If Germany is to shoulder a quarter part of her burden, it will be necessary for her political and economic situation to be most favourable, and for the courage and enterprise of her people to stand high.

France has, at last, to make a final choice whether she wants an organised and courageous Germany perhaps paying a vast tribute, or whether she prefers a disorganised and weak Germany certainly paying nothing. If France is ready for the former alternative, some sort of an economic settlement would be easy to arrange on paper, as the above argument shows. But if France chooses the latter, which she may well do, not because she undervalues the tribute, but because she suspects that the tribute is impossible anyhow (that a strong Germany will not pay it and a weak Germany cannot)—then no agreed settlement is worth discussing. We must each follow our own path.

Cabinets and governments (and newspapers, too) are inevitably occupied with momentary situations. If we can abstract ourselves from such, we are forced to acknowledge that the idea of the vast, continuing tribute may prove for profound and permanent reasons, a political impossibility, even if it is not also an economic impossibility; and that British policy, even in its present form, moderate and plausible though it appears, is still remote from certain essential facts, which M. Poincaré may have dimly grasped. The material difference between us and him lies much more in our different conceptions of the future polity of Europe and of international relationships generally, than in his expecting more cash than we do from reparations.

In the same issue of the *Nation* under 'Events of the Week' Keynes drew attention to the increasing depreciation of the mark and took the editorial privilege of saying what he thought of the German banking establishment.

From The Nation and Athenaeum, *28 July 1923*

Meanwhile, there are increasing indications that Belgium is preparing to diverge from France, at least to the extent of sending Mr Baldwin a more encouraging reply than M. Poincaré is likely to send. In this respect delay may bear some fruits. In Germany, on the other hand, the perils of delay are rapidly increasing. The *rate* of depreciation of the mark is a more important indication than its absolute depreciation; it is the increasing rate of depreciation which spells the decay of government. The mark is now worth only about one-tenth of what it was worth six weeks ago. Nothing like this ever happened even in Russia or in Austria at their worst. It is due mainly to the fact that the tax revenue of the German government has now sunk practically to zero (2 per cent of the expenditure in the first ten days of July), whilst resistance in the Ruhr costs them a large sum measured in real resources; and partly to the undeniable financial incompetence of Dr Hermes, the Finance Minister, and Herr Havenstein, the president of the Reichsbank. As a result, the government is all but bankrupt. An ever-growing proportion of the population is abandoning moderation and allying itself to the extremists either of the left or of the right. Food riots in Breslau and the savage mob murder of the public prosecutor of Frankfurt must unhappily be accepted as indications of what will occur on a large scale if Mr Baldwin allows M. Poincaré to entrap him for much longer in empty and insincere conversations.

This paragraph was preceded by a comment by another writer on Poincaré's two most recent weekend pronouncements against British policy. In the 'Life and Politics' column of the same date Keynes encouraged Lloyd George, who had spoken out in the House of Commons against the latest of these rural 'Sunday sermons'.

From The Nation and Athenaeum, *28 July 1923*

It is very refreshing to hear Mr Lloyd George his natural self again—not explaining away the past, but letting fly with good, strong, heartfelt invective against M. Poincaré. 'There were many incidents and episodes which discouraged. There was M. Poincaré. He wished M. Poincaré would not make speeches on a Sunday. (Laughter.) It was a day sacred to good-will, and hardly the day to unscrew cylinders of carefully distilled hatred, ill-will, suspicion, and anger among the nations. (Cheers; and, one can almost hear from the back, "That's the stuff to give him.")' That *is* the stuff to give him, and Mr Lloyd George will regain the ear of the country if he can voice feelings which are growing very passionate, and which the proprieties of members of the Cabinet will never satisfy.

In the next week's issue the acting editor was able to insert in 'Life and Politics':

From The Nation and Athenaeum, *4 August 1923*

Mr Keynes's article in last week's *Nation and Athenaeum*, suggesting that the best immediate settlement of reparations would be to fix the nominal German debt at 50 milliards, to divide this according to the Spa percentages, and to cancel inter-allied debt, has been the subject of a leading article of qualified approval by the *Journal des Débats*, which has a semi-official position in Paris, and of wholehearted agreement by the *Popolo d'Italia*, which is the organ of Signor Mussolini in Rome. The reason for this is to be found, no doubt, mainly in Mr Keynes's unequivocal proposal to cancel debts—a proposal never yet made officially by the British Government. But the reaction to Mr Keynes's scheme in France and Italy indicates that Mr Baldwin still has one valuable inducement in hand, from which no British Prime Minister has yet attempted to get the full value—though the appropriate time for using it may have passed by for the moment. The occupation of the Ruhr, which from being a means has become an end in itself, is now the main obstacle to some sort of a provisional settlement.

A month later, when a contemporary put forward a much harder view, he took notice in the same column as follows:

From The Nation and Athenaeum, *1 September 1923*

Last Saturday the *Morning Post* published a two-column signed article (by Mr John S. Hecht) maintaining that Germany could pay reparations in goods to the value of £1,000 million a year, and claiming that this is a conclusion at which a commission of inquiry would arrive if it were composed of 'honest and intelligent men', and if 'economists and financiers' were excluded from it. The argument is that 70 million Germans can produce £80 worth of goods per head per annum, and can live comfortably on £65 worth per head per annum, whence the result. Probably not even the readers of the *Morning Post* really believe this sort of thing any longer. Yet it is not so very easy, without a little help from the 'economists and financiers', to refute it briefly and clearly. How many readers of *The Nation and the Athenaeum* feel confident that they can do so?

The text of the arrangements for the funding of the British debt to the United States was published on 9 July 1923. Various details of the agreement gave Keynes cause for reflection.

From The Nation and Athenaeum, *4 August 1923*

THE AMERICAN DEBT

A week or two ago the details of Mr Baldwin's settlement with the United States were published in full for the first time in a White Paper [Cmd. 1912]. It includes some interesting features which were not clearly noticeable in the summaries which were issued when the agreement was first made.

The total indebtedness is $4,600 million carrying interest at 3 per cent for ten years and at 3½ per cent thereafter. In addition, a portion of the capital debt, gradually increasing in accordance with a table of payments, is to be discharged each year. For example, in 1923 $138 million (3 per cent on $4,600 million) must be paid in interest and $23 million in repayment of capital, making $161 million altogether (equivalent to £35 million at the current rate of exchange of $4.59 to the £). In 1933 $152 million (3½ per cent on $4,340 million, assuming that $260 million capital has been repaid meanwhile in accordance with the schedule) must be paid in interest and $32 million in repayment of capital, making $184 million altogether. In 1950 $127 million will be payable for interest and $53 million for capital, making $180 million; and the annual total will remain round about this figure until 1984, by which time the aggregate total of the annual instalments will have mounted up to more than ten thousand million dollars.

It scarcely requires illustrations to bring home the magnitude of this burden. We shall be paying to the United States each year for sixty years a sum equivalent to two-thirds the cost of our Navy, nearly equal to the State expenditure on education, more than the total burden of our pre-war debt, more than the total profits of the whole of our mercantile marine and the whole of our mines together. With these sums we could endow and splendidly house *every month* for sixty years one university, one hospital, one institute of research, etcetera, etcetera. With an equal sacrifice over an equal period we could abolish slums and rehouse in comfort the half of our population which is now inadequately sheltered.

For these reasons, and on account also of the technical problem involved in purchasing over the exchanges $500,000 every weekday, on the average, for sixty years, we must examine with care every slight opportunity which the agreement may give for alleviating the burden. In this respect the United States Treasury has been generous, and has allowed several useful options, which may operate to our advantage in course of time. In the first place, we are entitled for five years (i.e., up to 1927) to fund half the interest due and add it to the *corpus* of the debt. Our Treasury will be well advised to take advantage of this provision, so far as is required to enable us to redeem the balance of our bonds held by the public in the United States, which carry a much higher rate of interest than 3½ per cent (our 5½ per cent bonds now stand below 102).

There is a further provision by which we can pay in any bonds of the United States, issued or to be issued subsequent to 1917, taken at par and accrued interest. Since such bonds are now obtainable round about 98, this allows us at the moment a discount of 2 per cent; and at some future time we may secure a far greater advantage than this. For the rate of interest sometimes goes up and sometimes goes down. Whenever it goes up higher than the rate current at some date when the United States was issuing bonds, such bonds will fall to a discount. Over a long period of years, there are sure to be times when this option will have a value.

The most important provision, however, if we take a long view, is that which gives us an option to pay either in United States gold coin, *or in gold bullion.* That is to say, we shall get the full advantage of any future depreciation in the value of gold, whether by the discoveries of chemists or because of the demonetisation of the metal or for any other reason. If the legal-tender dollar becomes depreciated in terms of gold, the option to pay in U.S. bonds becomes valuable. If the legal-tender dollar becomes appreciated in terms of gold (as, for example, by a closing of the U.S. mint to gold in the interests of price stability), the option to pay in gold bullion becomes valuable. Over a long course of years one or other of these

195

events is extremely likely to occur. In effect we are entitled to pay in legal-tender dollars or in gold bullion, whichever is the less valuable; and of the double option I believe myself that the right to pay in gold bullion is the one we are likely to make use of.

At all events, the result is to give us a big interest, so far as the American debt is concerned (there may be some offsets in certain contingencies, if we take our national balance sheet as a whole, in respect of sums owed by others to ourselves), in gold having as low a value as possible. If the commodity value of gold were to rise to what it was in 1914, the real burden of the American debt would be increased 50 per cent; and if it were to fall to what it was in the summer of 1920, the real burden would be decreased nearly 50 per cent. There has been no attempt whatever to stabilise the value of the debt in terms of goods and services. The cheaper gold is, the less we have to pay; and vice versa.

There is no other example of international obligations on this scale, covering so long a term of years, being fixed in terms of gold bullion. The arrangement may have a considerable reaction on future currency policy. For whilst it will be in our interest for gold to fall in value, we shall certainly want to avoid the rise of sterling prices which would occur if sterling was allowed to depreciate along with gold.

Since at the present moment gold is tending to appreciate, those who favour a policy of stabilising prices are willing to allow sterling to fall, if necessary, in terms of gold. But this is, very likely, a temporary phenomenon. In the long run, gold, left to itself, may depreciate; and in this case, the policy of price stabilisation will favour a recovery of sterling to its gold parity and *even higher*. This development is much to be hoped for; for in that case price stabilisers will be able to claim 'respectability' as well as wisdom, and will be freed from the moral taint which seems to attach at present to anyone who does not object to a fall of the sterling exchange. When price stabilisation does not require a devaluation of the old standard, but even involves raising it above its old parity, many sturdy prejudices against such an innovation will disappear.

On every ground, therefore, it is a British interest (except for shareholders in gold mines) that gold should fall in value. On the other hand it is a pure delusion to suppose that to increase the value of sterling lightens the burden of the American debt. The *Daily Mail* and other critics of some views, expressed in *The Nation and Athenaeum* in recent weeks, believe that if the gold value of sterling (e.g.) is doubled, the burden of the American debt is halved. If the increased gold value of sterling is due to the diminished commodity value of gold (i.e., stable sterling prices), this result follows. But if the increased gold value of sterling is due to the increased commodity value of sterling (i.e., falling sterling prices), the result does not follow at all. *Nothing* can alleviate the burden of the American debt except a fall in the commodity value of gold; and if this occurs, it does not matter in the least, so far as this debt is concerned, whether the gold value of sterling rises or falls.

The readers of *The Nation and Athenaeum* must excuse me for bringing economics from the decent seclusion of the back page into this part of the paper. But these problems are acquiring so much importance, and are going to be the subject of so much political controversy, that they must be dragged out of academic groves into the limelight of the big world. After all, questions of currency are not a bit more difficult than the theory of free trade—indeed, with a little familiarity they will prove much easier. A hundred years ago statesmen, pushed from behind by economists, began the great fight for free trade. Another issue, hardly less important, is now ripe for the statesmen; and the public must take heed.

'Professor [*sic*] J. M. Keynes justly earned a reputation for his well-known book *The Economic Consequences of the Peace*, but Heaven only knows what has happened to him since', wrote D. M. Mason in a letter to the editor of the *Nation* published 11 August 1923. Mason, a 'sound currency' man whose views Keynes once analysed for Asquith (*JMK*, vol. XVI, pp.75-8), continued:

> On the supposition that gold may be demonetised, and the United States mint be closed to gold in the interests of price stability...he argues that it is a British interest...that gold should fall in value. Most people who have suffered...from high prices—either paper or gold—would like to see gold become more valuable, and exchange for a great amount of commodities. Then his amazing statement that 'it is a pure delusion to suppose that to increase the value of sterling lightens the burden of the American debt'. Why then trouble about the depreciation and debasing of the currency? According to Professor Keynes, let us work the printing press day and night, get down the value of the pound to a shilling, and this will lighten the burden of the American debt, stabilise prices, and ensure prosperity all round...As to his statement that if the commodity value of gold were to rise to what it was in 1914...the real burden of the American debt would be increased fifty per cent, and if it were to fall to what it was in the summer of 1920 the real burden would be decreased nearly fifty per cent, I entirely disagree. Things don't work out like that in practice.

Keynes's reply, dated 11 August, appeared the following week.

To the Editor of The Nation and Athenaeum, *11 August 1923*

Sir,

There is no controversialist more difficult to answer than he who says that two and two is five. What is one to say? Where is one to begin?

I find no common solid ground from which to start in discussing this question with Mr D. M. Mason. I am reduced therefore to repeating that 'it is a pure delusion to suppose that to increase the value of sterling lightens the burden of the American debt'. But I throw out the suggestion that perhaps the reason why Mr Mason thinks this statement 'amazing' is because he thinks it identical with the statement 'to *decrease* the value of sterling lightens the burden of the American debt'. So far from their being identical, the first statement is true and the second is false. I was trying to convey the idea that, since the American debt is not fixed in terms of sterling, the burden of it is not affected by the value of sterling, one way or the other.

Yours etc.,

J. M. KEYNES

The British government produced the promised draft reply to Germany on 20 July. It called for the ending of passive resistance, the progressive evacuation of the Ruhr, an impartial enquiry into Germany's capacity to pay and means of payment, and the initiation of Allied discussions with the intention of arriving at a final settlement. The French reply and similar Belgian reply of 30 July were uncompromising; they refused to negotiate until Germany abandoned passive resistance and refused to leave the Ruhr until they were paid. They opposed the idea of an impartial enquiry as taking the power of deciding Germany's capacity to pay away from the French-dominated Reparation Commission.

Baldwin reported these developments to the House of Commons on 2 August in an attempt to enlist world opinion in support of the British stand, and promised an early publication of the documents exchanged.

Keynes commented on the British draft reply in the *Nation's* 'Events of the Week'.

From The Nation and Athenaeum, *4 August 1923*

Our draft reply to Germany, as described by Mr Baldwin, follows, on the whole, expected lines, though it is weak and non-committal all through. But in one passage it embarks on dangerous ground. Mr Baldwin advises Germany 'to withdraw without further delay the ordinances and decrees which had organised and fomented the policy of passive resistance'. We have no right to advise Germany to lay down her only weapon, unless we are prepared to guarantee to her fair play in the event of her acting on our advice. Is Mr Baldwin in a position to do this? Is it not quite likely that we shall, in the last resort if France persists, abandon Germany to her fate? And if there is any possibility of this, are we entitled to urge her to a particular course in the expectation of advantages which we cannot securely promise her? We hope that the full publication of documents will disclose that this advice was to be definitely contingent on certain undertakings from France.

Keynes also had little praise for Baldwin in 'Life and Politics'.

From The Nation and Athenaeum, *4 August 1923*

At last Mr Baldwin has told the House of Commons what he is doing. The effect is to raise doubts whether the present government is capable of dealing with the situation. The result of an enormous amount of drafting and debate is singularly unimpressive. Mr Baldwin means well. But he has no constructive ideas, no springs of energy, and no definite aim. Add to this much divergence of opinion within the Cabinet itself, and the result is naturally feeble. Not in this spirit or with these weak impulses will Great Britain inspire the world or restore the peace of Europe. Mr Baldwin seems more in his element in sentimental reminiscing at his old school.

The documents are to be published. That is necessary. We are to expound our case to the world. That is right and overdue. But the documents are not likely to contain much which we do not know already. And our attitude is far too undecided to rally the moral forces of the world.

Andrew McFadyean, secretary to the British delegation to the Reparation Commission, reacted to the Baldwin statement by writing to Keynes from Paris on 3 August,

on the hypothesis that you have some influence, more or less direct and not merely through the medium of the *Nation*, upon the German government. I suggest that you should strongly advise them to test the legality of the Ruhr occupation without further delay. Let them ask the Reparation Commission to interpret paragraph 18 [of the Treaty of Versailles], and on the Commission, as is inevitable, either refusing or failing to interpret, let them ask for a ruling by the World Court or other impartial body; conceivably they might omit the first step.

I have never understood why the Germans did not take this step in January. I am personally convinced that it is imperative now...until that aspect of the question is tested 99 per cent of France (and even a large majority of French people who are opposed to French policy) believe that she is acting well within her rights...

As far as I can see yesterday's government declaration really leaves us just where we were. I cannot persuade myself that publication of the documents is in itself a constructive policy or marks an appreciable advance, and I feel convinced that the main difficulty of the British government resides in its unwillingness or its inability to raise the supreme moral question. [Lloyd] George was the only man who mentioned it!

Just at this point, however, Keynes attacked on another front, in a column-long letter to *The Times*.

THE RUHR IMPASSE
THREE COURSES FOR ENGLAND
A BOLD OFFER TO FRANCE

To the Editor of The Times, *6 August 1923*

Sir,

Mr Baldwin's draft Note to Germany and M. Poincaré's reply are, in most particulars, pretty much what everyone expected. Mr Baldwin is feebler than we hoped; M. Poincaré as unbending as usual. Only one point in the documents themselves requires comment.

With the object, presumably, of satisfying the diehards in his Cabinet and in his party, Mr Baldwin has contingently undertaken to advise Germany to abandon passive resistance. Does Mr Baldwin understand what responsibility he takes on himself if he gives this advice? There are only two conditions in which he is entitled to take the line of a well-meaning third party advising Germany for her own good to abandon her only weapon. He can advise her in this sense in return for a firm and specific promise of fair treatment from France obtained by him as intermediary. Failing this, he has no right to speak unless he is prepared himself to guarantee fair treatment if his advice is taken. The latter guarantee he is not in a position to implement; for in the last resort he has no sure means at his command to influence France. If his advice was contingent on a specific promise from France and falls to the ground in the absence of such a promise, Mr Baldwin ought—if only for the effect on feeling in Germany—to have made this clear in his speech. He did not make it clear—rather the contrary. Nevertheless, we must hope that the actual Note sent to Germany, if any Note is sent, will, in face of the present position, refrain from any such advice. We are in danger of dishonouring ourselves in the same way that President Wilson dishonoured himself after the Armistice. He induced Germany to lay down her arms under promise of a peace based on the fourteen points, and then found himself impotent to carry out his promise. We may be playing on Germany the same trick again, if we induce her to give up passive resistance in the expectation of a reasonable settlement.

The position as a whole is as plain as a pikestaff. M. Poincaré thinks it to his advantage that Germany should collapse; he believes that there is reasonable expectation of this within (say) two months; he feels pretty confident that Mr Baldwin will *do* nothing whatever; he is prepared to be reasonably polite with the object of spinning out conversation for the requisite two months; but he has no intention of making the slightest real concession. Why should he? on his own presuppositions.

M. Poincaré makes two mistakes. The first mistake— namely, that the collapse of Germany is to his advantage—is widely appreciated outside France. Nevertheless, one immediate aspect of it is worth mentioning. The Ruhr is fed by the rest of Germany—at great expense and only by the exercise of the central authority of Berlin. If this authority is broken, whether by collapse at the centre or by capitulation at the Ruhr circumference, the organisation of food supplies will fail. Suppose ten million people throw up their hands, submit to France, and cry: 'We will do whatever you desire, but feed us', what will M. Poincaré do then! The value of the net surplus of the Ruhr in full prosperity is not enormous; at the present time it is certainly less than nothing. If France were to have the Ruhr thrown on her hands, she would not know what to do with it. If Germany breaks down, it is then in fact that M. Poincaré's difficulties will begin.

His second mistake may not be a mistake after all. Mr Baldwin's exaggerated regard for French susceptibilities, the notorious divisions within the British Cabinet, even the speeches of Lord Grey, have combined to persuade M. Poincaré that Great Britain will cling to the *entente* at all costs, and that he has nothing at all to fear from her so long as he keeps his head. He calculates that the final breakdown in Germany will find the strong, silent man in Downing Street still talking. Who can say that he is wrong? Mr Baldwin is partly fooled by M. Poincaré, but mainly he fools himself on purpose, because he has no idea what to do next when once he stops fooling. Indeed, the problem is of extraordinary difficulty. Most people in Mr Baldwin's place would do the same as he does.

Nevertheless, the problem would be vastly simplified if the British Cabinet could make up its mind which of the three broadly alternative policies it means to pursue. If we are going to do nothing, the sooner we say so the better. For, as Mr Chamberlain pointed out in the House of Commons, our present indecision merely prolongs the agony. If we wish to defeat M. Poincaré's policy of producing a breakdown in Germany, no half-measures are useful. We must break the *entente*, encourage Germany, and get busy to fix up new diplomatic combinations. This is what Mr Lloyd George would probably do if he was in power now. I see no prospect of Mr Baldwin's Cabinet adopting such a course.

The remaining alternative is to make one more attempt to act, not against France, but on France, by offering her something which she prefers to her present prospects. Perhaps this is impossible. Nothing but an offer of extreme boldness would have a chance. Let me outline what I would offer France—not because I like it, but because if one is to play at all the great game of world politics one must fling big stakes on the table. Let us tear up all the correspondence to date and propose, openly before the world, as follows—

If France would agree

(1) to evacuate the Ruhr;

(2) to fix the nominal German liability at fifty milliards;

(3) to allow the rate at which this liability is discharged to be determined by a committee of the Reparation Commission on which would sit an American representative with a vote along with British, French, Italian, and Belgian representatives:

Then Great Britain would agree

(1) to cancel all inter-Ally debts;

(2) to allow the claims of the other Allies an absolute priority over her own on future receipts from Germany.

Failing acceptance of this by France, Great Britain would proceed

(1) to withdraw her troops from the Rhinelands and to leave France alone, with no aid or sympathy from Great Britain, to work out her present policy to its bitter conclusion;

(2) to preserve in their entirety British rights to a share of the sums collected from Germany;

(3) to require the payment of France's debts to Great Britain up to 100 per cent of France's receipts from Germany from time to time.

The situation is an almost desperate one, in which, as the result of British foreign policy having lacked strength and wisdom for five years past, M. Poincaré holds nearly all the cards. Unless Mr Baldwin is more of a man of action than he has shown himself so far, he hasn't a dog's chance.

Yours faithfully,

J. M. KEYNES

'Counsels of despair', Wickham Steed characterised Keynes's advice in a letter to the editor, 7 August, causing W. R. Heatley to remark in the same columns, 9 August:

I do not like the offer Mr Keynes would make to France, any more than Mr Keynes does himself, but it has at least this merit, that it is something tangible to discuss. Even a counsel of despair is better to have before us than to abandon ourselves to the dangerous policy of helpless drift.

'Five years since signing armistice will have elapsed November eleven', telegraphed the editor of the New York *World*, Herbert Bayard Swope, on 16 August.

The World seeks for publication that day symposium of opinions of leaders of thought throughout earth on developments these years and their promise of good or ill for future stop Are the nations in closer accord are they coming closer whats their greatest need how may it best be secured stop...

Keynes kept the telegram with a doodled-over piece of rough paper on which he pencilled what appears to have been his reply:

To burn people's hearts with words; to persuade with words that Peace is the need of every big and little country. Will you join in?

As it happened, the British Note of 11 August, the work of Curzon, was a strong one, even belligerent. It stated that the amount of reparation Germany was actually able to pay could only be determined by an impartial enquiry—not by adding together the different claims against her. The demands of France could only result in a permanent occupation of the Ruhr. As for Britain, Curzon said, reaffirming the Balfour Note, she would ask France and Italy to repay her only the amount which, together with her reparation receipts from Germany, would allow her to repay her debt to the United States.

Among the 55 paragraphs of the Note was one quoting the opinion of the British legal profession that the Franco-Belgian occupation of the Ruhr was not authorised by the Treaty. Returning to the subject of McFadyean's letter, Keynes chose this aspect of the Note for comment in the *Nation*—a proof copy of which he sent to Baldwin.

The reference to his earlier writing on the matter of legality two years before was to his two *Manchester Guardian* articles written at the time of Lloyd George's ultimatum to Germany, 'The Latest Phase of Reparations' (*JMK*, vol. XVII, pp. 221-5) and 'The Proposed Occupation of the Ruhr' (*JMK*, vol. XVII, pp. 225-30).

From The Nation and Athenaeum, *18 August 1923*

THE LEGALITY OF THE RUHR OCCUPATION

'The highest legal authorities in Great Britain have advised His Majesty's Government that...the Franco-Belgian action in occupying the Ruhr...is not a sanction authorised by the Treaty.' These words, from the new British Note, modify so profoundly the juridical and diplomatic situation, that I should like to discuss them by themselves in their reference to the future and to the past, apart from the many other issues raised by the Note in its entirety.

The effect of this opinion is to declare that the Franco-Belgian invasion is, by international law, what it appears to be by commonsense—an act of war; and that M. Poincaré's elaborate pretences of legality are without foundation. If France disputes, as no doubt she does, this interpretation of the Treaty, she has bound herself by Article 13 of the covenant of the League to submit the dispute to arbitration.[3] Moreover, she is doubly bound to accept arbitration, because the same annex of the reparation section of the Treaty upon which she bases her case provides that the Reparation Commission itself

[3] Article 13 binds members of the League to submit to arbitration whenever any dispute shall arise between them as to the interpretation of a treaty, as to any question of international laws or as to the existence of any fact which if established would constitute a breach of any international obligation.

can only interpret the Treaty by unanimous vote; so that, as soon as one member dissents, the Commission is for this purpose *functus officio* and the general provisions of the covenant come into force. Lord Curzon invites M. Poincaré to accept arbitration; but he has not yet pointed out that M. Poincaré is bound to accept the invitation.

If France repudiates her obligation under the covenant, it is still competent (under Article 14) for either the council or the assembly of the League to refer the question to the permanent court of international justice for an advisory opinion.

In the event of the arbitral court supporting the opinion of the law officers of the British Crown, the occupation becomes an act of war. But the process of law does not stop, as formerly it did, there. At this point Article 17 of the covenant, which provides for the case of a dispute between a member of the League and a non-member, comes into operation. By this Article the State which is not a member of the League 'shall be invited to accept the obligations of membership in the League for the purposes of such dispute, upon such conditions as the council may deem just'. If this invitation is accepted, all the provisions of the covenant which delay recourse to acts of war come into force, particularly Article 12, by which the members of the League 'agree in no case to resort to war until three months after the award by the arbitrators or the report by the Council'.

Lord Curzon's Note makes no reference to Articles 17 and 12 of the covenant, for the obvious reason that they are equally effective against the action threatened on former occasions by the British government itself under Mr Lloyd George. But once we have set out on the pathway of legality, there is no turning back. The extraordinary significance of the thirty-second paragraph of the British declaration of 11 August 1923 lies herein. The British government has committed itself to the view that the occupation of the Ruhr is a lawless act of war. It is impossible after this that we should not proceed to invoke the full force of the covenant of the League. For the first time, the covenant is clothed with power and majesty, and steps out of the clouds to the dusty floor of Europe.

It is a moment when all of us must withdraw former criticisms and stand with the full strength of union behind Mr Baldwin and Lord Curzon in their difficult and dangerous task. Nevertheless, it is not possible to overlook entirely the reflection which the new decision throws backwards on past events. More than two years ago the present writer published at full length all the legal points mentioned above, and expressed the opinion now endorsed by the law officers and on the same grounds. At that time Mr Lloyd George chose to ignore such considerations. Between March 1920 and May 1921 the invasion of Germany beyond the Rhine was threatened five times and carried out twice. In three out of the five threats, and in one out of the two occupations, the British government participated. Lord Curzon attempts to argue that even so, the British government cannot be convicted of inconsistency, because the threats and the occupation in which they participated were never claimed to be in pursuance of special rights under the Treaty of Versailles, but were in the nature of a renewal of war. He forgets that in the ultimatum delivered by word of mouth to Dr Simons on 3 March 1921, by Mr Lloyd George, speaking on behalf of the Allied governments, the occupation of three towns on the right bank of the Rhine was threatened as a course justified 'under the Treaty of Versailles' by the fact that Germany was 'deliberately in default'. He forgets also that, if Mr Lloyd George was not acting in pursuance of special rights under the Treaty, he was precluded by the covenant from a 'renewal of war' except after due process and delay under the auspices of the League. We now have, therefore, the highest legal authority for the view, always entertained by many laymen,

that on three occasions Mr Lloyd George violated international right. It is better that we should acknowledge this than
remain consistent in wrong courses. In time, I expect, we shall
attempt to redress the other great violation of right
committed by Mr Lloyd George in claiming reparation for
pensions on legal quibbles even more flimsy and worthless
than those put forward in the present case. The Note of 11
August at least makes a beginning in that vindication of law,
without which disarmament and peace can never be
established.

Keynes added a footnote to this article the following week in the form
of a letter to the editor (dated 22 August).

To the Editor of The Nation and Athenaeum, *25 August 1923*

Sir,

I beg leave to make a small correction in the article by me
which you published under the above heading. I omitted to
refer therein to an amendment which has been introduced
into the Treaty making provision for what is to happen when
there is a failure of unanimity on the Reparation Commission
on a point of interpretation of the Treaty. I failed to mention
this amendment because I was not aware of it—it is not
included in the text of the Treaty currently issued by the
Stationary Office—and has only come to light in the 'Report
on the work of the Reparation Commission' published last
week.

As the result of a deadlock in January 1920 on a point of
interpretation, advantage was taken of §22 of annex II of the
reparation section (by which the governments represented on
the Commission can amend this annex by unanimous
decision) to add the following §13 (*bis*) to the annex:

In case of differences of opinion between the Delegates on the interpretation of the stipulations of this part of the present Treaty, the question will

be submitted by the unanimous agreement of the delegates to arbitration. The arbitrator will be selected unanimously by all the delegates, or in default of unanimity will be nominated by the council of the League of Nations. The finding of the arbitrator will be binding on all the interested parties.

The phrase 'will be submitted by the unanimous agreement' is oddly drafted, and the force of 'unanimous' is not clear. Probably France will argue that, failing unanimity, there is no compulsion to arbitrate. Yet this is not consistent with '*will* be submitted'.

At any rate, the position seems to be that a dispute about interpretation between the governments must go to arbitration under the covenant, and a dispute between the reparation delegates must either go to arbitration under the above clause, or result, once more, in a deadlock which inhibits the Reparation Commission from action—which is the position I assumed in my article; so that in any case it all comes to the same thing. In the case of a dispute about interpretation, France is compelled to go to arbitration *before she can act.*

Yours, etc.,

J. M. KEYNES

Curzon's Note of 11 August encouraged some degree of German confidence. Although Cuno's government finally fell that same day, Gustave Stresemann was able to form a stronger group and overcame a Communist attempt at a general strike. But the Ruhr stalemate continued. Keynes wrote in 'Life and Politics':

From The Nation and Athenaeum, *15 September 1923*

The Press has been busy for a week past constructing out of the flimsiest materials the legend of an impending settlement in the Ruhr. The Sunday before last Herr Stresemann repeated what was essentially the old German offer. The papers told us that a new situation had been created by his important proposals. Last Sunday M. Poincaré replied with unabated

violence and contempt, reiterating his demand for unconditional surrender. The papers told us that he had welcomed
the new German offer. This week the stories became more
explicit, and on Tuesday New York started buying European
currencies excitedly in the belief that the end of our troubles
was at hand. Yet no solid foundation is discoverable for all
this confidence. The truth seems to be that the German
industrialists have been renewing their attempts to satisfy
their French colleagues and are ready to make tempting
offers, which the Frenchmen would be glad to accept. But this
has been the case for some time past, the French steel interests
being no longer the obstacle. It is also true that Germany is
fast approaching complete financial exhaustion and is only
too ready to climb down—if there was anything for her to
climb down on to. Her difficulty is that she has nothing more
to offer. Unless she capitulates it is hard to see how she can
go beyond what has been already proposed and rejected. If
it was a question of Germany's 'will', M. Poincaré would have
had his satisfaction by now. But he demands the moon.

Herr Stresemann's rejoinder on Wednesday to M.
Poincaré indicates no more than that Germany is exceedingly
anxious to come to terms. It is probable, indeed, that Germany would humble herself to the point of capitulation, if
that would end her troubles. But even this would bring her
no mitigation. It is also rendered nearly impossible by the
internal political situation. As it is, the left hand is beginning
to know what the right hand doeth, and communist and
nationalist are fixing up a temporary partnership. Count
Reventlow writes for *Die rote Fahne*, and Radek joins in
mourning the execution of the nationalist Schlageter. Germany is lurching to an unknown fate. Meanwhile, Mr Baldwin, under cover of Corfu and Tokyo, goes on saying
nothing. More than three months have passed since the
German Note was received, and it remains unanswered. It is
still possible that good would result from a sincere and

friendly reply, offering to study the German financial problem in collaboration with the German government, to see what can be done.

No longer able to support the drain on her finances, Germany called an end to passive resistance on 26 September. Melchior, writing to Keynes on the 29th after a holiday in Bavaria and a Vienna business trip, commented on the internal situation of the country.

From a letter from C. MELCHIOR, *29 September 1923*

Affairs in Germany have developed in a way which logically was to be anticipated. The passive resistance could only be maintained for a certain time, because Germany's growing economic and financial ruin, which inevitably accompanied it, could not be borne without help from abroad for any length of time. Although the passive resistance has now been given up, I still believe that it was right to respond to the invasion with passive resistance. There are moments in the lives of nations as in the lives of individuals, at which it may become imperative to offer resistance, even if the chances of success are but remote—it is already an exigency for a nation's history. Moreover the German government at the beginning of this year could not but count with [on] the eventuality, though remote, of the political attitude of those Allied powers, who did not take part in the invasion, undergoing a reaction, which would have had *practical* effects on the French and Belgian position. Nothing of the sort, however, happened, and the calculation proved to have been a mistake. I, nevertheless, believe that the former Cabinet was compelled to take this chance, poor as it was.

For the moment I do not consider the situation in Germany really alarming, although with the extraordinarily deep agitation prevailing in many quarters of the population, nothing certain can be predicted. We may see local communistic riots in Saxony and Thuringia, perhaps also nationalistic commotions in Bavaria, but it is generally believed that the 'Reichswehr' and 'Schutzpolizei' are loyal to the constitution and will for the present be able to quell any disturbances.

Further developments will virtually depend on France's attitude, who will now have to put her cards open on the table. If her victory in the Ruhr appeases her prestige–hunger, and if she wants to come to an economic settlement with Germany on the reparation problem, I do not foresee any internal difficulties. If, however, France wants to attain on any account her political aims regarding the Rhein and direct her efforts merely towards Germany's prostration and destruction, it will, of course, be impossible to say anything at all as to what turn things may take in Germany.

It would greatly interest me to hear your views on the political situation.

Keynes answered, according to Melchior—there is no copy of the letter in question (7 October) with his papers—by asking what England could do now to help Germany and Europe. The state of the world seems to have been more than usually heavy on his mind. One of the results of his thinking was a memorandum for General Smuts, who was in London to attend the imperial conference of dominion prime ministers.

This paper is untitled, consisting of 'Drafts' I, II and III, each proposing a different course of action for dealing with the reparation situation. There is no indication as to whether Keynes prepared this memorandum at Smuts' request or, as is more likely, volunteered it; it is marked simply 'Prepared for General Smuts / 5. 10. 23'.

MEMORANDUM FOR GENERAL SMUTS

Draft I

H.M.G. are of opinion that the payment of adequate reparations by Germany cannot be secured unless

(1) the amount and method of payment are fixed in accordance with Germany's capacity;

(2) the Ruhr is evacuated and restored to German control; and

(3) the financial and currency system of Germany is reconstructed with outside assistance.

Under the Treaty no progress can be made with (1) unless the powers entitled to reparation are in agreement. After prolonged discussion with their Allies H.M.G. must regretfully recognise that no sufficient measure of such agreement exists at present. Action under this head must, therefore, be delayed for the present, although they themselves remain of the opinion that the right course is to accept the proposal of the German government of 7 June to submit this question to the judgment of an impartial body.

213

Under the other two heads, however, action is possible, and also urgently required by the rapid progress of events.

(2) The occupation of the Ruhr is not authorised by the Treaty. It impairs Germany's economic resources; and it fosters a political situation which, if it resulted in separatism, would largely destroy the possibility of future payments.

H.M.G. have, therefore, decided to act under Articles 11, 13 and 17 of the covenant of the League of Nations, requesting the summons forthwith of the Council of the League to consider the Ruhr occupation.

(3) With a view to the reconstruction of the German financial system, H.M.G. are inviting the German government to join with them in appointing a joint Anglo-German Commission to investigate and to make recommendations.

(The objection to (2) is that it is doubtful whether the League can take any effective action in view of the Article requiring unanimity by the Council. An alternative would be as follows)

Draft II

A solemn appeal by the parliament of Great Britain and the dominions of the British Empire assembled in conference, addressed to the President and the Congress of the United States, reciting

(1) the responsibility of the U.S. arising out of her participation in the war and in the peace conference;

(2) the imminent dangers of the present state of Europe;

(3) the deadlock in the Reparation Commission arising out of the absence of the American delegate not contemplated by the Treaty; and begging the U.S., in the interests of the world, to appoint a delegate, and (alternatively or in addition) to agree to send a representative to a conference to be summoned in London, consisting of representatives of each of the principal Allied and Associated powers, and one representa-

tive each of the little entente, the neutral powers of Europe and of Germany (or of such of them as will attend) to consider the Ruhr occupation in all its aspects.

Draft III

(This draft ignores both the League of Nations and the Ruhr, and merely makes such reply to the German Note of 7 June as lies in our power, acting alone.)

Reply by H.M.G. to German Note of 7 June

'Since receipt of this Note H.M.G. have tried and failed to frame a reply jointly with their Allies. Nevertheless they are not willing to abandon the attempt to discover a basis for agreement, and with this object in view they propose the setting up of three bodies charged with the duty of preparing the necessary data, as follows.

1. *Germany's capacity to pay.* H.M.G. propose the appointment of a Commission of Three, nominated by themselves, by the President of the U.S. and by the government of Italy, together with an assessor nominated by the government of Germany, to enquire and to report.

2. *Germany's means of payment and guarantee.* H.M.G. propose the appointment of a joint Anglo-German Commission to develop and to put into concrete shape the proposals of §3 of the German Note under reply.

3. With a view to the reconstruction of the German financial system, H.M.G. invite the German government to join with them in appointing an Anglo-German Commission to investigate and to make recommendations with a view to early action.

Pending the reports of these bodies, H.M.G., whilst reiterating their view as to the illegality and inexpediency of the Ruhr occupation, advise the German government, under full reserve as to its present rights and future action, to withdraw,

215

for a provisional period of six months, all economic and financial assistance to the Ruhr, to hand over the government of the Ruhr to French administration, and to request the inhabitants of the Ruhr to obey, so far as they can, all French instructions.

Smuts wrote 9 October, 'Many thanks for your suggestions. I incline to the following reparation plan': and then outlined his own ideas which involved fixing specific amounts and arranging for postponement of payments.

The lack of agreement and co-operation between France and Britain at this time contributed to a defeat for the League of Nations over the matter of Corfu. The Italians had bombed and occupied the island in retaliation for the murder by Greeks of Italian members of a border commission. Greece appealed to the League and was strongly supported by Sir Robert Cecil; Mussolini denied the League's competence in the particular case and was backed by France in a bid for Italian support. The outcome was that Mussolini was able to turn the dispute over to the conference of ambassadors where the question was settled technically by the payment of a fine by Greece.

Keynes was incensed at the public attitude towards the Corfu incident. In 'Life and Politics' he remarked editorially:

From The Nation and Athenaeum, *8 September 1923*

Comments on current events, not wholly confined to the Rothermere Press, show that the most elementary principles of the League of Nations are still thought a suitable subject for a sneer. The *Evening Standard,* for example, of last Tuesday (in 'A Londoner's Diary') enquires 'what does it matter to us who has Corfu?', argues that the League has no standing in the matter because its business is to deal with disputes, whereas 'in this case there is nothing to arbitrate about; and, strictly speaking, the matter is not a dispute at all' (!); and concludes (with apparent satisfaction) 'it is quite possible that this question may bring the League within sight of dissolution'. What an outlook to the present state of the world such sentences exhibit! All the same, the objects of the League may make more progress, when they become matter for sharp controversy and strong feelings, than they can ever make as a mere occasion of tepid platitude about which we are all supposed to agree.

Taking Corfu as his example, Lord Grey addressed a long letter to *The Times*, published 9 October 1923. His words were directed in particular towards the conference of prime ministers then in session and discussing foreign policy. 'Recent events', he declared, 'have shown us, with horrid clearness, Europe sliding surely, though it may appear slowly, towards the abyss.'

Of the great powers, Grey remarked, only Britain and France had not fallen into the hands of dictators. Declining to discuss the French Ruhr policy as 'out of place here', he asked whether the two countries could co-operate on questions other than reparations.

Keynes was bitter about what he felt was a half-hearted stand.

From The Nation and Athenaeum, *13 October 1923*

LORD GREY'S LETTER TO 'THE TIMES'

The only thing that will prevent the catastrophe of another great European war is that there should be, in every case, a genuine attempt to settle disputes between nations by the just decision of an impartial authority before resort is had to force.

Thus Lord Grey in Tuesday's *Times*. His text is the episode of Corfu; his pessimism is caused by the compromise with justice used to settle it; he writes with strength and feeling on the sanctity of Treaties and the need to pursue justice with courage. 'It is essential', he says, 'that the representatives of the British Empire should be clear as to whether they are united in the policy of upholding the covenant of the League ...The future liberties of Europe depend upon regulating disputes between nations by justice and law; and upon maintaining the sanctity of treaties and thus making peace secure.

That is the policy for which the League of Nations was created to be the instrument.'

How does he proceed? He mentions that in the view of Great Britain. France's Ruhr policy 'must postpone, if not destroy, the prospect of getting reparations', and 'will hinder, if not prevent, the restoration of Europe'; and merely concludes that, since we and France hold exactly opposite views on the Ruhr and reparations, we must just agree to differ. In a letter which is all about justice and law and Treaties he forgets, it seems, the lawlessness of the one act of unprincipled force which matters above all others. Is Lord Grey entitled in such a context to omit mention of the fact that in the opinion of our highest legal authorities the occupation of the Ruhr is an act of war, and that Articles 11 and 17 of the covenant prescribe in such cases the intervention of the League?

We hope that we misunderstand Lord Grey; for if not, the feebleness and muddleheadedness of the foreign policy he offers us must fill all Liberals with despair. If, in fact, Lord Grey is in favour of the British government bringing the question of the Ruhr before the League, we beg him to say so. If not, is he not subordinating the cause of international legality to his desire not to quarrel with France, just as he charges others with subordinating it to their desire not to quarrel with Italy? If Lord Grey does not wish the imperial conference to demand the reference to the League of the great outstanding question of the hour, what other practical recommendation relating to the League has he in his mind, which would be more than words?

For, unless he means more than he says, he leads us nowhere. Although we and France hold exactly opposite views on the Ruhr and reparations, he seems to suggest that that is no reason against our co-operating on all other questions! And his only suggestion by which 'a situation that is becoming increasingly perilous may yet be saved' is that France may come to realise that the future of parliamentary government in Europe depends upon disputes between nations being regulated by justice and law! He shows not even a suspicion that France may have a definite and scarcely concealed policy for the future of Europe which is destructive of everything he cares for, that this is at the bottom of the whole diplomatic situation, and that our problem is not how to co-operate with France (for co-operation implies common aims), but how to defeat her.

J. M. KEYNES

The intensity of Keynes's feelings at this time appeared even when he was canvassed to support Lord Buckmaster, one time liberal M.P. for Cambridge (1906–10) and formerly Lord Chancellor (1915–16), as Rector of the University of Edinburgh.

To ALEXANDER ROSS, *13 October 1923*

Dear Sir,

Naturally, I warmly support the candidature of Lord Buckmaster for the office of Lord Rector, but it is not easy to express oneself adequately on these occasions in a few words. I offer you the following to do what you like with.

'If I had an opportunity of showing my feelings at this time about political affairs I should want to use it in relation to the foreign situation. We are most of us oppressed and terrified by the developments in central Europe, enraged by what appears to be the policy of France, and disgusted by the weakness and ineptitude of our own government. We do not know where to look for wise guidance. Lord Buckmaster is one of the very few former holders of high office in the State who have an unbroken record of wisdom, courage and foresight in their utterances on public events since the Armistice. In casting a vote for him for the office of Lord Rector I should feel that it was some symbol of my discontent with our ways and practices in the past five years, and at the same time of my confidence that there do still exist in Great Britain, though not in office, a few statesmen whom one can respect.'

Yours faithfully,

[copy initialled] J.M.K.

Melchior wrote on 13 October, thanking Keynes for his letter of the 7th.

From a letter from C. MELCHIOR, *13 October 1923*

To your question, as to what could now be done on the part of England, I can give you only my absolutely private opinion, because I have—at least for the present—no personal contact with the leading men now in office.

My private views are, that Germany will continue her endeavours to arrive at negotiations, be it direct ones with the Allied governments, be it with the Reparation Commission. In my opinion England could do two things in order to calm the situation in Germany and therewith subsequently also in whole central Europe.

(1) A counter-action against France's exertions to bring about the neutralisation of the Rhinelands. England can neither have an interest in this neutralisation. France is certainly not going for a long time to come, to annex the Rhinelands and the Ruhr, because she cannot digest eleven million Germans, and because she will not have the deputies of those countries in Paris in her Parliament. But if France secures for herself the railways and the right to keep garrisons there permanently and moreover removes the customs frontier to the east frontier of those districts, abolishing it in the west against France and finally introduces the francs currency, she will have created a State which economically and politically is absolutely dependent on France. I do not believe that this will last, because the feeling of solidarity of the Germans will be too great, but it will then probably require in later days a new great European war in which the attempt would be made to liberate the Rhinelands.

(2) How we shall get through this winter in Germany, I do not see yet. Foreign credits, which in my opinion need not be particularly large, might be of very great help in this respect. That these credits, if given on a purely commercial basis, could only reach a very moderate height, is sure. The question is, whether the English government would think it right to encounter the threatening chaos in Germany by way of admitting or favouring credits which from a purely commercial point of view might perhaps not be considered reasonable.

As regards my visit to London I should be quite ready to come, but, as I have said, I am not in the same personal contact with the present Cabinet as with the former one, and my visit to London could therefore only have purely private character. Perhaps I may however, also have occasion to go to London on business...

In his militant mood Keynes reacted against rumours growing out of Smuts' speeches to the Imperial Conference.

To JAN CHRISTIAN SMUTS, *21 October 1923*

Dear General Smuts,

It is rumoured in the newspapers that you are interesting yourself in the details of reparation schemes. I cannot help writing to say that I hope this is not so. Surely at this moment of time such things are utterly useless.

No action now has any value except something that frightens France or encourages Germany or both. If we are not prepared to take such action, either for lack of courage or for better reasons, then there is nothing to be done. But plans about fifty milliards (or whatever it is) are as remote from realities now as plans about four times that amount used to be. The more I reflect upon it, the more convinced I am that no advantage can accrue to this country from still continuing to base policy on the infliction of imaginary milliards. Europe is not going to be saved by devices based on the hope of collecting, even at this time of day, substantial reparations for this country.

Ever yours sincerely,
J. M. KEYNES

I shall be in London in the middle of this week.

To which Smuts replied:

From JAN CHRISTIAN SMUTS, *22 October 1923*

My dear Keynes,

Thanks for your note. I agree with you that the reparation question is being swallowed up in a much graver situation. Tomorrow night I shall speak on this situation at the South African dinner and hang my remarks on the peg of the reparation question. You cannot and should not avoid that question, but place it in its proper perspective to what is now happening on the Continent. I hope I shall be able to do so. Look me up when you come to London.

Yours ever,
J. C. SMUTS

The 'much graver situation' worrying Keynes and Smuts concerned the numerous risings against the German government. The nationalists in Bavaria and Communists in Saxony and Thuringia continued to give trouble, while in the Rhineland the separatists, encouraged by the French, declared an independent republic.

Smuts's speech at the South Africa Club dinner on 23 October attracted much attention. He urged an immediate conference of the powers interested in reparations and emphasised the importance of the presence of the United States. The possibility of both these propositions actually materialising was higher than before; President Coolidge had endorsed the original Hughes suggestion of an impartial tribunal and Baldwin and Curzon had invited the Allies to a conference, intimating that America would join them.

Keynes was generally pleased with what Smuts said.

To JAN CHRISTIAN SMUTS, *26 October 1923*

Dear General Smuts,

I am sorry that I was not able to get hold of you during my weekly visit to London. I enjoyed your speech enormously, and wanted to say how grateful I felt to you for it. I expect that the general line you adopted is the one right for the occasion; especially as I now gather from several sources that there is a real chance of the United States accepting an invitation to participate in a conference. (I do not know whether you see *The Nation* regularly. I am now the chairman of the company owning this paper, and besides contributing myself am generally in close touch with what appears there.)

I cannot much complain of your references to the reparation question. But all the same I do feel that there is here a difference of opinion between us. If you have in mind some such figure as 50 milliard gold marks you must not include me amongst the experts who are alleged to be in unanimous agreement about this. To have the nominal German debt fixed at this figure would represent real progress. But I am perfectly convinced that there is not the faintest chance of Germany's paying anything approaching this sum. Nor do I agree that from the point of view of her industrial competition with ourselves we should have less to fear if she was held down to very burdensome reparation payments than we should have to fear otherwise. Indeed, I think we should have to fear more.

As regards the possibility of 50 milliards, I have briefly three things to say. (1) This is a good deal higher than the total figure for reparations which I used to estimate in Peace Conference days when I was trying to put the figure as high as I possibly could, and when circumstances were far different from what they are now and far more favourable to German payments. My figure at that time never exceeded 40 milliards. And the arguments which led me to make it as low as that at that time lead me to make it much lower now.

(2) My figure of 40 milliards at that date included what Germany would discharge out of various surrenders and deliveries which she would make once and for all. These have now been made and cannot therefore be taken into account in calculations for the future. People generally forget what an enormous sum Germany has paid already. I enclose an article on this point which I am publishing in next Saturday's *Nation*. It is quite a mistake to fix Germany's future liability on the assumption that she has not paid anything already.

(3) Since 1919 an enormous lot has happened to diminish

both the expedience and the practicability of large payments; besides which experience has opened our eyes, I think, to many obstacles which have existed all the time, but of which we were not as vividly aware then as we are now.

I had quite another subject on which I wanted to say a word to you. It now looks as though you might be staying in England until well into December. If this is the case is there any chance of persuading you to come to the Founders' Day Feast at King's on December 6th? I have been asked by the College to convey to you an invitation to come as one of their guests. It would be a great pleasure to see you in Cambridge, and a great advantage and satisfaction to the undergraduates of the College to have you amongst them. This banquet is not, like so many that you are attending, one primarily composed of old gentlemen. All the scholars and all the third year men of the College are present, and it would be to them that you would be showing yourself and (I hope) speaking.

Ever yours sincerely,
J. M. KEYNES

The article that Keynes sent to Smuts follows.

From The Nation and Athenaeum, *27 October 1923*

HOW MUCH HAS GERMANY PAID?

With the German government's formal announcement of its bankruptcy and the total cessation of all payments, including deliveries in kind, the first phase of reparations, during which Germany has continuously paid large sums—probably up to the full limit of her capacity—has come to an end. It may be that no more will ever be paid. This is, therefore, an appropriate moment for reviewing and estimating her past performance.

The mind of the public has been extremely confused by the variety of estimates which have been current, varying from German official claims that she has already paid more than £2,000 million to Press headlines that she has paid nothing at all.

Apart from differences of opinion as to the estimation of particular items, there are two sets of figures which have to be distinguished—namely, the total financial burden thrown on Germany by the Peace Treaty, and the portion of this which reckons, under the terms of the Treaty, towards the discharge of reparations. Certain sacrifices imposed on Germany are excluded altogether from the items reckoning towards reparations, although they cost Germany just as dear as the items which are not excluded; whilst the method prescribed by the Treaty for calculating, for the purposes of the reparation account, the value of certain other items, undoubtedly yields a lower figure than their real cost to Germany. Thus the cost to Germany of what she has paid and delivered is much greater than the sum credited to her in the books of the Reparation Commission.

Now, if we are considering what progress Germany has made towards meeting her Treaty liabilities, the latter figure alone is relevant. But if we are seeking a measure of Germany's effort to carry her burdens or of the punishment imposed on her, it is the former figure which matters.

Let us begin with the sums credited to her in the books of the Reparation Commission, which are indisputable, and present the lowest estimate of her effort on any computation. These fall into three categories:

	£ million (gold)
Cash	95
Deliveries in kind	189
State property in ceded territories	127
	411

Of these sums £19,600,000 was returned to Germany in the form of coal advances (under the Spa agreement). On the other hand, currency, worth about £35 million, and goods

225

and services, worth at least a further £35 million, have been furnished to the armies of occupation and commissions of control. Further, the Reparation Commission has still to estimate and credit the value of State property in the ceded area of Upper Silesia, estimated by Germany, I think, at about £50 million. If we adjust for these various items, the total sum is £511 million.

Let us allow, next, for items reckoned in the reparation account below their real value. The largest and most indisputable of these is coal and coke. If the value of these deliveries had been calculated at the world market price instead of by the formula prescribed by the Treaty, it is estimated that an additional £70 million (or thereabouts) would have been credited. There are also several other important items, in which there is a wide difference between the value placed on them by the German government and that assessed by the Reparation Commission, as follows:

	German valuation £ million	R. C. valuation £ million
Saar mines	50	20
Mercantile marine	290	35
Ceded State property (not including Upper Silesia)	275	127
Armistice deliveries	175	59
Total	790	241

Thus the German valuation is more than three times that of the Reparation Commission. A part of this discrepancy can be explained, without imputing bad faith to either party, by a difference in the principles of valuation adopted. The German government naturally consider what the property is worth to them and the Reparation Commission equally what it is worth to them—which may be all the difference between a going concern and bankrupt stock. It might be quite consistent with the terms of the Treaty to value some of the most essential parts of Germany's industrial equipment as scrap iron; but this would not be a correct measure of the burden thrown on Germany. Indeed, its tendency to impoverish whatever it touches and to convert organised equipment into rubbish is one of the characteristics—we can almost say one of the objects—of the Treaty of Versailles. Two items, however, since they relate to known and definite objects, are particularly striking—the Saar mines and the mercantile marine. The difference between the valuation per ton of output placed by the Reparation Commission on the Saar mines and that claimed by France for the destruction of her own mines, and the difference between the valuation per shipping ton placed on the German mercantile marine and that claimed for the destruction of Allied shipping, are so wide as to seem obnoxious to justice. It should be added that the discrepancy in the shipping valuation partly depends on whether the boom values current at the date of delivery are taken or the slump values current at the date of valuation. It is instructive, because it well illustrates the outrageous character of the reparation business, to note that the valuation placed on the whole of the German mercantile marine is sufficient to pay the interest on Germany's reparation liability, as assessed by the same authority, for a period of less than six weeks, while the surrender of the Saar mines pays the perpetually accruing interest bill for less than one month.

Since the German valuation has been built up item by item and offered for criticism and cross-examination, we may fairly assume, after allowing for all possible exaggerations, that the measure of the burden thrown on Germany by the deliveries is not less than half the figure claimed, that is to say £395 million, as against the £241 million credited under the terms of the Treaty. No one, I think, could put the cost to Germany, as distinct from the value to the Allies (which in some cases is less than nothing), at a lower figure than this.

Our table is then as follows [at the top of p. 228].

I think that this can be regarded as a conservative estimate of the burden thrown on Germany under these heads.

	£ million
Credits with the Reparation Commission (less Spa coal advances)	391
Cash and goods supplied to armies of occupation	70
Ceded property in Upper Silesia	50
Addition for world market price of coal	70
Addition for real value to Germany of various surrenders	154
	735

We now come to certain items, which, under the terms of the Treaty, do not count at all towards reparation, but are none the less a charge on Germany. The most important are the following:

(1) the sums owed to Germany by her former allies;

(2) the German colonies and State property there situated;

(3) State property in Alsace-Lorraine;

(4) 'restitutions' in replacement of specific Allied property removed by Germany from invaded territory;

(5) German ships seized in enemy ports;

(6) German private property seized and liquidated abroad;

(7) payments by Germany in discharge of private debts.

The face value of the first item is £850 million. But whilst it represents a real loss to Germany, its market value is undoubtedly *nil*. I know of no reliable estimate of items (2), (3), (4) and (5). On the basis of partial data I should put these items, but without much confidence as to the accuracy of the figure, somewhere round £100 million altogether.

Items (6) and (7) are of a different character. The proceeds have been applied to the discharge of German private debts, and to this extent they represent, not a net loss, but a liquidation of liabilities. A net burden has been thrown on Germany only to the extent that the assets have not been applied to discharge the liabilities of her own nationals,[4] or have been sequestrated and in part unapplied (as in the United States), or have been sold at a price less than their value to their

[4] Under the Treaty, any surplus can be applied to discharge the private debts of Germany's former allies.

German owners as a going concern. Nevertheless, apart from this net burden, the fact that this amount of capital previously lent to Germany has been called in, thus diminishing her working capital abroad and her liquid reserves against emergencies, has clearly diminished her capacity to make foreign payments during the period since the Armistice almost as much as though it were a net loss. The figures are very large. The German government's estimate of the value of the property liquidated abroad is £585 million;[5] and the amount of cash payments under the clearing house system is £30 million. The estimate of the value of the property liquidated appears too high if it is intended to represent its present value, but probably not too high as a measure of its pre-war value.

Summing up, I am of the opinion that the financial cost to Germany of her efforts to meet her Treaty liabilities and of her surrenders under the Treaty between the date of the Armistice and the date of the occupation of the Ruhr has exceeded £1,000 million; and if we include the sums which she has had to find in this period to discharge private debts, the figure reaches £1,300 million.[6] In addition to this, Germany's pre-war investments in Russia, Turkey, and Austria-Hungary, and her war loans to her allies, have been rendered valueless by the course of events; and there has, of course, been an enormous loss of 'goodwill' in her business connections and organisation.

Allowing for the change in the value of money and for the relative wealth and population of France in 1871 and Germany in 1919, the figure of £1,000 million represents a real burden on Germany per head more than double that

---

[5] M. Tardieu has estimated it a little higher, namely, at £650 million.

[6] In order to reach an independent estimate, I made this calculation before opening the valuable volume *Germany's Capacity to Pay*, by Moulton and McGuire, lately published by the New York Institute of Economics. The corresponding estimate of these writers is £1,290 million up to 30 September 1922, which almost exactly agrees with my figure, allowing for the fact that I carry my calculations up to a later date. There are, however, some differences between us regarding one or two of the items which make up the total.

thrown on France by her payment of £200 million after the Franco-German war. If we remember that Germany had fought the most exhausting war in history for four years, and had lost, one way and another, the bulk of her foreign assets, whereas France had her previous resources of foreign investments and the like almost intact, it is clear that the German effort to pay has represented enormously more than the equivalent of the French indemnity—as indeed we can easily judge, after the event, by the comparative effects on the wealth and prosperity of the German people in 1923 and the French people in 1873.

In face of these facts, the broad outlines of which are not open to dispute, it is an outrageous thing that certain sections of the Press should be filled with charges that Germany had paid next to nothing, that she has evaded her liabilities, that by bluff and chicane she has cheated her creditors. These statements and suggestions are untrue.

Keynes's valuation of the German mercantile marine in 'How Much has Germany paid?' was disputed by Sir B. A. Kemball-Cook, an assistant British delegate to the Reparation Commission. In a letter marked 'Personal' he showed that the German valuation could not properly be compared with the Reparation Commission valuation because the German figure included other classes of ships than the merchant marine.

'Are you sure, also,' he wrote,

of the accuracy of your statement that 'the difference between the valuation per shipping ton placed on the German mercantile marine and that claimed for the destruction of Allied shipping is so wide as to seem obnoxious to justice'?

Explaining the different periods that the Allied and German claims were based upon, he concluded. 'I do not think that it can be said that the difference was so strikingly great as to justify your stricture'.

In his reply Keynes referred to his correspondence with 'Alpha' about the French claim for damages (*JMK*, vol. XVII, pp. 303–13).

To SIR B. A. KEMBALL-COOK, *13 December 1923*

My dear Kemball-Cook,

Many thanks for your letter of 12 November, and apologies for not answering it sooner. I have been diverted from these matters by the publication of a new book [the *Tract*] and by a certain amount of electioneering at the general election.

Some of the facts and figures which you give in your letter were not known to me. And indeed they could not have been known to me, I think. In fact, I am not clear that I could use them in public discussion even now, since you mark your letter 'Personal'. I do not see what one can do when one is criticising the work of the Devil's Kitchen, except base one's observations on the best available information publicly published. This is particularly so as regards the details of the ultimate claim against Germany. The Reparation Commission published the details of the claims as submitted by the claimants, but none of the items as accepted by the Commission. I admit that it is not possible to pass an absolutely final judgment until the Reparation Commission publishes, item by item, its adjudication of the several claims. In the meantime I think one is justified in forming a judgment on the basis of the broad indications available. On this basis I remain of the opinion that impartial justice was not done, and that the result is not the same as would have been produced by a strictly judicial and impartial body.

I ought to add, however, that it is often rather difficult to distinguish between injustices inherent in the terms of the Treaty and injustices arising out of the decisions of the Reparation Commission on the basis of the Treaty. I agree that there is often a tendency to do some injustice to the Commission by imputing to them results which were inherent in the Treaty itself, and where they were probably giving a sound legal decision on the basis of the Treaty's terms. This sort of point particularly arises where certain sacrifices or payments rendered by Germany are excluded, by the terms of the Treaty, from reckoning towards reparation account.

The outside critic is unfortunately hampered, not only by the lack of published information. I do not know whether you saw a recent criticism of my book [*A Revision of the Treaty*—the remainder of this paragraph appears in *JMK*, vol. XVII, p. 309]...

I am sorry that in the particular matter of shipping I should have led you, in whose sense of justice I feel confident, to think that I have in some degree misrepresented the position. But I plead that it is not my fault, and that in the absence of the full publication of facts and figures covering the whole field it is necessary to go on somewhat broad lines and to be impressed, as I was, by the wide discrepancies between the German valuation of their fleet, the Reparation Commission valuation of the figure due to them in respect of ships, and the claim of the Allied governments in respect of Allied shipping. The apparent discrepancies between the magnitudes of the three figures were so striking as to require public defence in detail—which they never yet had.

Yours sincerely,
[copy initialled] J.M.K.

When Smuts answered Keynes's last letter on 30 October events had progressed far enough for him to be relatively optimistic. Poincaré had replied negatively to the British invitation to an Allied conference, insisting on impossibly hampering conditions. In the meantime, however, Germany had applied to the Reparation Commission to investigate her capacity to pay, and through the efforts of Bradbury two committees were appointed, one to enquire into ways of balancing the German budget and stabilising the currency, and a second to look into the repatriation of German capital. This proved to be the needed breakthrough; the work of these two committees led eventually to the setting up of the Dawes Plan.

From JAN CHRISTIAN SMUTS, *30 October 1923*

My dear Keynes,

Many thanks for your note and for what you say about my speech. The experts will now once more start the task of Sisyphus and try to settle the figures. My feeling is that events are moving very fast and that they will cut the Gordian knot. Meantime I hope we shall succeed in getting America into the business before the great crisis arrives. It will be something if we have not to face the storm alone.

I am sorry I cannot accept the invitation for Founders' Day. I shall be gone by that time.

With best wishes
Ever yours
J. C. SMUTS

'I am talking over matters quietly with Melchior', Smuts added at the end of his letter. Melchior had acted on his plan to visit London mentioned in his letter of 13 October (p. 220). Keynes saw him on 30 October. Melchior had two conversations with Smuts, 27 and 29 October, describing the economic and political scene in Germany while Smuts explained British attitudes. At Smuts's request Melchior worked out a memorandum of his ideas for the financial reconstruction of Germany. He sent Keynes a translation of his detailed account of the two meetings, which Keynes kept with his papers.

Chapter 5

A BREATHING SPACE—THE
DAWES PLAN, 1923–1928

The break-up of Germany seemed very near in October 1923. Separatist movements continued to be supported by the French, while the official abandonment of passive resistance left the only opposition to the occupation to come from the trade unions. These, with their demands for an eight-hour day, were fought by the German industrialists, who combined with the French for their own interests to shut down works and factories. The payment of reparations stopped; the Stresemann government signified its willingness to pay to the Reparation Commission but declared that to do so was financially impossible. Periodicals like *The Nation* printed letters to the editor describing the pitiful living conditions in Germany under inflation and carried the advertisements of relief organisations soliciting contributions.

The British government with the backing of the Imperial Conference and the promise of American co-operation proposed yet another enquiry into Germany's capacity to pay. This was impeded by Poincaré insisting on impossible conditions, but finally in December 1923 an agreement was reached to set up a twofold investigation under the auspices of the Reparation Commission, with the active participation of the United States. Two committees of experts were appointed to enquire into the possibilities of (1) the restoration of Germany's financial stability, and (2) the expropriation of German capital exported abroad. These came to be known respectively, by the names of their chairmen, as the Dawes Committee, after the American general Charles Gates Dawes, and the McKenna Committee, after Reginald McKenna. The experts began work in Paris in January 1924.

Keynes wrote nothing about these developments until the committees reported in April 1924. In the meantime, during the autumn election called by Baldwin on the issue of protection, he spoke on Liberal platforms and wrote on free trade in *The Nation. A Tract on Monetary Reform* was published in December 1923; he continued to explore the subject of money in articles for *The Nation* on gold, the speeches of the bank chairmen, and the French franc (*JMK*, vols. IX and XIX).

The Expert Committees reported on 9 April. Keynes asked for an early copy of the Dawes Report, which was sent to him, hot from the drafting table, by J. C. Stamp, one of its most influential framers.

'The drafting committee work was most difficult, as the Latins strove to pull down and tone out everything—it was a great fight,' Stamp exulted in his accompanying note written on the way home from Paris.

Everyone in France is saying—'What will Keynes say?' So go easy on the vials of your wrath at present. *You* shall run the next kindergarten under an alias.

The novelty of the Dawes Plan was that it separated the matter of the collection of reparation payments from the question of transferring them to foreign countries so as not to upset the stability of the German exchange. Payments were to be made in gold marks, to be converted into foreign currencies only to the extent that the foreign exchange market would permit.

Keynes was sceptical of the Report as a whole and withheld judgment, but he praised it none the less as 'the finest contribution hitherto to this impossible problem'.

From The Nation and Athenaeum, *12 April 1924*

THE EXPERTS' REPORTS

I. *The Dawes Report*

This report seeks to attain three prime objects: to restore the economic integrity of Germany; to secure a breathing space of peace and quiet; and to combine the possibility of large payments by Germany hereafter, if, when the time comes, she is able to make them, with full protection for Germany if, when the time comes, she is not able to make them. These are essential features of any proposal which is to prove both politically practical and economically tolerable. The experts have assisted the attainment of these objects. Therefore they deserve the thanks of the world—thanks belonging to the immediate present, which transcend, for the moment, criticisms directed to the question whether the complicated scheme here adumbrated for future years is the sort of thing that could ever really come to pass in the world of actual happenings.

The experts insist that their plan depends on restoring to Germany the control of railways, customs, and administration throughout her empire. 'Our whole report', they say, 'is based on this hypothesis.'

If political guarantees and penalties intended to ensure the execution of the plan proposed are considered desirable, they fall outside the committee's jurisdiction. Questions of military occupation are also not within our terms of reference. It is however our duty to point out clearly that our forecasts are based on the assumption that economic activity will be unhampered and unaffected by any foreign organization other than the controls herein provided. Consequently, our plan is based upon the assumption that existing measures, in so far as they hamper that activity, will be withdrawn or sufficiently modified as soon as Germany has put into execution the plan recommended, and that they will not be reimposed except in case of flagrant failure to fulfil the conditions accepted by common agreement.

In case of such failure it will be for the creditor governments jointly 'to determine the nature of sanctions to be applied and the method of their rapid and effective application'. This is explicit and satisfactory. If, however—as seems probable—the French insist on the perpetuation and recognition in some form of a military occupation of the Ruhr, two questions are raised. First, such occupation cannot be compatible in practice with the financial and economic integrity of the German empire, if the French military authorities are to retain the powers of daily interference which they are now exercising in the Palatinate and in the Rhinelands. In any event, therefore, the occupation must be limited to the presence of French troops in barracks, with no administrative powers in normal circumstances and no authority to act except in grave emergency on the instructions of the Allies as a whole. Secondly, the perpetuation of the Ruhr occupation into a period when Germany will be no longer in technical default involves a revision of the Treaty of Versailles on *any* interpretation of that Treaty. France has maintained that the Ruhr occupation is amongst the sanctions permitted by the Treaty when Germany is in technical default. No one has maintained that it is permissible in general and at all times. The recognition by the other Allies of a continuing French occupation of the Ruhr must be conditional, therefore, on its voluntary acceptance by Germany in return for what she considers counterbalancing advantages, and on the precise conditions of the occupation being laid down by Treaty in terms free from the ambiguities of the Treaty of Versailles. It may be difficult to frame conditions which will be acceptable both to France and to Germany. In their attitude towards this crucial diplomatic problem it will not be permissible for the British government, in face of the unanimous declaration of the experts and in face also of the declared policies of the predominant parties in the House of Commons, to show the slightest weakness.

Do the experts' proposals secure the second prime object, a breathing space? This is the part of their scheme about which I feel most doubtful. The effective moratorium is to last for only one year. During this year Germany's liability for Treaty payments abroad is limited to £10 million (gold), and for Treaty payments at home to £40 million (gold), against which she is to receive a foreign loan of £40 million (gold)— equivalent to about £44 million sterling. It appears, but this is not quite plain, that if it proves impracticable to raise so large a loan, then her liability will be reduced proportionately. If the loan is raised, which will be difficult, she might be able during this first year to strengthen her position. In the second year she is to pay altogether £61 million (gold) entirely out of her own resources, including an internal loan. In the third year she is to pay £60 million (gold); in the fourth year £87,5000,000 (gold); and thereafter £125 million (gold). This presumes a very rapid recovery of Germany's balance of payments with the outside world, and only the progress of events can provide a certain answer. The proposals for the third and fourth years are based on hypothetical estimates of the yield of taxation by that time, which are at least as likely to be wrong as to be right. If these estimates prove wrong, will Germany, or will she not, be once again in technical default? However this may be, to limit the effective moratorium to so brief a period makes the fundamental mistake of cutting off Germany, during the initial period of her presumed recovery, from accumulating her prosperity at compound interest. It is impossible that Germany should make large payments hereafter, if her entire surplus production is to be taken away almost from the outset, before she has had time to build up again her store of working resources. The shortness of the period, which will probably elapse before episodes of so-called 'default' begin again, also has the defect that there will be no sufficient time for any sensible relaxation of political rancours and fears. Nevertheless, the rigours of the moratorium, as well as of the permanent, period are to be mitigated by the proposals governing the conditions of remittance which are explained below.

When we come to the 'permanent' proposals, we find the most original, and also the most perplexing, of the committee's contributions. They lay down two independent conditions governing the maximum of possible reparation: the annual payment must not exceed 'the difference between the maximum revenue (of the budget) and minimum expenditure for Germany's own needs'; but neither must it exceed the maximum amount which can be transferred to foreign countries without upsetting the exchange stability of the German currency. 'It is quite obvious that the amount of budget surplus which can be raised by taxation is not limited by the entirely distinct question of the conditions of external transfer. We propose to distinguish sharply between the two problems.' The sharpness with which this vital distinction is conceived and worked out is the most important part of the committee's scheme. It has not received sufficient emphasis in the preliminary Press comments.

First, the budgetary surplus (supplemented by contributions from the railways and from industry): as a result of an elaborate survey and on the basis of a weight of taxation at least commensurate with that imposed in the Allied countries, the committee venture a definite figure—namely, £125 million (gold). This figure itself is subject, however, to important modifications in certain contingencies. First, if the commodity value of gold rises or falls by more than 10 per cent, the above figure is to be adjusted proportionately. Secondly, if the future prosperity of Germany rises or falls above or below the committee's expectations as measured by an index, based on the statistics of foreign trade, the budget, railway traffic, consumption of sugar, tobacco, beer and alcohol, population and coal, then in this case also the above figure is to be adjusted proportionately. Thirdly, if in the long run this figure exceeds what it proves practicable to remit outside Germany, the lower of the two maxima is to prevail, and the contribution from the budget is to be limited to the amount that can be remitted abroad.

Germany can scarcely expect better terms than these. The figure of £125 million is itself, apart from possible abatements, equal to the lowest amount mentioned hitherto in any official project, namely, the *minimum* in the Bonar Law proposal of January 1923. The amount may prove too high, but there are safeguards for its reduction. The committee have avoided the danger of mentioning any definite capital equivalent of the annual payments.

Next, the maximum amount to be remitted outside Germany: here the committee venture on no figures at all. It is, they say,

by comparison with the budget, incapable of close calculation, unmanageable and too elastic...It would be both speculative and unjust to attempt to forecast the possibilities of the future exchange position and to determine Germany's burden in advance with reference to a problematic estimate of it. Experience, and experience alone, can show what transfer into foreign currencies can in practice be made. Our system provides in the meantime for a proper charge upon the German taxpayer, and corresponding deposit in gold marks to the Allies' account; and then secures the maximum conversion of these mark deposits into foreign currencies which the actual capacity of the exchange position at any given time renders possible.

The means by which this is to be effected is as follows. The proceeds, derived from the assigned revenues, from the railways and from industry, are to be paid over in marks to a special account in the proposed new German bank of issue. This mark balance will be controlled by an Allied committee, who will transfer it to the Allies by the purchase of foreign exchange to the maximum extent possible 'without bringing about instability of currency'. If the sums paid into the account exceed what it is possible to remit abroad, the accumulations up to a normal maximum of £100 million 'will form part of the short money operations of the bank' within Germany. Accumulations beyond this sum are to be invested in bonds or loans in Germany. But when the unremitted accumulation reaches £250 million, it is not to be increased further, and the payments required from the German government will be reduced accordingly. This maximum figure can, however, be modified upwards or downwards by a two-thirds majority of the controlling committee.

I express no opinion at present as to whether a scheme of this kind is capable of being operated in practice on so vast a scale over a long period of years. But the project has this merit at least—that it endeavours to reconcile the possibility of very large payments hereafter with adequate safeguards in the event of optimistic forecasts proving wrong. If the plan is worked with skill and good faith, it seems to protect Germany from the dangers of oppression and ruin. We must be content for the present with the committee's own conclusion—'We do not deny that this part of our proposal will present difficulties of a novel character which can only be solved by experience. But what are the alternatives?'

There remains one feature of the plan to which Germans are likely to pay close attention—the various agents, controllers, and trustees to be attached, on behalf of the Allies, to the organs of German administration. It does not seem, on the first reading, that the proposed powers of these persons are excessive. Germany has much to gain by the Allies' receiving first-hand information from sources they trust about the real facts.

The report is the finest contribution hitherto to this impossible problem. It breathes a new spirit and is conceived in a new vein. It achieves an atmosphere of impartiality, and exhibits scientific workmanship and sound learning. Though the language seems at times the language of a sane man who, finding himself in a madhouse, must accommodate himself to the inmates, it never loses its sanity. Though it compromises with the impossible and even contemplates the impossible, it never prescribes the impossible. This façade and these designs may never be realised in an edifice raised up in the light of day. But it is an honourable document and opens a new chapter.

Keynes found his own earlier conclusions regarding the worth of German foreign assets vindicated by the McKenna Report, which he reviewed the following week.

From The Nation and Athenaeum, *19 April 1924*

THE EXPERTS' REPORTS

II. *The McKenna Report*

This report, of which the object is to estimate the value of the foreign assets owned by individual Germans, is of high general interest, but the practical effect is mainly negative. The report clears away illusions, and furnishes us with facts. It does not disclose any unsuspected resources immediately available for the payment of reparations, and it makes no practical suggestion directed to this end. Thus the common-sense view is confirmed, that German foreign assets are moderate in amount and quite beyond the reach of confiscatory legislation. The committee seem to take the view that these assets can only be made available to assist the payment of reparations in so far as they voluntarily return to Germany; and that the best way to promote this lies in the removal, rather than in the extension, of restrictive legislation.

The report arrives at a conclusion, definite within limits, and quotes separate estimates for each of the main items; but—rather oddly—it does not bring the individual items together in any balance sheet or show precisely how they lead up to the final result. Enough information, however, has been given to enable us to draw up a balance sheet for ourselves as below, subject to a few dubious entries.

The committee follow previous investigators in dividing their problem into two parts: first, the remnant of Germany's pre-war foreign investments, and second, the new acquisition of foreign assets since the war by the sale of marks, etc.

I. *Net foreign assets in 1919*

(All the following figures are in terms of milliards of gold marks. Those figures which are not separately stated by the experts are marked with a query.)

Foreign assets in 1914	28·0	Foreign trade deficit and loans to Allies during the war	15·2
Profits in occupied territories during the war	5·7–6·0		
Sale of gold during the war	1·0	Loss by depreciation, liquidation, and sequestration	16·1
Income from foreign assets during the war	1·3 (?)	Sale of securities during the war	1·0
		Net assets remaining in 1919	4·0
	36·3		36·3

Thus Germany's pre-war investments have fallen from 28 milliards (£1,400 million) to about 4 milliards (£200 million); that is to say, she has lost six-sevenths of them. This estimate

242

of 4 milliards agrees closely with the figure which I published in 1919 in *The Economic Consequences of the Peace* (pp. 161–8) [*JMK*, vol II, pp. 110–14], where I gave 5 milliards for the maximum size of the remnant and 2 to 5 milliards for the maximum which the Reparation Commission could reckon on from this source. It is higher than a figure which I published in September 1922, as applicable to that date (namely, ½ to 1 milliard) [p. 47], and somewhat higher also than the figure of 2 to 3 milliards, given by the American Institute of Economics in their recent volume *Germany's Capacity to Pay*. These discrepancies are explained by the McKenna Report starting from a higher *initial* figure for the pre-war period. Hitherto 20 to 25 milliards has been the generally accepted figure (I have summarised the various pre-war estimates—*Economic Consequences of the Peace*, p. 162) [*JMK*, vol. II, p. 110], whereas the McKenna Report sets out, as we have seen, from a figure of 28 milliards. Since this estimate appears to have been made on the authority of the German government itself, it must be accepted. The difference seems to be due to the McKenna figure (1) including the value of foreign partnerships and participations and not merely stock exchange securities, (2) estimating the value of securities at their face value, and (3) giving the gross total without deduction for property in Germany owned abroad. After allowance under these heads, the experts are very close indeed to the earlier estimates cited above.

II. *Net post-war acquisition*

The McKenna figures for the post-war period, set forth in the same manner, are as follows [top of p. 244].

These estimates will finally dispel the legendary figures which had been accepted by the credulous. It is curious to recall that so recently as 29 August 1922 *The Times* in a leading article estimated at eight or nine hundred millions

Sale to foreigners of mark balances and bank notes	7·6–8·7	Adverse trade balance and cash payments to Allies since the war	9–10
Sale of gold	1·5	Foreign notes in Germany	1·2
Sale of German property and German securities to foreigners	1·5	*Net* acquisition of foreign assets since the war	1·7–3·8
Remittances, tourists, shipping, etc. (net), German private property in ceded territory	1·3–3·3 (?)		
	11·9–15		11·9–15

sterling the sum 'safely invested in foreign securities or lodged in foreign banks' on German account.

Remembering the comments with which my own estimates of these figures were received in certain quarters, I am justified in comparing them with the final verdict. In an article published in the 'Manchester Guardian Commercial' *Reconstruction Supplement,* on 28 September 1922 [pp. 47–58], I estimated that by 30 June 1922 (by which date indeed the bulk of the business had been done), the sales to foreigners of paper mark balances and bank notes and German property and securities amounted to 9 milliard gold marks; the McKenna Report puts the figure up to 31 December 1923 (eighteen months later), at between 9·1 and 10·2 milliard gold marks. (It appears, however, that a greater proportion than I reckoned was held in bank balances and a smaller proportion in notes, property, and securities.) I estimated the adverse trade balance and cash payments to the Allies at 8 milliards; the committee put the figure at 9 to 10 milliards eighteen months later. I estimated the value of the foreign notes held in Germany at 1 milliard; the committee put the figure at 1·2 milliards—again for the later date. Allowing for the difference in date and for the fact that I did not reckon private German property remaining in ceded territory, Silesia, Posen, Danzig, etc., as representing new acquisitions of foreign capital, the general accuracy of these conclusions —conclusions reached inevitably on data far more imperfect

than those available to the committee—is narrowly confirmed.

If the Dawes Report opens a new chapter, the McKenna
Report closes one of the strangest in modern history—a most
perfect example of tragic irony and the turning of the tables
on those guilty of the excessive. For five years Germany's
victors have squeezed the lemon with both hands, have heard
the 'pips squeak' and felt their own hands ache, have seen
a trickle flowing into the bowl—only to discover in the end
that every drop has come, not from the lemon, but from the
hands themselves. What Germany has appeared to pay in
reparations is nearly equal to what the foreign world has
subscribed in return for worthless marks. The same illusion,
the same ill-calculating ignorance, which generated oppres-
sive and impossible demands, have brought forth also these
vast losses, before which the losses of all previous bubbles are
nothing. A million foreigners, we are told, have acquired bank
balances in Germany, and each of these accounts has cost its
owner on the average about £400. It is these lively gentlemen
who have paid the bill so far. These are the rich ones—the
bankers, the financial experts. Beyond them are the many
millions, the housemaids and the hairdressers, who have
bought a few shillings' worth or a few pounds' worth of crisp
Reichsbank emissions, fresh with the press of ink—until all
the world knows the smell of a new German note.

It is not reasonable to believe that this prodigious process
has been brought about by the conscious guile and subtlety
of the German people. The same sink, which has swallowed
up the voluntary, gambling surplus of the foreign world, has
swallowed up also the indispensable, relied-on savings of the
mass of the German people. Germany has been the scene of
the most extensive redistribution of national wealth from the
many to the few ever experienced within a like space of time,
until she has become the outstanding example of distributive
injustice. The death of the great Stinnes, who saw first and

most passionately the glorious chances which civil disturbance, whether it be political or economic, must always offer
to the bold and debonair freebooter, brings down the curtain
with a just appropriateness. The extravaganza is over, and
common sense resumes her quiet sway.

Hugo Stinnes was a German industrialist, owner of steel foundries and
electrical works, who profited from the circumstances of the Ruhr
occupation.

After some delay because of elections in France and Germany, the Allies
and invited representatives of the United States met in London on 16 July
for the adoption of the Dawes Report. Although not explicitly stated, the
crux of the Dawes scheme—well understood—was to be the release of
Germany from foreign occupation in order to work out her own recovery.
Britain, Italy and Belgium were agreed on this, and the new radical French
premier, Edouard Herriot, who had succeeded Poincaré, paid some lip
service to the idea. But Herriot was not sure enough of his position to
disregard the French obsession with security, and his nervousness that
Poincaré might be swept back into power was shared by England's new
Labour Prime Minister, Ramsay MacDonald, who went to what Keynes felt
to be extreme lengths to conciliate France. Important issues were blurred
and the power of individual Allies to take action or make reprisals, so
dear to France, remained as before.

Keynes wrote to Melchior on 21 July, the day the conference's committee
reported, a letter of which he kept no copy but to which Melchior referred
in his reply of 24 July giving his own reaction. Keynes also addressed his
objections to the readers of *The Nation*.

From The Nation and Athenaeum, *26 July 1924*

THE LONDON CONFERENCE AND
TERRITORIAL SANCTIONS

One item, amongst the conclusions of the conference so far
disclosed, is so vital, both to the acceptance of the ultimate
scheme by Germany on the one hand and by the investors
of the world on the other hand, that it deserves to be picked
out for isolated emphasis and warning.

The Dawes scheme can provide no solution unless it marks a complete break with the past régime of Ruhr occupations and the like. A month ago this was universally accepted in this country. In the exhausting combat of daily debate it would seem that the natural desire for compromise has allowed the sharp distinction, between what is proposed for the future and what has happened in the past, to be slurred over. The penalties to be enforced in the event of a German default are merely superimposed on the existing conditions of the Treaty of Versailles, and no attempt is made to clear up doubts as to the position under that Treaty. From the report of the first committee of the conference, as published on Monday, it appears that any powers of individual action at present possessed by Allied governments under the Treaty of Versailles remain unmodified. Nor is there any definition as to whether the penal measures contemplated include territorial sanctions.

Fortunately, the bankers, who have been consulted, have had the public spirit and the good sense to ask that, as a condition of the loan, the possibility of future Ruhr expeditions should be clearly excluded. We have reason to be grateful to the British and American financiers who are refusing to be a party to Mr MacDonald's subterfuges.

At the moment of writing, the future course of the conference is still obscure. But even if the bankers succumb to the politicians, it is extraordinarily short-sighted to suppose that any settlement can be reached acceptable to Germany, or, indeed, one which can be reasonably preferred to Germany, which does not clear up all doubts. Mr MacDonald and M. Herriot cannot expect that ambiguities, introduced with the object of avoiding the discussion of awkward questions, can be left unchallenged by Germany.

It seems to me both right and inevitable that the German government should immediately ask certain questions if they are presented with the text reached by the first committee of the London Conference. They are bound to ask: (1) Do the penal measures contemplated include territorial sanctions? (2) Is a single power acting in isolation entitled to apply either territorial or other sanctions? (3) Is the military occupation of the Ruhr, a continuation of which appears to be contemplated in some shape or form, legitimised by all the members of the London Conference? If so, to what section of the Treaty of Versailles do the assembled powers unanimously appeal as justifying this occupation?

If the German government ask these questions, they are entitled to a reply. Is there any reply to which both the British government and the French government can subscribe? Is it not a continuation of the worst traditions of our post-war diplomacy to present unanimously to the Germans a document the most important adherents to which interpret it in different ways and are well aware that each interprets it in a different way? There should be some decent limit to the divergence between a politician's declarations out of office and in office. It is not creditable to Mr Ramsay MacDonald—to whom personally, if rumour is to be credited, and not to his Cabinet or to his party, the surrender is to be attributed—that it should have been left to international financiers to recall him to a sense of honest behaviour between nations.

Keynes pursued the idea of the necessity for precision in agreement in a letter to *The Times*. 'Satan alone could separate us,' MacDonald had declared dramatically at the end of the conference's first phase. Herriot had been warmly welcomed back in Paris and his policy was unanimously approved by the French Cabinet. But the conference had left unsettled questions, in particular the continuing French occupation of the Ruhr and France's freedom to take action if Germany were in default. The terms adopted by the conference had been intended to ensure that Germany could not be considered in default unless she had defaulted actually and wilfully, but they left a loophole for separate action by the French, which Keynes seized upon in his letter written on 6 August and published two days later.

To the Editor of The Times, *8 August 1924*

WILFUL DEFAULT IN REPARATIONS
An omission in the agreement

Sir,

The point, raised by Mr Lloyd George yesterday in the House of Commons, about the curious absence of specific reference to 'voluntary default' by Germany in the report of the recent conference, may be very important. Mr Mac-Donald's reply was obscure and confused. We have learnt by experience that inexactitude of word in agreements relating to reparations may have so much significance that it is worth while to state the position as clearly as possible.

The reparation chapter of the Treaty of Versailles deals first (part VIII, annex II, § 17) with 'default' by Germany in the performance of her obligations. In the event of such default, it is the duty of the Reparation Commission to give notice of it to the interested powers. It deals next and separately (§ 18) with the measures which the Allied governments are entitled to take in case of 'voluntary default'. Now, in view of the complicated and hypothetical character of the Dawes Report, it is likely that at some future date Germany will be in default, and that this will be a question of fact relatively easy to answer. The difficult and important question will be, not whether Germany is in default (which may need no argument), but whether her government could have avoided it—i.e., whether it is a wilful (or voluntary) default.

One might, therefore, have supposed that the recent conference, after setting up a complicated procedure of adjudication and arbitration, would have explicitly related this procedure, not merely to the declaration of 'default', but to the declaration of 'voluntary default'. But not so. The phrase 'voluntary default' of § 18 of the relevant section of the Treaty of Versailles never occurs. We hear only of the mere 'default' of § 17. Then, partly to repair, by a side wind, this grave

249

omission, a later section of the report of the first committee prescribes that the signatories agree not to apply the sanctions of § 18 of the Treaty of Versailles unless a default has been declared 'within the meaning of section III of part I of the experts' report'. On referring to this section, which is part of the descriptive introductory matter, and is not drawn up in precise form, we find no mention either of 'default' or of 'voluntary default', but a new phrase—namely, 'flagrant failure to fulfil the conditions' (*manquement flagrant aux conditions*). Thus it is the duty of the adjudicating body to report not the 'voluntary default' of § 18, but 'flagrant failure to fulfil the conditions'; and it is in this event that France reserves to herself the right to apply territorial sanctions acting alone.

Now the word 'flagrant' is, generally, rhetorical, meaning 'glaring' or 'notorious', and has, so far as I am aware, no legal signification. It might be open to M. Poincaré to argue hereafter that a 'flagrant failure' means an obvious failure in some important respect, in distinction from a doubtful, petty, or merely technical failure. But this is not the same thing as a voluntary or wilful failure. If, for example, Germany does not succeed in raising by taxation, for the purpose of reparation, more than two-thirds of the amount laid down by the Dawes Report, this might be correctly described as a 'flagrant' failure, but it might not, all the same, be voluntary or wilful. The sums contemplated by the experts may prove in certain circumstances, as they themselves would admit, to be beyond Germany's fiscal capacity. Germany's liabilities under the Dawes scheme rise if the 'index number of prosperity' rises; but there is no provision for them to fall if the index falls. Thus the actual phrasing leaves a loophole for separate French action in the not improbable event of the Dawes scheme breaking down as an instrument of reparations by no fault of Germany. What object is there in the circumlocutions which have been adopted? Would it not be better to say plainly, if that is what we mean, that the subject of adjudication by the agreed abitration bodies, failing which no sanctions are to be taken by anyone, is 'wilful default by the German government in a matter of importance'?

All this is, of course, apart from the fundamental questions —what kind of sanctions are lawful in the event of wilful default, and by whom applicable—which the conference did not touch.

Yours, etc.

J. M. KEYNES

Keynes's first version of the final paragraph of this letter read (and was crossed out) in his handwritten draft:

the fundamental questions...which the conference has not attempted to tackle so far, but a clear answer to which is a prior condition of an honest European settlement. At present Mr Ramsay MacDonald and M. Herriot are preventing 'Satan from separating them' by offering Germany a proposition which, as the former admitted in the House of Commons on Monday, each of them interprets in a different sense. If the German delegates were to enquire which meaning holds good they will doubtless be accused of a base intrigue to separate two [here the word 'loyal' appeared, with 'faithful' inserted—both words were crossed out] Allies.

Andrew McFadyean, writing Keynes the same day as the publication of the letter, 'which I was prepared to see after what you said to me the other day', mentioned 'one point on which you have gone a little bit astray'.

It does not destroy your main argument, but it is just worth while drawing your attention to it. Since the famous declaration of default, there has been no difference between default in paragraph 17 of annex II and the voluntary default of paragraph 18, for the Reparation Commission formally and unanimously interpreted the 'default' of 17 as meaning the 'voluntary default' of 18. The decision, which is not without importance, was published at the time, but it is quite intelligible that it should have been forgotten outside the Commission.

An attendant result of the adoption of the Dawes Plan was the reimposition by Britain (and other Allies) of a 26 per cent duty on German imports. This device for collecting reparations—by which the British Treasury received the duty for which the German government reimbursed the German exporter—had been dropped in its original form when the German government had ceased to reimburse exporters during the moratorium in 1923. Its readoption was the occasion of confusion, as evidenced by 'A.G.G.', a *Nation* contributor to 'Life and Politics', whom Keynes set right in the following letter, and perplexity on the part of the public. (The latter was demonstrated by the Orientalist who wrote to *The Nation* ironically thanking Mr Keynes for explaining why he had to pay 'reparations' on Persian books from a Berlin bookseller.)

To the Editor of The Nation and Athenaeum, *20 September 1924*

Sir,

The reimposition of the 26 per cent on German imports into this country may or may not be wise; but it is not such a senseless proceeding as 'A.G.G.' makes out in your issue of 13 September.

It is not true, as he suggests, that the English consumer paid the duty all along, because for a time the German government reimbursed the German exporters. It was only in 1923, when the German government ceased to do this, that the duty became purely protective; and it was for this reason that it was reduced to 5 per cent. Under the Dawes scheme, however, the German government resumes the reimbursement of German exporters. This, presumably, is the Treasury's first reason for reimposing it.

Nor is it true, as 'A.G.G.' says, that 'the British Exchequer only got a portion of it, for it went to the general reparations account'. The British Exchequer retained the whole of it. It is correct that the sums received have to be brought, theoretically, into the general reparations account; but it is there used mainly to offset the excessive share which would otherwise be received by France on account of the coal deliveries. When one Ally has obtained, as a result of deliveries or otherwise, more than its share, the matter has not been adjusted in practice by that Ally paying cash into the pool; and adjustment has been postponed pending the time when problematic cash payments by Germany may be available to balance the account—the greater part of which payments hitherto have gone in satisfaction of Belgium's priority.

During the next two years this aspect of the matter will be more important than ever, and this is, doubtless, the second of the Treasury's reasons for reimposing the duty. For the Dawes Report recommends (1) that during the first two years the sums available for reparation should be spent almost exclusively within Germany, i.e., on deliveries in kind and armies of occupation, etc.; and (2) that payments under the Reparation Recovery Act should reckon as deliveries in kind. Since the coal deliveries go to France, Italy and Belgium but not to us, we shall get next to nothing out of Germany's payments in the first two years, which are to amount to £111 million (gold) under the Dawes scheme, unless we reimpose these duties; and if by inaction we allow a very big credit to pile up to our account in the books of the Reparation Commission, we shall be lucky if we ever get it paid.

The Reparation Recovery Act is a clumsy and tiresome method of collection. But it is not protectionist, except to the extent that any piece of troublesome machinery impedes trade; and the Dawes Report has so arranged matters that it is our only offset to the coal deliveries for two years at least. And—if the deliveries in kind turn out, as they well may, to absorb the whole of Germany's surplus for payment—it will be *permanently* our only possible source of reparation receipts. If Germany is made to pay reparations, I do not think that we should wholly forgo our share.

Yours, etc.,

J. M. KEYNES

The agreement of the London Conference to accept the Dawes Plan was signed by all the parties concerned on 30 August 1924, in spite of a certain amount of lingering opposition from the Poincaré diehards in France, those businessmen who were fearful of competition in England, and the National Socialist party in Germany. Keynes did not give his considered opinion of the plan until a month later. Through his close association with McFadyean, Stamp and McKenna, he had an intimate knowledge of the economic and political complexities involved in its framing and there was no question as to his sympathy with its aims. In spite of his usual optimism, his early scepticism towards the plan had hardened into a conviction that it was doomed, eventually, to failure.

The article that he wrote for *The Nation*, 'The Dawes Scheme and the German Loan', was also published in Germany in *Wirtschaftsdienst*, Hamburg, and in the United States in the *New Republic*, in the latter under the title 'What the Dawes Plan Will Do'.

In the *New Republic* version, as in all Keynes's articles published by the *New Republic*, all references to 'we', 'us' and 'our' were changed to 'British'. The third section, on the loan as an investment, was omitted in this version, and in the first paragraph, where Keynes wrote of Britian being 'honourably committed' to the loan, he added: 'This fact has been generally appreciated in London, and it is for this reason that the violent agitations of the Rothermere Press against the loan have had no effect.'

From The Nation and Athenaeum, *4 October 1924*

THE DAWES SCHEME AND THE GERMAN LOAN

The Dawes scheme was adopted by general consent. Everyone knew that it involved a loan to Germany, of which this country would be expected to take up from a quarter to a third. The object of this loan was not to help *us*, but to provide a bait to secure the acceptance of the scheme as a whole by France and by Germany. We are, therefore, honourably committed to the loan, and it is much too late to back out on the ground that this is not the part of the scheme from which we ourselves gain direct advantage. It is, in fact, certain that we shall not back out. The Bank of England will undertake to float our fair share of the loan, and it is within the power of the Bank to see the matter through.

This being regarded as settled, we need not be afraid of speaking candidly about the prospects opened out by the Dawes scheme. I will endeavour to answer four questions which are often asked.

1. *Is the loan an essential part of the experts' scheme?*

Economically and financially—no; diplomatically and psychologically—yes. Since Germany is not expected to have an effective surplus for a year or more, the obvious course was to postpone for a year or more the date at which she should commence to pay. But this was not agreeable to France. It was disagreeable to French opinion out of proportion to the amount of money involved. It was deemed, therefore, to be worth the while of Great Britain and the United States, in order to gain French acquiescence, to take on their own shoulders the burden of the first batch of payments— particularly if this could be arranged on terms which would give a fair prospect of eventual recoupment from Germany. This was one half of the diplomatic argument. The fact that popular opinion in Germany also attached importance to a foreign loan out of proportion to the amount of money involved furnished the other half. It is absurd, perhaps, that either German or French opinion should be swayed by the expectation of a loan, equal in amount to no more than what Germany is to pay over in the first eight months of the scheme (by next July Germany will have paid back to the Allies the equivalent of the whole proceeds of the loan—a loan which she will not have touched before the end of this month), and equal to what Germany is supposed to be going to pay every four months for ever, when the Dawes scheme shall have come into full operation. But crowds are not clever at arithmetic. The great international loan has been talked about for years. It is the one matter on which France and Germany have always been agreed—the plan by which the reparation bill should be shouldered, in the first instance at least, by Great Britain and the United States. An appearance of some slight concession to this point of view had, therefore, both in France and in Germany, a decisive psychological influence.

2. *Will the Loan have an immediate and large effect in increasing Germany's competitive power in international markets?*

I do not think so. Both those who believe that the loan will restore Europe and therefore restore us, and those who believe that the loan will restore Europe and therefore destroy us, greatly exaggerate its effect. The amount which the loan will place at Germany's free disposal is small compared with her need of working capital. It is probably less considerable than the sums which have been already invested in Germany during the past few months under the stimulus of high rates of interest. Nor can we expect that it will pave the way for private foreign investment in Germany of much larger sums at ordinary rates of interest. Counteracting considerations, of the kind to be examined below, will continue to deter foreigners from investing in Germany except as a speculation—that is to say, with the knowledge of risk but with expectations of possible profit on a corresponding scale.

The smallness of the sum which the loan will place at Germany's free disposal is due to a fact which is often overlooked. The new State Bank, imposed on Germany by the Dawes scheme, is compelled to hold an amount, equal to 33 per cent of its note issue and 12 per cent of its deposits, in gold or in foreign banks. The existing gold reserves of the institutions which are to be consolidated into the new bank fall considerably short of the amount thus required to cover the existing note issue and the existing deposits. Moreover, both of these are much below the levels of note issue and of deposits which Germany would need in normal conditions. It is difficult to estimate just what the circulation and the deposits of the new bank will be. I calculate, roughly, that about a third of the loan would have to be left behind in the form of deposits in foreign banks, in order to bring the reserves up to the figures requisite in existing conditions.[1] But more than the whole of it would be needed for this purpose if conditions were to return to normal. The Dawes committee themselves seemed to contemplate that the bulk, if not the whole, of the loan should be used in this way, i.e., not to finance imports but to furnish a ground, satisfactory to public opinion, for an increase in the internal note circulation. Probably, in practice, at least a half of the loan will have to be retained abroad to provide a margin for some immediate expansion in circulation and in deposits.

Thus a considerable part of the sums raised for Germany in London and New York may never leave London or New York, but will remain deposited in those centres. In short, Germany will borrow money from us at (say) 8 per cent and will simultaneously lend half of it back to us[2] at (say) 2 per cent. It is not plausible to suppose that this transaction will either ruin us or vastly increase the quantities of cotton or copper or the like which Germany will be able to buy.

One important qualification to this remains to be mentioned. The new bank is to be allowed, subject to virtual unanimity on the part of the members of its governing boards, to let its reserves fall below the prescribed figure on the payment of a fine and the maintenance of a high bank rate. For example, with a bank rate of 10 per cent per annum, the bank could afford to pay a fine of 10 per cent on its reserve deficiency, which, under the Dawes scheme, would permit a reduction of the note reserve from 33 to 23 per cent. Something of this kind may happen in practice—10 per cent is, in fact, the existing bank rate in Germany. Nevertheless, on balance the loan cannot do much to relieve the existing stringency in Germany, since it is only on condition of a

---

[1] This makes no allowance for the redemption (in April 1926) of the Dollar-Schatzanweisungen, against which part of the Reichsbank's gold is pledged.

[2] I write *us*, but perhaps I should write *U.S.* For it seems to me doubtful whether English banks can be expected to pay interest on deposits at call repayable in gold (i.e., in dollars). Thus the bulk of Germany's additional reserves may have to be employed as New York call money.

continuance of this stringency that most of it can be used. The tying up in this way of Germany's very limited liquid resources is a mistake in the Dawes scheme.[3]

3. *Is the loan a satisfactory investment?*

One can scarcely answer this until the terms of the loan are published. We may assume, however, that as regards interest yield they will be liberal; for liberal terms will cost Germany nothing (the service of the loan is to be deducted from the sums due from Germany in subsequent years). The loan is likely, therefore, to compare favourably in yield with other loans to foreign governments.

Is the loan well secured? If it is to be a first charge on *all* payments by Germany, whether in cash or kind, its service is evidently well within Germany's financial capacity. In this case there will be nothing against it, except the incalculable 'political' risk attaching, in my opinion, to *all* loans to foreign governments. But on this interpretation the loan will be made, in effect, on the credit of the Allied governments which receive the payments in kind; for, in the not unlikely event of the transfer committee being unable to remit cash, those who have received in kind will have to repay the bondholders in cash.

If, however, it is only a first charge on the cash remittances which the transfer committee may be able to effect over and above the deliveries in kind, and if the latter (including one thing and another) may amount to as much as £40–50 million per annum, then it is not well secured. On this important point the Dawes Report is silent.

[3] The bank section of the Dawes Report is, technically, much weaker than the rest, and I am in full agreement with the responsible German authorities who have been criticising its technical faultiness, notably Professor Kurt Singer and Dr Hahn.

4. *Does the Dawes scheme 'settle' the reparations problem?*

The phrase 'Dawes scheme' has become an incantation inscribed on a closed sphere. The diplomatic solution has depended on a tacit agreement not to look inside or to ask irreverent questions. Almost everyone has connived at this, because no one could propose any alternative *next* step for the diplomatists. But those who believe that the Dawes scheme is workable or settles the problem are certainly deceived.

The arguments in favour of accepting the Dawes scheme as the next step were, and are, two: first, that under cover of it the French may leave the Ruhr; second, that an attempt has been made by its authors so to contrive that, as time goes on, it will itself furnish the demonstration of its own impracticability. But this is far from ridding us of the disease of reparations. It gives us a short breathing space; that is all. For, as a concession to diplomatic difficulties, the Dawes committee have embodied in their scheme two fatal faults.

In the first place, they do not, in spite of the loan, allow Germany the respite which she needs. Germany's economic weakness is now attributable almost wholly to one single cause—the exhaustion of her liquid and circulating capital. The course of events during and since the war has reduced this factor of production to a level below what is necessary for efficiency by—at a guess—something like £500 million. It is impossible that this shortage should be made good mainly by foreign credits. The outside world might furnish up to (say) a quarter of it, over a period of time, at usurious rates of interest—that is to say, with an expectation of from 10 to 20 per cent per annum, the payment of which would be a heavy burden. Foreigners will not invest large sums in Germany at normal rates of interest so long as the Dawes scheme hangs over her. For the most part, therefore, the shortage cannot be made good in any other way than by Germany's own annual savings being allowed to accumulate at compound interest for a certain period. But this is not compatible with arrangements for skinning her annually. The Dawes experts might have given more attention to making provision for the replenishment of Germany's working capital. Many Englishmen fear that the Dawes Plan will injure British industry because, under it, Germany, subjected to the compulsion of foreign task masters in effective charge of the economic system of the country, will deluge our markets with the fruits of sweated and semi-slave labour. In short, they assume that the plan will work. Let them have no such fears. The plan will not work in its entirety; and that part of it which will be operative for a time may actually hinder the recovery by Germany of her full competitive strength. In saying this I do not dissent from the view that a Germany over-stimulated by force to produce exports competitive with ours, in conditions which our working classes would not tolerate, is injurious to our interests. On the other hand, I do not believe that the restoration of normal prosperity to Germany will be to our disadvantage. [The last two sentences were omitted from the *New Republic* version.]

In the second place, the Dawes Plan pretends to erect a system which is not compatible with civilisation or with human nature. It sets up foreign control over the banking, the transport, and the fiscal systems of Germany, the object of which will be to extract from the German people the last drop of sweat. In such circumstances every patriotic and public-spirited German will feel it to be his duty and preoccupation, henceforeward, to do everything he can to bring this system to confusion and to an end. And if, by a miracle, the system were to work, it would not be long before most Englishmen, for various reasons, would desire the same thing.

No reparations will ever be obtained from Germany except such moderate sums, well within her powers, as she will voluntarily pay. The Dawes scheme pretends to attempt more than this. Therefore it will fail. But I venture to think that the foreign controls and the elaborate machinery of the scheme have not been contrived by its authors in a spirit of oppression, but for the purpose of perfecting the demonstration, when the breakdown comes, that every possible precaution had been taken, and that the breakdown was, therefore, due to nothing else but the inherent impossibility of the task which had been set.

Adoption of the Dawes Plan revived public hope in the eventual repayment of the war debts. Keynes contributed to a discussion of the subject in the *Daily Herald*.

From the Daily Herald, *5 August 1924*

DEBT PAYMENTS FROM OURSELVES TO AMERICA
AND FROM GERMANY TO THE ALLIES

I agree for the most part with the various authorities who have written for the *Daily Herald* about this question, particularly with Professor [A. L.] Bowley and Mr Norman Angell. So far as the receipt of payment goes, the great distinction is between payments which can be relied on to continue and precarious payments upon the continuance of which it is impossible to rely, but which have a very upsetting effect on existing industries.

But there are two points perhaps worth adding. So far as our payments to America are concerned, they will probably take the form, not of our exporting more or of our importing less, but of our reducing the volume of our new investments abroad. So far as this is the case we suffer no immediate disturbance in the level either of our production or of our consumption. It merely means that, over a long course of years, our *future* income from foreign investments will be less than it would otherwise have been. The fact that it is relatively easy for us to make our debt payments to America is because we have a surplus available for foreign investment. It is easier

261

to make the necessary adjustment out of this available surplus than it would be by readjusting our actual trade.

My second point relates to German reparations. Germany will have to pay in the main by exporting staple articles in the manufacture of which she is a competitor with us. On the one hand this is very likely to injure us. By accepting, or being forced to accept, a lower standard of life than ours, Germany may conceivably be able to compete, disastrously for us, with our products. Indeed, we may find ourselves in the paradoxical situation of being committed—unless our government is very careful—to putting extreme political and even military pressure on Germany to force her to continue injuring our own trades. In so far as the proceeds of reparation are payable to ourselves we have an offset to the damage thus done. But one has to remember, if one is calculating the self-interest of Great Britain, that only about a quarter of the receipts from reparations are due to be paid to us. This makes a great difference. The greater part of Germany's exports may compete with us, and three-quarters of the accruing proceeds will be paid, not to us, but to others.

I believe that we have an interest in restoring Germany, and Europe generally, to a state of peace and prosperity. But we have no interest—quite the contrary—in putting pressure on Germany to reduce the standard of life of her workers to a level at which she can sell products competing with ours in the world market at a price which is incompatible with the maintenance of a proper standard of life here.

Some paragraphs Keynes wrote two months later provide information on the behaviour of governments as debtors. They were part of a leading article entitled 'The Case Against the Russian Loan' in *The Nation*'s Russian Treaty Supplement of 18 October 1924. (The rest of the article was written by Hubert Henderson, except for three short final sections by Harold Wright.

THE DAWES PLAN, 1923–1928

From The Nation and Athenaeum, *18 October 1924*

DEFAULTS BY FOREIGN GOVERNMENTS

The record of defaults by foreign governments on their external debt are so numerous, and indeed so nearly universal, that it is easier to deal with them by naming those which have not defaulted than those which have.

All foreign governments which have borrowed any considerable sum on the London market[4] have been in default in whole or in part on the service of their external debt within the past twenty-five years, with the exception of Chile and Japan. It should, however, be added that the defaults by Peru have been insignificant, and those by Uruguay not very important unless we go back to 1891.

The defaulting governments include those of all the states of Central and South America, with the above-named two or three exceptions. Other important defaulters within the past twenty-five years include Mexico, China, Egypt, Turkey, Greece, Spain, Portugal, Russia, Austria, Hungary, Bulgaria, and Roumania.

Indeed, it is not an exaggeration to say that it has been very exceptional in the history of foreign investment for a foreign government to keep its engagements.

In addition to those countries which have technically defaulted, there are several other countries which have borrowed externally in terms of their own currency and have then allowed that currency to depreciate to less than half of the nominal value at which the loans were contracted, and in some cases to an infinitesimal fraction of it. The more important countries in this group are Belgium, France, Italy, and Germany.

With the prospect of reparation payments materialising under the Dawes régime, the American Debt Funding Commission approached France for

---

[4] The governments of Scandinavia and Holland, none of which have borrowed more than relatively small sums, are amongst the exceptious.

a settlement of her debt to the United States. France, the last remaining debtor to settle, was widely rumoured to be seeking more favourable terms than Britain had been able to obtain, and the British feared that they themselves would go unpaid. Keynes, who had opposed the British settlement and foresaw his country ending up with nothing in return for her loans to France and Italy, argued in *The Nation* that these debts were not ordinary debts and suggested a compromise agreement between Britain and the United States to divide any payments that were made proportionately between them.

This article also appeared in *Wirtschaftsdienst*, *Corriere della Sera* of Milan, and the *New Republic*. The *New Republic* version (21 January 1925) differed from *The Nation* only in the division of its paragraphs, a result of the article being received by cable rather than by mail.

From The Nation and Athenaeum, *10 January 1925*

THE INTER-ALLIED DEBTS

Most of the politicians and business men of America—but not all of them—tell us that they look on these debts just like any ordinary commercial debt for goods sold and delivered. We, in Great Britain, are acting on that principle. The United States have asked us to pay and we are paying. Nevertheless, there are three sufficient reasons for not treating France and Italy in a like manner—the origin of the debts, the evils which would follow on an attempt to exact them, and the practical impossibilities of collection. I sympathize, therefore, with the distinction, which M. Clémentel, the French minister of finance, has recently made, in calling these debts 'political' debts, and the other obligations of the French government 'commercial debts'. The inter-allied debts are a matter of politics and not of law or contract. It is as mistaken to treat them as things of contract as it was to treat the theoretical liabilities of Germany under the Treaty of Versailles as things of contract.

If we consider for one minute the origin of the debts, it is obvious that they are not just like other debts. Let me put the argument as it may reasonably appear to a Frenchman.

Each of the Allies threw the whole of their strength into the struggle—it was, as the Americans say, a 100 per cent war. But—wisely and properly—they did not all use their strength in the same way. For example, the effort of France was mainly military. On account of the number of men she put into the field in proportion to her population, and because part of France was occupied by the enemy, France did not possess, after the first year, sufficient economic strength to equip her armies and feed her people, as well as to fight. Our military effort, though very great, was not so great as that of France; but our naval effort was much greater than hers; and our financial effort also was far greater, since it fell on us—until America came into the war—to use our wealth and our industrial strength to help to equip and feed the other Allies. America's effort, on the other hand, was mainly financial. Both absolutely and in proportion to her population, her military effort, measured by the number of men she placed in the field and by her casualties—important though it was to the result—was on an altogether smaller scale. On the other hand, the part which America played in equipping and feeding the Allies was enormous, and we could not, without such help, have won the war. Thus each Ally made essential contributions to the result. But they did not all make them in the same way.

Now it has never occurred to us or to America to charge France and Italy for the British or American shells fired off from British or American guns. Yet, when British or American shells were fired off from French or Italian guns, the real cost to us or to America was much less, since France and Italy supplied the gunners, suffered the casualties, and are paying the pensions. Yet in this case we propose to charge France and Italy for the shells. In fact, when American men and guns and shells had time to reach the front, so that France was wholly relieved within the sector which they took over, there is no idea in anyone's mind that France should be charged money for the aid which America thus gave to her. When Great Britain sent men as well as supplies to the Italian front, there is no idea of charging Italy anything. But when the American men and guns had not reached the front, and only American shells or American wheat or American petrol reached the French armies, so that France had to find the men to use the equipment and to suffer the human losses, then France is to pay for the shells, the wheat, and the petrol. There is no rhyme or reason in this, no justice or common sense.

Why, then, were these sums lent, instead of being given outright at the beginning, which would have saved all this trouble? There was, at the time, an excellent reason against this—namely, that, if the money had been given outright, it would certainly have promoted extravagance and a lack of responsibility in spending. A large part of the financial conduct of the war consisted in establishing financial controls, that is, in preventing one department or one Ally spending sums out of the limited total resources available, which could be spent to better advantage by another department or Ally. It was hard enough for the Treasury to control our own spending departments, and it was impossible, except indirectly, to control the spending departments of our Allies. If every official of the Allied governments, down to those with the least feeling of responsibility and the least power of imagination, had known that it was someone else's money he was spending, the incentives to economy would have been even less than they were.

I have had no connection with the British Treasury for several years. But I am sure that their dealings with their Allies during the war were mainly directed to the enforcement of necessary economy and to seeing that our limited resources were spent to the best advantage. These transactions were not looked on at the time in the light of investments or of commercial advances. And I am sure that the same was true of the American Treasury. If the American public now think that in 1917 and 1918 they were engaged, not in war, but in investment, their memories are very short.

But, apart from the history of the debts, the attempt to exact them now will have no other result than to breed international ill-will. We should just have the German reparation problem over again between each of the former Allies. Hatred, dissension, and—in my belief—not even money would be the result of trying to collect this sum year by year for a generation.

Not even money—for France not only believes conscientiously that justice does not require her to pay, and also that she cannot pay, but payment in full would, in view of the history of German reparations, so deeply outrage her most genuine feelings that she would not do it, even if it were in her interest.

For let us look at the demand in relation to the Dawes scheme. If France were to pay interest and sinking fund, even at a low rate of interest, on what she owes to us and to the United States, it would come to rather more than £60 million a year, which is almost exactly equal to the *whole* of France's share of German reparations under the Dawes scheme, on the assumption that this scheme works out in full. Does anyone believe that France, in whatever circumstances, or under whatever threats, will agree to hand over to Great Britain and the United States every penny that she gets from Germany, and perhaps more?

What, then, ought we to do? Looking back, I believe that it would have been an act of statesmanship and wisdom on the part of Great Britain if, on the day of the Armistice, we had announced to our Allies that all they owed us was forgiven from that day. It is not easy to take that line now. For one thing, we ourselves have undertaken to pay to America half a million dollars every weekday for sixty years, and day by day we are paying it. This sum is equivalent to two-thirds of the cost of our navy, and is nearly equal to the total of our

State expenditure on education. It is more than the whole of the profits of all our merchant ships and all our coal mines added together. With an equal sacrifice over an equal period we could abolish slums and rehouse our population in comfort. That we should pay on this scale, and not be paid ourselves, must influence our attitude. Therefore, the idea that America should get better terms from France than we get, because of her brusquer attitude, is, for good reasons, intolerable to British opinion. It is impossible, now, for us to forgive the debts of France and of Italy unless America does the same. We cannot tolerate even the suggestion that America, whom we are paying, should get better terms than we get from those who owe us both. A frank discussion between Great Britain and America must, therefore, be the first step to a settlement. And if I may make a suggestion as to the lines of compromise which such a settlement might take, it is this. Let a certain moderate proportion of what France and Italy may receive from Germany each year, out of payments made under the Dawes scheme, be devoted to the payment of the French and Italian debts to their Allies; let these sums be divided between Great Britain and the United States in the proportion of what each is owed; and let this be in final discharge.

It is not appropriate to invite France to make an offer, as the American Debt Funding Commission is now doing. For this is merely to ask France to expose herself to humiliation. But if Great Britain and the United States could agree together to make to her a proposal on the above lines—say, one-third of what she may receive from Germany from time to time hereafter—there is a chance of an honourable settlement.

In the same issue as Keynes's article appeared the *New Republic* disagreed editorially with his contention that these were no commercial debts, arguing that the money borrowed enabled the debtor nations to pursue their own particular national interests more efficiently. The war was not fought for a common cause and many of the separate national aims of the war and the peace were antagonistic to those of the United States. 'If the debts must be scaled down or cancelled, let it be done as a repudiation necessarily arising out of the economic situation, not by the subterfuge of calling them something else than debts.'

At the financial discussions which shortly took place in Paris the French finance minister, M. Clémentel, proposed a compromise similar to Keynes's suggested solution, although offering about half the amount he mentioned. This Keynes welcomed, as an indication that France might be willing to offer more to obtain a settlement. Winston Churchill, who attended the Paris meeting as Chancellor of the Exchequer in the recently returned Conservative government, had taken as his text, however, the Balfour Note—which implied that Britain's combined receipts from Germany and the Allies must equal her payments to the United States.

In 'The Balfour Note and Inter-Allied Debts', first published in *The Nation and Athenaeum*, 24 January 1925, and reprinted in *Essays in Persuasion* (*JMK*, vol. IX, pp. 44-7), Keynes took issue with this stand. In practice, he said, the principle of the Balfour Note would work so that the less Germany paid, the more France would have to pay (in order to make up the British debt to the United States), an obvious impossibility, and the exact opposite of Keynes's solution—that the less Germany paid, the less France should pay.

Mr Churchill pronounced a *credo* in the Balfour Note before he went to Paris. He has repeated it on coming back. 'The Balfour Note', he says, 'remains for us a dominating guide of principle set up freely by our own hands.' There is some saving grace in the last seven words. Let me plead with Mr Churchill, if he wants a settlement, that freely by our own hands we should take it down again.

This was Keynes's opening paragraph as the article first appeared in *The Nation*. He omitted this paragraph and the two concluding paragraphs of the original article when he edited it in 1931 for *Essays in Persuasion*. In 1929 he upheld the Balfour Note in words echoing Churchill's when it was attacked by Philip Snowden (pp. 318-25).

Here is the original ending:

Such a settlement would increase, instead of diminishing, the interest of ourselves and the United States in the Dawes scheme. We should have, between us, a bigger interest than France. We might, in this way, obtain a moderate contribution towards our American debt, corresponding to that part of it which we contracted, indirectly, on French account. We should certainly place ourselves in a strong moral and diplomatic position to claim a moderating and pacific influence in the Franco-German problems which still lie ahead.

The Balfour Note would be dangerous, if it were not moonshine. Mr Winston Churchill will waste his time and spoil his reputation for common sense, if he lets himself be deceived by its superficial plausibility. There is nothing to be said in favour of the Balfour Note, except in comparison with the confusions of the present American position. For the American Isolationists, indeed, there is only one logical policy —complete cancellation.

The first year of the Dawes Plan passed and Keynes was involved in other things than reparations and war debts—Britain's return to the gold standard and *The Economic Consequences of Mr Churchill*, his own marriage and his first visit to the U.S.S.R., marked by the publication of *A Short View of Russia*. The appearance of the first report of Parker Gilbert, the Agent-General for Reparation Payments, gave him an occasion, however, to call attention to the report itself and assess the developing situation.

Germany had prospered under the first year of the Dawes Plan, ironically unhampered by some of the burdens experienced by the victorious nations. Yet Keynes put his finger on a troublesome blot—a trend towards falling prices and rising unemployment resulting from the credit restriction prescribed by the Transfer Committee following the principles of 'sound finance'. He saw the governor of the Reichsbank, Dr Hjalmar Schacht, achieving the same perverse results as Montagu Norman, governor of the Bank of England.

From The Nation and Athenaeum, *6 February 1926*

GERMANY'S COMING PROBLEM

The prospects of the second Dawes year

The agent-general, the commissioners, the controllers, all the jackdaws set up to keep a close eye on Germany, have issued their first reports.[5] They are clear and sensible documents, full of justice and common sense, and do credit to the corps of international civil servants, who—as one of the few good fruits of the Treaty of Versailles—are now, under the aegis of the Reparation Commission and the League of Nations, playing so big a part in the life of Europe.

The first Dawes year has been, it seems, plain sailing. The machinery has been introduced smoothly, with abundant good faith on both sides. The experts' forecasts of the yields from taxation and from the railways have proved conservative, and there are comfortable surpluses. The Dawes loan has duly greased the wheels. Deliveries in kind and collections under the Reparations Recovery Act have so nearly covered the annuity that it has not been necessary for the Transfer Committee to purchase foreign exchange except for the service of the loan. The fiscal benefits, which accrue to a country practically cleared of internal debt, State, local, and municipal alike, and owning its railway system free of encumbrances, a country, moreover, which practises disarmament and has no entanglements, expenses or responsibilities abroad, are becoming evident in practice. Mr Parker Gilbert points out that at the date of stabilisation the entire National Debt of the Reich in paper marks had a gold value of less than £50.

Apart, therefore, from reparations Germany is a finance minister's paradise. She is a standing proof that a country

[5] In particular, the 'Report of the Agent-General for Reparation Payments' is a most able paper of first-rate importance, which should be closely studied by anyone who is interested in the German situation. It has not received in the Press the attention which it deserves.

can live through a capital levy far more unjust and far more drastic than Socialists have yet proposed, and survive to enjoy the benefits. No National Debt, no private mortgages, no Navy, no Mesopotamia. Truly the fruits of defeat are very tempting! But all the same a spectre looms up. She is not through with reparations—she has not even begun. In spite of the excellent results which the commissioners and controllers relate, one feels in their reports a note of gravity and of uneasiness. They well know that their real troubles are ahead and not behind.

Last year the reparation annuity cost Germany about £47 million, out of which the Dawes loan furnished £40 million. Apart from this, Germany borrowed abroad some £33 million by long-term external loans, and a large additional sum in the form of short-term credits. The Reichs-Credit A.G. has recently estimated the adverse balance for 1925, including the reparation annuity, at £200 million, met partly by loans and partly by German citizens bringing their capital back home. This figure is surely too high. But it would seem that, apart from the reparation annuity, Germany has a deficit of at least £50 million per annum on foreign trade account. The published totals for exports and imports confirm this conclusion, even if we suppose that the former are 10 per cent below and the latter 10 per cent above the true figure. Moreover, the volume of foreign loans and the trade figures since October indicate that the same state of affairs still continues. The problem of the Transfer Committee during the next three years is to convert this deficit of £50 million into a surplus of £100 million.

How to do it? The orthodox prescription is to keep prices down by curtailing credit. No adequate export surplus will ever develop unless the price level is kept down—all experts agree on that. Accordingly the Agent-General watches the credit policy of the Reichsbank with a keen eye. So far the Reichsbank has co-operated loyally. It has been maintaining a high and effective bank rate, rations credit, and keeps the volume of currency much below the country's needs at the present price level.

What should we expect *a priori* from a credit policy on these lines? So long as the price level is rising, even a very high rate of interest, up to 15 per cent, is no burden on industry. If prices are rising at the rate of even 5 per cent per annum, we can have boom conditions in industry in spite of a 10 per cent rate for business loans. But so soon as prices cease to rise, and, worse still, if they begin to fall, a 10 per cent rate becomes a crushing burden. This, I think, is the clue to the history of German business in the past year.

In September 1924, when the Dawes scheme began, the mean between the wholesale index number and the cost-of-living index stood at 124. By December 1924 this had risen to 131, by March 1925 to 135, and by July 1925 to 138½. Till then the burdens of dear money had been fully compensated, so far as business was concerned, by the rising price level. Meanwhile, the volume of currency, largely as a result of the import of gold out of the proceeds of the Dawes loan, was increasing much faster than prices—the total German circulation rising by steady increments until in July 1925 it was 30 per cent greater than in September 1924, as compared with a rise in prices of (say) 8 per cent[6] during the same period. To such a tune, naturally and inevitably, business and employment stepped briskly. Between the same dates real wages rose nearly 10 per cent, the percentage of workers unemployed fell from 12·4 per cent to 3·5 per cent, and the percentage on short time from 27·5 per cent to 5·2 per cent; whilst the tonnage of traffic handled on the railways increased by nearly 50 per cent. By July 1925 railway traffics were 99 per cent of pre-war, and two months later real wages

---

[6] A change in the basis of calculation of the cost-of-living index may be partly responsible for the 12 per cent rise given by the figures quoted above. It is safer to assume an 8 per cent rise.

also were 99 per cent of pre-war. Germany's economic recovery seemed almost complete.

But though God sent a gourd to shelter Jonah in his afflictions, God also sent a worm. And in the latter half of 1925 the worm of deflation gnawed his way through. The Reichsbank's policy of credit restriction gradually became fully effective. The price level ceased to rise, so that there was no longer any compensation for the 11 per cent rate charged by the Reichsbank for loans. The volume of the currency was held in check at a figure which was hardly more than two-thirds of the pre-war requirements, after allowing for loss of territory on the one hand and for the rise of prices on the other. In fact, in the autumn of 1925, Germany was trying to carry on a volume of production with a volume of banking credit and monetary resources very inadequate to the existing price level. Provided the Reichsbank stood firm at the sources of credit, it was certain that either the volume of production must give way, or else the level of prices. As is apt to happen on these occasions, it was the volume of production which yielded. The usual symptoms began to make their appearance —bankruptcies greatly increased, the prices of industrial shares fell (during 1925 the *Frankfurter Zeitung* index fell 42 per cent), and the percentage of workers unemployed and on short time steadily increased. The numbers in receipt of unemployed relief rolled up rather slowly at first, increasing from 195,000 on 1 July 1925 to 364,000 on 1 November. But thereafter the rate was so rapidly accelerated that by 15 December the unemployed numbered 1,057,031, by the end of the year the total had reached 1,486,000 and on 15 January 1926 it stood at the appalling figure of 1,750,000. Governor Schacht [Hjalmar Schacht, President of the Reichsbank] has topped his million unemployed in Germany by the remorseless working of the same beautiful and reliable technique by which Governor Norman had previously achieved a comparable figure in England.

Now to put 10 per cent of the working population of Germany on to the relief fund does not help reparations. But the Transfer Committee is faced with a difficult dilemma. If it acquiesces in the Reichsbank's relaxing its hold on credit and allowing the German price level to follow its tendency to approximate to the world level, it will have to abandon hope of developing an adequate export surplus in the near future.

It has always been evident to me that the problem of reparations must become, as soon as we got to real business —which is *now* for the first time—a problem of the real wages of the German workers. The German worker has very nearly recovered his pre-war real wages. If we take Germany's losses of capital and of markets into account, it seems unlikely that this fortunate state of affairs can be compatible with the development of an export surplus adequate to meet the full reparation annuity. The work of the Transfer Committee must become, more and more obviously as time goes on, a struggle to reduce the German workers' standard of life. The first stage of the Dawes plan has been to give Germany a much-needed breathing space, and to replenish her resources with foreign loans. This stage has naturally benefited the workers. The serious unemployment now prevalent is, as I read it, the first episode of the second stage—it is the result of an attempt to reduce prices and wages by the method of credit restriction. It is conceivable that this method may be partly successful in bringing down wages. But the Transfer Committee needs a combination of good trade and low wages in order to effect its objects, and I doubt if the method of credit restriction can bring off the double event. Perhaps the Committee will be compelled to attack wages, which is its real objective, in some more direct way.

'Sound' finance has Germany by the throat, just as it has England. I expect that it will not be shaken off except by a political storm. Big business in Germany is very ready to work loyally with the Dawes commissioners, partly for love of a quiet life, partly in order to preserve good relations with foreign financial interests. But a situation may not unlikely arise in which no German government which obeys the behests of the Transfer Committee can retain the votes of the electorate. If that happens, what threats will the Allies offer to overawe the German public? A campaign by the Western powers for the explicit purpose of forcing down the standard of life in central Europe will not be a bull point for the capitalist cause, and may give to the forces of unrest further East the opportunity for which they wait.

The mild and peaceful reports of the first year's doings do not correct my instinct that I profoundly dislike the whole business. We must hope that those in charge will continue to pursue quiet and sensible courses, will hesitate to push anything to its logical conclusion, will ease out the credit situation as much as they can, and will be content for some time yet with moderate results. There is evidence of a considerable relaxation in the pressure for credit during the past month. But this may be as much due to the falling off in production as to a change of policy by the Reichsbank. At present Germany is the economic danger spot in Europe.

This article was published simultaneously in France in the *Petit Journal*, Paris ('Un Jugement pessimiste sur l'Avenir du Plan Dawes'), and on 17 February 1926 in the *New Republic* as 'Germany's Coming Problem', featured as the lead article of the issue. The *New Republic*'s editor, Herbert Croly, thought it 'of quite extraordinary interest' (letter of 4 February 1926). Keynes himself regarded it as 'the most important article, from the German point of view, which I have written for some little time past' (letter to his literary agent, Roy Hopkins, 19 February).

Unfortunately the article as it appeared in Germany was a travesty. By accident it had been sold to the organ of the extreme Nationalists, the *Berliner Lokalanzeiger*. 'The tone of your article,' reported Dr Lothar Frank (in a letter of 10 February), 'in itself pessimistic enough, is worked out still more pessimistic[ally] and some economic conclusions simply omitted. On the other hand there is some rather strong language you didn't use at all.'

Keynes complained to Hopkins (13 February) that the article had been largely curtailed, with the result of altering the balance and effect:

sentences to which I attached great importance have been omitted: the whole of it has been vilely translated, and several passages are so different in detail from what I wrote, that the German version is better described as an abstract or paraphrase of what I wrote (and not a very competent one at that) rather than a translation.

He was upset to the extent of threatening to break off his relations with the agency. In a second letter to Hopkins, 19 February, he wrote:

It has had the effect of absolutely cutting me off from presenting my ideas properly before the German authorities. I have actually had a letter from the statistical department of the German government pointing out the serious discrepancies between the version printed in the *Nation* and that published in Germany. And suggesting that some action is necessary on my part for the protection of my reputation—though what can possibly be done at this stage to remedy matters I do not know.

A change in the schedule of German payments due to the country's prosperity caused Keynes to look again later in the year at the working of the Dawes scheme and to ask whether the payments were being made by exports, as would be desired, or by foreign loans.

This article was published in *The Nation and Athenaeum*, *Wirtschaftsdienst*, *L'Oeuvre*, and the *New Republic*.

From The Nation and Athenaeum, *11 September 1926*

THE PROGRESS OF THE DAWES SCHEME

An important modification was made last week in the schedule of Germany's payments. According to the original scheme Germany was to pay £50 million in 1924–5, £61 million in 1925–6, £60 million in 1926–7, £87,500,000 in 1927–8, £125 million thereafter, subject to increase according to the index of prosperity. But the payments in 1926–7 and 1927–8 were to be subject to a modification not exceeding £12,500,000 per annum upwards or downwards according to the yield of the controlled revenues.

The yield of these revenues up to date has made it probable that Germany would become liable for the additional sums, thus raising her payments to £72,500,000 in 1926–7 and £100 million in 1927–8. But it has now been agreed that in lieu of these two contingent additional payments amounting to £25 million altogether, Germany shall pay a fixed additional sum of £15 million in 1926–7, thus making the payments for the next two years £75 million in 1926–7 and £87,500,000 in 1927–8.

By this means Germany probably escapes from £10 million; the upward progression of the annuities is rendered more gradual; the business of budgeting is made less doubtful; and the Allies get a little money a little sooner. The new arrangement is certainly an improvement, and that it should have gone through so quietly reflects credit on everyone concerned.

It will be seen that the effect of the change is to increase Germany's liability this year to £75 million as compared with £61 million last year. It is important, therefore, to examine in what form Germany has paid so far, and to what extent her capacity to pay has been based on foreign loans rather than on a true excess of exports.

During the first year no remittances were made in cash (i.e., by the purchase of foreign exchange) except for the service of the Dawes loan, nearly the whole amount of the annuity (£50 million) being covered by deliveries in kind, the expenses of inter-Allied troops and commissions inside Germany, and the proceeds of the British and French Reparation Recovery Acts. During the second year just ended, out of the annuity of £61 million only about £3 million has been remitted in cash (apart from the service of the loan). In order to find £75 million in the third year (1 September 1926–31 August 1927) deliveries in kind may be somewhat increased, but the Transfer Committee will probably find themselves for the first time in the position of having to purchase substantial amounts of foreign exchange from the Reichsbank.

So far the receipts of the German Budget have fully

attained and have even exceeded the estimates of the Dawes commissioners, and the scheme as a whole has proceeded as smoothly as anyone could have expected. The difficulties of the transitional period have been overcome. What of the normal period which is now almost in sight? In 1928–9 Germany will have to pay double what she has paid in the year just ended. What are the prospects of her doing so? Ought we to prepare our minds for a new reparations crisis not later than 1928–9?

Probably we ought. But the answer largely depends on the further question how far Germany has been paying out of her own resources, and how far by merely handing back to the Allies the proceeds of foreign loans.

German issues on the international loan market between 1 September 1924 and 30 June 1926 have been summarised by *Wirtschaftsdienst* as follows (in round figures):

	In the U.S. (£ million)	In Great Britain (£ million)	Elsewhere (£ million)	Total (£ million)
The Dawes loan	—	—	—	42
Other loans, September–December 1924	6	1·75	—	7·75
January–December 1925	62	9	2·5	73·5
January–June 1926	42	6	4·25	52·25
Total	110	16·75	6·75	175·5

During this same period the Transfer Committee transferred altogether in one way or another about £97 million —say, £100 million. Thus, on this showing, not only has Germany borrowed the whole of her reparation payments, but nearly as much again in addition.

Before we can draw this conclusion, however, there are some important adjustments to be made. The above is the nominal total of the loans and is subject to deduction in respect of the expenses of issue and the discount below par in the price of issue. Probably we should deduct about 10 per cent to cover this, bringing the net receipts down to £158 million. Further, during the same period, Germany has been repaying out of the proceeds of these loans a substantial amount of foreign indebtedness incurred in previous periods. On the other hand, the above does not include the operations of foreign syndicates and individuals who have brought fairly large amounts of ordinary shares on the internal market in Germany. Lastly, German private balances remitted abroad during the period of instability have probably, on balance, been returning home again rather than otherwise.

Taking one thing with another—the figures of visible trade, the service of pre-existing foreign indebtedness, the increase in the Reichsbank's holding of gold and foreign exchange, etc., I should have been inclined to guess that Germany's net foreign loans during the Dawes period up to the end of last June were pretty nearly equal to the Dawes payments at some figure approaching £100 million. In this case practically the whole amount of the reparations so far have been provided by the foreign lender, and mainly by the United States.

The Agent-General for Reparation Payments seems, however, in his report lately published, to take another view; and his authority in such a matter is not to be lightly disregarded. He writes as follows.

In their earlier phase foreign credits provided funds with which to pay a substantial share of the excess of imports in German foreign trade, and to furnish the Reichsbank with additional reserves of gold and devisen. More recently, notably during December 1925 and the first four months of 1926, the foreign loans, though on a reduced scale, have coincided with an excess of exports over imports. This fact, supplemented by other evidence known to the banks, has led the German authorities to the conclusion that for several months past the aggregate foreign debt of Germany has not changed materially, and that the large volume of long-term issues placed abroad during that period has largely taken the place of a short debt already owed abroad but now repaid. It is clear at any rate that latterly there has been a tendency for certain German issues placed abroad to flow back again into the hands of German investors, and that the German banks have themselves become substantial holders of liquid funds abroad. It is too soon, however, to tell how far these conditions may prove to be permanent.

This is a cautious statement and relates only to a short period. During this period Germany was suffering from a severe industrial slump during which her imports of essential raw materials fell to a figure which would spell industrial ruin if it were to continue. Moreover, the German harvest of the previous autumn had been exceptionally abundant, and the period of the year was one when the balance of payments always tends in favour of Western Europe. I am not disposed, therefore, pending further evidence, to modify very much my *prima facie* conclusion expressed above.

If this is right, reparations and inter-Allied debts are being mainly settled in paper and not in goods. The United States lends money to Germany, Germany transfers its equivalent to the Allies, the Allies pay it back to the United States government. Nothing real passes—no one is a penny the worse. The engravers' dies, the printers' formes are busier. But no one eats less, no one works more. I paint the broad picture—not the details. For the effect of systems of taxation is to shift the burdens as between individuals.

The sums written on paper mount up, of course, at compound interest. Germany is paying on the average about 7½ per cent net for her foreign loans. Thus the annual interest on the debts incurred in the last two years comes to about £10 million per annum. How long can the game go on? The answer lies with the American investor.

There has been lately a revival of discussion about the cancellation of inter-Allied debts. The more this is talked about, wisely, foolishly, or indiscreetly, by M. Clemenceau, American senators and journalists, or anyone else, the better for an ultimate understanding. But the moment when cancellation will become a living topic, an unavoidable burning issue of practical politics, will be when the circular flow of paper is impeded and the artificial equilibrium is broken. It will be for the American investor in due course of time to give the word—and for the American public to find the solution.

Three-quarters of the way through the third Dawes year the Agent-General for Reparation Payments presented an interim report which Keynes interpreted as a warning. Regarding the 'transfer problem' as intractable—'The Dawes scheme will break down in accordance with plan' —he urged Germany to take care of her budget problem to preserve her international reputation for probity.

This article was published in the *New Republic* (3 August 1927) with the title 'The Coming Crisis in Reparations' and in *L'Oeuvre*, but did not appear in *Wirtschaftsdienst*. The reason for this was the immediate translation and publication of quotations from *The Nation* version by other German newspapers before *Wirtschaftsdienst* could make use of their own advance copy.

From The Nation and Athenaeum, *16 July 1927*

THE PROGRESS OF REPARATIONS

Mr Parker Gilbert, the Agent-General for Reparation Payments, has presented us with his interim observations on the state of Germany without waiting for a year to elapse since his last report. It is evident why he wishes to put the facts on record quickly. In spite of the moderation of his language and of his conclusions, Mr Gilbert's Report, dated 10 June 1927, is a warning to Germany and to the world—a warning which deserves closer attention than it has received from the daily Press.

At the end of May 1927 the third quarter of the third annuity year was completed. The first annuity (1924–5), met mainly from the Dawes loan, was £50 million; the second (1925–6) was £61 million; the third (1926–7) now in course of discharge is £75 million; the fourth (1927–8) will be £87,500,000; and the fifth (1928–9) £125 million. The annuity is not, however, evenly distributed through the year, with the result that in the three-quarters of the third annuity year just elapsed only three-fifths of the annuity has been paid. Thus Germany has not contributed so far at a rate exceeding £61 million a year. The big jump now comes. In the year beginning June 1927 Germany is due for nearly £100 million, soon rising to £125 million. We are, therefore, just entering on the critical period.

But this is not all. Hitherto the burden on the German budget has been triffling; from now on it increases rapidly. In 1924–5 the German budget contributed *nil*; in 1925–6 £12,500,000; and in the first nine months of 1926–7 £12,165,000. From June 1927 onwards the budgetary contribution will be at the rate of about £25 million per annum rapidly rising to £62,500,000.

It has therefore become urgent to consider what progress has been made towards supporting these greatly increased burdens, first on the budget, and secondly on the balance of international payments. These two matters are the subjects of Mr Gilbert's warnings.

As regards the budget the outlook is certainly serious. The position has been getting worse instead of better. In 1924–5 there was a handsome surplus, and in 1925–6 a small deficit. But in 1926–7 there is an excess of expenditure over revenue provisionally calculated at £42,500,000, and for 1927–8 an estimated deficit of the same amount; and after deducting items of a capital nature against which it is reasonable to borrow there is still a deficit. Something drastic will have to be done if the expenditure of 1928–9 is to be covered.

This state of affairs is not due to the yield of the taxes falling below the expectations of the Dawes Committee, whose estimates have been fully borne out. It is due to the growth of expenditure and to the failure to reorganise the financial relations of the Reich to the states and communes. The states and communes regardless of their real financial necessities are entitled to draw from the Reich 75 per cent of the income tax and corporation tax, 30 per cent of the turnover tax, 96 per cent of the tax on real estate transactions, the automobile tax and the betting tax, and 50 per cent of a portion of the tax on companies. The immediate and automatic disappearance out of the coffers of the Reich of so large a proportion of so many of the most productive sources of revenue, actual and potential, must aggravate the difficulties of the Reich in devising sound fiscal measures which will turn its deficit into a surplus.

Nevertheless in Mr Gilbert's opinion—and I have no doubt that he is right—the problem is certainly soluble, and 'should yield readily enough to a steady application of sound principles of budget-making'. 'The problem of checking the rising tide of government expenditures has become acute,' but the estimates still 'provide a substantial margin of safety'. It is desirable that German political parties should heed in time Mr Gilbert's categorical warning.

When we turn to the transfer problem, the figures look—as many of us expected that they would—much more intractable. Up to date the German trade balance has contributed nothing to the payment of reparations, long-term foreign credits having substantially exceeded the Transfer Committee's external remittances whether by deliveries in kind or otherwise. Germany has only paid the world what the world has been ready to lend her. Indeed, she has arranged to borrow considerably more than she has paid, if all kinds of borrowing are included.

The trade figures after correcting errors of valuation and including deliveries in kind have been as follows [top of p. 285]. There has never been any export surplus except during the trade slump in the early part of 1926 which resulted in a heavy falling-off in the imports of raw materials.

Now the invisible items, other than reparations, can scarcely

	£ million
Year ending 31 October 1925 Excess of imports	161
Year ending 31 October 1926 Excess of exports	63
Six months ending 30 April 1927 Excess of imports	61
Total for 2½ years: net excess of imports	159

be favourable to Germany—allowing for the growth of private debt to foreigners—to any material extent, and may be unfavourable. If, therefore, Germany is to pay the reparation annuity of 1928–9 otherwise than by borrowing it from abroad, she must convert an import surplus which has averaged £60 million per annum into an export surplus of £100–120 million. What proportion does this bear to Germany's present trade? The figures, which are as follows, are not encouraging:

German exports (£ million)

Year ending 31 October	Food	Raw materials and semi-manufactured	Finished goods	Total
1913	53·5	114	337·5	505
1924–25	26	82	331·25	439·25
1925–26	24	116·5	348	488·5
1926–27*	23·5	120	344	487·5

* (On basis of first six months' results doubled.)

Thus apart from foodstuffs and beverages German exports are somewhat above the pre-war level in value, but presumably somewhat below it in volume—perhaps by 10 per cent allowing for loss of territory. For the past three years the figures have been very steady with a slight upward trend. If we subdivide the exports into groups the same conclusions hold, except that there has been a large falling-off in the value of coal exports since the conclusion of the British coal strike.

It follows that in order to cover the 1928–9 annuity in full without recourse to foreign loans German exports must now take a great leap forward and increase by some 36 per cent, or, allowing for the import of raw materials embodied in the exports, between 40 and 50 per cent. Some further improvement we may reasonably anticipate. But is so great a transformation feasible in two or three years? Considering that more than a third of Germany's exports consist of coal, iron and steel, and textiles—and if we add in chemicals and machinery considerably more than half—would any of her industrial competitors welcome it? Remember, too, that this great expansion will only occur if Germany's chief industrial competitors put overwhelming pressure on her to knock them out of their own existing markets. Does anyone—does M. Poincaré—think this probable?

There is, indeed, nothing new in all this. Nothing new—except that time passes and that dates which were distant creep nearer. The Dawes scheme will break down in accordance with plan. The question is—what will be the price of its modification? How considerable a crisis will have to be provoked in Germany's affairs before the facts are admitted? It is this question which from now on should be the preoccupation of the diplomatists.

This brings us back to the problem of the budget and to Mr Gilbert's warning. It is probable that the authors of the Dawes scheme did not expect their plan to work. The objectives to which they were moving were, first, to gain time, but, above all, so to arrange that, when the breakdown came, it would come as something inevitable and involuntary. Their object was to segregate that part of the problem which it would lie within Germany's power to fulfil given goodwill, from that part which was really beyond her capacity—in other words, to separate as clearly as possible the budget problem from the transfer problem. Here lies the significance of Mr Gilbert's words. The present financial policy of the German government runs the risk of reintroducing just that confusion which it was the object of the Dawes Committee to eliminate. If, when the transfer problem comes to a head, Germany is regularly meeting her annuities out of revenue and without recourse to borrowing of any kind, then it should be possible to discuss necessary modifications in a cool spirit; for the German Treasury would have fulfilled its side of the bargain. But if her budgetary policy is open to criticism, if her expenditure is higher than it should be, then there is a danger that the question of Germany's 'goodwill' may creep back into the diplomatic arena—and give M. Poincaré his opportunity. I hope that Germany will give the Dawes idea a chance by putting her budget in order as soon as she can.

The prediction of Keynes's penultimate paragraph was much noted. G. P. Auld—'Alpha', the critic of *A Revision of the Treaty* (*JMK*, vol. XVII, pp. 303–13)—took it as his text to contradict in his book published at this time, *The Dawes Plan and the New Economics*. When, six weeks later, the third year of the Dawes Plan was completed, the Agent-General announced that Germany had met in full all payments falling due. In spite of this reassurance, the correspondent reporting the facts in the *Manchester Guardian*, 2 September 1927, was prompted to question whether the fourth year to come would be so satisfactory. 'Especially since Mr Keynes's celebrated article in *The Nation* the newspapers have fallen into the habit of taking the imminent breakdown of the Dawes scheme altogether for granted.'

The *New Republic* of 7 December 1927 carried an article outlining a comprehensive plan for settling all reparations and war debts at one stroke, the whole scheme to be tied in with a world agreement to keep the peace. This was the brainchild of an American private citizen, Salmon O. Levinson, a Chicago lawyer whose speciality was the reviving of ailing corporations. His proposal was well received by American bankers and in Democratic circles and he hoped to interest British opinion.

Levinson's scheme would fix the bill for reparations at $6,000 million—the amount to be found by an international private loan to Germany. Allied debts to the United States would be reduced to $4,000 million and paid out of reparations. The British debt to the United States and the Allied debts to Britain would be cancelled.

The *New Republic*'s editor, Herbert Croly, asked Keynes, 'Whether in your opinion the plan has any essential weakness, and whether, if it were proposed at a suitable time by the American government, it would have any chance of success' (letter of 8 December 1927). Keynes's reply, written 20 December and published by the *New Republic* as a letter, pointed out the transfer problem.

To the Editor of the New Republic, *18 January 1928*

Sir,

Mr Levinson's proposal of 'A Financial Path to Peace' published in the *New Republic* of 7 December must have attracted many readers by the generosity of its outlook. I am convinced that the main principles which Mr Levinson lays down must be the basis of any durable settlement: that is to say, German reparations must be fixed at a definite and moderate amount; inter-Allied government debts must be fixed on a similar principle; the one must be set off against the other; and the financial settlement must be made, if possible, the opportunity for an experiment in world peace.

Moreover, the figures which Mr Levinson has chosen, perhaps more as illustrations of his argument than as definite proposals, strike me as being of something like the right order of magnitude all round. Such a settlement as he adumbrates would constitute a reasonably generous offer by the United States, and at the same time a reasonably lenient treatment of Germany.

If, therefore, I venture to express a doubt as to the details of the technical financial arrangements which Mr Levinson proposes to bring about the settlement he desires, it is not out of any want of sympathy with his ideas, but only with a view of avoiding possible disillusionment and disappointment later on.

Mr Levinson wishes to convert annual payments over a number of future years into capital sums to be discharged at once, and he invokes the aid of the financiers of the world to bring this about. But if private financiers are to be brought in—and I fully appreciate the advantages of getting rid of financial payments between governments spread over a great number of years if this can possibly be done—we must not forget that by shifting the task from governments to private finance we do not in any way modify or mitigate the problems of transfer as between different countries. No country at the present moment, with the possible exception of France and the United States, is in a position to transfer large capital sums in cash to other countries. It follows that, broadly speaking, any financial arrangements must be concluded in the same financial centres as are to receive the proceeds of the loan when floated. It would not be possible for any country to finance by way of loan sums much larger than it would be due to receive on balance under the proposed settlement.

Now, Mr Levinson does not indicate with precision in what proportions he would expect the proposed international loan to be divided between different financial centres. If he contemplates a division on the above principle, namely that the financiers of no country shall be required to finance more than its government is due to receive under the settlement, well and good. But it is not clear that this principle is appreciated by him. And indeed its practical implications are exceedingly inconvenient. For under the proposal more than two-thirds of the proceeds would be receivable by the United States, whilst, in accordance with the terms of the Balfour Offer, to which I am sure Great Britain would be ready to adhere, the net sum due to Great Britain would be nil. Thus, if the principle set forth above were to be accepted, by far the greater part of the loan would have to be floated in New York, and none of it in London. In practice, I am sure that London, in the interests of a settlement, would be prepared to go beyond this and would strain its resources to the utmost to participate. But our resources for such an operation are obviously very limited.

The practicability of the broad outlines of the scheme must depend, of course, on persuading the various governments concerned to fall in with the idea. But the technical financial means depend not only on goodwill, but also on capacity.

J. M. KEYNES

Keynes took the occasion of the appearance in English translation of two books by German financiers who were intimately involved in the diplomacy of reparations and the financial recovery of Germany to review the progress of recent history. These books were *The History of Reparations* by Carl Bergmann and *The Stabilization of the Mark* by Hjalmar Schacht.

From The Nation and Athenaeum, *7 January 1928*

THE FINANCIAL RECONSTRUCTION OF GERMANY

Two books[7] have lately appeared, both of them in an English translation also, by the two financial diplomatists who, on the German side, have played, perhaps, the greatest individual parts in the extraordinarily rapid financial recovery of Germany from the ruin of 1919–23—Herr Carl Bergmann and Dr Hjalmar Schacht. Both books have been written not only with the authority of persons who have themselves played a major part behind the scenes in the unrolling of the events described, but also with a remarkable objectivity of vision and evenness of temper. They pass by the external chronicles and well-worn tables of statistics which do duty time after time in the ephemerals of lesser authorities, and are persistently concerned with trying to tell us what really happened and what was really unimportant. The volumes are, therefore, definitive contributions to the history of our times, which should be on the shelves of every historical or economic library.

Herr Bergmann was behind the scenes continuously from the appointment of the organization committee of the

[7] *The History of Reparations,* by Carl Bergmann (Benn, 21s), and *The Stabilization of the Mark,* by Hjalmar Schacht (Allen & Unwin, 8s 6d).

Reparation Commission in 1919 to the adoption of the Dawes Plan in 1924. He was one of the most successful of that invaluable class of persons who do not occupy gilded chairs, but establish friendly informal relations with the opposite side and are the vehicles of those private communications exploring the possibilities of the situation, yet committing no one to anything, which are the indispensable preliminary to success in formal conference, especially in those conferences which concern more parties than two. It is a class of persons capable of much mischief, it is true, as well as good; for to retain any measure of sincerity along with the requisite pliability of temper is a hard task. It is their duty, like a good hostess, to encourage everyone to talk, to spread an atmosphere of ease, to snub no one and nothing, to be on much the same terms with the great and the small of the social scene alike, never to contradict, never to show impatience, never to appear to step ahead or be before their time, to encourage even inanities if perhaps they may develop into something, and to maintain all the while, if it be possible, a certain standard of consistency and intellectual integrity. Such gifts are required to smooth the edges of international life and to combine the advantages of secret with open diplomacy. Of such gifts Herr Bergmann showed himself a great master, to the advantage of his country and of the world, and through five years, in which nothing was ready and little was honourable and most things were turned upside down, he did not lose the respect of the many different characters whom he was so sedulously and ingeniously edging along the path that they should go. At any rate, it helps history if such a person, when it is all over and what was indiscreet yesterday has become discreet today, sits down with a cool head and a steady pen to tell his tale.

On 16 June 1919 the German delegation left Versailles for Weimar, in order unanimously to recommend its government to reject the terms of peace, because it saw no possibility of fulfilling the Allies' demands; but the Weimar government, not dissenting from the truth of this conclusion, deemed that expediency required them to sign. From that day on, the contest for sanity and wisdom had to be fought simultaneously along the two lines represented by the decisions of the delegation and of its government respectively. It was my endeavour in a series of books and articles during those years to declare the eventual destination, conceding as little as possible to the diplomatic demands for half-truths or quarter-truths—or 10 per cent truth to start with; and to throw down with violence the idols of the market place. It was Herr Bergmann's part to put up patiently with nonsense, even sometimes to talk a little of it, and to be for ever concerned with the next possible step and content with it, provided that the direction was right. Reading again the history of those years from the angle of Herr Bergmann's vision, one feels indeed a certain inevitability—that the various stages, however imbecile and disastrous in themselves, had to be passed through. But one feels also the extraordinary wastefulness and futility and lack of real necessity in the events of that period.

The footprints of even the greatest historical events are not slowly obliterated; and those who have come out at the other end are inclined to belittle the evils overpassed, like yesterday's toothache. Herr Bergmann's story serves to recall the nature of the risks which were run, the evils which were imposed and endured, and the final fruitlessness of the whole business. So early as 24 April 1921 the German government transmitted an offer to accept reparation terms which would have been more onerous than the Dawes Plan. And it is certain that the embodiment in the Treaty of Versailles of anything approaching the Dawes Plan would have been accepted by Germany with enthusiasm and regarded by the whole world as an act of appeasement and honourable generosity towards defeat.

Thus for no ultimate gains whatever, the risk of general revolution was incurred, the collapse of Germany in particular was twice threatened, the middle classes of central Europe were beggared, millions of persons suffered penury and starvation, the Ruhr was invaded, and the economic progress of the whole of Europe, including Great Britain, was put back by at least ten years.

When we turn to Dr Schacht's book, we are concerned, in the main, with a different period and a different method. Dr Schacht tells, it is true, from its beginning the story of the collapse of the German currency, and this part of his narrative, being an account of the internal economy of Germany as affected by external events, is a useful complement to Herr Bergmann's account of the way in which these external events came to pass. But his main theme is the remarkable achievement of the restoration of the German financial system to a position of confidence and efficiency within the brief period of three years after Herr Bergmann's diplomacy had done its work. Dr Schacht is a diplomatist too, in his way; but his way is not particularly smooth. Dr Schacht has shown himself one of Germany's strong men. He has won his victories by determination and strength of character, by great obstinacy and courage in the face of opposition, and by holding tenaciously to a few simple principles, rather than by any especial subtlety of intellect or method. He deserves to be proud of the results. No one would have believed, when he became currency commissioner in 1923 and succeeded Herr Havenstein shortly afterwards as President of the Reichsbank, that within four years the financial reconstruction of Germany could possibly have been carried to its present point.

Dr Schacht's simple principles were the following: that in the conditions of the German currency collapse of 1923 a straightforward return to the gold standard was essential; that a limitation of the volume of the currency was fundamental and much more important, in the particular circumstances of the case, than discount policy; that he must stand up like a man to vested position, particular interested parties, and political pressure, or perish in the attempt; and, above all, that the restoration of confidence would be cumulative, just as its collapse had been, and that, therefore, to begin the restoration of confidence would be half the battle. All these principles were sound and right; and nothing else was necessary. So far as concerned the gold standard, Germany could obviously be the one to act as pioneer in currency improvements. In general the rapidity of Dr Schacht's success was a confirmation of the advice tendered by the foreign experts called in by the German government in 1922, before the invasion of the Ruhr, that the currency problem would be susceptible of treatment by the recognised methods much more easily and rapidly than was commonly supposed, as soon as the Reparation Commission should make the necessary decisions permitting any solution at all.

Dr Schacht's reorganisation would, of course, have been impracticable without the adoption of the Dawes Plan in 1924. But its most remarkable historical feature is the fact that the mark was first stabilised before the adoption of the Dawes Plan and whilst the Ruhr was still occupied; the Ruhr occupation, by terminating the normal reparation payments, having brought about indirectly the necessary relief to the exchange. 'Three dates', Dr Schacht concludes, 'constitute landmarks in the recovery of the German currency. On 20 November 1923 the mark was stablised at the rate of a billion paper marks to one gold mark; on 7 April 1924 the enforcement of credit rationing finally assured the success of the stabilisation; and lastly, on 10 October 1924 the addition of the 800 million gold marks of the Dawes loan to the working capital of the country provided just that economic backing which the situation required.'

In his references to the future, Dr Schacht touches on some matters which are still controversial, in particular the part to

294

be played by foreign loans in the discharge of payments due under the Dawes Plan. As between the policy of putting off the evil day by Germany's borrowing as much as the world can be persuaded to lend her, and the policy of facing an earlier crisis by restricting payments so far as possible to what can be made out of current surplus, Dr Schacht plumps for the latter. Dr Schacht has made enemies by so valorously laying about him, and there are problems still ahead which may need a Bergmann as well as a Schacht. But I believe that, in his country's interests, the policy which he is now advocating is probably right; though my sympathies have always been, perhaps, a little too much with those who are facing the facts of tomorrow and too little with the diplomatists who are helping us to last out today!

Incidentally Dr Schacht, whilst deprecating foreign loans by German states and cities, implies that the service of such loans will rank for exchange transfer ahead of reparations, provided that the German government have duly discharged the latter in terms of marks. This is directly opposed to the opinion just expressed by Mr Parker Gilbert, the Agent-Gerneral for reparations, in his latest report, where he claims that the service of loans to German states ranks after reparations for transfer as well as for payment. But in this matter I believe that the weight of responsible opinion is against Mr Gilbert's contention.

A word of praise is due to the translators of the two volumes, Sir Andrew McFadyean and Mr Ralph Butler.

In April 1928 Keynes and his wife Lydia Lopokova visited Russia and stopped in Hamburg and Berlin on their way there and in Berlin on the return journey. In Germany Keynes had an opportunity to talk with Melchior, who at this time was the German representative on the League of Nations Financial Committee, and with the head of the Reichsbank, Dr Schacht (letter to Sir Richard Hopkins, 19 April 1928).

On Keynes's return to England he gave a broadcast talk on 'The War Debts' (3 May), linking them with the discussion of the 'final settlement' of reparations which it was becoming evident must soon be arranged to succeed the Dawes Plan. The talk was published in *The Nation*, 5 May 1928, and in *Wirtschaftsdienst*. It also appeared in the *New Republic* as 'A London View of the War Debts', 23 May 1928, accompanied by an editorial comment titled 'An American View of War Debts'. In this edition of Keynes's writings it is to be found where Keynes included it in *Essays in Persuasion* (*JMK*, vol. IX, pp. 47–53).

In this article Keynes began by returning to some old themes—the origin of the debts and the British willingness for cancellation—and went on to explain the separate settlements that in fact were made.

The American settlement with Great Britain is twice as onerous as that with France, and eight times as onerous as that with Italy. Great Britain, in her turn, has made arrangements with France and Italy, and has in both cases let them off lighter than has the United States—the British settlement with France being 10 per cent easier, and that with Italy 33 per cent easier than the corresponding American settlements. Thus, while the other Allies have been largely relieved, England is left with the task of repaying her whole burden, subject only to the mitigation that the rate of interest charged, namely 3·3 per cent, is moderate.

Balancing the theoretical receipts of what Britain was to get in reparation from Germany against the burden of what she herself had agreed to pay to the United States, Keynes concluded that Britain was to end up receiving nothing. The United States, on the other hand, would benefit by what she received both in paid-up debts and on her own account as reparation.

If all, or nearly all, of what Germany pays for reparations has to be used, not to repair the damage done, but to repay the United States for the financial part which she played in the common struggle, many will feel that this is not an outcome tolerable to the sentiments of mankind or in reasonable accord with the spoken professions of Americans when they entered the war or afterwards...

Obviously, Great Britain must pay what she has covenanted to pay, and any proposal, if there is to be one, must come from the United States ...I continue to hope that in due course, and in her own time, America will tell us that she has not spoken her last word.

In 'An American View of the War Debts' the *New Republic* recorded a 'vigorous dissent' and again took issue with Keynes's moral arguments. Although agreeing that both reparations and debt settlements must be scaled down and as a practical matter considered together, the editors insisted that this must be justified by economic circumstances, rather than the 'dubious moral attitudes' with which Mr Keynes and his associates—so well qualified to urge economic reasons—were 'veiling the controversy'.

Keynes replied to this criticism in a letter dated 4 June, which was published with an added note by the *New Republic* editors.

To the Editor of the New Republic, *4 July 1928*

Sir,

Your leading article of 23 May, criticising my contribution on the war debts, has made me try to find out just where we differ. For that is the first step to reaching an ultimate agreement. Am I right on the following points?

(1) I argued that in settling the war debts, regard should be paid to their origin and the circumstances in which they were made. The *New Republic* does not agree, and looks on them as being in the same category as any other investment.

(2) I suggested that, if the net result of the settlements including reparations were to leave the United States as the sole beneficiary, this would not be an outcome tolerable to sentiment or in sufficient accord with the professions of Americans when they entered the war. The *New Republic* disagrees and sees nothing distasteful or inconsistent in this outcome.

(3) I proposed, not that the United States should make unconditional concessions; but that when the Dawes scheme comes up for revision the war debts should be considered along with reparations, and that any concession by the United States should be used to facilitate a reasonable re-settlement of the latter. Here, I understand, the *New Republic* and I are in agreement.

(4) Since we are thus in agreement on practical policy, it is a pity that we should differ in the abstract. The *New Republic* urges me, therefore, to base my case on the *expediency* of using a revision of the war debts as a means of obtaining a better settlement of reparations; and to avoid 'dubious moral attitudes' about the origin of the debts. I have no doubt that the advice is wise. I am guilty of having sacrificed

297

propaganda to a desire to express my feelings. But perhaps I may plead, in mitigation of sentence, that when certain sentiments are felt strongly by the inhabitants of a whole continent practically without exception, it is difficult—however advisable—to conceal them. Nor am I sure that it is the best plan in the long run, when two nations genuinely entertain divergent sentiments, that one of them should dissemble, even in the hope of obtaining a pecuniary advantage. For what half the world feels will be discovered sooner or later.

J. M. KEYNES

The *New Republic* added:

We have not the slightest objection to the expression by Mr Keynes of his feelings and those of many other inhabitants of the Allied nations concerning the debts. The desirability of communicating to Americans what these feelings are was one of the reasons for the publication of his article. Our editorial was published for the purpose of informing him, on the other hand, of the opinions held by many Americans, in the hope that they might have some influence on his feelings. To take up his specific points:

(1) We have never believed that the war debts belonged in the same category as other investments. Accurate and careful regard to the circumstances in which they were made does not, however, prove that from our point of view they are not morally binding as debts.

(2) We do not see the connection between reparations and war debts in any such terms as Mr Keynes here states it. Reparations are only one possible source of revenue for the Allied governments. One might as well say that there is something distasteful about the United States being the sole beneficiary of a certain part of the income tax receipts of France or Great Britain.

(3) The United States would not logically be in a position to make concessions about the debts conditional upon concessions about reparations if she had admitted that the debts are not rightfully due to her.

(4) If one believes that the debts are rightfully due, but ought to be revised downward, it would be, for him, a resort to mere expediency to argue for revision upon the ground of a lack of obligation to pay them. Our conviction is that debts and reparations ought to be revised downward because they will be either difficult or impossible to pay, and such obligations should not be continued so far into the future. The reason they are so

difficult is that they are international obligations not arising out of productive use of human resources. This certainly has an important moral aspect of its own.—THE EDITORS.

Keynes also replied personally to two American correspondents. Of his exchange with one of them, a Mr Amberson, only the copy of his own letter remains, as he returned Amberson's letter with numbered references to points taken up. Keynes's letter is dated 17 May, so that Amberson must have read the article in *The Nation*.

From a letter to MR AMBERSON, *17 May 1928*

(4) I agree with this paragraph...I do not consider that America had any 'obligation' to do anything whatever, and I can sympathise with the view of those Americans who would have preferred to remain neutral...

(6) I am entirely in sympathy with the aims and objects put forward in this paragraph. If America could make some proposal of cancellation the occasion of a contribution to the cause of peace, I should be unreservedly in favour of her doing so. Indeed, I do not suggest for a moment that any mitigation should be offered by America unconditionally. The whole point of my article was that it should be associated with some scheme for the reasonable settlement of reparations, my argument being that it would be very difficult to secure a proper settlement of reparations unless the inter-allied debts are considered at the same time. If some contribution could be made at the same time to the cause of disarmament, I should be very glad. But I am sceptical. Some things can be bought with money and some cannot. If a new world order can be purchased for cash, as you suggest in the paragraph I have numbered (7)—which I doubt—I am inclined to think that the price would be somewhat higher than the figures we are now talking about. But a good European is liable to resent an American suggesting that he can

be made good and virtuous by the offer of an adequate quantity of American dollars.

There are two points I should like to add, the first to avoid misunderstanding, the second because it is really essential to a proper understanding of how people here feel.

The first point is that, in virtue of the Balfour Note, any concession which may be made by the United States will be for the benefit of Germany and the European Allies, and not for the benefit of this country. Because we claim that we have already made a proper financial sacrifice and that America as yet has not, it must not be deduced that the further sacrifice which we think America should make is to come into our own pockets. I should add to this, however, that in view of the doubts as to Germany's capacity to pay the whole of her present liability, indirectly we might benefit financially by American concessions to a small extent. It would be impossible to calculate this exactly, but I should not put it above £5 million per annum, a sum which I should agree with you in reckoning trifling as compared with the other issues involved.

The other point relates to the practically universal feeling in Europe that there has been a discrepancy between the way in which Americans have talked at different dates; that there is a certain inappropriateness between the sort of things that were said at one time and the sort of things that were done at others. This is quite a different thing from saying that America was under any 'obligation' to do anything. Moreover, if Americans had announced from the first that they were advancing money, not to save civilisation, or any phrase of that kind, but as the best business investment available in the circumstances, no one would have objected to their maintaining the same business attitude subsequently. Against Americans who were pacifists in 1917 and did not much care about the intervention of their country at any time, no charge of inconsistency lies. But they are a very small minority. The feelings which most Europeans have about the majority are not usually or conveniently mentioned in public.

Yours very truly,

[copy initialled] J. M. KEYNES

A reader of the *New Republic*, John M. Micklin, who was a member of the sociology department at Dartmouth College in Hanover, New Hampshire, wrote to Keynes (24 May 1928) protesting his 'tacit assumptions' as to American responsibility.

From JOHN M. MICKLIN, *24 May 1928*

If, as you say, Europe is disgusted at America for belying her lofty idealism by playing the international Shylock please remember that many Americans are disgusted with Europeans for obfuscating stern hard facts with an appeal to mawkish sentiment. You are practically asking this country to pay for the blunders, the stupidities and the age-old enmities of Europe. Is this 'moral'—how English-speaking peoples love to conjure with this term—or is it even good sportsmanship?... I have yet to read in any European journal a correct statement of the position of the better informed classes in this country... You should not confuse the high-flown moral idealism and the talk of fighting a common battle for freedom, 'making the world safe for democracy' and the like that fell from the lips of American leaders in the height of the conflict with the matured and disillusioned and hard-headed opinions of the nation today. It is just this disillusionment and thorough grasp of the hard facts that make all your talk of moral responsibilities offensive to the masses of this country.

Keynes replied:

To JOHN M. MICKLIN, *11 June 1928*

Dear Sir,

I have sent the *New Republic* a short letter for publication with reference to their leading article criticising my contribution on the war debts. Probably you will see this in due course.

In reply to your letter, I would just add this. Undoubtedly we all have various legal claims in connection with war debts and reparations. We most of us agree that it is not desirable that we should stick out for these legal claims in full. In Europe we think there are two reasons for this: first, the circumstances out of which the debts arose; secondly, the desirability of clearing up the future situation. Personally, I lay at least as much stress on the first as on the second. Since my own country has offered to go further than any other in the direction of abating her legal claims, I am at liberty to speak freely. Americans who share your view are prepared, I gather, to act to some extent on the second of the above reasons, namely the desirability of clearing up the future; but not on the first of the reasons. Moreover, they are very fond of urging on us that if Europe really wants the cash she had better conceal her true feelings about the American position on the first point. I daresay this is true.

No one, however, reading your letter would readily guess that my country had undertaken to pass on in full to others any concession which yours might make, nor that the occasion proposed for a concession was a better and a final settlement of German reparations. Having been close to the Paris negotiations which led to the iniquitous reparations clauses, I know that your country carries a share of responsibility which is not negligible for securing a just settlement of that matter at long last.

Of course, it is important that each country should understand the state of mind of the other. In that spirit I welcome your letter as a piece of sociological information. But I suggest that in the same spirit you should welcome my article. For I confess that I was more concerned, when I wrote it, to express the sentiments generally prevailing in this country, which I share, than I was to put the case in just that form which would be most likely to extract concessions out of the United States. You find this very shocking. But is it? Perhaps it is.

Yours faithfully,

J. M. KEYNES

P.S. Would you have any objection to my publishing your letter and this reply in the press of this country, probably in *The Nation*? If you agree to this, will you be kind enough to send me a cable with the word 'Yes'. Would it be correct to describe you as Professor Micklin?

Micklin thanked Keynes (26 June) for a prompt and courteous letter but said his own was 'not so well considered as to deserve publication'. He went on, at greater length than in his first letter, to tackle what he considered the real issue of Keynes's reply, 'the assumption of a cultural and moral solidarity which is largely fictitious'. He recalled that in his own student days in the Germany of 1897–1900 he had felt American culture was 'but a phase of European', but today the gap between America and Europe had been consciously widened.

Was this nation responsible for the intrigues, alliances (secret), economic rivalries, hoary prejudices and hates that finally led to this war...Did we have any say in the diplomatic negotiations (except in the interest of peace) that finally precipitated England and the rest into this bloody strife? Were we responsible for the wasted blood and treasure, the 'legal claims' incurred...? Our responsibilities came...when unforeseen issues arose as a result of four years of conflict, namely, the freedom of the seas imperilled by the submarine, and the growing need for world stabilisation and assured peace.

Like the *New Republic*, with no conscious irony, Micklin lectured Keynes that the real issue was economic rather than moral. He finished by saying, 'I wish that some day we might be able to sit down quietly and talk the matter over', and in a long postscript he acknowledged,

Repudiating vigorously the assumption that the circumstances out of which these debts arose hold equally for America as for England and the continent, this country may recognise that it is for the good of all concerned for her to abate her debt claims or wipe them out entirely if this should prove necessary or wise (which I much doubt). A contented and prosperous Europe is after all a far more valuable asset to this country, as Americans are now fast coming to see, than the mere dollars and cents of the war debt.

Chapter 6

SEARCH FOR A FINAL SETTLEMENT—THE YOUNG PLAN, 1928–1930

Under the Dawes Plan there was growing apprehension that Germany would not be able to continue borrowing the loans from which she had met all her payments to date. In addition the Dawes Plan had never mentioned a final figure for these payments, which were revisable, to be adjusted up or down according to an index of prosperity. German opinion required not only a reduction in the amount of reparations but the naming of a definite sum—the 'final settlement' advocated by Parker Gilbert, the Agent-General.

Accordingly in September 1928 a new committee of experts, including German representatives, was announced under the chairmanship of the American industrialist, Owen D. Young, who had been a member of the Dawes Committee. The Young Committee met for the first time in Paris on 9 February 1929. Among the experts were Sir Josiah Stamp and Lord Revelstoke (replaced on his death by Sir Charles Addis) who were the British members, J. P. Morgan and Thomas W. Lamont representing the United States, and Dr Schacht, accompanied by Melchior, as an adviser attending on behalf of Germany.

Keynes felt this conference had been called too soon, as may be seen in the following letter that he wrote to the editor of a New York financial information service. The article enclosed with his letter was 'The Transfer Problem', to be published in the March 1929 issue of the *Economic Journal* (*JMK*, vol. XII).

To L. H. SLOAN, *20 February 1929*

Dear Mr Sloan,

I see in a recent budget of news from Washington published by 'Standard Statistics' that responsible opinion in America is expecting a favourable outcome from the present reparations conference. I doubt whether responsible opinion in this country shares that view.

I enclose an article which will be published in a few weeks' time dealing specifically with the theory of the transfer problem. But the main point is the following.

Germany would naturally be willing enough to accept a reduction of the present annuity, and she would raise no objection to her bonds being sold on the international market, if the international market would take them. But the only concession which it would be practicable for Germany on her side to make would be to forgo her transfer protection. She would be extremely ill-advised to do this, and I cannot believe that it is really within the realm of practical politics to suppose that she will. That is to say, the fundamental difficulty before the negotiators in Paris arises out of the fact that there does not actually exist any basis for a deal. Germany will not relinquish transfer protection except for a reduction of the annuity to a figure far below what anyone would contemplate.

I think it is correct to say that the best opinion in this country regards the conference as premature. There is no particular eagerness in British circles to do otherwise than gain a little more experience of the existing arrangements. Therefore there will not be, as on previous occasions, any overwhelming pressure from the British side to get something done.

So you will see that the prospects of any positive results emerging are somewhat remote.

Yours very truly,
J. M. KEYNES

Keynes also sent a copy of his article to Stamp in Paris.

To SIR JOSIAH STAMP, *20 February 1929*

My dear Stamp,

It was very good of you to send me a copy of your new volume of collected essays. A good many of them I had read before, but several of them were new, and reading them has relieved the tedium of influensa. I was very glad to see that in your Ball Lecture you let fly against the really ridiculous curriculum to which the poor economists at Oxford have to submit.

Meanwhile I see that you are being bored in Paris. So much nonsense has been written lately (and even more, I suspect, spoken) about the theory of the transfer problem that I felt I ought to try and write down what seems to me to be the truth. The result is the enclosed, which will appear in the March *Economic Journal*.

I cannot imagine that Germany will lightly abandon transfer protection. And if she won't, where does there exist any sort of basis for a deal? However, you know all this much better than I do.

Yours ever,

J. M. KEYNES

Stamp's letter was undated, but informative.

From SIR JOSIAH STAMP

My dear Keynes,

Very many thanks for your note with enclosure. The latter is inimitably neat—a quality which has been characterising all you do increasingly of late. It is timely, and I am circulating it to the British and American members, and certain French. Curiously I had already dictated a note of certain points, including this, where everything I may say is 'barred' by *authority*! This I was sending you, if not for your advice, at any rate for commiseration. Anyway, you might in a word suggest some way of approach, which I've not thought of, to reopen, in case any one of these points become of importance again in the main subject.

It is *still* a madhouse, in a way—but all are mad in a very genteel way, the main occupation being elaborate proofs, from different angles, of sanity.

One half sit round a hat, saying with Coué reiteration: There *is* a rabbit—there *is*. The other half try to make a noise like a succulent lettuce.

There is a general conviction that the more eminent the conjurors convened, the more certainty is there of the existence of the rabbit.

Of course, this *can't* be the final stage—tho' all aver solemnly that it is. (3 years under Dawes might have made it possible.) The only thing, now one is in for it, is to make as good an approach shot as possible, so that the next effort may hole out.

Transfer protection—at one moment a blessing, the next a curse. Even *good* people won't give a considered conclusion on this.

Yours ever,

J. C. STAMP

Stamp's enclosed typewritten notes were marked *Personal.*

1. Dr Schacht repeatedly states, whenever the question of depreciation of the mark under pressure of necessity to make external payments in excess of the export surplus plus foreign loans arises, that depreciation of the mark is *impossible*. 'It could not happen under my management.' When pointing out that we are considering periods beyond his term of office, he says—'It cannot happen so long as the rules which I have laid down are followed.' He will therefore not allow that *any* sign of impending difficulty can be given by the exchange value of the mark. His line of reasoning is that the offer of a larger number of marks for foreign currency can be checked by reducing the number of marks in circulation. He says that the circulating medium would disappear until only one mark was left rather than that the exchange should go to a discount. He lays this down with great vigour and will not follow any ordinary line of economic argument that the consequences of the measures taken to bring about this particular result might be worse in other directions.

2. McKenna's contention, which he says himself is vital to the validity of his final political argument about the Rhineland, is that, under pressure of circumstances when political and commercial forces are in the exchange market with marks to get foreign currencies, in practice the commercial would always get priority and succeed and leave the political in the lurch. It is not put to him that the political can be given such power by special measure as to get in first with priority, but only that they would tend to rank *equally* in the struggle. This he strongly denies on the practical contention that each bank will act as a clearing house of marks against sterling for its own customers. Each trade operation sets in motion its own demand and offer of one of two currencies. There would be a private arrangement within the walls of the bank to clear these against each other before the balance of demand was released to the open

exchange market. He is extremely definite and dogmatic that this is what *every bank would do* and that the political demand for currency would have no chance until this process had been exhausted.

3. Transfer problem. The French, and to a less degree the Belgians, are now given over *entirely* to the most recent view that this problem does not exist. This has been chiefly brought about by articles by [Albert] Aftalion and [Jacques] Rueff, of which [Jean] Parmentier [French member of the Young Committee] has given me translations. He regards them as conclusive. As far as I can see, they are very lucid and clear expositions of the usual fluid 'Hawtrey' line of thought, but seem to be by men who have only recently begun to think of the problem and have not seen all round it. There is no evidence of any examination of the question of elasticity of demand nor of commercial opposition in receiving countries, nor of rapidity of the necessary change-over of capital assets into the appropriate kind in Germany. Parmentier agrees that the export surplus thus created is, in the last resort, a question of degree, and will not postulate that the theory is correct at *any* point, but simply considers that in the political figures we are discussing we are well within all economic possibilities and dangers.

Schacht's exposition of the range of suitable exports and the proportion existing between these and necessitated imports leaves him quite untouched. This makes Parmentier very difficult on setting any *practical* figure that Schacht is justified in taking uncontrolled responsibility for.

Francqui [the Belgian delegate] won't even discuss the problem and Moreau [Governor of the Bank of France] I don't think appreciates it.

Keynes's interest showed in the detail of his reply.

To SIR JOSIAH STAMP, *7 March 1929*

My dear Stamp,

Thank you very much for your most interesting letter. I confess that I am considerably shocked by the various arguments set out in your typewritten enclosure. For they really do seem to me, most of them, to be the most terrible nonsense. In case it may be of some use at a later stage, I give below the best short answers which I can think of to the various contentions.

1. I assume that Schacht's argument as to the impossibility of the depreciation of the mark under his management assumes that transfer protection continues unabated. On this assumption the main threat to the stability of the mark will obviously arise out of attempts by foreign lenders to withdraw some part of the money now lent at short notice. A possible order of events seems to me to be: (a) the continuance of transfer by the Agent-General at the expense of depleting the Reichsbank's reserves of gold and foreign exchange down to their legal minimum; (b) the suspension of transfer when the minimum is in sight; (c) the suspension of transfer operating as a danger signal to foreign short lenders, who in their attempts to repatriate even one-tenth of the £300 million which Schacht says is lent short in Germany will face him with the alternative of letting the mark depreciate or abandoning his reserve proportions. If he chooses to create simultaneously a credit crisis within Germany by restricting credit, that will do nothing whatever to restore the faith of the foreign lender; nor, once he is feeling the least nervous, will he be tempted to leave his money behind by the promise of a rate of interest even 2 or 3 per cent higher than at present. In fact, Schacht's remedy consists in threatening to throw the greater part of the German population out of work. This is not a threat which will influence the foreign financier one way or another, and if carried out it is bound in the long run, though not, I agree, in the first few weeks or months, to turn the balance of trade against Germany. In fact, what you attribute to him seems to me to be the most dreadful nonsense.

2. McKenna's argument, in contradistinction to Schacht's is based, I assume, on the situation which would exist in the event of the abolition of transfer protection. Anyhow, I should agree that so long as transfer protection exists the commercial will, in effect, get priority and leave the political in the lurch. His argument about each bank giving priority to its own customers seems to be an ingenious little invention,

which I cannot believe for one moment that he himself takes seriously. Which of the following propositions would he deny?—

(*a*) There will always exist an open market quotation for the mark.

(*b*) The Agent-General will always be able to deal on as large a scale as anyone else at the market quotation, and if he presses his sales can force the market quotation down.

(*c*) The banks will put through deals between their own customers at whatever the market quotation may be, for otherwise they would simply be cheating those who had sterling to convert into marks for the benefit of those who had marks to convert into sterling.

If he answers, as he surely must, each one of these propositions in the affirmative, than it follows that in practice the Agent-General and private people will always be able to remit on precisely equal terms.

3. I need not, perhaps, say any more about the transfer problem, in view of my journal article. I shall be interested to learn whether it produces any effect on Parmentier.

If I was in Schacht's place, I should refuse to abate transfer protection in the slightest degree, and in all other respects accept and concede practically whatever is likely to be offered or asked. If I were in your place I should join with Schacht in seeking to maintain complete transfer protection, and in any other respect serve up whatever the other parties find tastier.

It seems to me, by the way, to be a good debating point that if the French and Belgians disbelieve the reality of the transfer problem, there can be no objection, from their point of view, to the maintenance of transfer protection, since if they are right it is extremely improbable that it can ever be operative. If transfer protection is retained, that will mean in effect, whatever may be done in detail, that we shall jog along with the Dawes scheme unchanged in essence until we begin to have some real experience about Germany's capacity.

Yours ever,

[copy initialled] J.M.K.

Keynes also sent copies of the article to Basil Blackett, who attended the committee at the beginning and end of its task, and to Melchoir, who wrote (in German) from Paris:

From C. MELCHIOR, *4 March 1929*

My dear Keynes,

Many thanks for your kind letter of February 26 and your very interesting article.

I share your view that the reparation will eventually be paid by depressing the standard of life of the industrial working classes and of the employees and besides by maintaining exaggerated direct taxation. This probably will lead to very serious social and political disturbances, if it would mean a drastic reduction of the money wages. So probably the solution of the reparation problem would necessarily lead to the attempt to either maintain or slightly increase the level of prices. These questions must be very seriously studied in case a solution will be found. Whether this will be possible cannot yet be foreseen.

Please remember me to Mrs Keynes.

With kindest regards,

Yours very sincerely,

C. MELCHIOR

Schacht read 'The Transfer Problem' in the *Economic Journal* and wrote a short note in German to Keynes about it (1 March 1929). The article, he said, got to the kernel of the reparations problem—German real wages and standard of living—which, Schacht said, he himself had always been concerned about.

On 2 March Keynes received a cable from Professor Irving Fisher of Yale University asking for a 1,000-word article on his views of the Paris conference 'especially discussion transfer and fixed payment problems'. Fisher asked for this in interview form for use in his weekly economic service which he supplied to the financial pages of 75 American newspapers with a combined circulation of about 7 million. He mentioned a 'small honorarium'. Keynes had his article, a layman's version of the transfer problem, on the way even before Fisher's letter of the same date as the cable arrived giving details.

To IRVING FISHER, *6 March 1929*

Dear Professor Fisher,

In response to your cable, I enclose a statement of my views about the prospects of the Paris Reparations Conference. I am not sure whether it covers exactly the ground you wanted. But I could not do more in a thousand words. Indeed, I think I have exceeded the limit you suggested. Please feel free to modify the questions in any way you are inclined, and to make any cuts in my answers which considerations of length require. Indeed, sub-edit it as you will, provided the sense of what I am saying remains unchanged.

You put me in a slight difficulty by not stating in your cable the amount of the honorarium you propose. Whilst I have not written a great deal lately, I am more or less a professional journalist so far as the international Press is concerned, and I have a regular standard of charges for the United States, which it is not policy for me to abate or modify. My general rule has been to make $100 my minimum figure in any circumstances, and in the case of contributions written specially for America the rate is generally somewhat higher. However, in the circumstances I leave myself in your hands.

Yours very truly,
[copy initialled] J.M.K.

Fisher was pleased and gratified with the 'interview'. He wrote (5 April 1929):

...I like very much your method of dealing with the subject and, as you will see from the enclosed clippings of the article very little editing of your text was needed.

Your reasoning interests and impresses me and I only regret that there is not an opportunity for detailed discussion of some of the points which you make. Although I do not entirely agree with you (as you doubtless anticipated) I believe that your comments are highly valuable and I am glad to have a part in disseminating them.

The interview duly appeared under such headlines as that of the New York *Evening World* below. An introductory passage by Fisher read: 'So far as space permits, his [Keynes's] views on the present conference on reparations are presented here in the following interview which he has granted me.' The questions were Keynes's own. The amount of the honorarium was $150.

From the New York Evening World, *25 March 1929*

PROF. FISHER DISCUSSES REPARATIONS PROBLEMS WITH JOHN M. KEYNES

Mr Keynes, do you think that the conference now being held in Paris about the revision of the Dawes scheme for reparations is opportune? In certain respects I think that Mr Parker Gilbert has been quite right in pressing for an immediate conference to consider revision of the German liability. For one thing, the fixed annuity now reaches its maximum figure, namely $625 million, and very shortly this will be supplemented to a certain extent by reference to what is called the index of prosperity. There is much to be said for some downward revision of this large sum before any untoward consequences are produced. There is also another reason which I think may have weighed with Mr Parker Gilbert. It would certainly facilitate any new scheme if it could provide for a certain quantity of German government bonds being mobilised through sales to investors throughout the world. Now the huge scale on which Germany has been borrowing for the last three or four years is beginning to exhaust her possibilities of credit. The longer the delay, therefore, the less chance there will be of floating a large-size German loan. If matters are allowed to drift on until Germany has exhausted her credit it will obviously be more difficult to secure a solution satisfactory to Germany's creditors than it is now.

All the same, I think on the whole that the committee is

premature and is unlikely to secure solid results. In the four years which have elapsed since the Dawes scheme was started Germany has paid the instalments due from her entirely by borrowing abroad, and not at all by means of an export surplus. Indeed, she has borrowed very greatly more than she has paid in reparations. Now it is evident that the borrowing cannot continue for ever, if only because money accumulates at compound interest. German borrowing during the past four years has already amounted to such a figure that it requires some $250 million a year to meet its annual service. But it is only when this process of borrowing comes to an end that we can begin to gather experience of what figure Germany can safely be asked to pay. That experience we totally lack up to date. We really have no more evidence as to what she can pay than we had five years ago when the Dawes Committee first met. I imagine that at that time the committee themselves and everyone else supposed that in five years' time a good deal of evidence would have collected as to Germany's capacity, that the sums demanded could be revised in the light of that experience, and that the control system could be brought to an end. But as things are, we are no nearer to a real knowledge of Germany's capacity to pay than we were.

I appreciate that from the scientific point of view we are not much further forward than we were for forming a sound estimate. But public opinion changes with time and governments become more reasonable. May there not perhaps be some better basis for a settlement now than there was five years ago, even though our positive knowledge has not increased as much as we hoped it would?

It is difficult to say. One hopes very much that for the sort of reasons you suggest it will be found possible to make some revision. But the difficulty which I foresee is this. There are various concessions which it would be practicable, and perhaps right, for the Allies to make. They could evacuate the Rhineland; they could remove the system of controls at present established in Berlin, and so on. Above all, they could reduce the annuities below their present figure. But what is there that Germany can be asked to concede on the other side? It seems to me that there is little or nothing which she can be asked to give up, except to surrender that part of the Dawes scheme which is called transfer protection, that is to say, the arrangement by which the payments by the German government are made in marks, whilst the responsibility for changing these marks into foreign currency lies with the Allies and not with Germany. The only real concession which Germany could make would be to take over responsibility for furnishing to the Allies not marks but foreign currency. But this brings us back to what I have just been saying about our want of experience as to the export surplus which Germany can produce. For I can hardly believe that Germany would accept the responsibility of transfer unless the annuity were to be reduced to a figure much lower than the Allies could be expected to accept save in the light of a more extended experience than exists at present. The *impasse*, which I believe the experts in Paris will find themselves in, is due to this. Put shortly, there is not any basis for a deal. It may be that the conference will simply end in certain concessions being made to Germany without much of a *quid pro quo*. This will be all to the good. But I should not expect that such concessions will be very big ones. I doubt, therefore, whether we shall really get a final settlement until we have more experience as to the export surplus which Germany can safely remit.

I see that you lay a good deal of stress on the question of an export surplus, and on the possible difficulty which will be experienced in developing such a surplus. I suppose this means that you attach importance to the distinction between what is generally called the budgetary problem and the transfer problem, that is to say, the distinction between the problem of raising taxes in Germany and that of remitting the proceeds abroad?

315

I know that a school has grown up, very acceptable to French opinion, which argues that if you can collect the money by sound methods of taxation it will not be very difficult to remit it over the exchange. But I cannot agree with their line of argument. You do not automatically create an export surplus merely by collecting taxation within Germany. For after all, what is the reason why Germany's exports are no larger than they are at the moment? It is certainly not that her export industries cannot get the necessary labour, for there is a surplus of labour in nearly all the leading export industries. Undoubtedly, the reason why she has no more exports is because her costs of production do not enable her manufacturers to compete in international markets on a larger scale. She can only export more if she cuts down her costs of production, and it is roughly true to say that she can only cut down her costs of production materially if her wages are reduced. Now, it has been calculated that in order to produce an adequate export surplus she would have to increase her exports of finished goods by at least 40 per cent. By how much would she have to reduce her wages in order to produce this result? I do not know. But the amount of reduction of wages which would be necessary is the measure of the difficulty of the transfer problem. Germany's capacity to pay otherwise than by borrowing can only be increased by improving in some way her competitive position in international markets. As a matter of fact, the breathing space allowed during the last few years has permitted German wages to rise very considerably from the abnormally depressed level of 1924. Since 1924 gold wages in Germany have risen 40 per cent and real wages 23 per cent, with the result that real wages in Germany are now about 8 per cent higher than they were in pre-war days, with the result that so far Germany's competitive power has been weakened rather than strengthened.

If putting pressure on Germany to pay a large sum means

316

strengthening her competitive power, how do you think this will affect British interests?

Very adversely indeed. It becomes a question of how far Great Britain wants to force down German wages in order that Germany may steal her export industries away from her, and how much pressure Great Britain is prepared to put upon her in order to compel her to achieve this result. The great wisdom of the Dawes Plan as it now stands is this. The Dawes scheme provides that any surplus accruing to Germany through what you might call the natural situation is to be remitted over the exchange. But when as much has been remitted in that way as is feasible the Dawes scheme prevents any undue pressure being put upon Germany to force down her standard of life. Quite apart from humanitarian consideration, this arrangement seems to me to suit British policy. Great Britain does not want to press down the German standard of life so as to compete with her own exports because she is quite sure that it would finally have the effect of driving down her own standard of life. I should expect, therefore, that the British delegation in Paris would support the German delegates in wishing to maintain a large measure of transfer protection until we have a clearer view of the situation than we have at present.

I have asked you how you think that British interests are affected. May I complete this by asking you how you think it would affect American interests?

This question is easily answered. The direct American interest in the payment of reparations is not very great. America's main direct interest nowadays results from the very substantial sums which her citizens have invested in Germany. Now, the transfer protection clauses of the Dawes scheme protect the exchange value of the mark by providing in effect that the Allies can only remit reparations after Germany has duly met her commercial obligations, including interest on borrowed money. Once the transfer protection is removed, the position is no longer as secure, from this point of view, as it was before. I do not think that there can be any doubt that the interest of American investors in German bonds requires very decidedly that the transfer protection instituted by the Dawes scheme should be retained.

On 16 April 1929 Philip Snowden, the Labour Party's designate as Chancellor of the Exchequer, lashed out in the House of Commons against the Balfour Note. Attacking the Conservative policy on war debts, he bitterly criticised the Note on which it was based as unfair to British taxpayers in preventing the collection of the war debt deficit, and declared that the Labour Party considered itself free to repudiate its principles.

A number of factors made the situation delicate. The Labour Party was about to challenge the Conservatives—successfully—in the May general election. Britain had made France an offer, as yet unaccepted, for settling her debt. The Young Committee were in the process of scaling down Germany's reparation payments and it appeared that Britain was to receive less than her former share. If there were no Balfour Note Britain would then be able to make up the deficit in her debt payments to the United States by demanding more in payment from the Allies. France and Italy, fearing this reaction, might insist on larger reparation payments from Germany to meet the threat to themselves of larger British demands. But the Labour Party, like the other two parties, was solidly committed to the Balfour Note and Snowden had to back down.

The incident occurred on a Tuesday, the deadline for copy to be printed in that week's *Nation*. Keynes's reaction was immediate. While, in 1925, he had written, 'There is nothing to be said in favour of the Balfour Note' (p. 270 and *JMK*, vol. IX, p. 47), in 1929 he felt the circumstances had changed.

From The Nation and Athenaeum, *20 April 1929*

MR SNOWDEN AND THE BALFOUR NOTE

In Tuesday's budget debate Mr Philip Snowden was guilty of a remarkable outburst of which one can hardly believe either that it was, or that it was not, a premeditated and considered statement.

He described the famous Balfour Note, regulating the

relationship between our payments to the United States, our receipts from reparations, and our claims on our Allied debtors as 'infamous', and declared that the Labour Party 'hold themselves open, if the circumstances arise, to repudiate the conditions of that Note'.

Mr Snowden is at liberty to criticise the wisdom of our settlement with America. I agree with him (and Mr Bonar Law) in believing that this settlement was a disastrous mistake and that Mr Baldwin was one of the worst and most expensive ambassadors that this country has ever employed.

Mr Snowden is also at liberty to criticise the wisdom of the Balfour Note. There are many persons of good judgment who think that we made a mistake—not in giving the concessions to our Allies which that Note gives—but in giving them at that time and without an adequate *quid pro quo*, instead of keeping what we had in hand to assist us in our future negotiations relating to German reparations and European peace and amity generally. The irritation which it caused in the United States has also been a just ground of criticism. But I do not remember that the Labour Party announced at that time that they considered its terms to be 'infamous'. The Balfour Note was, when it was published, a great gesture on the part of this country in the interests of international generosity and moderation. It represented a profound reaction from the spirit of the Treaty of Versailles. These sentiments were in accord with those which the Labour Party were then professing. The main criticisms which they made were in the other direction, namely, that the writing-down of British claims was not sufficiently generous.

Further one can agree that the delay on the part of France to ratify the offer which we have made would entitle a future government to reopen the question, if they were to think it wise to do so. It is, indeed, possible and even probable, particularly in connection with a new reparations settlement, that it might be advisable to modify the terms which we have

319

offered to France, provided the modification was consistent with the conditions of the Balfour Note.

But none of these considerations affect the point that to talk of repudiating the conditions of the Balfour Note itself is wild and irresponsible, grossly unfitting on the lips of one who has been Chancellor of the Exchequer and hopes to be again. I cannot believe that Mr Snowden can have been aware of the implications of what he was saying. For with our Allies, other than France, funding agreements have been signed, sealed, and delivered. The Balfour Note forms part of the actual text of these agreements in every case except that of Roumania.

The result is that, even if France were to be deprived of the benefits of the Balfour Note, they would, under the terms of these existing agreements, enure not to the advantage of this country, but to the advantage either of Germany or of those Allies, mainly Italy, with whom we have already made agreements. To delete the Balfour Note from the draft agreement with France would mean raising our terms to them in order to give unanticipated advantages to Mussolini.

The doctrine of the continuity of foreign policy is a dangerous one, which should not be accepted without reserves. But this is quite a different thing from holding oneself free to break financial engagements, even if this country may have acted with an impulsive and premature generosity. It would be a blow at sound, businesslike practices in international affairs. It is not by greedily grasping at cash that we shall never see and to which we are no longer entitled, that we shall escape from the financial tangles which still survive the war period.

Mr Snowden asked in the House of Commons: 'Does the Chancellor of the Exchequer, then, maintain that an agreement which is made by a government supported by a party which happens to have a temporary majority in the House of Commons commits every other party in the State to the confirmation and the acceptance of that agreement in the future? If that be so, it is a doctrine to which I cannot subscribe.'

But if the agreement is neither a piece of domestic legislation nor a terminable treaty with a foreign power but a financial bargain for the funding of debts, it is surely a doctrine to which he *must* subscribe. The only possible exception could be if the official Opposition in Parliament had given the most explicit and deliberate warning to the foreign power concerned at the date when the agreement was before the House of Commons. I believe that, when the Italian agreement was before the House, Mr Snowden expressed his dislike of the principles of the Balfour Note—in a short dialogue he and Mr Churchill agreed with one another that it erred on the side of generosity—but he certainly gave no warning that the Labour Party would, if they were returned to power, repudiate the document under discussion when once it had been signed on behalf of His Majesty's Government.

It is worth adding in conclusion that Mr Snowden's arithmetic as to the relative severity of the terms accorded by ourselves and the United States to our European Allies is quite erroneous and misleading. The arrangement of the progression of the annuities through time is different in the two cases, the actuarial equivalent of which he has not taken into account. It is true that the American terms are, generally speaking, somewhat severer than ours, but not to the extent that he pretended. Indeed, if we had made settlements on identical lines with the American, we should have received up to date a *smaller* sum than we actually have received. The American severity lies all in the future; and who can say that it will actually be enforced? The Americans have not said their last word—though there is nothing more likely to stiffen their backs than such utterances as Mr Snowden's.

In Paris Dr Schacht presented the conference of experts with the maximum offer that he considered Germany could reasonably make. When this was not accepted, he left for Berlin to consult with his government. At this point it was feared that the conference had broken down. On 18 April Keynes produced an article for the *Daily Express*, published on Monday the 22nd, which was half an expansion of his reaction to Snowden's demonstration and half an explanation of the significance of 'the latest news from Paris'.

As a matter of course Keynes offered this article by mail to the *New Republic*; the *Republic*'s new editor, Bruce Bliven, however, asked him to cable 1,000 words on the conference's latest developments. Keynes telegraphed the latter half of the article, leaving out all reference to Snowden. Starting on page 7 of his manuscript, he wrote a new and still more up-to-date opening, added two paragraphs elaborating the importance of transfer protection, changed a few tenses and all the 'we's' to 'the Allies' and the '£'s' to '$'s', and deleted the reference to Mr Churchill's Budget surplus. It appeared as 'The Reparations Crisis' in the *New Republic*, 1 May 1929.

The version of the article given here is from the *Daily Express*. Keynes's original wording where it differs substantially and the additional material inserted in the *New Republic* version are shown in square brackets. Keynes headed his manuscript 'Allied Debts and Reparations. Mr Snowden's Wild Outburst', but the *Daily Express* circumspectly dropped his subtitle.

From the Daily Express, *22 April 1929*

ALLIED DEBTS AND REPARATIONS

In Tuesday's Budget debate Mr Snowden denounced the famous Balfour Note as 'infamous', and in the humiliating discussion which followed on Wednesday he refused to modify his declaration that the Labour Party 'hold themselves open, if the circumstances arise, to repudiate the conditions of that Note'.

Mr Snowden's outburst was particularly unfortunate, because many of the ideas which probably lay at the back of his head are ideas with which many of us keenly sympathise. How easy it would have been for him, with a little less obstinacy and rather better information about the facts, to have made good sense on Wednesday of rash and hasty words uttered on Tuesday! But, as he said [—alas!—] he is 'not of the apologising sort', even when something quite indefensible has been said which *must* be explained away.

Mr Snowden's feeling that our handling of the problem of inter-governmental indebtedness has been badly managed, is not confined to the ranks of the Labour Party. Bonar Law's passionately held conviction that Mr Baldwin's American debt settlement was a disastrous blunder has been far more widely shared in this country than has ever found expression in print.

There are, too, many who felt at the time, and have been strengthened in their opinion as time goes on, that the Balfour Note—splendid gesture, as it was, on the part of this country, as an act of international generosity—was a wasted gesture, an impulsive and premature concession. It would have been wiser to have kept it (and our other concessions) in reserve for the occasion of a satisfactory *all-round* settlement. It must, for example, be hampering our representatives in Paris in the reparations conference, now in progress, that, having already conceded so much, to have nothing more to offer wherewith to oil the wheels of compromise and negotiation.

But there is another point of greater practical significance than repinings about the past—namely, British policy to France today. Mr Snowden would have had public opinion behind him, if he had limited himself to emphasising that, in view of the long delay on the part of the French government in ratifying the very generous offer which we have made to them, a future British administration is unquestionably entitled to reopen its terms, provided the modification is consistent with the Balfour Note.

As the *Evening Standard* has put it: 'The Foreign Secretary [Austen Chamberlain] has declared that he loves France like a woman, and no Frenchman will ever believe that a chivalrous English gentleman could ever present a bill to the woman that he loves, save as a light-hearted pleasantry.' It is high time that we treated our entirely masculine neighbour as man to man.

The French policy, practised both towards ourselves and towards the United States, of squeezing out the best terms they can and then refusing to bind themselves on the assumption that these terms will always remain open, so that they can have an option for nothing for an indefinite period, is—looked at coolly—rather bold [quite intolerable]. A warning from Mr Snowden that these free options do not run for ever and that we are still capable of resuming a more businesslike relationship, might have strengthened the hands of our diplomacy and would certainly have been received by the country with relief and even enthusiasm. I cannot help thinking that this is really what was in Mr Snowden's mind. But he blundered when he got on to his feet and then turned obstinate.

For what he actually said was ill-informed in fact, misconceived in effect and indefensible in substance.

His threat to repudiate the clause of the Balfour Note, which provides that we shall not claim from our Allies and from Germany together a greater sum than the United States asks from us, is indefensible in substance, because this clause forms part of the actual text of the funding agreements already signed and finally concluded with all our Allies except France. It is wholly out of the question that any government could repudiate these agreements. I understand that on third thoughts (in a statement made to a journalist on Thursday), Mr Snowden admits this. [This sentence was added.] Moreover, the Balfour Note dates back to 1922, and continued to hold the field, unqualified and unwithdrawn, throughout the period when the Labour ministry was in office!

It is misconceived in effect. For to cut the benefits of the

Balfour Note out of the draft French agreement, which is the only withdrawal still open to us, would not help the British taxpayer in the least. The benefits of the Note, if any, withdrawn from France must necessarily accrue, under the agreements already made, either to Germany or to our other Allies, mainly Italy.

It is ill-informed in fact. For the debt Settlements which we have already made *plus* our reasonable expectations from German reparations actually fall quite a long way short of what we are entitled to receive under the terms of the Balfour Note itself! That is to say, we are at present by way of offering appreciably *more* than the Balfour Note concessions. It follows that we could raise our terms to France quite materially, whilst still allowing them, like our other Allies, the benefits of the Note. If further concessions are made to Germany in respect of reparations, this will widen still further the margin between our actual receipts and the maximum set on them by the Balfour Note. It is hard to believe that Mr Snowden can have known all this.

In truth the positive side of the Balfour Note—namely, that we propose to do our best to break *even*—is more closely bound up with the reparations problem than its negative side—namely, that we do not propose to do *more* than break even—is with the draft French agreement.

Meanwhile, the reparations conference in Paris has, it seems, reached a deadlock. If so, this is exactly what was to have been expected from the outset.

[Keynes started the *New Republic* version at this point. The opening sentences read:

The latest news from Paris makes it unlikely that an agreement will be reached, though one still hopes that there may emerge at least the appearance of a resettlement. If, however, there is a final breakdown, this will be in accordance with the most reasonable expectations.

Here Keynes picked up his text:]

325

For the truth is that the conference was held too soon. It would have been better to have jogged on for a year or two more under the Dawes scheme without talking about it. [Keynes had 'without talking'.] This was always the view of responsible British opinion. The conference is the fruit of Mr Parker Gilbert's over-optimism and his excusable impatience to get rid of the existing complicated machinery.

The dilemma which has faced the conference is easily explained. The object of the discussion was to reduce the annuities due from Germany and to fix the period over which they are payable.

The difficulty is that, Germany having paid hitherto by means of borrowed money, we really have no more evidence as to her capacity to pay than we had when the Dawes Committee met five years ago. Thus it is hard to find compelling reasons to induce the Allies to make large concessions, unless Germany on her side can offer something in return.

Now there is only one important concession left which it is open to Germany to make—namely to forgo the 'transfer protection' afforded her by the Dawes scheme. 'Transfer protection' means that the duty of the German government is limited to making payments in German marks. It is the responsibility of the Allies to change these marks into foreign currencies, and to cease exchanging them as soon as to do so endangers the mark exchange. This protection is of such tremendous advantage to Germany that she cannot be expected to give it up, except in return for a reduction of the annuities to a much lower figure than the Allies can be expected to concede without more compelling evidence than exists at present as to Germany's capacity to pay. So long, therefore, as Germany is asked to give up 'transfer protection', there is certain to be a wide gap between the Allied minimum terms and the German maximum offer.

The latest news from Paris indicates that Dr Schacht's minimum price for giving it up is (1) a reduction of the annuities by about one-third; (2) a limitation of the period over which they are paid to thirty-seven years; and (3) some vaguely outlined territorial concessions [corrected in the *New Republic* to 'Concessions relating to raw materials'] which are certain to be refused. This brings the dilemma to a head. For Dr Schacht would certainly be foolish to offer a larger 'unprotected' annuity. Indeed, he would have been rash to offer so much if he had not coupled it with other conditions which ensure its rejection. On the other hand, it is too much to expect the Allies to come down to his figure until it is proved that they cannot get more. In short, there is not, and never has been, the basis for a 'deal'. Nor will there be one, without a longer experience of the working of the Dawes scheme.

[The last two sentences were replaced in the *New Republic* by the following:

Doubtless, Dr Schacht would be prepared to improve his offer, provided that transfer protection remained; but in that case, he would be getting something for nothing as compared with the Dawes scheme.

Nevertheless, for the Allied representatives to allow transfer protection to continue is probably the best chance of securing a settlement, for I doubt whether the general public is right in thinking that the amount of the annuities is the crucial point at issue. The vital question is as to the part of the annuities, if any, which is to be unprotected and therefore unconditional.

But there is another paradox...

Keynes himself had actually written 'probably the best chance of preventing a breakdown of the negotiations'—a reflection of his feeling for the precariousness of the situation.]

But this is not the end of the difficulties. Neither Great Britain nor the United States really desires the removal of 'transfer protection' in their own interests. For the Dawes scheme was a highly ingenious technical invention. 'Transfer protection' protects two other kinds of interests besides Germany's.

In the first place it protects the foreign investor, for it means that his claims come first. The proceeds of reparations can only be remitted when this is possible without interfering with other remittances at the par of exchange. If Mr Owen Young were to press Germany to surrender 'transfer protection', the Americans who have lent to Germany would have their investments endangered through the possibility of a fall in the mark exchange. Moreover it would be much more difficult for Germany to go on borrowing.

In the second place it protects the British, Italian and French industrialists from undue German competition. Under the Dawes scheme Germany has to pay the equivalent of her 'natural' trade surplus. We cannot obtain more, unless we give a special stimulus to German exports, either by forcing down German wages or by taking large deliveries in kind, or by giving her a preference, or in some other way. That is to say, the Dawes scheme gives us all we can get without using artificial means to compel German industry to compete with ours more intensively than would occur otherwise. Do we want to do this?

I take rather a grave view of possible developments in the near future. For five years Germany has been more than paying her way by borrowing, with the result that six months ago she had built up quite a comfortable reserve of gold and foreign currency. Partly on account of the position in Wall Street, her ability to borrow large sums has come to an end. As a result of this her reserves have been melting away—the published figures of the Reichsbank showing a loss of £26,500,000 since 1 January, of which she lost no less than £8 million last week. At this rate the surplus reserves will disappear entirely in a few months or even a few weeks.

The breakdown of the Paris Conference is likely to accelerate this process. For at the beginning of this year it was calculated that foreign financiers had deposited something like £200 million in Berlin recallable at short notice. A withdrawal of 10 per cent of this sum would be very inconvenient.

I am disposed, therefore, to predict that the 'transfer protection' of the Dawes scheme will come into operation very shortly and that Germany will cease for the time being to make any reparation payments at all. In this case Mr Churchill's Budget surplus may already have disappeared before the election is over.

Early in May Keynes contracted with the American United Press Association to write an article for world distribution as promptly as possible after the outcome of the conference was known. His summing up, which transmits some of the relief that was felt by those involved in the four-month ordeal, was ready for publication 7 June, the day the conference ended. He retained the British rights for *The Nation*.

The reference to 'the Belgians' in the first paragraph of this article is to a Belgian move to get compensation for the loss in value through inflation of a sum of German marks left behind in Belgium after the Armistice and credited to their reparation account.

From The Nation and Athenaeum, *15 June 1929*

THE REPORT OF THE YOUNG COMMITTEE

What a nightmare it must have been! The hot gilt rooms, the babel of tongues, the shifts and counter-shifts, the Belgians, the unutterable boredom, and rising from the soil the miasmas of the Paris Press! We owe deep gratitude to Mr Young and Mr Morgan and Sir Josiah Stamp and the rest, who might have been occupied in the tranquil realism of business, yet have voluntarily subjected themselves for four interminable months to turn and twist on a polyglot grill. Have they reaped the reward of their devotion to duty?

The outlines of their construction have not yet risen distinctly out of the cloud of dust and the builders' rubble. The conference was premature—it would have been better to await some further experience of the Dawes Plan. Once summoned, nevertheless, it was important that it should not dissolve in futility. But what matters in the Young Plan is not

the exact figures or the miserable disputes which have pro-
tracted the negotiations, but one or two big ideas. I do not
believe that Mr Owen Young and Sir Josiah Stamp would have
thought it worth while to put up with the caterwaulings for
all these weeks if there was not something large behind; they
would have gone quietly home to their own affairs. These
great business-diplomats must have believed that there was,
after all, something worth while at stake. Let us see if we
can find it.

The technical problem and the diplomatic problem

Two objects which ought to have been kept separate have
been inextricably interwoven in the committee's contorted
deliberations; on the one hand, to determine Germany's
capacity to pay, and on the other, to discover the minimum
sum which, having regard to the Allied debts to America,
would be sufficient to permit an acceptable division of the
proceeds. The first was a matter for experts, the second for
diplomats.

But diplomacy has inevitably predominated over
expertism—for the simple reason that not much fresh information has come to hand relevant to Germany's capacity
to pay since the experts of the Dawes committee did their
work. Inasmuch as these annuities have only now reached
their maximum and have been paid exclusively out of
foreign loans, we still lack any compelling evidence based
on experience. Germany has paid so far—therefore it is not
certain that she cannot go on paying. But she has failed to
develop the necessary export surplus or even to begin to
develop it—therefore there is no proof that she can go on
paying. There is nothing to compel the former Allies to abate
their demands; and there is nothing to convince Germany
that she can comply with them.

The experts, *qua* experts, have, therefore, had little to say

330

except that the Dawes annuities, particularly now that they are due to be augmented by the so-called 'index of prosperity', are—as we knew five years ago—much too high, and that a change in the downward direction would be a further move towards sanity and reason. Having delivered themselves of these remarks of limited usefulness, they have had to doff their black robes of knowledge and to put on the tight, parti-coloured uniforms which diplomats wear. The problem has shifted from the still insoluble problem how much Germany can pay to the question how little the Allies can be induced to demand.

The latter figure has been fixed within narrow limits by two equations. It was governed, first, by the Allies' determination to demand from Germany at least as much as what the United States demands from them. Great Britain asks no more than this. The others require a modest surplus for themselves.

But there was a second equation limiting the committee's freedom of movement. The division of the receipts between the Allies was finally fixed several years ago by the 'Spa percentages'. Great Britain has stood adamant that she would not allow the Spa percentages to be materially modified to her disadvantage, so long as they yield her less than she is entitled to under the terms of the Balfour Note. (The small concessions from Great Britain, to which Sir Josiah Stamp has agreed, are not, in my opinion, unjustifiable or really detrimental to our interests. I hope that the new government will stand by him. The assignment to France of an excessive proportion of the unconditional annuity is, in spite of the guarantee fund which France is to put up, much more dangerous to our prospective receipts than the rearrangement of our nominal annuities.)

Thus the existing Dawes annuities set the maximum. The Allied debts to America and the Spa percentages give, taken in conjunction, the minimum. But Belgium and France could not be satisfied diplomatically without some surplus over and

331

above this minimum. Mr Owen Young's first problem, there-fore, was to settle the reasonable amount of this surplus and then to employ every device of obstinacy and tact to force it on the others. Some weeks ago he announced his decision. The average annuity was to be £102,500,000 a year instead of the Dawes annuity of £125 million, or (say) £135 million when augmented by the index of prosperity.

Now from Germany's point of view this is a reduction—and, therefore, to the good. Moreover, there was a further mitiga-tion which could be offered her. The average annuity could be spread so as to be lighter in the near future and heavier in later years. This has been a characteristic of all the repara-tion settlements. It is a feature which commends itself to the 'experts', because Germany's capacity is certainly less now than it will be later on; and it commends itself to Germany because a burden which is thrown in to the future may be, and hitherto always has been, removed when the time comes. On this occasion it is proposed that the annuity shall start at about £90 million, and rise to £121 million.

Thus next year Germany will pay under the Young scheme only some two-thirds of what she would have had to pay under the Dawes scheme.

So far, so good. But Germany could not expect to get this reduction as a mere gift without a *quid pro quo*. What concessions from her could the Allies ask?

Germany's concessions

They were two in number. The Dawes scheme left it uncertain over how many years Germany must pay. Germany has argued that thirty-seven years is all that can be required under the Treaty of Versailles. The Young Plan asks Germany to put her signature to a duration of fifty-eight years from today and sixty-eight years from the Treaty of Peace. But the amount of the annuity is to be much reduced after thirty-seven years from today.

In the second place the Dawes scheme allowed to Germany what is called 'transfer protection'. That is to say, her liability was limited to payment in marks, and the Allies were only entitled to remit the money outside Germany to the extent that this proved possible without upsetting the exchange value of the mark. Germany could be asked, therefore, to undertake an unconditional liability for the payment in foreign currency of a part of each annuity. The amount of this 'unprotected' portion is the question on which, in my judgment, Dr Schacht was most justified in showing obstinacy. It is also the question on which the Allies were least justified in pressing him too far. For if the unprotected portion is dangerously large, the foreign loans already made to Germany will be placed in jeopardy and the prospects of getting further loans will be much diminished. Now it is certain that at present Germany cannot pay even the reduced annuity without the help of further loans. Thus to shake her credit by forcing on her too large an 'unprotected' transfer might hasten a crisis. Germany has agreed to an unconditional transfer of £33 million a year. Even this may embarrass her seriously in the near future.

But there is a further feature of the new scheme which, in my judgment, is dangerous, and therefore objectionable compared with the Dawes scheme. The liability to transfer the *whole* of each annuity in foreign currencies rests henceforward on Germany, and her right of postponement, instead of being unlimited in duration, is restricted to two years. Moreover, Germany's task is made more difficult by a great reduction, and extinction after ten years, of the deliveries in kind. Practically, no doubt, the two years will, in the event of a postponement taking place, be devoted to the labours of yet one more committee of revision. But formally the experts allege 'that the total amount of the annuity proposed is one which they have every reason to believe can, in fact, be both paid and transferred by Germany'. They affirm that their proposals 'with the conditions and safeguards that accompany them will be within Germany's capacity to pay', adding that they 'realise the responsibility of this declaration'. They do not, however, even mention the fact that Germany has paid hitherto by borrowing. Nor do they say whether the transfer of the annuities is compatible with Germany's present standard of life or her present rates of money wages relatively to other countries. Thus the real economic issue—as distinct from the immediate diplomatic necessities—is, as usual, shirked, and the consciences of the experts are saved by suppressed qualifications.

The immediate prospects

I am not sure, therefore, that the Young scheme, regarded from a limited technical standpoint, is worth the pains it has cost.

What was the matter with the Dawes scheme? Merely, that there was a prospect of 'transfer protection' and a temporary cessation of German payments coming into operation at an early date.

Does the Young scheme avoid this? I doubt it. Of course, it is easier for Germany to remit £90 million than £135 million. But it would seem that even to pay the former sum, it will be necessary for the present that Germany should borrow abroad at least £100 million a year and perhaps a good deal more. Will the rest of the world go on lending to her at this rate? It is unlikely.

Moreover, the problem of Germany's capacity to pay remains where it was. Given the level of the world's economic prosperity, Germany's capacity will be fixed, first, by the willingness of the rest of the world to take her goods, and, secondly, by the degree to which she can depress the efficiency wages of her workers relatively to efficiency wages elsewhere. It depends on nothing else. It is a human problem—to be

334

settled by time and men's natures. The confabulations of Paris do not alter it; they have not even discussed it.

Where, then, are we to look for the large conceptions? I see the possibility of them in two quarters.

The international bank

The scheme has been complicated by what appears, at first sight, a portentous piece of machinery. The tasks of remittance and of supervision are to be entrusted to a new international bank having the substantial capital of £20 million. I conceive that the objects of the bank are twofold. It renders possible the substitution of banking management for political management and the demobilisation of the elaborate system of supervision and control devised by the Dawes scheme. But it also provides a nucleus for the super-national currency authority which will be necessary if the world is ever to enjoy a rational monetary system. This is a very big idea about which we shall be wise to reserve judgment.

The United States

The total obliteration of the war debts remains today, as it has been for ten years, the only solution ultimately compatible with the world's needs and the promptings of the world's conscience. Each successive conference is to be judged, therefore, not by its technical details, but by the progress it makes to this goal. On this test the Young committee deserves, I am sure, our gratitude and our applause.

For it has achieved one result of very great importance. By the goodwill of its American members, the committee has defined with a new precision the relation of the United States to the war debts. What Germany must pay is linked up by a strict formula to what America demands. Two-thirds of the benefit of any concession on her war debts which the United

335

States may see fit to make hereafter, is to go to the reduction of Germany's payments and only one-third to the former Allies themselves.

Thus the way is cleared for future action. Generosity on the part of America will necessarily redound to appeasement and mercy. If America in exercise of *her* rights presses the former Allies, they in exercise of *their* rights will transmit the pressure to the standard of life of German workers who were babes or unborn when the war was hatched. But if America substitutes generosity for rights, the Allies have bound themselves to pass on to Germany the major part of the relief. This broad outcome is Mr Owen Young's best achievement. He has deliberately allowed his committee—even encouraged it—to 'pass the buck' to his own country.

During the conference Owen Young had been criticised in the English Press for seeming to force on Britain a reduction of her share of the reparations receipts as agreed at Spa in 1920. *The Nation* published an editorial taking him to task; although in 1929 Keynes no longer kept up the scrapbook of his unsigned writing, it appears from other evidence to have been substantially his work.

From The Nation and Athenaeum, *11 May 1929*

GREAT BRITAIN AND REPARATIONS

The long-drawn discussions of the reparations conference in Paris have taken an unexpected and disconcerting turn. For four weary months, the committee of experts have wrestled with their thorny task, their highly technical deliberations having been from time to time lit up by fierce outbursts in the Press of Paris and Berlin. More than once they have reached a deadlock which appeared insoluble, but have contrived to avert a breakdown by agreeing to explore some new suggestion. The strain on individuals has been immense. Lord Revelstoke has died; Sir Josiah Stamp's indefatigability must have been severely taxed. But, throughout, the part played by the British delegation has been exactly what we should all desire, moderating, patient, and resourceful. In the attempt to bridge the gulf between the demands of the creditor states and the offers of Germany, the influence of Britain has been cast, as everyone has recognized, on the side of accommodation. Until this week, it has not seemed possible that we could be put in the position of appearing to obstruct a settlement.

Yet, if reports from Paris are correct, this is what has now occurred. It is proposed to solve the problem of reconciling French demands and German offers by reducing the British share of reparation payments; and this proposal, which not unnaturally is acceptable both to France and Germany, is sponsored by the American chairman, Mr Owen Young.

It is not surprising that the British delegation should have been taken aback by this proposal, and should feel some resentment at its having been put forward by Mr Owen Young. After a long and vexed controversy, which behind the scenes was almost as acrimonious as that over the figures Germany should be required to pay, the distribution of reparation payments among the various creditor states was determined by the Spa agreement of July 1920. Ever since then the Spa percentages (France 52 per cent, the British Empire 22 per cent, Italy 10 per cent, Belgium 8 per cent, etc.) have been the one fixed and settled point in the reparations question. They were left untouched by the London Conference of 1924 which established the Dawes Plan. Upon what principle of equity can it be argued that they should now be revised to our disadvantage?

As regards the merits of the percentages themselves, infinite argument is, of course, possible—in more than one direction. Our own Spa percentage of 22 is much less than the share we claimed. Our position until Spa was that the French and British shares should be in the ratio 5:3, which would have meant a British percentage of more like 30. But it is impossible at this stage to reconsider *ab initio* the merits of the distribution. An equitable case for revision can only be based on some change since 1920 in the relevant circumstances. If, for example, the events of the last nine years had shown that the economic life of France was being crippled by the burden of war costs, while Great Britain had entered on a new lease of buoyant progress, there might be something to be said for modifying the existing arrangement in France's favour. But the course of events has been the opposite of this. In recent years France has made an astonishing industrial advance, while the prosperity of Britain has been checked by persistent, large-scale unemployment to a degree which no one in 1920 would have thought likely.

It would seem, indeed, that Mr Owen Young has been moved to put forward his proposal not by any principle of equity, but by the principle of least resistance. He has found the French difficult, and the British helpful. The British were prepared to go further than the French in the direction of scaling down the aggregate demands on Germany. Might they not be willing, then, to abate their share of the aggregate demands? In view of the British desire to come to terms, a settlement might possibly be found in this expedient; and this seemed to be the only chance. Such reasoning would be natural enough to Mr Owen Young, at his wits' end to find an acceptable compromise. But it is no less natural that the British delegation and British public opinion should resent it. We did not expect that the reasonableness and moderation of the British attitude would be exploited to our special disadvantage and we are not in the least likely to acquiesce in any arrangement which is so inspired.

The exact terms of Mr Owen Young's proposal have not, at the moment of our writing, been disclosed. The communications from Paris in the newspapers stress the point that it would disallow our claim to the arrears which arise, under the principle of the Balfour Note, from our past payments to the United States. If this were all, we should not regard it very seriously. We are not very likely in any case to recover those arrears. We shall only do so, under the Spa percentages, if Germany makes larger reparation payments than we think it likely she will make. If, accordingly, the redistribution proposed by Mr Own Young were confined to the higher reaches of the theoretical reparation payments, leaving the Spa percentages untouched for the lower reaches, we should not feel much concerned. But, so far as we can gather, this is not what is proposed. On the contrary, the chief significance of the writing-down of the maximum British claim appears to be that in this way a logical basis is supplied for reducing substantially our share of *all* reparation payments, including in particular the part which is to be 'commercialised'. The comments which we have made above are made on this assumption.

It is quite out of the question that any British government will agree just now to any such proposal. Mr Snowden has denounced the Balfour Note as representing an 'infamous' sacrifice of British interests; and the Labour Party have backed him up to the extent of declaring officially, in the terms of the amendment moved last week by Lord Parmoor in the House of Lords, that the debt settlements 'have imposed unfair burdens upon British taxpayers'. In these circumstances, it is politically quite safe for the Government to refuse all concessions, while it would be politically dangerous to make any. If the reparations conference breaks down owing to our refusal to make concessions, the Labour Party will be debarred from complaining, as they otherwise might have done, that the government has sacrificed the interests of European appeasement in a spirit of short-sighted greed. Indeed, the danger of the present situation is not in the least that a British government will be unduly ready to bargain away British interests for the prestige of a settlement, but rather the opposite. It may prove difficult for the government to make concessions which it might be reasonable for us to make, and which our representatives in Paris may wish us to make. It may prove difficult for Great Britain to maintain her traditional moderating rôle.

The prospects of a reparations settlement cannot be said, therefore, to have been advanced by the recent negotiations in Paris. It seems not unlikely that, after five years of quiescence, we are about to enter on a virulent and embittered phase of the reparations controversy; and not unlikely either that the next Chancellor of the Exchequer will have to face a substantial hole in an early budget as the result of a failure in reparation receipts.

This was read a month later, after the conference was over, by Keynes's old acquaintance Thomas Lamont, one of the American delegates, as he was returning to the United States on the *Aquitania*. Assuming Keynes was the author, he wrote a long letter, dated 14 April, from on board ship, giving the true story of what had happened.

When the creditor experts had made their offer of 2,123 million marks which was rejected by the Germans offering 1,650 million marks, the conference seemed on the verge of breaking up. Young then talked privately with both the Germans and the Allies and, with the knowledge of all the parties that he was doing so, proposed a hypothetical figure for discussion based on the top figure that he had learned the Germans would accept. The substance of his memorandum showing how he had made up the figure reached the press without the explanation that the proposal was only a suggestion for discussion. Lamont enclosed for Keynes a clipping from *The Times*, which had eventually printed Young's own explanatory words from the memorandum.

Lamont assumed that the *Nation* article was written by Keynes and Keynes in his reply to the letter, which follows, does not deny it; indeed, he tacitly appears to admit responsibility. More recently, he said, he had written 'another article', that of 15 June (p. 329), of which he enclosed a copy. It is possible that Keynes and Hubert Henderson might have discussed the substance of the unsigned article and that Henderson, whose style of editorial writing was very like Keynes's, might have been the author. (Both Keynes and Henderson at the time were very much occupied with the Liberal plan to cure unemployment and the publication of their pamphlet *Can Lloyd George Do It?* during the 1929 election.) But while joint or

340

other authorship is possible, the sharp vexation expressed at what appeared to be an advantage unfairly taken seems the reaction of someone who was personally deeply involved—as Keynes was.

To THOMAS W. LAMONT, *26 June 1929*

My dear Lamont,

Very many thanks for your letter of June 14th about the reparations conference. I am glad to know just what happened. I agree that Mr Owen Young was somewhat maligned. I had really supposed at the time that there must be some element of misrepresentation. But the hue and cry raised in this country was of course aimed not so much at him as at the whole suggestion of any serious nibbling at the Spa percentages. The object was not personal, but intended to make it clear that any such arrangement should be ruled out of the field of reasonable possibility.

More recently, since the committee reported, I have written another article, of which I enclose a copy. On longer reflection, I feel that I should probably have been prepared to sign the report as an Englishman, but should almost certainly have refused to do so as a German. Also, I fancy there are certain points with regard to the constitution of the proposed bank which need rather careful criticism. Indeed, there is a good deal about the bank which might be reconsidered, and I should have thought that it might have been made clear that the 'take it or leave it as a whole' injunction need not be taken as applying to the details of the bank and its constitution.

I have been very glad to hear from you again—it is some time since we met. There is just a possibility that I may be coming over to the United States, for the first time since the war, some time in the first half of next year. If so, I shall venture to let you know, and will hope to see you.

Yours sincerely,
[copy initialled] J.M.K.

Towards the end of May Irving Fisher had cabled again to Keynes asking for another article in interview form 'whenever results of Paris conference are in your opinion sufficiently definite to warrant evaluating conclusions'. Keynes's interview of himself repeated in part the substance of the *Nation* article, with greater emphasis, however, for American readers, on the Young Plan's definition of the relation between Allied debts to America and Germany's debts to the Allies. He also called attention to the closeness of the new reduced annuity figures to the figure he justified as a final settlement with Germany in *The Economic Consequences of the Peace*.

Fisher in his introduction to the interview supplied the quotation:

I believe that it would have been a wise and just act to have asked the German government at the Peace negotiations to agree to a sum of $10,000 million [£2,000 million in the English edition] in final settlement [*JMK*, vol. II, 85].

From the New York Evening World, *24 June 1929*

PROPOSED INTERNATIONAL BANK
AND NEW U.S. POLICY ARE BIG
IDEAS OF YOUNG DEBT PLAN

John Maynard Keynes, interviewed by Irving Fisher, finds annuities fixed almost at figures predicted by him ten years ago

Mr Keynes, do you think that the immense pains expended by the experts on the new Young Scheme are justified by the results?

Yes. I have been one of the sceptics as to the utility of the recent Paris Conference. I have taken the view that it was being held prematurely and that the Dawes scheme should have been given a further trial. But in the result I feel that something substantial, and perhaps something important, has really been achieved. If I am right, the world owes a real debt of gratitude to the experts, and primarily I should suppose to the two American delegates, Mr Owen Young and Mr J. P. Morgan, and the chief British delegate, Sir Josiah Stamp. Indeed, I can hardly believe that these great business men would have been content to spend four months in Paris on what must have been most tiresome and disagreeable negotiations unless they had believed that there was something of real importance for the world to be attained by it.

Could you sum up in a few words the effect of the whole thing so far as Germany is concerned?

Germany has had to make two concessions in order to get a reduction in the amount of the Dawes annuity by about one-quarter. Under the Dawes scheme she would have had to pay from now onwards $625 million a year plus an augmentation to be determined by an 'index of prosperity'. You may take it that this would have raised the annual figure by at least $25 million, making the total $650 million. Under the Young Plan the average annuity is reduced to $512,500,000. Moreover, in the early years the annuity is to be a lower figure still, starting at $437,500,000. Thus, to begin with, Germany's payments will be reduced by about a third. This is a substantial reduction and—perhaps I may add—the annuity has now been reduced almost to the exact figure which I said was practicable when I wrote *The Economic Consequences of the Peace* ten years ago.

What concessions has Germany had to make on her side as some compensation for these reductions?

Apart from details, there are two undertakings to which Germany has had to put her signature, which did not appear in the Dawes scheme. The Dawes scheme left it doubtful for how many years Germany was to pay, and she herself has always maintained that she is not liable for more than 37 annuities under the terms of the Treaty of Versailles. According to the Young Plan, the annuities will continue at their normal figure for 37 years, and then at a greatly reduced figure for a further 21 years. Thus Germany has had to abandon her contention as to the date at which the annuities should terminate. Indeed, under the Young Plan, payments will still be continuing 68 years, or more than two generations after the signature of the Treaty of Peace. I confess, however, that I regard this as a minor matter. The future will look after the future.

But there is another concession of much greater immediate significance. Under the Dawes Plan Germany had no responsibility for converting the payments she made in terms of marks into foreign exchange. She has now agreed, however, that her liability for paying some part of the annuity in foreign currencies shall be unconditional, namely, a sum of $165 million a year. Eventually she ought to have no difficulty in providing this sum. But in the near future it may be embarrassing. I doubt if it has been wise on the part of the Allies to press Germany to concede this amount of unconditional transfer, since it certainly weakens Germany's credit, and therefore her opportunities for borrowing from private investors all over the world.

You suggested that Mr Owen Young and his colleagues were induced to stay on in Paris, not so much because they attached importance to the particular figures of their plan, but because there were some big ideas in it which were worth salving.

Yes, I am convinced that the importance of the Young Plan does not lie in any of the figures which I have mentioned, but in certain big conceptions which are to be found a little below the surface. I fancy that Sir Josiah Stamp may be primarily responsible for one of them, and Mr Owen Young for the other.

The first big idea is that of the proposed international bank. Whether this has really been accepted in advance by the central banks of Europe I do not know. But one must presume that the experts have good reason for supposing that it will be. The international bank is to command gigantic resources —something like $250 million in addition to its capital of $100 million. These resources and the organisation proposed would create an unnecessarily large and cumbrous piece of machinery if the only object of it was to take over the duties of Mr Parker Gilbert's transfer committee and to facilitate the technical operations of remitting reparations to the creditor nations. Obviously, the authors of this great instrument have

344

a more important destiny than that in mind for it. What can this be, except to provide the world with machinery which may be appropriate and useful for some great currency reform in the future? If we are to manage our monetary affairs in a rational manner in the years to come, unquestionably we shall need some super-national authority of great influence which will provide an organisation for the collaboration of the central banks of the world—including in due course, I hope, the Federal Reserve system of the United States. I believe that the Paris experts are taking advantage of the reparation situation to call into being a mammoth institution which may in future years take its place beside the League of Nations and the International Court of Justice as one of the super-national institutions with which the world of the future will endeavour to keep its international arrangements in order.

The second big idea relates to the new position which the United States takes up under the new plan in relation to the war debts problem as a whole.

How can the United States be taking up a new position when its government has stood ostentatiously aside from any participation in it?

The Young Plan defines the relation between the Allied debts to America and Germany's debts to the Allies with a new precision. The sums which Germany is to pay for reparations are definitely divided into two parts, one of which corresponds to the sums which the Allies have to pay to the United States and the other to reparations proper in excess of this sum. I may add that the amount allocated to reparations proper is a comparatively small proportion of the whole. But not only so. The scheme provides what is to happen in the event of the United States at some future time reconsidering her attitude towards the war debts. Any concession which the United States may make in future to any of her Allied debtors will under the Young Plan redound to the extent of two-thirds

345

to the benefit of Germany, and only to the extent of one-third to that of the Allies themselves.

I think it is a matter of extraordinary importance to have this precise relationship defined. America will now know beforehand the exact consequences of any concessions which she may feel justified in making. The Allies have in effect announced that the extent to which they press their legal rights against Germany will depend upon the degree in which the United States presses her legal rights against them. There can be nothing unreasonable in this. Not only so, but it creates a situation in which the problem before American citizens is put to them in far clearer and more definite terms than before. Moreover, it is of high importance that it should have been a leading American citizen who has taken a prominent part in formulating the problem just in this manner. I hope that Americans will not feel annoyed by this emphasis on the connection between the debts of the Allies and the reparations due from Germany. For there is no getting out of the reality of this connection. At any rate, Europe has every reason to be grateful to the two Americans who have been ready to take on themselves the odium, if there is any, of putting the above arrangement into black and white.

Privately Keynes did not expect the Young Plan to be successful. In a letter to Andrew McFadyean commenting on the manuscript of McFadyean's book on reparations, he said, 'I think I should have dared to express a more definite disbelief in the Young Plan'. After querying a specific point in the manuscript, he asked some informed questions on his own account about what was going on in Germany. (McFadyean at the time was writing from Berlin.)

From a letter to ANDREW MCFADYEAN, *5 January 1930*

1. What do you think of the credit of the German municipalities? Some people hold over here investments in the short-dated mark loans of, for example, Heidelberg or Munich.

2. Are any estimates yet available of Germany's borrowings during 1929 in short-term and in long-term respectively?

3. One would rather expect that as a result of the now somewhat prolonged cessation of long-term borrowing, Germany's liquid foreign assets must be running down somewhat seriously. Is there any positive evidence of this?

4. Does Schacht's obvious anxiety to escape any sort of responsibility for the working out of the Young Plan mean that he anticipates the possibility of, or is by no means over-anxious to avert, some sort of a payments crisis in the course of 1930?

My own prophecy would be that the Young Plan will not prove practicable, even for a short period, unless the mark exchange is allowed to depart from its present parity, and I should not be at all surprised to see some sort of crisis in 1930. For I much doubt whether Germany will be able to borrow really large sums either in London or in New York; whereas Paris, which ought to be her source of borrowing, will probably seek to keep German loans at bay for the present in order not to block the way for their precious mobilisation schemes which are due in 1931.

McFadyean, replying 9 January, answered the financial questions in detail and said he thought that Schacht's attitude had to do with his political ambitions: 'He must see that part responsibility for the Young Plan is rather a millstone round the neck of a would-be conservative leader...' For his own part, he wrote:

I am inclined to believe, though I admit that in some respects it has rather a flimsy basis, that Germany will scrape through for the time being. The question of loans is, of course, the crux of the matter but I believe if the Young Plan comes into force fairly soon she will succeed in scraping together enough foreign assets to keep going: some of them by floating long-term loans, more of them by a dangerous addition to the short-term indebtedness, and others of them by a more extensive sale of German shares and participations in German enterprise. But it is a gloomy outlook and I won't pretend that there is not a good deal in my view which is little more than feeling...

It was a time of depression and disillusion and one journalist-observer, taking the name of 'Logistes', chose as his title for an account of England's role in recent history *The Dupe as Hero*. This was both too simple and too ignoble an explanation for Keynes, who in reviewing the book for *The Nation* offered his own analysis.

From The Nation and Athenaeum, *3 May 1930*

A DUPE AS HERO

This book is described as being by a journalist 'of distinction and wide influence', who once held 'a position in Whitehall'. But the contents give no further clue to the authorship, and provide no reason why it should have been published anonymously. It consists of a narrative of various matters relating to inter-allied debts and reparations from the beginning of the war down to last year. The upshot is that Great Britain has allowed herself to be the financial dupe of those who were her allies and associates in the war.

The events of which the author reminds us are not novel. But just as the time seems to have come for war plays and war novels, so it may be a moment when the public can look more calmly than before at some of the less pleasing financial details. The author reminds us that by the time the United States entered the war Great Britain had exhausted her resources in financing her allies as well as herself. The point had come, therefore, when, although she could go on financing her own war expenses, she could furnish no more money to France and Italy unless she borrowed an equal amount from the United States. Accordingly, from 1917 onwards she borrowed about a thousand million pounds from the United States and lent a like sum to France and Italy. After the war France and Italy were allowed to repudiate five-sixths of their debt to Great Britain. Great Britain agreed to pay the whole of her own debt to the United States. She also allowed France to receive more than half of the reparations payable by Germany, and accepted for herself less than a quarter. The author adds that Great Britain is also paying more than any other country towards the expenses of the League of Nations, and that by 1929 France had become the second richest nation in the world after the United States.

The author might have left out some of these items and added one or two others. I see nothing to complain about in our contribution to the League of Nations. In view of the Armistice terms on which we agreed, we could not legitimately claim for ourselves or deny to France very different shares from those which have been arranged. We are still a great deal richer than France. But the author might have added that immediately after the war we rejected the expedient of a capital levy, and by our return to the gold standard in 1925 at the pre-war parity with gold we riveted the internal war debt on the backs of the taxpayer, not only unreduced by a capital levy, but substantially augmented by an appreciation in the value of money.

Taking everything into account, it is not very surprising that we are suffering certain embarrassments from which other nations are free. Why did we do all this? The author suggests no explanation beyond that one which is indicated by his title. I think three causes were at work, combined in different proportions in the case of different episodes. The explanation is partly to be found in our being very inferior poker players compared with those with whom we were playing the game. France and the United States were probably just as keen to carry on the war in 1917 and 1918 as we were. But they succeeded in persuading us that we should be jeopardising the whole position if we refused to agree to the very onerous arrangements to which we did in fact agree. I think it is arguable that we could have escaped a large part of these obligations by simply refusing to shoulder them, without any serious prejudice to the conduct of the war. The same thing was true in the case of the funding of the debts both with America and with France and Italy. We played our cards badly and allowed ourselves to be bluffed. By playing a delaying game we should quite certainly have made better terms.

The second ingredient was a sort of noble idealism. We felt that it was right to shoulder the burdens which we were asked to shoulder, and that it would have been in some way mean, or dishonest, or cowardly to try to avoid them. The third ingredient was a 'back to pre-war' conservatism, of which perhaps we are gradually getting cured. Until quite lately those who have been in power in Great Britain have been quite determined to refuse to accept as inevitable any radical change from the pre-war situation. They have been determined that we should carry on precisely as we have always been accustomed to carry on—no capital levies, no attempt to escape our obligations, no monkeying with currency.

We are now inclined to wonder whether it was wise to be so conservative, so noble, and so bad at poker. But there are certain indignities which we might be spared. It has been rumoured that during the Naval Conference there were some amongst our Continental friends who were inclined to sneer at our alleged pacifist ideals, saying that these pretended motives were certainly not our real ones. 'Look at the figures of your unemployment,' they said. 'It is there we find the motive for the Naval Conference. Obviously a state of affairs has come about in which *you* cannot afford to pay for a Navy. But *we* can.'

Chapter 7

HOW IT ENDED

The Young Plan was discussed by representatives of the governments concerned meeting at The Hague in August 1929 and January 1930 and was eventually adopted by all of them. It was hoped that this would be a permanent settlement, but events had changed everything within a year. The Young Plan looked forward to Germany building up an export surplus during an assumed general expansion of world trade; instead Germany continued to meet her obligations by foreign borrowing at a high rate of interest. Germany was the first country to be hit by the depression; she reached her post-war industrial peak in 1929. With her large population and the rationalisation of industry that put people out of work, she already had two million unemployed in 1929, which grew to six million by the end of 1931.

Loss of confidence in Germany and the general world depression led to the withdrawal of her foreign loans; she was unable to renew them to make payments, and gold drained out of the country. Early in June 1931 the Brüning government issued a declaration that Germany was making every possible sacrifice to meet her obligations. This had the effect of making all her creditors very nervous, particularly in the United States, her largest source of capital.

On Sunday, 21 June 1931, President Hoover took action and proposed a moratorium of one year on all inter-governmental payments. With the exception of France, all the interested governments accepted. France feared the cutting off of even the scaled-down reparation payments of the Young Plan and agreed to the moratorium only after days of bargaining on the understanding that the suspended payments would be repaid with interest after two years.

Keynes's preoccupation at this time was with unemployment, but he still held a watching brief for war debts and reparations. In any case it was clear that the German economic situation not only had parallels to the English situation, but also had immediate world-wide repercussions.

Keynes sailed from England on 30 May 1931, at the conclusion of the

Macmillan Committee proceedings, on a five-week visit to the United States, his first since he accompanied Lord Reading on the British financial mission in 1917—the primary reason for his trip being to give the Harris Foundation lectures in Chicago. The week before the President's move, he was in New York meeting influential Americans and picking up information which he passed on to Hubert Henderson, now attached to Prime Minister MacDonald's Economic Advisory Council, of which Keynes was a member.

'Consider German position most serious', he cabled his business associate Geoffrey Marks on 16 June.

> Average opinion here not discounted position, being inclined to think bad news propaganda, whereas reverse true. In responsible circles two schools thought, one for patching situation by collecting support for Reichsbank and hoping stop drain by announcing this. Other school for letting matters take their course in belief this would prepare way to more radical solution. Believe that patching up proposals are breaking down, in which case severe crisis may not be long delayed, but have good grounds for belief that crisis might lead to very favourable developments here which would surprise you. When things look worst they may quite possibly be at best. Send copy above Henderson.

The following day he sent a long letter of elucidation to Henderson. Its beginning and ending appear to have been dictated from a Wall Street office with the middle section added afterwards in Keynes's own hand.

The letter began with 'a few notes bearing on the German situation, though they are very apt to be out of date by the time they reach you'—a description of the present standing of German debt held by the American banks and a discussion of a 'patching up' scheme being considered to alleviate the situation.

From a letter to HUBERT HENDERSON, *17 June 1931*

[The section of the letter in Keynes's handwriting began here.]

I hope you did not find my cable to Marks, of which I asked him to send you a copy, too mysterious. What lay behind it is the following. I spent part of last weekend with Eugene Meyer, the governor of the Federal Reserve Board. The German question was, of course, boiling, and he was constantly on the telephone with the President, Morgans etc. I was alone with him and he talked to me with astonishing freedom about all that was going on—so much so, that I can't but think he wanted me to pass something on. He was taking the line that he was opposed to the Federal Reserve system having anything to do with any patching up scheme or giving any assistance at the present stage. They would help nothing, he said, which was not on a permanent, sound economic basis. His public attitude was calculated to produce the impression that he was in favour of letting things rip. He then disclosed to me in private his own policy if he could persuade the President—to cut down all war debt payments by 50 per cent for a period of five years, the benefit to be passed on to Germany. He did not think it at all impossible that the President would be prepared to take this up at the right time. The President had at one time discussed on his own initiative the question of a total remission (*not* suspension) for two years. Thus it would seem wrong to suppose that the U.S. administration will prove hostile to a sound scheme, when they think that the time has really come. Most people think that the President could succeed in putting over Congress (but not before December) any scheme he might sponsor. But Meyer is determined not to use his cards too soon, and would like the situation to develop rather melodramatically in a way which would strike public opinion as to the absolute necessity of action.

[Here the typed part of the letter resumed.]

As regards the general position here my impressions are still very confused. The market seems trying to go up rather than down, apart from the influence of central European developments. Several good judges expect a mild recovery in the coming months due to a recovery of retail trade. It is held that consumption articles have been consumed for some time at a greater rate than they have been produced. But apart from this I see absolutely no foundation whatever for a real recovery. There seems no prospect of construction programmes being on a much greater scale for ages to come.

353

The bond market is intolerably slow to move. At the same time there are real dangers in the local banking situation, since, owing to the depreciation of their bond holdings and the deterioration of the security behind their farm mortgages and their real estate mortgages, there is probably a vast number of banks which are not solvent and could not stand a drain. At any moment bank runs are liable to break out almost anywhere in the country. All this tends toward a mania for liquidity by anyone who can achieve it. The banks try to turn into absolutely liquid resources all that part of their assets which is saleable at the respectable price. There is also quite an appreciable hoarding of currency by the public. After allowing for diminished payrolls it would seem that there are additional hoards of currency amounting to as much as 10 per cent of the normal total circulation.[1]

On the other hand, both the New York Federal Reserve Bank people and Governor Mayer are absolutely along the right lines as to what ought to be done. They are only held back from open market operations by the opposition of others (for many of the leading banks are opposed to it for perfectly balmy reasons) and partly because of certain technical difficulties which I need not go into, and of doubt as to whether there will be much effect. But they will do what they can in the right direction whenever opportunity offers...

[At the bottom of the final page was added, in Keynes's own writing:]

Will you hand on to the P.M. any part of the above which you think will interest him?

The extract given here was what Henderson passed on to the Prime Minister.

The day after Keynes wrote this, 18 June, he cabled directly to Henderson at the Economic Advisory Council offices, 2 Whitehall Gardens, in code:

[1] Currency in circulation $250 million more than last year, whereas it probably ought to be $250 million less. This is largely in Chicago district and there may be a reflux when confidence is restored. If there was a reflux, the Federal Reserve system (after allowing for recent gold imports) would find themselves deluged with gold.

Bentley Code Probable American banks continue gradually withdraw German funds position many banks here so weak they will run no risks merely to help general situation moratorium or other suspension not fully discounted by average banks and announcement may make matters worse.

His reports from the midst of things were appreciated. 'Your information, written as it was before the Hoover offer, is most helpful is enabling one to assess the significance of what has happened since', Henderson thanked him (26 June).

On his return Keynes wrote 'A Note on Economic Conditions in the United States', a 35-page memorandum for the Economic Advisory Council, of which the final section was devoted to 'The War Debts' and an impression of what had happened since the Hoover moratorium.

From A Note on Economic Conditions in the United States, *16 July 1931*

THE WAR DEBTS

My impressions regarding the American attitude to this question can be summed up briefly:

(1) Mr Hoover's pronouncement was an unqualified success in *all* quarters. I did not discover anywhere a shadow of opposition even to the prospects of the 'next step' which everyone assumed must follow. The papers which had previously been intransigent concealed or discarded their opinions in response of the obvious popular feeling—except the Hearst papers, and Mr Hearst was, I think, out of the country at the time. It seemed to me clear that popular opinion is entirely purged of its former passions and will readily accept whatever the administration may propose.

(2) Indeed it is not going too far to say that this is the most popular thing the president has yet done. When I arrived, his stock stood incredibly low. There was not a soul who would say a good word for him. But this 'constructive' step changed the whole situation. With the elections in sight the

Democrats would doubtless be willing to work up the old feelings. But two things restrain them. Partly the obvious change in public sentiment. Chiefly, perhaps, that they are just as dependent on Wall Street for funds as the Republicans are, and Wall Street is unanimous in desiring a solution, indeed they cannot possibly afford that there should not be one. It is the slump, as well as the lapse of time and the inherent reasonableness of Americans, which is partly to be thanked for the change in mind.

(3) Quite apart from political considerations, social or otherwise, the immense short-term indebtedness of Berlin to New York (and indeed to American member banks all over the country) made some action by the president almost imperative. The total indebtedness of Berlin to American banks before the run began was estimated at $200 million, and the five largest New York banks were owed, I was told, an average of $20 million each—sums far larger than they could afford to see in jeopardy on the top of their other troubles. Thus the pressure of big finance on the Federal Reserve system, and of the reserve system on the Treasury and the president, was overwhelming. If Mr Hoover has refused to move, that, on the top of his previous extreme unpopularity, might well have ruined him. He acted at the very last moment when he had practically no other choice left him. I was convinced that this was so a week before he actually moved.

(4) But now that a move has been made, it is of first-class importance that the main architects should have been the president, Mr [Andrew] Mellon [Secretary of the Treasury] and Mr Ogden Mills [Assistant Secretary of the Treasury], and that they should have got great credit out of it. For these are the individuals who have been hitherto the great stumbling blocks. Now, however, they are somewhat committed to seeing it through, and will probably themselves wish to make, if they can, a good job of what they have put their hands to. I do not think that anyone in Washington

356

is so foolish as to conceal from himself that what has been done is only a beginning.

(5) The two chief dangers in the situation are these. There was an *extreme* irritation in Washington against the French —and I am speaking of a date before their latest exploits as engineers of ruin. Both the President and Mr Ogden Mills, the Acting Secretary of the Treasury, spoke of them in my presence with extraordinary bitterness. The other danger is lest Germany should tumble down altogether on reparations *before* the time has come for the Americans to make their further concessions. It might, paradoxically enough, be more difficult for the United States to make concessions which overtly benefited their former associates only than concessions which were associated with the voluntary reduction of what these associates are demanding from Germany.

(6) The scheme of a large long-term loan to Germany— though here I may be speaking rashly and without enough knowledge of the immediate diplomatic circumstances— seems to me to be quite chimerical, having regard to what America is likely to, and is able to do constitutionally, as well as a bad idea from our own point of view.

[initialled] J.M.K.

The Hoover moratorium had the effect of seeming to prove Germany's bankruptcy. The withdrawal of foreign money continued and a crisis developed, culminating on 'Black Monday', 13 July; German banks were closed for two days, future payments restricted and all foreign exchange business put under Reichsbank control. The Bank for International Settlements renewed the Reichsbank's rediscount credit and an international conference was called in London to see what could be done. A committee of German bankers and foreign bank creditors was set up and drafted a 'standstill' agreement which' provided that Germany's foreign creditors would not withdraw their short-term money for six months ending 29 February 1932. The standstill agreement helped Germany but embarassed her creditors. France was especially anxious to return to the Young Plan.

Keynes wrote the following paper on the reparations problem as it was in the autumn of 1931 for the Prime Minister's Advisory Committee on

Financial Questions. This committee was appointed when Britain went off the gold standard in September; its members were Reginald McKenna, Lord Macmillan, R. H. Brand, Walter Layton, Sir Josiah Stamp, Sir Arthur Salter and Keynes. The memorandum (CAB 58/169) was dated 30 November 1931.

A NOTE ON THE GERMAN RIDDLE

There is the reparations problem to solve—much as usual. But to understand the exact nature of the present situation, it is important to disentangle clearly from the reparation problem proper the extra complication created by the private debts problem.

I

Since 1923 at least the French government has never ceased to claim in the most explicit terms that in some sense reparations have 'priority' over private debts. But this claim has never had the slightest practical importance until recently, for the two reasons following.

(1) There was no practical means to enforce it compatible with the freedom of exchange transactions in Germany. For so long as any person in possession of German marks was free to exchange them for foreign currency, the private debtor, who had no responsibility for the maintenance of the exchange, could in practice always get in first; and the reparationers had to take what was left. This was, indeed, expressly recognised by the 'transfer' clause of the Dawes scheme, foolishly surrendered by Germany in exchange for the Young scheme which contains no such clause. Moreover even under the Young scheme the Reichsbank has the responsibility of maintaining the gold value of the mark. Thus, assuming freedom of exchange transactions, both these schemes meant that the solvent private debtor had a sort of priority in practice.

But now that exchange is controlled by the Reichsbank

down to the last pfennig and is doled out in rationed amounts for 'approved' purposes, the situation is completely changed. There is no longer any practical obstacle to arranging demands for foreign exchange in an order of priority, or to putting reparations higher on the list than the repayment of private debts. Thus the old French claim, hitherto academic, suddenly becomes of the greatest possible practical importance.

(2) But there is also a second reason. So long as new loans to Germany were largely in excess of the repayment of old ones, there was no room for the advantageous exploitation of the French doctrine. The increase of private debts was *facilitating* the payment of reparations. In fact it was only through the incurring of private debts that reparations were paid at all. Thus the French (and other recipients of reparations) had nothing to gain and everything to lose by trying to enforce a practical application of the French doctrine. But this did not prevent France from persistently maintaining her doctrine as an academic proposition for the time being but with important potentialities at some later stage of the proceedings.

Now that the tide of private debts has turned and Germany is asked to repay capital previously lent to her, the occasion for resurrecting the French doctrine has obviously arrived; and in a very acute form. For if France were to concede 'priority' for the private debts, meaning by this not only the service of the long-term debts (many of which have heavy sinking funds) but also the capital repayment over as short a period as possible of the short-term debts estimated at £500 million, this would obviously mean the total cessation of reparation payments for many years to come. Thus the French are not being merely tiresome; they are maintaining the essence of their position. And it is impossible to expect them, at this stage of the negotiations, to moderate their claim.

359

II

The first step towards disentangling the problem must be to delimit the legitimate meaning of 'priority'. France cannot mean that she has a first claim on the gross receipts of foreign exchange accruing in the hands of the Reichsbank from the sale of exports. Obviously the cost of imports must first of all be deducted. So also, it is reasonable to argue, must the normal annual service of the German foreign debt; for otherwise Germany's credit would be permanently destroyed. And other invisible items on *income* account, both *plus* and *minus*, must be allowed for. It is the resulting surplus over normal current requirements, on which France must be presumed to be asserting a prior claim. This is the only *reasonable* position she can take up. Her demand is thus reduced to the intelligible claim that she cannot be expected entirely to forgo reparations merely because Germany's short-term creditors have simultaneously fallen into a panic and collectively require the impossible—since no debtor country (and few creditor countries) can be expected to repay all its short-term liabilities at the same time. The international short-term lending system, like all banking contrivances, is one which allows the *individual* creditors and debtors to change but presumes no rapid large change in the aggregate outstanding.

If we assume that this is agreed, then the first step is for the experts to estimate what net surplus, interpreted as above, is likely to be available.

At this point the necessity for compromise intrudes itself. Since Germany's short-term creditors have in fact fallen into a panic (an event for which, as a matter of fact, France herself is largely responsible), Germany's future capacity to pay anything to anyone is largely dependent on restoring her credit. In short it would be highly injudicious of France to insist on a hundred per cent priority. Thus there can be no solution unless Germany's prospective surplus, arrived at as above, is divided into two parts—one for reparations, and the other for the restoration of confidence in her private credit. If France will concede this, then the bargaining begins.

III

We can now return to the short-term debt problem. It is obvious that the proportion of the *total* short-term debt which Germany can be expected to repay at an early date under a compromise scheme would be, at the best, very small. For example, an allocation of £20 million per annum to this purpose would be exceedingly optimistic; and this is only 4 per cent of the alleged total of £500 million short-term debt. Thus it would be impossible to go on pretending that these short-term debts were other than frozen; and this presents an acute problem for the acceptors of German bills. The same problem would, however, arise almost as acutely if reparations were entirely obliterated. The 4 per cent might become 7 or 8 per cent; but that is all. A demand on the part of the whole body of short-term creditors to be entitled to withdraw their credits at the rate of (say) 25 per cent per annum cannot be met in any circumstances. Also it is quite out of the question that the British Treasury could be properly invoked to guarantee or render liquid *all* the German short-term debt to British acceptors, etc., irrespective of the solvency of the individual German debtor. The technical problem, therefore, is to segregate the grand total into separate parts for which separate treatment is appropriate.

To find a solution, we must return to the facts mentioned at the beginning of this note as being responsible for creating the problem, namely the control of exchange by the Reichsbank which prevents *solvent* German debtors from meeting their foreign obligations. If this obstacle in the way of solvent debtors could be overcome, then the problems arising between foreign creditors and insolvent or unliquid German debtors could be left, as usual, to the individuals concerned.

I suggest, therefore, some technical contrivance on the following lines.

(1) The Reichsbank to create bonds (up to a maximum of (say) £150 million) guaranteed by itself and constituting a first charge on its holding of gold and foreign currency, expressed in the various foreign currencies in which Germany owes money under the Stillhalte, bearing 7 per cent interest and repayable over (say) 10 years in equal instalments.

(2) Any German debtor under the Stillhalte, who is both solvent and liquid, to be entitled to buy such bonds for Reichsmarks, either at once or at any time, so long as free exchange dealings are not permitted and the maximum of the issue had not been reached.

(3) If the plan were to work, it would, of course, be necessary for the Reichsbank not to use the issue of these bonds as an instrument of deflation in any drastic or unreasonable way, i.e. the normal volume of its assets in the shape of bills, etc., would be increased by approximately the same amount as the volume of bonds created; so that German institutions in possession of first-class bills expressed in Reichsmarks would be able to turn these into Reichsbank bonds by discounting the former at the Reichsbank. Thus the working capital of Germany, already provided by foreign money markets, would continue to be at Germany's disposal through the intermediary of the Reichsbank. The German debtor would draw mark bills instead of sterling bills, discount these mark bills at the Reichsbank, obtain Reichsbank bonds in exchange for them, and use these bonds to discharge his foreign liability which the Reichsbank would have assumed in his place.

(4) This plan has the great advantage that it automatically separates the German debtor, who is sufficiently solvent and liquid to be able to acquire Reichsbank bonds, from the debtor

who is not. The same automatic test is applied as if there were freedom of exchange operations. In effect the Reichsbank is provided with facilities for selling forward exchange to the amount of £150 million against cash or its equivalent in German currency.

(5) The foreign creditor to agree to accept Reichsbank bonds in discharge of Stillhalte debts in whole or in part. Subject to the provision of this facility, each foreign creditor to deal with his German debtor direct, just as he would if there were no exchange restrictions.

(6) The Bank of England to undertake, subject to its usual discretion in the making of advances, to lend at bank rate to its usual customers against the security of these Reichsbank bonds during the whole period of their currency.

(7) The Treasury to undertake to make good to the Bank of England any ultimate loss resulting from this undertaking, which could only occur in the event of the default both of the Reichsbank and of the customer of the Bank of England to whom the advance is made.

From our point of view these would be no reason against proceeding with such proposals at once in advance of a general reparations conference and merely in connection with the Stillhalte renewal negotiations. If France were to object, this would put *her* into the position of wanting to link up private debts and reparations into the same discussion.

When it comes to the reparations conference proper, in some ways the most critical decision for His Majesty's Government to take is whether we are prepared to advocate (and, indeed, to press for) the European powers putting up publicly a definite proposal to U.S.A. asking for the cancellation of war debts against reparation concessions. For all the rest is the usual sort of bargaining.

J. M. KEYNES

In January 1932 Keynes made a brief visit to Germany. A letter from Max Warburg, dated 8 January, ends with the message that he is looking forward to meeting Keynes in Hamburg. Keynes gave a lecture in Hamburg and on 11 January, according to Heinrich Brüning in his *Memoirs*, had a 'long conversation' with the German Chancellor in Berlin, during which Brüning on his own account tried to persuade him that an 'inflationary' programme would shake the foundations of any reasonable finance policy in Germany. There is no mention of this meeting in Keynes's papers.

According to Keynes's engagement diary, which does not show any record of the German trip, he had appointments to see Stamp on 12 January, and the Prime Minister and the 'B of E' (Bank of England) on 13 January. He saw the Prime Minister again on 15 January before an Economic Advisory Council meeting.

His strong reactions to his German impressions were put down immediately into an article. He sent an advance proof of it and the letter that follows to Alexander Shaw, chairman of a shipping company and a director of the Bank of England, who had sent him a copy of an address of his own on war debts and reparations to a gathering of business men. 'It was, I thought', wrote Shaw (11 January), 'a very good sign that the mention of your name was received with loud cheers.'

To the HONOURABLE ALEXANDER SHAW, *13 January 1932*

Dear Mr Shaw,

Many thanks for sending me a copy of your address. I had seen the newspaper report and was delighted that you were speaking out so plainly.

It is frightfully difficult to know how to influence American opinion. I have recently collected together a number of papers of mine bearing on all this, which I have published under the title *Essays in Persuasion*; and that will be coming out in an American edition in a week or two's time.

I am just back from a short visit to Germany. The position there is really appalling. And everyone naturally attributes all the miseries of the acute deflation which is occurring to reparations, with the result that there is now a strong moral determination on the part of almost everyone that reparations must come to an end.

I was in Hamburg as well as in Berlin. Business there is almost at a standstill. The shipping people are suffering impossible losses. You may be interested to know that my impression is that the German shipowners cannot possibly continue to compete for any length of time at the present level of gold freights.

Yours sincerely,

[copy initialled] J.M.K.

Keynes's visit coincided with Chancellor Brüning's announcement, on 9 January, that Germany could not resume reparation payments after the expiration of the Hoover year. Late in 1931, at Germany's request, the Bank for International Settlements had convened a Special Advisory Committee to investigate once again her capacity to pay. Meeting in Basle in December the committee reported that Germany would not be able to transfer the conditional part of the reparation annuity due in July 1932. 'The Basle Report', Brüning declared,

> shows not only Germany's matter-of-fact inability to pay but, beyond that, the causal connection between German reparation and the present world situation... It is as clear as day that Germany's position makes it impossible for it to continue political payment. It is fully as plain that every attempt to maintain intact a system of such political payments must lead to disaster not only for Germany but for the whole world.

And, on 12 January, in a phrase that came often to be repeated, Mussolini's newspaper *Il Popolo d'Italia* of Milan urged the world to 'wipe the slate clean of the tragic book-keeping of the war'.

Keynes's article was published in *The New Statesman and Nation*; the two weeklies had joined the year before. It appeared as 'Britain for Cancellation' in the *New Republic*, 27 January 1932. Keynes clearly felt that the article was important and he decided to cable it to the *New Republic* so that it would not be out of date by the time it was received. He wrote to the editor, Bruce Bliven, on 18 January: 'The article has had a good deal of publicity here and it seems that the solution to be adopted is likely to be along the lines suggested.' Bliven 'made a hasty last-minute rearrangement and put it into the issue then on the press' (letter of 29 January).

From The New Statesman and Nation, *16 January 1932*

AN END OF REPARATIONS?

Germany today is in the grip of the most terrible deflation that any nation had experienced. A visitor to that country is offered an extraordinary example of what the effects of such a policy can be, carried out *à outrance*. Indeed, the position is worse than a mere deflation need create. For a deflation might generally be expected to lower costs relatively to foreign costs and thereby assist exports. But in this case it is combined with a strangling exchange control which, by maintaining the mark at a fancy figure (14½ marks to the £) in relation to the currencies of the non-gold countries, has simultaneously *raised* the relative cost of German goods in foreign markets and is thus destroying her trade. The result reaches, or goes beyond, the limit of what is endurable. Nearly a third of the population is out of work. The standards of life of those still employed have been cruelly curtailed. There is scarcely a manufacturer or a merchant in the country who is not suffering pecuniary losses which must soon bring his business to a standstill. The export trades, until recently so flourishing, are rapidly losing their foreign orders. Parents see no careers or openings for their offspring. The growing generation is without the normal incentives of bourgeois security and comfort. Too many people in Germany have nothing to look forward to—nothing except a 'change', something wholly vague and wholly undefined, but a *change*. And it is now more than seventeen years since the outbreak of war.

Hamburg, living in a stupor, many miles of ships laid up silent in its harbour, with the elaborate traffic control of a great city but no traffic to be seen, is a symbol of Germany under the great deflation—a worse visitation, if it is to be continued, than even the great inflation was a few years ago. Germany today, still spick and span as ever, is like a beautiful machine at a standstill, ready to spring to life at the press of a button, but meanwhile inanimate. But while the machine sleeps, its crew cannot sleep.

We need to have an imaginative apprehension of all this. The reparations problem has become a matter of human feelings, of deep popular gusts of passion, and, consequently, of very simple reactions and decisions. It is high time for the 'experts' to leave the room. If they have ever contributed anything, they have nothing further to contribute. It is a moment for the statesmen of the world to handle the matters which they are supposed to understand, namely, to record in set terms the unreflecting but absolute decisions of the common mind.

For although it is scientifically true that the situation thus delineated was created by a complex of events of which reparations and war debts have been only one, the common man cannot be expected to see it this way. If he is to think and feel about it at all, as today he must, he has to simplify it. And if he is determined on a 'change', he can only demand what is concrete and appears to him to be within his mere power to effect.

Has not, then, the time come to invoke the power of simple ideas which all can understand? It is not worth while to send the 'experts' into closets to calculate whether there may not be conceivable circumstances in which someone could pay sixpence some day. I am sure that it is the will of the British people, felt today with a rare force and unanimity, that the government of this country should stand, openly and with determination, for the total cancellation of reparations and war debts. We should not be disturbed by the fact that this country has in the main already made its own contribution of generosity to the appeasement of the world, and that the paper sacrifices now asked for (for that is all they are) are mostly from others; though if there is anything further which can be justly asked of us, we should concede it. The country wants the Prime Minister to take up a stand beside Italy in support of Dr Brüning's appeal.

This should be our declared policy. But it need not be incompatible with a respect for the diplomatic difficulties and for the difference of pace with which the public sentiments of the countries concerned are moving. It is rumoured in the Press that our Treasury has been discussing with the French a project of a moratorium of two or three years and some sort of another Dawes Committee at the end of it. The City views this expedient with hostility and alarm; and I believe that the City, for once, is right. In any event, it would be impossible for the German Chancellor, in the face of the present vehemence of opinion in his own country, even to discuss it. If this policy were to be pressed, it could only end in a total repudiation by Germany of all future liability. We must set our faces invincibly towards a final settlement within the present year.

Nevertheless, there would be immense advantages to the world in an agreed settlement, over against a forced, universal default. It is worth while to exercise the utmost patience and all the arts and usages of conciliation and political wisdom. It would even be worth while, in spite of what I have just said about the sixpences, for Germany to agree, and for us to urge Germany to agree, to pay modest and reasonable sums hereafter, if it was clear that this would make a settlement possible. For what may be conceded for the sake of peace is not the same thing as our own preferred policy.

But this does not mean that the position is ripe for a final settlement at Lausanne this month or next. There are several reasons why this is almost certainly impossible. Europe is seething with pure politics, and so is America. In this country all is plain for the time being. But abroad the political kaleidoscope is such as to make any observer dizzy. In particular, with elections both in France and in Prussia only a few weeks off, we may be sure that the statesmen of neither country can make today those concessions which they may feel in their hearts to be wise and may have the authority to put over a few months hence. Moreover, opinion all over the world is advancing with seven-league boots. But it is not equally advanced everywhere. Time and the silent pressure of events are still doing good work and should not yet be interrupted.

It happens that a short adjournment is singularly easy without raising any fundamental problems. Under the Hoover moratorium Germany is due to commence making payments on 15 July next, but the war debt payments to America do not recommence until 15 December. Thus it is possible to extend the moratorium to Germany by five months without bringing to a head our own position *vis-à-vis* America. The decisions to be taken at Lausanne might, therefore, take the form (1) of a promise from the Allies to make to Germany within the present year a precise and definite proposal for the final determination of her liabilities, together with any further concessions which they are able to offer to make her task easier and more palatable, and to bring the war atmosphere to an end with a shake of the hand and a sincere offer of friendship; (2) of an agreement to watch the development of the economic crisis for a further six months before making this offer; and (3) with these objects in view, of an extension of Germany's moratorium to 15 December and an adjournment of the conference for six months.

'From all I hear,' wrote Alexander Shaw on 15 January,

the course which you envisage in your article as likely to happen is anticipated by those who were at Basle the other day and the world will be stretched upon the rack for at least another year or so. The concluding words of your article are entirely in accord with what I heard yesterday from a person whom you know, whom I had better not mention.

Shaw was a director of the Bank of England. Keynes had also sent an advance copy of his article to Montagu Norman. Norman, marking his letter 'Personal', wrote 18 January that it seemed to him 'to express many truths succinctly and with conviction; I hope it has been widely read'.

On 2 February Neville Chamberlain, speaking in the House of Commons as Chancellor of the Exchequer, said:

the policy of His Majesty's Government is that a comprehensive settlement of reparations must be reached as soon as possible. We believe ...that this aim can best be realised by means of a general cancellation of reparations and war debts.

The British government had called an international conference at Lausanne in January, but it was not a good time for it. The United States— only the autumn before in favour of an international agreement to tide the world over the depression—had turned isolationist. Germany was also uncompromising, demanding a political solution by the end of the year. The conference was postponed until June, with the United States not attending. It was her attitude that there was no connection between reparations and war debts, and she insisted on negotiating separately with each of her debtors.

Public opinion was pessimistic but Keynes continued to hope for cancellation. In a letter marked *Private*, F. W. Leith Ross, the Government's chief economic adviser, wrote (23 May):

I gather that our views about Lausanne are pretty close and that you think it would be desirable to try and get a general declaration in favour of an all-round cancellation of reparations and debts, leaving on America fairly and squarely the responsibility for further difficulties about these wretched questions. I wish you would urge this line on the P.M., who I think is rather apprehensive that it will create trouble between us and America. Of course it may, but it seems to me that we can never get progress on these questions if we are to try and avoid trouble with everybody...

Keynes applauded the spirit advocated by O. R. Hobson in an article published by the *Financial News*, 26 May 1932. Hobson urged that Britain should take the lead at Lausanne by renouncing all her claims to reparation and to repayment of war debts. Keynes wanted to see the involvement of the Europeans and also the United States.

To the Editor of the Financial News, *28 May 1932*

Sir,

I am in strong agreement with the view which Mr Hobson expressed in his article of 26 May, that everything is to be hoped from boldness at Lausanne, and nothing from timidity. It would be a disaster if the conference were to end without a clear-cut pronouncement from our government.

All the same, I feel that Mr Hobson's proposal of independent action by Great Britain is a *pis aller*—far better than an indeterminate conclusion, but not the best possible. The European powers should aim, I think, at drawing up a scheme which they themselves consider adequate to the case, provided that the United States will play their part. It is not necessary that the scheme should relate solely to reparations.

It might well be advisable that it should also cover disarmament and the currency problem. But, whatever the scheme may be, whether simple or complex, it should then be forwarded to the United States, with an invitation to the administration of that country to enter into conference with the European powers for its adoption or amendment. I can scarcely conceive that the United States administration would, in present circumstances, return a direct negative to an overture of this kind. Indeed, on the contrary, I believe that they are anxious for some kind of constructive initiative from this side of the Atlantic.

Yours, etc.,

J. M. KEYNES

Hobson's article had been called 'A Policy for Lausanne'. Keynes decided on his own policy—and offered it to *The Times*.

To GEOFFREY DAWSON, *12 June 1932*

Dear Dawson,

I offer you the enclosed as an article for publication on the right hand middle page of *The Times* one day this week. It has to be an article, not a letter, owing to my arrangements for publication in other parts of the world. For my own past I think it would do much good if this should appear in *The Times*. But you may not think so. If you are indisposed to take it I should be exceedingly grateful if your secretary could let me know to this effect at the earliest possible moment, so that I can make other arrangements.

Yours sincerely,
[copy initialled] J.M.K.

The article was to be published in 15 June, the day before the opening of the conference. Keynes sent an advance copy to the Prime Minister.

To the RIGHT HON. J. RAMSAY MACDONALD, *13 June 1932*

Dear Prime Minister,

I should have liked very much to have had a few words with you before you left for Lausanne. But I know that you would be excessively busy and so did not ring up your secretaries. I have now put my point of view, as it has crystallised, in the enclosed article, which will be published in various quarters towards the end of this week.

According to common rumour the policy is attributed to you of standing for complete all-round cancellation. Of course, I am in favour of this as the ideal and it seems to me the right starting point. But I feel most strongly that America must be a party to any real settlement; that we cannot wait for this until after the American elections; and that as a matter of fact the American politicians would probably welcome some device for lifting the whole issue out of party politics. At present it is an embarrassment to Democrats and to Republicans equally.

However, I need not enlarge on my point of view, since it is set out in the enclosed. I do not expect you will disagree from the point that it is fifty times better to have a final settlement now than to delay any part of it. If in the next six months things go worse, the delay will have proved fatal. If they go better, I think we may find the Americans more difficult to handle than now.

All the best wishes in the great task you are engaged on.

Yours sincerely,

[copy initialled] J.M.K.

The article appeared in *The Times* in the spot Keynes had specified. The European journals he had offered it to cabled 'Accept'.

From The Times, *15 June 1932*

A POLICY FOR LAUSANNE

The Conference and the U.S.: Mr Keynes's view

In the article below—on which comment is made in a neighbouring column—Mr J. M. Keynes, the well-known economist, suggests a plan of action to be followed by the powers attending the Lausanne Conference, which begins tomorrow. He admits the impossibility and even inadvisability of total cancellation of reparations at the present moment, but suggests that the reparation-receiving states should devise as definite a plan as possible for the settlement of reparation and war debts and communicate it to the American government forthwith.

Never was a conference impending from which less was expected. Pessimism is almost universal. But perhaps this is a good sign. Moreover, there are two reasons, drawn from the characteristics of human nature, for being a little hopeful. In the first place, all the parties to this conference enter it hoping little and fearing much. Thus their inner intention will be cooperative, since they all dread a breakdown or a fiasco. In the second place this conference differs from all former reparation conferences in a peculiar respect which deserves attention. Previously the object has been to devise a formula which should conceal fundamental differences of opinion. But today the object is to devise a formula which will conceal a fundamental similarity of opinion, which is much easier to accomplish without sacrificing the substance.

The main risk to the success of the conference lies in a different direction. It springs from the doubts which Europe feels as to the wisest way of approaching America. This

373

perplexity may encourage a hazy policy and promote delays. Yet time and clear-cut decisions were never more important. What outline of a definite plan can we devise?

A plan of action

It is, I suggest, the proper business of the European powers assembled at Lausanne to prepare a complete plan for the settlement of the war debts on lines which they themselves consider wise and prudent and as fair as the circumstances permit. Such a plan will necessarily be contingent on certain action by America. But the conference must not be afraid of that. For the American view, that it is for the debtors to make proposals rather than for the creditor, is reasonable. The first step, therefore, is for Europe to tell America in the most open and precise manner what it considers the circumstances to demand.

We all know that it is against both the economic facts and the probabilities of the behaviour of nations to expect that substantial sums will change hands hereafter in discharge of the war debts. The object of the conference should be to reconcile these admitted facts with the maintenance of the rule of law. It is of great importance for the future of international relations that Treaties should not be broken and that debts should not be repudiated. But the sanctity of contract can only be preserved so long as concessions are made to circumstances. If changes by agreement are unreasonably withheld, the prestige of reasonable contract will be jeopardised. For countries, such as Great Britain and France and the United States, which stand for the rule of law between nations as the safeguard of future peace, and which are also the leading creditor nations of the world, these considerations should be of overwhelming importance. At the same time I agree with Sir Arthur Salter [British delegate to the League of Nations, in his *Recovery: the Second Effort* published March 1932] that

374

the plan should probably stop short of the total cancellation of war debts. For this would offer no basis of discussion and mutual concession, and it would throw almost the whole share of the burden upon the United States.

While the plan should reduce the war debts as much as possible, the proposals of the British government should be governed by two fundamental principles. In the first place, Germany should be asked, after such necessary interval as may be agreed, to make what Sir Arthur Salter has called a token payment—a recognition, that is to say, of liability, but one which does not throw a heavier burden than can easily be borne by this generation of Germans. An agreement to make such a payment should be accompanied by a handshake all round and a declaration to let bygones be bygones. If the moral atmosphere and the accompanying gesture are right I do not believe that Germany would refuse. In the second place, Great Britain must be prepared to offer a larger payment to the United States than she herself receives.

After Lausanne

A plan devised on such principles as these would be subject, of course, to the assent of the United States, without which it would fall to the ground. It should, therefore, be publicly remitted from Lausanne to Washington, with the proposal that the Conference of Lausanne should forthwith proceed to Washington to discuss with President Hoover and with leading representatives of the Republican and Democratic parties the acceptance or the amendment of the scheme. The scheme itself should be strictly confined to the problem of war debts, but it should be made clear that the United States (but no other participant) would be free to raise other related issues in the discussion if it saw fit to do so. We should have to hope that all parties in the United States would join to lift this international problem out of the arena of party politics.

We know that a presidential election is impending. But we also know that to delay a settlement for many months more would be exceedingly dangerous. It might, indeed, be a relief to American politicians to take this issue outside the controversies of the presidential election. For they agree in their hearts and heads about what should be done far more completely than it is politic for their lips to pronounce on partisan platforms. However this may be, it is necessary that America should give her decision now. It is possible that a blank negative would be returned by President Hoover and that he would refuse to entertain a discussion. If so, even that would clear the ground. But surely he would shrink, and all responsible Americans would shrink, from the consequences of so hideous a negative. It would be a formidable responsibility to take before the world, and an unforgivable act. Nor would a conference in Washington preclude the United States from raising reasonable conditions of any kind. Indeed it would give it the opportunity to do so.

It may be that American politicians would like to escape from the responsibility of an answer. The advice which emanates from America suggests that this is so. But there is no surer thing than never to take the advice of an American as to how to behave to Americans. They always recommend you to fudge a little and to adjust your speech to an alleged implacable and unalterable 'public opinion'. Yet if you follow this course there is nothing they dislike more. American 'public opinion' is an instance of the Emperor's clothes in Hans Andersen's story. It only needed the voice of a little child to discover to the whole city that in fact the Emperor had nothing on. It may only need today the voice of Europe speaking with the candour and directness of a little child to discover to the citizens of America that in fact they hold no such opinions as each is attributing to the others.

Editorially on the same page, *The Times* doubted the wisdom of confronting Washington with a common front. The United States was about to become embroiled in a bitter election campaign; it would be better to wait until it was over. *The Times* agreed, however, that a first step was for the Europeans to come together themselves on a reparation settlement.

Not unexpectedly, MacDonald did not entirely take to Keynes's plan. He wrote from Lausanne, in a letter marked 'private', 17 June:

From the RIGHT HON. J. RAMSAY MACDONALD, *17 June 1932*

My dear Keynes,

Thank you very much for your letter of the 13th June which has just reached me. I saw your article in *The Times*. Our Treasury and Board of Trade have gone very carefully into the pros and cons of complete cancellation or partial cancellation and have put up a very convincing case that the former would be far more profitable to us than the latter. We shall just have to stand the racket of debate and examination. The conference has started very well indeed and it has shown more willingness to be expeditious than any international conference I have ever attended. The American situation is, of course, very embarrassing, but I do not at all like your suggestion. It is being considered from all points of view, however. It cannot be altogether dominated by political conditions in America. Economic conditions in Europe require very urgent treatment. However, we shall do our best.

I wish I had been able to see you and several others before I left, but those annoying operations completely upset my normal plans.

Yours always sincerely,

J. RAMSAY MACDONALD

To the RIGHT HON. J. RAMSAY MACDONALD, *21 June 1932*

Dear Prime Minister,

In reply to your letter I do not doubt or dispute that complete cancellation is far the best plan. I do not argue that it is not right to begin with that slogan. If you can achieve it, it will be a splendid thing.

My plan was based on what seemed to me a high improbability that you would succeed in getting both France and the United States to agree to this. And I much prefer my plan to any kind of postponement. In particular a plan reached by the Europeans and put into cold storage until after the

377

American elections seemed to me to be fatal. In the first place the postponement would entirely kill any favourable psychological reaction; and apart from that I should be afraid that if a plan was in existence every American candidate would get pledged against it in the course of the election. If, on the other hand, we were to force the issue now by presenting a European plan to America for immediate decision, I still confidently believe that there is a real chance of pulling it off.

But, as I have said, all this is based on the presumption that a complete cancellation is too much to hope for. If it is not too much to hope for so much the better.

I think you will have seen the currency plan which Henderson has put forward. I should like to say that I am very strongly in favour of it. This, or something which amounts to the same thing though dressed up differently, seems to me exactly what the situation requires. If you could settle reparations and then proceed on the lines Henderson suggests, I should begin to believe that our troubles are at an end.

Yours sincerely,
[copy initialled] J.M.K.

Henderson's 'currency plan', which he suggested to the British government as a proposal for the Lausanne Conference, was a scheme for a special currency to be issued by the Bank for International Settlements. It would be advanced to governments complying with regulations for use as they wished—for example, to pay external debts, improve the reserves of central banks, lighten taxation or spend on relief or public works. The currency, which would have no backing or cover of any kind, would consist of international certificates declared to have so much value in terms of gold. Keynes made use of a version of the proposal in *The Means to Prosperity* (*JMK*, vol. IX, pp. 355–64).

On 9 July 1932 the Lausanne Conference reached an agreement to end the Young Plan. Germany's reparation payments were reduced to 3,000 million gold marks, to be issued to the Bank for International Settlements in German government bonds which were not to be negotiated for three years. Any unnegotiated at the end of 15 years were to be abolished. Germany's creditors assented to a 'Gentlemen's Agreement' to the effect that this settlement depended on a satisfactory settlement with their own creditors. This, effectively, was the end of reparations.

Keynes congratulated MacDonald—and himself.

To the RIGHT HON. J. RAMSAY MACDONALD, *12 July 1932*

Dear Prime Minister,

My congratulations on your having secured all that was possible. I see that you are being criticised on the ground that, in effect, the arrangement is contingent on action by America. I have always considered this inevitable and you have probably submitted to it in its most innocuous form. The choice lay between this and putting up a solution to U.S.A. *at once* which I favoured. But this is a political issue where you are the more likely to be right.

It is a long time since June 1919 when I resigned from the British delegation in Paris in an enraged and tormented state of mind. The waste over the intervening years has been prodigious. But it is a comfortable feeling that at last it is cleaned up. For whatever America may do, this is necessarily the end so far as Germany is concerned.

The preliminary impediments having been cleared out of the way, it is now worth while to try to persuade the world to take strong doses of tonic to recover its economic health.

12.7.32   [copy initialled] J.M.K.

MacDonald replied to Keynes at Tilton from 10 Downing Street, in a 'Private' letter, on 13 July:

From the RIGHT HON. J. RAMSAY MACDONALD, *13 July 1932*

My dear Keynes,

Thank you so much for your letter. Lausanne was a great tussle. The United States was in the background all the way—present, not as a negotiator, but as a shadow. I cannot help feeling but that it will play up, however, though of course the election is most unfortunate. Had we gone straight to the United States, I am sure we would have got nothing, because, first of all, we could only have talked of ourselves and would have roused the suspicion of other European states; and had we succeeded in getting anything it could only have been in the nature of reduced, but continuing, reparations. I was not out for that. In the second place, however, I know that the United States would not have talked profitably.

You have indeed been vindicated again and again for what you did in June 1919.

I am a little bit knocked up, but hope to go ahead with further developments. I am flying to Lossiemouth on Saturday if I possibly can.

> Yours very sincerely,
> J. RAMSAY MACDONALD

Keynes was still left with the problem of the war debts. The first repayment scheduled after the expiration of the Hoover moratorium on 30 June 1932 was due 15 December. The presidential election over, Britain and France simultaneously presented the United States with almost identical notes on 10 November, asking for a reconsideration of their war debts in view of the fact that the Lausanne Conference had cancelled reparation. President Hoover, about to leave office, replied that the power to suspend payment was reserved with Congress, although he would recommend that Congress should consider the matter. The British government's Note of 1 December attempted to influence Congress by giving economic reasons why the payment could not be met, but only succeeded in influencing its members adversely. Congress asked for payment on 15 December as scheduled, with the United States insisting that the Lausanne agreement to cancel reparations had been made independently of American policy on war debts.

Keynes had something he wanted to say.

To the RIGHT HON. REGINALD MCKENNA, *9 December 1932*

Dear Reggie,

I have thought over the question of a pamphlet a good deal since our talk, but I feel that I can really convey the essence of what I have to say in an article; so I have written one and enclose you an advance copy of it. So far as this country is concerned, it will appear in the *Daily Mail* on Monday.

> Yours ever,
> [copy initialled] J.M.K.

Keynes also sent advance copies of the article to Leith Ross at the Treasury and to Sir John Simon, who was the Foreign Secretary at this time, using a note from Simon asking about a critical letter he had received from a King's College undergraduate, as an introductory excuse.

To the RIGHT HON. SIR JOHN SIMON, *8 December 1932*

Dear Sir John,

H— C— is a very charming undergraduate, by no means a scholar of the College, in his second year, who lives on the next staircase to me, the son of an old Kingsman of about my time. He is an idealistic young man, of very strong pacifist sentiments, and he was worked upon by reading the *Manchester Guardian* and other documents, to feeling that it really was his duty to do something about it, and to agitate for the suppression of private trade in arms. And he could think of no form of action, except writing to you!

When I called upon him to enquire about it, he was very shamefaced and apologetic, and said that he had doubtless made a fool of himself. It is very nice of you to have taken his letter so kindly, and you may be quite sure that he is a boy who deserves it and upon whom it will not be wasted.

Like everyone else, I suppose, I spend a good deal of time turning over the debt problem in my mind. This morning I have written a short article for Monday's *Daily Mail*, and enclose a copy in case you don't always see that organ.

Analysing the problem from the point of view of the Cabinet, there seem to me to be four alternatives—

1 Not to pay.

2. To pay quietly.

3. To pay firmly, with simultaneous notice that this is assuredly the last time, failing a satisfactory settlement.

4. To pay gloriously. That is, to announce at the same time that we were cancelling at that moment all war debts due to ourselves, declaring that we would not collect another brass

farthing from them, and reserving our future course pending further discussion with America.

Sometimes in the past fortnight I have been strongly in favour of no. 1. At times no. 4 attracts me. You will see that in the enclosed article I recommend no. 3. No. 2 is the one course for which I see nothing to be said.

Yours sincerely,
[copy initialled] J.M.K.

Keynes appeared on film in a newsreel commenting on this article. He also took some extra care with its language, writing to the literary editor of the *Daily Mail*, which was publishing it, to alter a statement that

Mr Hoover's point, that we bought food for civilians, who were occupied in war-tasks, as well as actual munitions, is a feeble sophistry

to

Mr Hoover's point...does not alter the case.

and toning down the words he had used about Congressmen, of whom he originally wrote,

When one reads the rubbish reported from Congressmen, much of it altogether beneath the intelligence and dignity of human nature,

to

When one reads what Congressmen say to reporters...

From the Daily Mail, *12 December 1932*

A BRITISH VIEW OF MR HOOVER'S NOTE

I cannot regard this problem as primarily one of the economic consequences of payment. It is a question of historic justice and of what is right and proper between nations. The evil consequences of payment are important, and were well brought out in the British Note. But if I was an American considering the matter purely from this standpoint without reference to any other considerations, I should require payment if I thought I could enforce it.

On these lines, therefore, Mr Hoover's reply is not without force. He is certainly right, for example, that if we take the post-war period as a whole, the maldistribution of gold has been due more to reparations than to America's demands, which up to 1929 were offset, only too generously, by her new lending. Thus by stressing this aspect too much, we leave out not only the strongest part of our case, but the real reasons why we feel so strongly. We shall not bridge the gulf between Westminster and Washington unless we can somehow convey across that distance the fundamental grounds why we profoundly believe that an uncompromising attempt to enforce the debt would be nothing less than a monstrosity. No one in England can read Mr Hoover's reply without the reaction that it leaves our case, as we ourselves feel it, quite untouched. Let me state this case in a few words, which any intelligent being can understand.

In the first place, there are not now and never were any profitable assets corresponding to the sums borrowed. The medieval Church was wise to make a fundamental distinction between usury and a share in emergent profits. The war debts are a case of pure usury. Mr Hoover's point, that we bought food for civilians, who were occupied in war tasks, as well as actual munitions, does not alter the case. We borrowed nothing except for the purposes of the war. It would be a good, not a bad, precedent for the future, to establish a distinction between money lent internationally to foster a war and money lent to build, for example, a railway. If anyone expects to make a profit out of financing war, there is no harm done if it turns out a bad risk. War loans should never be made except out of sympathy with the cause of the borrower, and the gradual repayment of the sum lent without interest is the most that should be expected. If I lend money to a man to help him expand his business, I am entitled to ask interest. But if I lend money to a friend to help him out of a tight place, where there can be no question of his earning a profit, I expect no more than the repayment of my loan.

Secondly, we only owe this money at all because of our greater eagerness in a common cause. I happen to have been during the war the Treasury official most directly concerned with the borrowing and the spending of the money, and I know this to be true. We ourselves were self-supporting. We borrowed the money to hand it over to our Allies, because the refusal to do so would have brought doubts and delays hazardous to the prosecution of the war. We were ready to agree to anything rather than run the risk of a hitch, and our greater wholeheartedness is the sole reason of our owing this money today.

Thirdly, the value received at the time was far less than that represented by the principal sum today. Again in order to avoid delay, we paid, with our eyes open, profiteering prices for what we bought, and the United States government collected back in taxation a considerable proportion of these excess profits; in addition to which the value of money has since suffered a catastrophic change. The replacement cost today of the wheat, cotton, copper, chemicals and munitions which we purchased, should be the true measure of this non-commercial debt.

Fourthly, the sanctity of contract, the preservation of which is a matter of serious importance to a country with the financial organisation of the United States just as it is to Great Britain, cannot be preserved except by the reasonableness of the creditor. It is not an immutable law of nature. The principle itself, if we consider it historically in the modern world, is largely a British conception, its prestige built up during the eighteenth and nineteenth centuries, which America has inherited from us. But it is because we are reasonable people that it has flourished amongst us, not because our laws are more forcible than elsewhere. Debtors are only honourable in countries where creditors are reasonable. If creditors stand on the letter of the law, debtors can usually show them how little the law avails. Internationally, contract has nothing to support it except the self-respect and self-interest of the debtor. A loan, the claims of which are supported by neither, will not be paid for long.

Fifthly, we ourselves are, on balance, large creditors of war debts. Though not at first, yet in the coolness of time we have shown that we are still reasonable, and that we practise what we preach. A final settlement, in which we alone were to make large payments in respect of war debts, would be monstrous.

Finally, it is the duty of a creditor not to frustrate payment. The only means by which we can pay large sums to America reduce in the long run to two. We can pay a few instalments in gold, but we do not produce gold and the debt is many times greater than our total stock. This, therefore, is an emergency, not a normal, means of payment. There can in the end be only two means of settlement—directly or indirectly, we must sell more goods to America or buy less from her. If Americans will send us a list of our produce of which they would like to buy more, we will take steps to ship it; and if they will schedule a list of those of their goods which they would like us to refrain from buying, we will try to cut down our purchases. Or we can achieve the same results by triangular trade through the intermediary of a third country. For example, we might in return for trade concessions, make a bargain with the Argentine, that they should buy from us goods which they now buy from the United States, thus providing us indirectly with exchange wherewith to pay our debt. If Congress desires us to negotiate on these lines, let them say so. But when we are told by Congressmen that a suggestion of buying less is a reprisal and that an offer to sell more is an injury, the obligations of honour wear extremely thin.

America has in Great Britain a debtor more sensitive to considerations of good faith than any other debtor in the world. Self-respect and self-interest are powerful motives with us to do our utmost for a friendly and fair settlement. What is our wisest course next Thursday? When one reads what Congressmen say to reporters, one's impulse is to bring things to a head at once. But patience is still the course of wisdom. We should agree to pay what is now demanded, so as to give America time for reconsideration. I see no reason why we should not ask to defer the capital portion of the instalment if Mr Hoover has power to postpone this without reference to Congress; and we should pay the balance out of the gold in the issue department of the Bank of England, modifying the fiduciary issue accordingly. But, above all, it is essential that we should declare plainly and at once that, failing a settlement which we consider satisfactory, this must be the end. Whatever narrow calculations of financial self-interest might urge, we will not continue to acquiesce in what we know with conviction to be utterly wrong. Unless our Cabinet conveys this to Congress, they will fail to represent the overwhelming weight of the national sentiment.

Margot Asquith wrote warmly (2 January 1933) enclosing a quotation from the article:

Dearest Maynard

I think enclosed the *only* good thing I've read on the American debt. You sd. have sent it to *The Times*, as those who read the *Daily Mail* are mostly in the Servants Hall. (I never take it in.)

McKenna, who had been in France, had read the article in the Paris *Daily Mail*. 'Needless to say I liked it very much', he wrote on 21 December,

though I should have liked still more an examination by you of the true amount which we owe to America. The Treasury and the Admiralty ought to be able to make out a powerful case based upon arithmetic. Dealing with the Middle West, argument and right and proper appreciation of what an ally in a war ought to do have little or no effect.

Yours ever,

R. MCKENNA

But *The Times*'s correspondent in New York (where the article appeared 12 December in the *Herald Tribune*) wrote that the position of friends of revision had not been made any easier by its publication—and in particular by Keynes's description of the war debts as 'pure usury'. While there was much in his argument to appeal to thoughtful readers, this writer said, 'at the moment it is not the argument but the phrase which is evoking comment'.

Britain ended by paying the instalment due 15 December in full but in six months was faced with the problem again when the next instalment became due 15 June 1933. The *Daily Mail* again presented Keynes's views, a few days before the World Economic Conference of 1933 gathered in London to discuss other matters.

From the Daily Mail, *8 June 1933*

AN ECONOMIST'S VIEW OF THE DEBT PAYMENT PROBLEM

Pay or default?—neither

In Tuesday's *Daily Mail* Viscount Snowden advised this country to pay America next week. Those who disagree with his conclusions will sympathise with some of his reasons. And it is obvious from his article that Viscount Snowden, in his turn, understands the other point of view. I believe that most responsible persons in America are finding themselves in the same double-mindedness.

I draw from this the obvious conclusion that we are being presented with a false dilemma—that we are in danger of being caught up in legalisms and of allowing them to override not merely the common sense but the deep realities of the case. 'Pay or default' is a dilemma which I refuse to accept at this stage. My recommendation is that we should do neither.

Tact essential

No one in either country supposes that the present legal position represents the final settlement. No one supposes that the final settlement can be reached, or even approached, before 15 June. It is equally in the interest of both countries that the least possible should transpire to injure the fragile fabric of international contract. Both countries are equally reluctant to give cause of offence to the other on the eve of a conference from which nothing can be hoped except on the basis of their fraternal collaboration.

387

In an article which I wrote for the *Daily Mail* last December I advised that we should pay the instalment then due, 'so as to give America time for reconsideration'. By our action in making full payment at that date we did all that was reasonable to give the new American administration time to consider its policy. For reasons which have seemed to him to be sufficient, and perhaps compelling, it has not suited President Roosevelt, in the midst of his other vast preoccupations, to take advantage of this interval to seek legislative authority for his ultimate debt policy or even to disclose what it is.

If Britain pays

Nevertheless a point has been reached where, if we were to repeat our action of last December, it might actually embarrass the President in securing the assent of Congress to what he doubtless intends to recommend at long last. So troublesome a problem as that of the debts will surely be allowed to drift, so long as nothing happens to bring it to a head.

I say that the nature of the solution between reasonable persons is, in such circumstances, obvious. Informal arrangements for delay, entirely outside the letter of the law, are a commonplace between ordinary people, both desiring time to agree, who are neither overweening nor litigious. The nature of the law, especially of that vaguer law between nations where there is no urbane court to smooth the path of two disputants who wish to compromise, is not so rhadamanthine as Viscount Snowden supposes.

Communications can still be exchanged between the governments of Great Britain and of the United States which would not affect or call in question the legal situation, but which would make it evident to everyone that, although payment is not being made, neither is there default.

Soundest step

The duty of our government, I suggest, is to address a letter to President Roosevelt telling him that we believe it to be in the general interest that the payment of the June instalment should be held in suspense pending further discussion; that we are taking this step without prejudice to the legal rights of the United States, which we do not dispute, or to the nature of the ultimate settlement; that we act because we see it to be unavoidable, things being as they are, that the onus of this initiative should fall on us rather than on him; but that we trust him to accept our action in the same spirit by which we ourselves are moved.

I should hope for a reply from the President that he understands what we mean, and that, while he has at this stage neither the power nor the wish to accept, by implication or condonation, any modification of the existing contract, he will not regard our holding this payment in suspense either as impairing the harmonious relations of the two governments or as prejudicing the discussions in prospect. If we have reason to believe that a 'token' payment, such as has been suggested, would render postponement more acceptable to American opinion, as constituting a recognition of legal liability, by all means let us make it.

Who in the world, unless he is malignant or mischief-making, would regard such a situation as default? If we look round at the abundance of genuine defaults, it must be obvious that the exchange of such letters as the above could not possibly impair international confidence, as Viscount Snowden fears. If, on the contrary, President Roosevelt were to charge us with default and bad faith, *if* that is his mood —which I am sure it is not—then there is no course of action from which good results could follow.

Candour and sincerity require a further word. The object of a postponement is to give time for an agreed settlement.

Conceivably a point may come when default would be forced on us as our only right course. But this cannot occur until the two governments have met to discuss a new settlement and have failed to agree; or—a contingency which one must not ignore—until Congress has refused to ratify a settlement recommended by those who have negotiated with us on their behalf.

If such unhappy events are in store for us we shall have to act, when the time comes, as the broad judgment of the nation would have us act. But it is ridiculous, meanwhile, to use about the present situation language which would be appropriate to what we should be doing then.

I do not read Viscount Snowden as impugning our ultimate liberty of action. For he emphasises throughout his article that it is only £12 million—that is to say, the amount of the June instalment—which is in question. In urging us to pay this sum on grounds, not of immutable principle, but of practical wisdom, I believe that he makes a mistake. To pay promptly on 16 June, after all we said and wrote in December, will prejudice the negotiations about to commence, and will render more difficult President Roosevelt's task of persuading Congress to accept a just and wise solution.

For it will create the impression that we may, after all, be intending to pay if necessary, and that our former declaration, as to the impossibility or disastrous consequences of continued payment, was so much bluff.

This time the British government made a token payment. According to President Roosevelt they were not in default; according to Congress, they were. Britain made no more payments and that was the end of war debts. And so Keynes left the subject—fourteen years, almost to the day, after he left the Treasury.

In World War II he had to return to 'the old, familiar, insoluble problems of "Reparations"'—his own phrase. He was a member of Treasury and inter-departmental committees and was involved in talks with the Americans. At the outset he attacked the matter vigorously but in the later stages, when what he described as 'nonsense' set in, he withdrew from the discussion (*JMK* Vol. XXVI).

DOCUMENTS REPRODUCED
IN THIS VOLUME

391

DOCUMENTS REPRODUCED IN THIS VOLUME

DOCUMENTS REPRODUCED IN THIS VOLUME

INDEX

397